The World's Best Poetry

Supplement II

Twentieth Century English And American Verse, 1930-1950

Poetry Anthology Press

The World's Best Poetry

Volume	I	Home and Friendship
	II	Love
	III	Sorrow and Consolation
	IV	The Higher Life
	V	Nature
	VI	Fancy and Sentiment
	VII	Descriptive and Narrative
	VIII	National Spirit
	IX	Tragedy and Humor
	X	Poetical Quotations; General Indexes
Supplement	I	Twentieth Century English and American Verse, 1900-1929
	II	Twentieth Century English and American Verse, 1930-1950
	III	Critical Companion

Survey of American Poetry

Volume	I	Colonial Period, 1607-1765
	II	Revolutionary Era, 1766-1799
	III	Early 19th Century, 1800-1829
	IV	First Great Period, 1830-1860
	V	Civil War and Aftermath, 1861-1889
	VI	Twilight Interval, 1890-1912
	VII	Poetic Renaissance, 1913-1919
	VIII	Interval Between World Wars, 1920-1939
	IX	World War II and Aftermath, 1940-1950
	X	Midcentury to Present; General Indexes

The World's Best Poetry

Supplement II

Twentieth Century English And American Verse, 1930-1950

Prepared by
The Editorial Board, Roth Publishing, Inc.
(formerly Granger Book Co., Inc.)

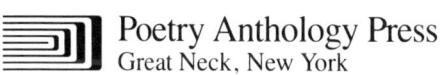

Poetry Anthology Press
Great Neck, New York

Acknowledgements

Permission to reprint copyrighted poems is gratefully acknowledged to the following:

DOUBLEDAY & COMPANY, INC., for "Dolor" copyright 1943 by Modern Poetry Assoc.; "The Lost Son" copyright 1947 by Theodore Roethke; "Moss Gathering" copyright 1946 by Editorial Publications, Inc.; "Open House" copyright 1941 by Theodore Roethke, from *The Collected Poems of Theodore Roethke*.
FABER & FABER PUBLISHERS, for "Autobiography;" "Brother Fire;" "Conversation;" "An Ecologue for Christmas;" "Explorations;" "June Thunder;" "Les Sylphides;" "The Mixer;" "Museums;" "Neutrality;" "Perseus;" "Slow Movement;" "Stylite;" "Sunday Morning;" "The Sunlight on the Garden" from *The Collected Poems of Louis MacNeice*.
FARRAR, STRAUS & GIROUX, INC., for "Canto amor" and "The Song of the Demented Priest" from *Short Poems* by John Berryman. Copyright 1948 by John Berryman. "The Monument" and "The Weed" from *The Complete Poems 1927–1979* by Elizabeth Bishop. Copyright 1983 by Alice Helen Methfessel. Copyright 1932, 1937 by Elizabeth Bishop. Copyright renewed 1967 by Elizabeth Bishop. "The Death of the Ball Turret Gunner;" "Losses;" "A Pilot from the Carrier;" "Second Airforce" from *The Complete Poems* by Randall Jarrell. Copyright 1944, 1945, 1948 by Mrs. Randall Jarrell. Copyright renewed 1971, 1972, 1973, 1975 by Mrs. Randall Jarrell. "Ode to the Confederate Dead" and "The Trout Map" from *Collected Poems 1919–1976* by Allen Tate. Copyright 1952, 1953, 1970, 1977 by Allen Tate. Copyright 1931, 1932, 1937, 1948 by Charles Scribner's Sons. Copyright renewed 1959, 1960, 1965 by Allen Tate.
HARCOURT BRACE JOVANOVICH, INC. for "Invitation to Juno;" "Legal Fiction;" "Missing Dates;" "Notes on the Local Flora;" "This Last Pain," from *Collected Poems of William Empson*, copyright 1949, 1977 by William Empson. "After the Suprising Conversions;" "As A Plane Tree by the River;" "Colloquy in Black Rock;" "The Drunken Fisherman;" "Mr. Edwards and the Spider;" "The Quaker Graveyard in Nantucket;" "Where the Rainbow Ends," from *Lord Weary's Castle*, copyright 1946, 1974 by Robert Lowell. "O" from *The Beautiful Changes And Other Poems* copyright 1947, 1975 by Richard Wilbur. "Still Citizen Sparrow" from *Ceremony And Other Poems* copyright 1950, 1978 by Richard Wilbur.
INTERNATIONAL CREATIVE MANAGEMENT, INC., for "Reading Time," from *A Turning Wind* copyright 1939 and 1967 by Muriel Rukeyser. "Boy With His Hair Cut Short;" "Mediterranean;" "More Of A Corpse Than A Woman;" from *U.S. 1* copyright 1938 and 1966 by Muriel Rukeyser.
NEW DIRECTIONS PUBLISHING CORPORATION, for "After the Funeral;" "Altarwise by Owl—Light;" "Ballad of the Long-Legged Bait;" "Ceremony after a Fire Raid;" "Ears in the Turret Hear;" "Fern Hill;" "The Hunchback in the Park;" "Poem in October;" "A Refusal to Mourn the Death by Fire of a Child in London" from *Poems Of Dylan Thomas* by Dylan Thomas. Copyright 1938, 1939, 1943, 1946 by New Directions Publishing Corporation. Copyright 1943, 1945, 1967 by the Trustees for the Copyrights of Dylan Thomas. "A Winter's Tale" and "Poem in October" first appeared in POETRY magazine. "23rd Street Runs into Heaven;" "Joe Hill Listens;" "Let Us Have Madness Openly;" "A Letter on the Use of a Machine;" "A Letter to a Policeman;" "Street Corner College," from *The Collected Poems Of Kenneth Patchen*. Copyright 1939 by New Directions Publishing Corporation. "The Bereaved Swan;" "The Heavenly City;" "Little Boy Lost;" "The River God;" "To the Tune of the Coventry;" "The Weak Monk;" from *Collected Poems* by Stevie Smith. Copyright 1937, 1938, 1950, 1957, 1966, 1971, 1972 by Stevie Smith. New Directions Publishing Corporation, Publishers and agents for the Estate of Stevie Smith.

(Acknowledgements are continued on page 440)

**Copyright © Granger Book Company, Inc. 1984
All rights reserved**

Library of Congress Catalog Card Number 82-84763
International Standard Book Number 0-89609-239-9

Manufactured in the U.S.A.

Poetry Anthology Press is a
division of Roth Publishing, Inc.
(formerly Granger Book Co., Inc.)

CONTENTS

Preface

Introduction

James Joyce (1882–1941)
    I Hear an Army Charging upon the Land 1

Andrew Young (1885–1971)
    The Black Rock of Kiltearn 2
    The Dead Crab 2
    The Scarecrow 3
    Stay, Spring 3

Hilda Doolittle (1886–1971)
    Helen 4
    Not Honey 5
    There Is a Spell, for Instance 6

Edith Sitwell (1887–1964)
    The Coat of Fire 10
    Dark Song 12
    The Drum 12
    Heart and Mind 14
    Most Lovely Shade 15
    An Old Woman 16
    Still Falls the Rain 21
    The Youth with Red-gold Hair 22

John Peale Bishop (1892–1944)
    Colloquy with a King-Crab 24
    A Frieze 24
    Ode 25
    The Return 27

Hugh MacDiarmid [pseud. of Christopher Murray Grieve] (1892–1978)
    At the Cenotaph 29
    Empty Vessel 29
    O Wha's Been Here Afore Me, Lass 30

Reflections in an Iron Works	30
Scunner	31
The Two Parents	31

Herbert Read (1893–1968)
Bombing Casualties in Spain	32
The Contrary Experience	32
Sic et Non	34
A World within a War	36

Edmund Blunden (1896–1974)
The Giant Puffball	44
The Midnight Skaters	45
Report on Experience	46
Solutions	46

Ruth Pitter (Born 1897)
But for Lust	48
The Military Harpist	48
The Tigress	50
The Viper	51

John Wheelwright (1897–1940)
Ave Eva	52
Bread-Word Giver	53
In Poets' Defence	54
Titanic Litany	55
Train Ride	56
The Word Is Deed	57

Malcolm Cowley (Born 1898)
For St. Bartholomew's Eve	59
The Hill above the Mine	60

Horace Gregory (1898–1982)
Dempsey, Dempsey	62
Hagen	63
Hellbabies	64
Salvos for Randolph Bourne	65
Tombstone with Cherubim	66
The Woman Who Disapproved of Music at the Bar	67

Leonie Adams (Born 1899)
    Country Summer 70
    The Runner with the Lots 71

Allen Tate (1899–1979)
    Ode to the Confederate Dead 73
    The Trout Map 76

Oscar Williams (1900–1964)
    The Elements 78
    Milk at the Bottom of the Sea 79
    The Road from Election to Christmas 80

Sterling A. Brown (Born 1901)
    After Winter 82
    Foreclosure 83
    Old Lem 85
    Remembering Nat Turner 87
    Sister Lou 88

Roy Campbell (1901–1957)
    Death of the Bull 91
    Choosing a Mast 92
    Luis De Camoes 94
    The Serf 94
    The Sisters 95
    Toledo, July 1936 95

Kenneth Fearing (1902–1961)
    C Stands for Civilization 97
    Devil's Dream 98
    Dirge 99
    Dividends 100
    No Credit 101

Stevie Smith (1902–1971)
    The Bereaved Swan 102
    The Heavenly City 103
    The Little Boy Lost 103
    The River God 104

    To the Tune of the Coventry Carol 105
    The Weak Monk 106

Richard Palmer Blackmur (1904–1965)
    The Dead Ride Fast 107

Cecil Day Lewis (1904–1972)
    All Gone 109
    As One Who Wanders into Old Workings 110
    Birthday Poem for Thomas Hardy 111
    Come, Live with Me and Be My Love 112
    The Conflict 112
    Departure in the Dark 113
    In the Heart of Contemplation 115
    In Heaven, I Suppose, Lie Down Together 115
    Maple and Sumach 117
    Nearing Again the Legendary Isle 117
    O Dreams, O Destinations 118
    Rest from Loving and Be Living 122
    The Sitting 122
    A Time to Dance 124
    You That Love England 125

Richard Eberhart (Born 1904)
    The Goal of Intellectual Man 126
    The Groundhog 127
    I Walked Out to the Graveyard to See the Dead 128
    Mysticism Has Not the Patience to Wait for God's Revelation 128

Robert Penn Warren (Born 1905)
    Revelation 131
    Pursuit 132
    Terror 133

John Betjeman (Born 1906)
    Parliament Hill Fields 136
    Upper Lambourne 138
    Youth and Age on Beaulieu River, Hants 138

William Empson (1906–1984)
    Camping Out 140

    Homage to the British Museum 141
    Invitation to Juno 141
    Flighting for Duck 142
    Four Legs, Three Legs, Two Legs 143
    Legal Fiction 144
    Missing Dates 144
    Note on Local Flora 145
    This Last Pain 145

W. H. Auden (1907–1973)
    The Airman's Alphabet 148
    At the Grave of Henry James 150
    A Bride in the 30's 154
    Carry Her over the Water 157
    Casino 158
    In Memory of Sigmund Freud 158
    The Lesson 162
    Miranda's Song 164
    Musée des Beaux Arts 164
    Perhaps 165
    Petition 167
    Song for St. Cecilia's Day 167
    Watch Any Day 169

Louis MacNeice (1907–1963)
    Autobiography 171
    Brother Fire 172
    Conversation 173
    An Eclogue for Christmas 174
    Explorations 178
    June Thunder 179
    The Mixer 180
    Museums 180
    Neutrality 181
    Perseus 182
    Slow Movement 182
    Stylite 183
    Sunday Morning 184
    The Sunlight on the Garden 185
    Les Sylphides 185

E. J. Scovell (Born 1907)
    Evening Scene 187
    The First Year (*sel.*) 188
    The Swan's Feet 188

Vernon Watkins (1907–1967)
    The Collier 189
    Indolence 190
    The Turning of the Leaves 191
    Zacchaeus in the Leaves 192

Kathleen Raine (Born 1908)
    The Crystal Skull 196
    Desire 197
    The Fall 198
    The Goddess 198
    Isis Wandered 199
    Love Poem 200
    The Pythoness 201
    The Silver Stag 201
    Worry about Money 202

Theodore Roethke (1908–1963)
    Dolor 204
    The Lost Son 205
    Moss–Gathering 210
    Open House 211

Richard Wright (1908–1960)
    Between the World and Me 212
    I Am a Red Slogan 214
    I Have Seen Black Hands 214

Edwin Rolfe (1909–1954)
    Definition 217
    Not Men Alone 217
    Room with Revolutionists 218
    Somebody and Somebody Else and You 220
    To My Contemporaries 222

Stephen Spender (Born 1909)
    An Elementary School Classroom in a Slum 227
    The Landscape near an Aerodrome 228
    Marston 229
    Polar Exploration 230
    Port Bou 231
    Seascape 232
    Song 233
    The Trance 234
    Two Armies 235
    What I Expected 236
    Winter and Summer 237
    Word 238
    Your Body Is Stars 238

Robert Fitzgerald (Born 1910)
    Colorado 240
    Souls Lake 241

Elizabeth Bishop (1911–1979)
    The Monument 243
    The Weed 245

Kenneth Patchen (1911–1972)
    Joe Hill Listens to the Praying 248
    A Letter on the Use of Machine Guns at Weddings 252
    A Letter to a Policeman in Kansas City 253
    Let Us Have Madness Openly 254
    Street Corner College 255
    23rd Street Runs into Heaven 255

Lawrence Durrell (Born 1912)
    At Epidaurus 257
    In Arcadia 259
    Nemea 260
    On Ithaca Standing 260
    A Water-Colour of Venice 261

Roy Fuller (Born 1912)
    The Hero 263
    Meditation 264
    November, 1941 265
    The Plains 265

F. T. Prince (Born 1912)
    The Tears of a Muse in America 267
    The Token 270

Anne Ridler (Born 1912)
    Christmas and Common Birth 271
    Deus Absconditus 272
    For a Christening 273
    A Mile from Eden 275
    Now Philippa Is Gone 276
    Piero Della Francesca 276

George Barker (Born 1913)
    First Cycle of Love Poems 278
    Galway Bay 283
    Holy Poems 284
    News of the World II 285
    News of the World III 286
    Resolution of Dependence 288
    Sacred Elegy V 290
    Sonnet of Fishes 291
    Summer Idyll 292
    Summer Song 293
    To My Mother 294

Muriel Rukeyser (1913–1980)
    Boy with His Hair Cut Short 295
    Mediterranean 296
    More of a Corpse Than a Woman 303
    Reading Time: 1 Minute 26 Seconds 304

Delmore Schwartz (1913–1966)
    For One Who Would Not Take His Life in His Hands 307
    The Heavy Bear Who Goes with Me 308
    The Starlight's Intuitions Pierced the Twelve 309

Karl Shapiro (Born 1913)
    The Dome of Sunday 312
    Elegy for a Dead Soldier 314
    Elegy Written on a Frontporch 318
    Haircut 321
    Nostalgia 322
    The Potomac 322
    V-Letter 323

John Berryman (1914–1972)
    Canto Amor 327
    The Song of the Demented Priest 329

Randall Jarrell (1914–1965)
    The Death of the Ball Turret Gunner 330
    Losses 331
    A Pilot from the Carrier 332
    Second Air Force 332

Laurie Lee (Born 1914)
    Day of These Days 335
    Milkmaid 336
    The Three Winds 337

Norman Nicholson (Born 1914)
    Caedmon 338
    Cleator Moor 340
    Michaelmas 341
    Song at Night 341
    The Tame Hare 342
    The Undiscovered Planet 343

Henry Reed (Born 1914)
    Lessons of the War 344

Dylan Thomas (1914–1953)
    After the Funeral 347
    Alterwise by Owl-Light 348
    Ballad of the Long-Legged Bait 353
    Ceremony after a Fire Raid 359
    Ears in the Turrets Hear 362

    Fern Hill 363
    The Hunchback in the Park 364
    Poem in October 366
    A Refusal to Mourn the Death, by Fire, of a Child in London 368
    A Winter's Tale 368

Alun Lewis (1915–1944)
    Dawn on the East Coast 374
    The Jungle 375
    The Peasants 377
    To a Comrade in Arms 378

David Gascoyne (Born 1916)
    An Autumn Park 379
    Ecce Homo 380
    An Elegy 382
    Jardin du Palais Royal 384
    Orpheus in the Underworld 385

Robert Lowell (1917–1977)
    After the Suprising Conversions 386
    As a Plane Tree by the Water 387
    Colloquy in Black Rock 388
    The Drunken Fisherman 389
    Falling Asleep over the Aeneid 390
    Mr. Edwards and the Spider 393
    The Quaker Graveyard in Nantucket 394
    Where the Rainbow Ends 398

William Sydney Graham (Born 1918)
    At Whose Sheltering Shall the Day Sea 400
    Gigha 401
    Listen. Put on Morning 401
    Night's Fall Unlocks the Dirge of the Sea 402
    To My Father 403

Keith Douglas (1920–1944)
    The Deceased 405
    Desert Flowers 406
    Mersa 406
    Time Eating 407

Richard Wilbur (Born 1921)
    O 409
    Still, Citizen Sparrow 409

Sidney Keyes (1922–1943)
    Early Spring 411
    Elegy 411
    Glaucus 412
    The Grail 413
    Holstenwall 413
    The Kestrels 414

Index 415

Preface

The publications of **Poetry Anthology Press** constitute a comprehensive conspectus of international verse in English designed to form the core of a library's poetry collection. Covering the entire range of poetic literature, these anthologies encompass all topics and national literatures.

Each collection, published in a multivolume continuing series format, is devoted to a major area of the whole undertaking and contains complete author, title, and first line indexes. Biographical data is also provided.

The World's Best Poetry, with coverage through the 19th century, is topically classified and arranged by subject matter. Supplements keep the 10 volume foundation collection current and complete.

Survey of American Poetry is an anthology of American verse arranged chronologically in 10 volumes. Each volume presents a significant period of American poetic history, from 1607 to date.

INTRODUCTION

The nineteen thirties is an especially noteworthy period in the history of English-language verse for the predominance of political poetry, in which the writer utilizes his art to promote political or social views and solutions. This trend was a reaction to the "new poetry," or modernism, of the second decade of the twentieth century, led primarily by William Butler Yeats, T.S. Eliot, and Ezra Pound. Modernism continued the romantic tradition of the nineteenth century in unique and original ways. In traditional romanticism, the poet subjectively examines man's relation to his environment by turning to his own experiences, fears, dreams, and aspirations. While the early twentieth century poets were still individualistic and continued to interpret life in personal terms, their approach was more intellectual, realistic and less lyrical. Moreover, the modernist poets internalized the pessimism which their predecessors applied to the external world; indeed they regarded their own sentiments with skepticism and their future with apprehension. Still, modernism did not concern itself with political or social issues. Though Eliot's "The Waste Land," one of the greatest modernist poems, depicted the decay and dehumanization of twentieth century man, its tone was not overtly political in that Eliot did not take stands on particular issues; the focus of "The Waste Land," as with most modernist and romantic poetry, was on the individual. For the modernist poet, one did not combine art and politics.

This division of art and politics ended in the thirties. By 1930, the myth of the Great War, begun with patriotic fervor in 1914 and continued through the twenties by the veterans of World War I, had been rejected and was replaced by rabid anti-war feelings. By 1931, most people were suffering in the world-wide depression. With the shattering of popular illusions, the end of optimism, and the fear of another global conflict came a feeling of immediacy: that the end of the world was at hand and that something had to be done. The pervasive social and economic conditions of the thirties, "the low dishonest decade" in Auden's words, as well as an ominous sense of doom, were dramatically and forcefully reflected in the work of the poets. Stephen Spender wrote of a common perception of being "hounded by external events." One of these "events," the 1936 Spanish Civil War, a literary "cause celebre," further galvanized the poets, producing a copious effusion of poetry, and resulting in an antagonistic polarization between the Loyalists and Nationalists.

Commitment to specific programs or credos, "real solutions," as it were, formed the basis of much of the poetic response to the challenge of the times. English and American poetry of the thirties was basically Marxist–inspired, and all of it was exuberant, enthusiastic, idealistic, and full of hope. It is important to note that while poets such as Spender, Day Lewis, and Auden had definite leftist sympathies, and indeed proposed certain communistic tenets in their poetry, they were not fully committed revolutionaries. Auden, in particular, had only a brief flirtation with the communist party, and though he did participate in a few labor demonstrations, his Marxist orientation was basically conceptual. What is interesting is that most poets of the time, even the isolated Louis MacNeice, had leftist ideals. Still, there were some poets who openly despised Marxism, most notably Roy Campbell, who wrote anti-communist propaganda.

In the United States, the "Proletarian Poets," including Horace Gregory, Muriel Rukeyser, Delmore Schwartz, Edwin Rolfe, Alfred Kreymborg, Kenneth Patchen, and Kenneth Fearing, were intensely involved with social themes and issues, and reflected contemporary class antagonisms and conflicts. Their poetry was often more passionate, direct, and objective than their British counterparts. But for both British and American poets of the thirties, the times and immediate dangers of economic depression and imminent war demanded that their revolution be a political one, as opposed to the artistic revolution of modernism and romanticism.

The virulent crusade against capitalism forged by the British and American poets during the early thirties, together with the frequent advocacy of communism, was dissipated at the end of the decade by a convergence of events: the advent of the Second World War, disillusionment with Marxism as practiced in the Soviet Union, the Hitler-Stalin pact, and the end of the Civil War in Spain. Gone too was the new idealism. The reality of war, along with the failures of many reform ideas, exposed the empty idealism of the thirties; the ardor and spirit of revolt turned to despair and frustration. MacNeice wrote that the war "made nonsense of the poetry that professes to be 'realist'." It was clear in 1939 that the thirties was, in Spender's phrase, "being wound up like a company in bankruptcy." Auden, as if to symbolize the end of the era of political advocacy in poetry, emigrated to the United States in 1939. By the mid-thirties expressionism and sensuality, as embodied in the verse of Dylan Thomas and George Barker, began to enjoy a revival.

With the sobering of political expression, idealism in poetry disintegrated into a variety of movements; thus, the poetry of the forties is not easy to categorize. The romantic tradition continued, albeit with variations and evolutions. Although still political, the poets of the forties turned away from doctrinaire programs and sought solutions in other areas. Dylan Thomas, whose blend of religion, myth, and modern psychology seldom touched on political events, became very popular with a number of raucous and wildly successful tours of the United States. At the other end of the spectrum, John Betjeman produced a sentimental body of work, dealing with English life and manners, which was firmly grounded in the tradition of English pastoral verse. In America, the war produced a number of significant poems, including those of Richard Eberhart, Karl Shapiro, and Randall Jarrell. Yet, these poets did not give rise to any new or widespread "schools" of poetry.

The twenty years between 1930 and 1950 produced a vast amount of truly great works, a representative sampling of which is included in this anthology. The period expanded the number of subjects a poet could consider. Along with the liberalization of content came greater experimentation with style and form. These two factors contributed to the fragmented nature of the poetry. Therefore, a great diversity characterizes the present anthology, including, the pastoral reflections of Betjeman, the moral and social outrage of Richard Wright, as well as the cool and controlled psychology of W.H. Auden. This reflects the times these poets lived in, for the period 1930-1950 was a transitional bridge to the contemporary world. The poetry found in this collection is thoroughly modern and speaks directly to the contemporary reader. It is vital to an understanding of present day culture.

James Joyce (1882–1941)

James Joyce was born February 2 in Rathgar, Dublin, the eldest son of what was to become a large family. He was educated at a series of Jesuit schools and the University College in Dublin. Joyce left for Paris in 1902 to study medicine; instead he read, wrote, and studied literature while living in abject poverty. In 1903 he returned to Dublin to care for his dying mother. Her eventual death played a major role in his artistic development, being an important theme in his masterpiece *Ulysses*. Joyce met and fell in love with Nora Barnacle in 1904. They were married in 1931. The young couple moved to Pola in 1904 where Joyce was a schoolteacher. It was in this year that he started to get his first short stories and poems published. *Dubliners,* a collection of short stories, appeared in 1914, and in the same year his novel *Portrait of the Artist as a Young Man* was serialized in the *Egoist*. *Portrait* was printed in full in 1916. Despite severe eye problems, Joyce worked diligently on his magnum opus, *Ulysses*, for the next six years. It was published in 1922 by Shakespeare and Company in Paris. Another major novel, *Finnegans Wake*, was completed in 1939 even though Joyce was near complete blindness. He died January 13, in Zurich, from a perforated ulcer.

I Hear an Army Charging upon the Land

I hear an army charging upon the land,
    And the thunder of horses plunging, foam about their knees:
Arrogant, in black armour, behind them stand,
    Disdaining the reins, with fluttering whips, the charioteers.

They cry unto the night their battle-name:
    I moan in sleep when I hear afar their whirling laughter.
They cleave the gloom of dreams, a blinding flame,
    Clanging, clanging upon the heart as upon an anvil.

They come shaking in triumph their long, green hair:
    They come out of the sea and run shouting by the shore.
My heart, have you no wisdom thus to despair?
    My love, my love, my love, why have you left me alone?

Andrew Young (1885–1971)

Andrew Young was born April 29 in Elgin, Scotland. He was educated at the University of Edinburgh and New College, Oxford. Young was the Vicar of Stonegate until 1959 and the Canon of Chichester Cathedral from 1948 to 1971. He won the Queen's Gold Medal for Poetry in 1952. Though the subjects for Young's poems center around the countryside, animals, and plants (he was a botanist), there is always a metaphysical or theological underpinning to his message.

The Black Rock of Kiltearn

They named it Aultgraat—Ugly Burn,
This water through the crevice hurled
Scouring the entrails of the world—
Not ugly in the rising smoke
That clothes it with a rainbowed cloak
But slip a foot on frost-spiked stone
Above this rock-lipped Phlegethon
And you shall have
The Black Rock of Kiltearn
For tombstone, grave
And trumpet of your resurrection.

The Dead Crab

A rosy shield upon its back,
That not the hardest storm could crack,
From whose sharp edge projected out
Black pin-point eyes staring about;
Beneath, the well-kint cote-armure
That gave to its weak belly power;
The clustered legs with plated joints
That ended in stiletto points;
The claws like mouths it held outside:-
I cannot think this creature died
By storm or fish or sea-fowl harmed
Walking the sea so heavily armed;
Or does it make for death to be
Oneself a living armoury?

The Scarecrow

He strides across the grassy corn
That has not grown since it was born,
A piece of sacking on a pole,
A ghost, but nothing like a soul.

Why must this dead man haunt the spring
With arms anxiously beckoning?
Is spring not hard enough to bear
For one at autumn of his year?

Stay, Spring

Stay, spring, for by this ruthless haste
You turn all good to waste;
Look, how the blackthorn now
Changes to trifling dust upon the bough.

Where blossom from the wild pear shakes
Too rare a china breaks,
And though the cuckoos shout
They will forget their name ere June is out.

That thrush too, that with beadlike eye
Watches each passer-by,
Is warming at her breast
A brood that when they fly rob their own nest.

So late begun, so early ended!
Lest I should be offended
Take warning, spring, and stay
Or I might never turn to look your way.

Hilda Doolittle (1886–1961)

Hilda Doolittle (H.D.) was born September 10 in Bethlehem, Pennsylvania to Helen Wolle and Charles Leander Doolittle, a professor of mathematics and astronomy at Lehigh University. The family moved to a Philadelphia suburb in 1895 when her father was appointed to a professorship at the University of Pennsylvania. H.D. grew up in an atmosphere of learning and creativity. In 1901 she met Ezra Pound, then a student at the University of Pennsylvania, at a Halloween party and the two fell in love. H.D. went to Bryn Mawr in 1904 but had to return to Philadelphia two years later because of poor health. In 1905 she and Pound became engaged, to the vehement opposition of her parents. For several reasons the engagement was broken in 1908 and Pound went to Europe.

Pound returned to America in 1910 and renewed his engagement to H.D. He convinced her to travel to London with him where she was introduced to the great literary figures of the day. It was in London that H.D. began to write poetry in earnest. In August of 1912 she presented two of her poems to Pound, "Priapus" and "Hermes of the Ways," which he immediately sent to the magazine *Poetry* for publication. The two poems were received with much critical acclaim and marked the beginning of a new movement in poetry, the Imagist school. As stated by Pound in an issue of *Poetry* the credo of Imagism consists of three principles: direct treatment of the subject of the poem, composition in new rhythms to fit the idea of the poem, and the use of only essential vocabulary. The result was hard, lean, and objective verse.

In 1914 H.D. married the poet Richard Aldington and they settled in London. In the same year Pound published some of H.D's work in his anthology, *Des Imagistes* and she came out with her own collection in 1916, *Sea Garden*. During World War I, H.D. edited the periodical *Egoist* with T.S. Eliot.

In 1918 a series of personal tragedies befell H.D. which would mark the turning point in her creative career: her brother died, she had a miscarriage, her father died, she and Aldington separated, and she contracted double pneumonia during a subsequent pregnancy. After her daughter, Perdita, was born in 1919, H.D. had a nervous breakdown and was taken to Greece by her friend Bryher (Winifred Ellerman) to recuperate. With Bryher and Perdita, H.D. spent the twenties traveling to America, Switzerland, and Egypt. In 1925 her *Collected Poems of H.D.* appeared. After going through analysis with Freud (1933–34), H.D. developed a more mature grasp of her life and her art. Many critics believe that her later work is her best. During World War II she wrote a great deal of prose and poetry, including *Writing On The Wall, Tribute to the Angels,* and *The Flowering of the Rod.* In 1960 H.D became the first woman to receive the Award of Merit Medal for Poetry of the American Academy of Arts and Letters. She died of a heart attack on September 28, 1961.

Helen

All Greece hates
the still eyes in the white face,
the lustre as of olives
where she stands,
and the white hands.

All Greece reviles
the wan face when she smiles,
hating it deeper still
when it grows wan and white,
remembering past enchantments
and past ills.

Greece sees unmoved
God's daughter, born of love,
the beauty of cool feet
and slenderest of knees,
could love indeed the maid,
only if she were laid,
white ash amid funereal cypresses.

Not Honey

Not honey
Not the plunder of the bee
From meadow or sand-flower
Or mountain bush;
From winter-flower or shoot
Born of the later heat:
Not honey, not the sweet

Stain on the lips and teeth:
Not honey, not the deep
Plunge of the soft belly
And the clinging of the gold-edged
Pollen-dusted feet.

Not so—
Though rapture blind my eyes,
And hunger crisp
Dark and inert my mouth,
Not honey, not the south,
Not the tall stalk
Of red twin-lilies,
Nor light branch of fruit tree
Caught in flexible light branch.

Not honey, not the south;
Ah, flower of purple iris,
Flower of white,
Or of the iris, withering the grass—
For fleck of the sun's fire,
Gathers such heat and power,
That shadow-print is light,
Cast through the petals
Of the yellow iris flower.

Not iris—old desire—old passion—
Old forgetfulness—old pain—
Not this, nor any flower,
But if you turn again,
Seek strength of arm and throat,
Touch as the god:
Neglect the lyre-note;
Knowing that you shall feel,
About the frame,
No trembling of the string
But heat more passionate
Of bone and the white shell
And fiery tempered steel.

There Is a Spell, for Instance

There is a spell, for instance,
in every sea-shell:

continuous, the sea-thrust
is powerless against coral,

bone, stone, marble
hewn from within by that craftsman,

the shell-fish:
oyster, clam, mollusc

is master-mason planning
the stone marvel:

yet that flabby, amorphous hermit
within, like the planet

senses the finite,
it limits its orbit

of being, its house,
temple, fane, shrine:

it unlocks the portals
at stated intervals:

prompted by hunger,
it opens to the tide-flow:

but infinity? no,
of nothing-too-much:

I sense my own limit,
my shell-jaws snap shut

at invasion of the limitless,
ocean-weight; infinite water

can not crack me, egg in egg-shell;
closed in, complete, immortal

full circle, I know the pull
of the tide, the lull

as well as the moon;
the octopus darkness

is powerless against
her cold immortality;

so I in my own way know
that the whale

can not digest me:
be firm in your own small, static, limited

orbit and the shark-jaws
of outer circumstance

will spit you forth:
be indigestible, hard, ungiving,

so that, living within,
you beget, self-out-of-self,

selfless,
that pearl-of-great-price.

Edith Sitwell (1887–1964)

Edith Sitwell, born September 7 in Scarborough, England, had a very peculiar and unhappy childhood. Her parents, Sir George Sitwell and Lady Ida Denison, were both dissatisfied with their marriage and Edith was an unwanted child. "Little E." was by any standard an ugly baby. She grew to an ungainly six feet, was rail thin, and had stooped shoulders. Her father openly resented her awkward appearance, and frequently chastised her for her aquiline nose. Edith was estranged from her parents and fearful of most people. She withdrew into the refuge of her imagination, and enjoyed relating tales to her two little brothers.

Though Sitwell had a strained and alienated relationship with her mother and father, she lived at home until she was 26 years old. During the summer of 1914, determined to become a writer, she left home to take up residence in London. She had abundant notebooks full of creative work, and had even published a poem, "Drowned Suns," in the *Daily Mirror*. Still, her first poetry collection, *The Mother*, was published by a vanity press. It met with good reviews and in 1918 she did not have to pay to get her second book, *Clowns' Houses*, published. After the appearance of this second book, Sitwell moved rather easily into the small literary world of London. Contrary to her childhood days, she was accepted by her peers and was soon quite popular.

From 1916 to 1921, Sitwell and her two brothers, Osbert and Sacheverell, edited the periodical *Wheels*, an experimental vehicle for new poets. "Wheelites," as they were dubbed by Aldous Huxley, were rebelling against the English literary establishment, especially the Georgian school. The periodical folded in 1921 due to lack of finances, (even with her later success, Sitwell was always in desperate financial straits).

In 1921 Sitwell and the young English composer, William Walton, collaborated on a combined poetical and musical composition. The result, *Facade*, premiered in January of 1922 to the ridicule of critics and horror of audiences. The music and poetry were not so bad, as were the unrehearsed and amateur performances of Walton and Sitwell. Still, they did not give up, and by 1926 *Facade* was a critical and commercial success. The poems of *Facade* represent an experimenatl stage for Sitwell. She was concerned not so much with meaning as with, in her own words, ". . . the effect on rhythm and speed of the use of rhymes, assonances, and dissonances . . ."

Sitwell's *Troy Park* (1925) abandoned her technical enquiries, returning to the tradition of the English romantic movement. The poems deal with an idealized childhood (many culled from the fantasy world she imagined as a child) and the past. Her other collections of the twenties—*The Sleeping Beauty* (1924) and *Rustic Elegies* (1927)—concentrated on feeling and meaning, rather than form and effect.

In 1929 Sitwell composed two poems, "Metamorphosis" and "Gold Coast Customs," which turned away from nostalgic content, reflecting on the base state of human beings. After these poems she did not write another for ten years. During the thirties Sitwell spent most of her time in Paris writing prose works, compiling anthologies, and putting together a history of the town of Bath.

With the outbreak of World War II, Sitwell returned to England. She moved into the family estate of Renishaw with her brother Osbert. At Renishaw she began to write poetry again, and in 1942 her *Street Songs* was published. This was the turning point in her career, for *Street Songs* captured precisley the mood of the time and immediately went through three printings. Her 1944 *Green Song* was even more popular. *The Shadow of Cain* (1947), a poem for the atomic age, established Sitwell as the spokesperson of the post-war modern era. She became a celebrity in England and America, going on several lecture tours and often appearing on the BBC. Sitwell even starred as Lady Macbeth in a production of *Macbeth* at the Museum of Modern Art. In 1954 Sitwell was made Dame Commander, Order of the British Empire. Her last book of poems, *The Outcasts*, was published in 1962, and in the same year she came out with a best selling novel, *The Queens of the Hive*. Dame Sitwell collapsed on the night of December 8 and died shortly thereafter.

The Coat of Fire

Amid the thunders of the falling Dark
In Tartarean darkness of the fog
I walk, a Pillar of Fire
On pavements of black marble, hard
And wide as the long boulevard
Of Hell . . . I, in whose veins the Furies wave
Their long fires, move where purgatories, heavens,
   hells and worlds
Wrought by illusion, hide in the human breast
And tear the enclosing heart . . . And the snow fell
(Thin flakes of ash from Gomorrah) on blind faces
Turned to the heedless sky . . . A dress has the sound
Of Reality, reverberates like thunder.
And ghosts of aeons and of equinoxes
(Of moments that seemed aeons, and long partings)
Take on the forms of fashionable women
With veils that hide a new Catastrophe, and under
Is the fall of a world that was a heart. Some doomed
   to descend
Through all the hells and change into the Dog
Without its faithfulness, the Crocodile
Without its watchfulness, and then to Pampean mud.
In the circles of the city's hells beneath the fog
These bear, to light them, in the human breast,
The yellow dull light from the raging human dust,
The dull blue light from the brutes, light red as rust
Of blood from eyeless weeping ghosts, light black as
   smoke
From hell. And those breasts bear
No other light. . . .They circle in the snow
Where in the dust the apterous
Fates turned insects whisper 'Now abandon
Man the annelida. Let all be wingless
That hangs between the abyss and Abaddon.'
The Catastrophes with veils and trains drift by,
And I to my heart, disastrous Comet, cry
'Red heart, my Lucifer, how fallen art thou,
And lightless, I!'

The dresses sweep the dust of mortality
And roll the burden of Atlas' woe, changed to a stone
Up to the benches where the beggars sway—
Their souls alone as on the Judgement Day—
In their Valley of the myriad Dry Bones under
　　world-tall houses.
Then, with a noise as if in the thunders of the Dark
All sins, griefs, aberrations of the world rolled to
　　confess,
Those myriad Dry Bones rose to testify:
'See her, the Pillar of Fire!
　　　　　　　　　　　　The aeons of Cold
And all the deaths that Adam has endured
Since the first death, can not outfreeze our night.
And where is the fire of love that will warm our
　　hands?
There is only this conflagration
Of all the sins of the world! To the dust's busyness
She speaks of annihilation
Of every form of dust, burned down to Nothingness!
To the small lovers, of a kiss that seems the red
Lightning of Comets firing worlds—and of a Night
That shall outburn all nights that lovers know—
The last red Night before the Judgement Day!
O Pillar of Flame, that drifts across the world to
　　Nowhere!
The eyes are seas of fire! All forms, all sights,
And all sensations are on fire! All smells, a ravening
Raging cyclone of wild fire! The nose, burned quite
　　away!
The tongue is on fire, all tastes on fire, the mind
Is red as noon upon the Judgement Day!
The tears are rolling, falling worlds of fire!
With what are these on fire? With passion, hate,
Infatuation, and old age, and death,
With sorrow, longing, and with labouring breath,
And with despair and life are these on fire!
With the illusions of the world, the flames of lust,
And raging red desire!
A Pillar of Fire is she in the emptying dust,

And will not change those fires into warmth for our
    hands,'
Said the beggars, lolling and rocking
The heedless world upon a heaving shoulder.

Dark Song (from *Facade*)

The fire was furry as a bear
And the flames purr . . .
The brown bear rambles in his chain
Captive to cruel men
Through the dark and hairy wood.
The maid sighed, 'All my blood
Is animal. They thought I sat
Like a household cat;
But through the dark woods rambled I . . .
Oh, if my blood would die!'
The fire had a bear's fur;
It heard and knew . . .
The dark earth furry as a bear,
Grumbled too!

The Drum

(The Narrative of the Demon of Tedworth)

In his tall senatorial,
Black and manorial,
House where decoy-duck
Dust doth clack—
Clatter and quack
To a shadow black,—
Said the musty Justice Mompesson,
'What is that dark stark beating drum
That we hear rolling like the sea?'
'It is a beggar with a pass
Signed by you.' 'I signed not one.'

They took the ragged drum that we
Once heard rolling like the sea;
In the house of the Justice it must lie
And usher in Eternity.

Is it black night?
Black as Hecate howls a star
Wolfishly, and whined
The wind from very far.

In the pomp of the Mompesson house is one
Candle that lolls like the midnight sun,
Or the coral combe of a cock; . . . it rocks . . .
Only the goatish snow's locks
Watch the candles lit by fright
One by one through the black night.

Through the kitchen there runs a hare—
Whinnying, whines like grass, the air;
It passes; now is standing there
A lovely lady . . . see her eyes—
Black angels in a heavenly place,
Her shady locks and her dangerous grace.

'I thought I saw the wicked old witch in
The richest gallipot in the kitchen!'
A lolloping galloping candle confesses.
'Outside in the passage are wildernesses
Of darkness rustling like witches' dresses.'

Out go the candles one by one
Hearing the rolling of a drum!

What is the march we hear groan
As the hoofed sound of a drum marched on
With a pang like darkness, with a clang
Blacker than an orang-outang?
'Heliogabalus is alone,—
Only his bones to play upon!'

The mocking money in the pockets
Then turned black . . . now caws
The fire . . . outside, one scratched the door
As with iron claws,—

Scratching under the children's bed
And up the trembling stairs . . . 'Long dead'
Moaned the water black as crape.
Over the snow the wintry moon
Limp as henbane, or herb paris,
Spotted the bare trees; and soon
Whinnying, neighed the maned blue wind
Turning the burning milk to snow,
Whining it shied down the corridor—
Over the floor I heard it go
Where the drum rolls up the stair, nor tarries.

Heart and Mind

Said the Lion to the Lioness—'When you are amber
   dust,—
No more a raging fire like the heat of the Sun
(No liking but all lust)—
Remember still the flowering of the amber blood and
   bone

The rippling of bright muscles like a sea
Remember the rose-prickles of bright paws
Though we shall mate no more
Till the fire of that sun the heart and the moon-cold
   bone are one.'
Said the Skeleton lying upon the sands of Time—
'The great gold planet that is the mourning heat of
   the Sun
Is greater than all gold, more powerful
Than the tawny body of a Lion that fire consumes
Like all that grows or leaps . . . so is the heart
More powerful than all dust. Once I was Hercules

Or Samson, strong as the pillars of the seas:
But the flames of the heart consumed me, and the mind
Is but a foolish wind.'

Said the Sun to the Moon—'When you are but a lonely white crone,
And I, a dead King in my golden armour somewhere in a dark wood,
Remember only this of our hopeless love
That never till Time is done
Will the fire of the heart and the fire of the mind be one.'

Most Lovely Shade

Most lovely Dark, my Aethiopia born
Of the shade's richest splendour, leave not me
Where in the pomp and splendour of the shade
The dark air's leafy plumes no more a lulling music made.

Dark is your fleece, and dark the airs that grew
Amid those weeping leaves.
Plantations of the East drop precious dew
That, ripened by the light, rich leaves perspire.
Such are the drops that from the dark airs' feathers flew.

Most lovely Shade . . . Syrinx and Dryope
And that smooth nymph that changed into a tree
Are dead . . . the shade, that Aethiopia, sees
Their beauty make more bright its treasuries—
Their amber blood in porphyry veins still grows
Deep in the dark secret of the rose
And the smooth stem of many a weeping tree,
And in your beauty grows.

Come then, my pomp and splendour of the shade
Most lovely cloud that the hot sun made black
As dark-leaved airs,—
                    Come then, O precious cloud,
Lean to my heart: no shade of a rich tree
Shall pour such splendour as your heart to me.

An Old Woman

I

I, an old woman in the light of the sun,
Wait for my Wanderer, and my upturned face
Has all the glory of the remembering Day,
The hallowed grandeur of the primeval clay
That knew the Flood and suffered all the dryness
Of the uncaring heaven, the sun its lover.

For the sun is the first lover of the world,
Blessing all humble creatures, all life-giving,
Blessing the end of life and the work done,
The clean and the unclean, ores in earth, and splendors
Within the heart of man, that second sun.

For when the first founts and deep waterways
Of the young light flow down and lie like peace
Upon the upturned faces of the blind
From life, it comes to bless
Eternity in its poor mortal dress—
Shining upon young lovers and old lechers
Rising from their beds, and laying gold
Alike in the unhopeful path of beggars
And in the darkness of the miser's heart.
The crooked has a shadow light made straight,
The shallow places gain their strength again—
And desert hearts, waste heavens, the barren height
Forget that they are cold.
The man-made chasms between man and man
Of creeds and tongues are filled, the guiltless light
Remakes all men and things in holiness.

And he who blessed the fox with a golden fleece,
And covered earth with ears of corn like the planets
Bearded with thick ripe gold,
For the holy bread of mankind, blessed my clay:
For the sun cares not that I am a simple woman;
To him, laughing, the veins in my arms and the wrinkles
From work on my nursing hands are sacred as branches
And furrows of harvest . . . to him, the heat of the earth
And beat of the heart are one—
Born from the energy of the world, the love
That keeps the Golden Ones in their place above,
And hearts and blood of beasts ever in motion—
Without which comets, sun, plants, and all living beings
And warmth in the inward parts of the earth would freeze.
And the sun does not care if I live in holiness:
To him, my mortal dress
Is sacred, part of the earth, a lump of the world
With my splendors, ores, impurities, and harvest,
Over which shines my heart, that ripening sun.

Though the dust, the shining racer, overtake me,
I, too, was a golden woman like those that walk
In the fields of the heavens:—but am now grown old
And must sit by the fire and watch the fire grow cold—
A country Fate whose spool is the household task.
Yet still I am loved by the sun, and still am part
Of earth. In the evenings bringing home the workers,
Bringing the Wanderer home and the dead child,
The child unborn and never to be conceived,
Home to the mother's breast, I sit by the fire
Where the seed of gold drops dead and the kettle simmers
With a sweet sound like that of a hive of bees;
And I wait for my Wanderer to come home to rest—
Covered with earth as if he had been working
Among the happy gardens, the holy fields
Where the bread of mankind ripens in the stillness.
Unchanged to me by death, I shall hold to my breast
My little child in his sleep, I shall seem the consoling
Earth, the mother of corn, nurse of the unreturning.

Wise is the earth, consoling grief and glory,
The golden heroes proud as pomp of waves—
Great is the earth embracing them, their graves;
And great is the earth's story.
For though the soundless wrinkles fall like snow
On many a golden cheek, and creeds grow old
And change—man's heart, that sun,
Outlives all terrors shaking the old night:
The world's huge fevers burn and shine, turn cold,
Yet the heavenly bodies and young lovers burn and shine,
The golden lovers walk in the holy fields
Where the Abraham-bearded sun, the father of all things,
Is shouting of ripeness, and the whole world of dews and
    splendors are singing
To the cradles of earth, of men, beasts, harvests, swinging
In the peace of God's heart. And I, the primeval clay
That has known earth's grief and harvest's happiness,
Seeing mankind's dark seed-time, come to bless,
Forgive and bless all men like the holy light.

II
Harvest
To Stephen Spender

I, an old woman whose heart is like the Sun
That has seen too much, looked on too many sorrows,
Yet is not weary of shining, fulfilment, and harvest,
Heard the priests that howled for rain and the universal darkness,
Saw the golden princes sacrificed to the Rain-god,
The cloud that came and was small as the hand of Man.
And now in the time of the swallow, the bright one, the chatterer
The young women wait like the mother of corn for the lost one—
Their golden eyelids are darkened like the great rain-clouds.
But in bud and branch the nature of Fate begins
—And love with the Lion's claws and the Lion's hunger
Hides in the brakes in the nihilistic Spring.
Old men feel their scolding heart
Reproach the veins that for fire have only anger.
And Christ has forgiven all men—the thunder-browed Caesar,

That stone-veined Tantalus howling with thirst in the plain
Where for innocent water flows only the blood of the slain,
Falling forever from veins that held in their noonday
The foolish companion of summer, the weepig rose.
We asked for a sign that we have not been forsaken—
And for answer the Abraham-bearded Sun, the father of all things,
Is shouting of ripeness over our harvest forever.
And with the sound of growth, lion-strong, and the laughing Sun,
Whose great flames stretch like branches in the heat
Across the firmament, we almost see
The great gold planets spangling the wide air
And earth—
            O sons of men, the firmament's belovèd,
The Golden Ones of heaven have us in care—
With planetary wisdom, changeless laws,
Ripening our lives and ruling hearts and rhythms,
Immortal hungers in the veins and heart
Born from the primal Cause
That keeps the hearts and blood of men and beasts ever in motion,
The amber blood of the smooth-weeping tree
Rising towards the life-giving heat of the Sun. . . .
For is not the blood—the divine, the animal heat
That is not fire—derived from the solar ray?
And does not the Beast surpass all elements
In power, through the heat and wisdom of the blood
Creating other Beasts—the Lion a Lion, the Bull a Bull,
The Bear a Bear—some like great stars in the rough
And uncreated dark—or unshaped universes
With manes of fire and a raging sun for heart?
Gestation, generation, and duration—
The cycles of all lives upon the earth—
Plants, beasts, and men, must follow those of heaven;
The rhythms of our lives
Are those of the ripening, dying of the seasons,
Our sowing and reaping in the holy fields,
Our love and giving birth—then growing old
And sinking into sleep in the maternal
Earth, mother of corn, the wrinkled darkness.
So we, ruled by those laws, see their fulfilment.
And I who stood in the grave-clothes of my flesh

Unutterably spotted with the world's woes
Cry, "I am Fire. See, I am the bright gold
That shines like a flaming fire in the night—the gold-trained
    planet,
The laughing heat of the Sun that was born from darkness—
Returning to darkness—I am fecundity, harvest."
For on each country road,
Grown from the needs of men as boughs from trees,
The reapers walk like the harvesters of heaven—
Jupiter and his great train, and the corn-goddess,
And Saturn marching in the Dorian mode.
We heard in the dawn the first ripe-bearded fire
Of wheat (so flames that are men's spirits break from their thick
    earth),
Then came the Pentecostal Rushing of Flames, God in the wind
    that comes to the wheat,
Returned from the Dead for the guilty hands of Caesar
Like the rose at morning shouting of red joys
And redder sorrows fallen from young veins and heart-springs,
Come back for the wrong and the right, the wise and the
    foolish,
Who like the rose care not for our philosophies
Of life and death, knowing the earth's forgiveness
And the great dews that comes to the sick rose:
For those who build great mornings for the world
From Edens of lost light seen in each other's eyes,
Yet soon must wear no more the light of the Sun
But say farewell among the morning sorrows.
The universal language of the Bread—
(O Thou who are not broken, or divided—
Thou who art eaten, but like the Burning Bush
Art not consumed—Thou Bread of Men and Angels)—
The Seraphim rank on rank of the ripe wheat—
Gold-bearded thunders and hierarchies of heaven
Roar from the earth: "Our Christ is arisen, He comes to give a
    sign from the Dead."

Still Falls the Rain

The Raids, 1940. Night and Dawn

Still falls the Rain—
Dark as the world of man, black as our loss—
Blind as the nineteen hundred and forty nails
Upon the Cross.

Still falls the Rain
With a sound like the pulse of the heart that is changed to the
    hammer-beat
In the Potter's Field, and the sound of the impious feet

On the Tomb:
             Still falls the Rain
In the Field of Blood where the small hopes breed and the human
    brain
Nurtures its greed, that worm with the brow of Cain.

Still falls the Rain
At the feet of the Starved Man hung upon the Cross.
Christ that each day, each night, nails there, have mercy on us—
On Dives and on Lazurus:
Under the Rain the sore and the gold are as one.

Still falls the Rain—
Still falls the Blood from the Starved Man's wounded Side:
He bears in His Heart all wounds,—those of the light that died,
The last faint spark
In the self-murdered heart, the wounds of the sad uncomprehend-
    ing dark,
The wounds of the baited bear—
The blind and weeping bear whom the keepers beat
On his helpless flesh . . . the tears of the hunted hare.

Still falls the Rain—
Then—O Ile leape up to my God: who pulles me doune—
See, see where Christ's blood streames in the firmament:
It flows from the Brow we nailed upon the tree

Deep to the dying, to the thirsting heart
That holds the fires of the world,—dark-smirched with pain
As Caesar's laurel crown.

Then sounds the voice of One who like the heart of man
Was once a child who among beasts has lain—
"Still do I love, still shed my innocent light, my Blood, for thee."

The Youth with Red-gold Hair

The gold-armoured ghost from the Roman road
Sighed over the wheat
'Fear not the sound and the glamour
Of my gold armour—
(The sound of the wind and the wheat)
Fear not its clamour. . . .
Fear only the red-gold sun with the fleece of a fox
Who will steal the fluttering bird you hide in your
    breast.
Fear only the red-gold rain
That will dim your brightness, O my tall tower of the
    corn,
You,—my blonde girl. . . .'
But the wind sighed, 'Rest.' . . .
The wind in his grey knight's armour
The wind in his grey night armour
Sighed over the fields of wheat, 'He is gone . . .
    Forlorn.'

John Peale Bishop (1892–1944)

John Peale Bishop was born May 21 in Charles Town, West Virginia, the son of a southern mother and a northern father, a division which he would deeply feel in his later years. Despite a long bout with a psychosomatic illness Peale had a typical upper middle class southern childhood. His father taught him to paint and up until the time he was 17 Bishop planned to become a painter. He attended the Mercersburg Academy where he became interested in poetry. In 1912 Bishop's first published poem, "To a Woodland Pool,' appeared in *Harper's Weekly*.

In 1913 Bishop went to Princeton where he established a great literary reputation. He wrote for *The Nassau Literary Magazine* and became a close friend of F. Scott Fitzgerald. The character of Tom D'Invilliers, in Fitzgerald's *This Side of Paradise*, was modeled after Bishop. In 1917 Bishop published his first book of poetry, a slim collection entitled *Green Fruit*.

After graduating from Princeton, Bishop accepted a commission in the United States infantry and fought in World War I. He returned to New York after the war and was an editor at *Vanity Fair* from 1920 to 1922. In 1922 he married Margaret Hutchins and they immediatly left for a two year sojourn to Europe. Returning to New York in 1924, Bishop began to work on a novel. Scribners, after initial encouragement, eventually rejected the book. During this period Bishop was alienated by American culture and found the twenties an uninspiring time. He yearned for Europe and after his novel was rejected he and his wife bought a chateau in Orgeval, France where they settled down to raise a family.

Isolated from literary circles, Bishop's productivity declined significantly, though he did manage to publish two books: a collection of short stories, *Many Thousand Gone*, in 1931, and a collection of poems, *Now With His Love*, in 1933. Bishop and his family grew tired of the expatriate life and moved back to the U.S. in 1933. He began to write more frequently and published a novel, *Act of Darkness*, and a book of poetry, *Minute Particulars*, in 1935.

In 1938 Bishop's family moved to a custom built house in South Chatham on Cape Cod, settling down to an elegant and cultured life. He wrote very little between 1938 and 1940. In December of 1940 his dear friend, Scott Fitzgerald, died and Bishop was inspired to write numerous troubled and noble poems. In 1941 he served in New York City as the publications director of The Office of the Coordination of Inter—American Affairs which brought him back to the mainstream of the literary world. This seemed to renew his enthusiasm for poetry and he continued to compose with great vigor until his death. Poor health forced him to retire to Cape Cod in 1942. He died on April 4, 1944.

Though John Peale Bishop was close friends with many of the great American writers of the twenties and thirties—Hemingway, Pound, Cummings, Edmund Wilson, and Fitzgerald—he was an alienated figure who never quite fit into any literary movement or school. This was consistent with his philosophy of writing: ". . . he (the writer) should, at whatever cost of violence, constantly set against any system, which at the moment is approved, the spontaneity and variety of life." Bishop has, for the most part, been ignored in recent (post-war) histories and anthologies of the period 1920–1940, despite his excellent reputation among leading critics and writers. Though his work is uneven, many of Bishop's poems, including the ones chosen for this anthology, are considered to be among the best examples of American poetry in the twentieth century.

Colloquy with a King-Crab

Dwarf pines; the wild plum on the wind-grassed shore
Shaken by autumn to its naked fruit;
Visions of bright winds across the bay:
These are, perhaps, sufficient images
To say what I have sought. These I have found.
Let these suffice with seas—though honesty is this,
To know what's sought from what the sands have found.
It needs no Proteus to announce the sea
Above the proclamations of loud surf—
Only the horseshoe crab, black carapace,
Project of life, though hideous, persisting
From the primordial grasp of claws on shore.
This crab is no abstraction, yet presents
No difficulty to the abstract mind,
His head all belly and his sword a tail,
But to the imagination is suspect.
Reject him? Why? Though voiceless, yet he says
That any monster may remain forever
If he but keep eyes, mind and claws intent
On the main chance, be not afraid to skulk.
This proletarian of the sea is not,
But scuttles, noble as the crocodile,
As ancient in his lineage. His name
Is not unknown in heaven. But his shell
Affords no edifice where I can creep
Though I consent like him to go on claws.

A Frieze

Arrested like marble horses
In timeless prancing: in the heave of haunches
A pause in the prancing:
Arrested like marble horses, spurred
By impetuous riders, by furious young heels
In a tumultuous curve of haunches.
Confounding seasons,
To the despair of Apollo,

The light on the restless arrested horses, the stayed
Feet, and the beautiful impetuous riders.
Love longs for life, love looks toward ecstasy.
But though the passionate motion ceases
Desire is incensed and urges
The sport for which immortality leases
This extravagant, time's prodigal body
With thoughts that exult though the body tire
Appeased but afflicted
With a pain of dissolute longing
Saved from diluvium of timelessness. Whence comes
This rage? Dimensionless and undiminishable
Lust of the timeless prancing, pause in the proud prancing,
Spurred by the furious heels of immortal horsemen?

Ode

Why will they never sleep
Those great women who sit
Peering at me with parrot eyes?
They sit with grave knees; they keep
Perpetual stare; and their hands move
As though hands could be aware—
Forward and back, to begin again—
As though on tumultuous shuttles of wind they wove
Shrouds out of air.

The three are sisters. There is one
Who sits divine in weeping stone
On a small chair of skeleton
And is most inescapable.
I have walked through many mirrors
But always accompanied.
I have been as many men, as many ghosts,
As there were days. The boy was seen
Always at rainfall, mistily, not lost.
I have tried changing shapes
But always, alone, I have heard

Her shadow coming nearer, and known
The awful grasp of striding hands
Goddess! upon
The screaming metamorphosis.

One has a face burned hard
As the red Cretan clay,
Who wears a white torso scarred
With figures like a calendar
She sits among broken shafts
Of stone; she is and still will be
Who feeds on cities, gods and men,
Weapons of bronze and curious ornaments,
Reckoning the evens as the odds.
Her least movement recalls the sea.

The last has idiot teeth
And a brow not made
For any thought but suffering.
Tired, she repeats
In idiot singing
A song shaped like a ring:
"Now is now and never Then
Dead Virgins will bear no men
And now that we speak of love, of love,
The woman's beneath
That's burdened with love
And the man's above
While the thing is done and done.
One is one and Three is three
Children may come from a spark in the sun
But One is one and never Three
And never a Virgin shall bear a Son
While the shadow lasts of the gray ashtree!"

Phantasmal marbles!

There was One who might have saved
Me from these grave dissolute stones
And parrot eyes. But He is dead,
Christ is dead. And in a grave
Dark as a sightless skull He lies
And of His bones are charnels made.

The Return

Night and we heard heavy and cadenced hoofbeats
Of troops departing; the last cohorts left
By the North Gate. That night some listened late
Leaning their eyelids toward Septentrion.

Morning flared and the young tore down the trophies
And warring ornaments: arches were strong
And in the sun but stone; no longer conquest
Circled our columns; all our state was down

In fragments. In the dust, old men with tufted
Eyebrows whiter than sunbaked faces gulped
As it fell. But they no more than we remembered
The old sea-fights, the soldiers' names and sculptors'.
We did not know the end was coming: nor why
It came; only that long before the end
Were many wanted to die. Then vultures starved
And sailed more slowly in the sky.

We still had taxes. Salt was high. The soldiers
Gone. Now there was much drinking and lewd
Houses all night loud with riot. But only
For a time. Soon the taverns had no roofs.

Strangely it was the young, the almost boys,
Who first abandoned hope; the old still lived
A little, at last a little lived in eyes.
It was the young whose child did not survive.

Some slept beneath the simulacra, until
The gods' faces froze. Then was fear.
Some had response in dreams, but morning restored
Interrogation. Then O then, O ruins!
Temples of Neptune invaded by the sea
And dolphins streaked like streams sportive
As sunlight rode and over the rushing floors
The sea unfurled and what was blue raced silver.

Hugh MacDiarmid (1892—1978)

Hugh MacDiarmid, a pseudonym for Christopher Murray Grieve, was born August 11 in Langholm, Dumfriesshire, Scotland. He was largely self-educated in the local library. His earliest works were written in English, but as he progressed he began to use a pure Scots dialect. MacDiarmid is considered by most critics to be the greatest Scottish poet since Robert Burns; he has been compared to Pound and Eliot as having one of the most original voices of the twentieth century. His poetry is devoted to resurrecting basic humanistic values in the face of an insincere and decadent society. Always a defender of the common man and underdog, MacDiarmid was the founder of the Scottish Nationalist Party. He died September 9 in Edinburgh, having written over 70 books.

At the Cenotaph

Are the living so much use
That we need to mourn the dead?
Or would it yield better results
To reverse their roles instead?
The millions slain in the War—
Untimely, the best of our seed?—
Would the world be any the better
If they were still living indeed?
The achievements of such as are
To the notion lend no support;
The whole history of life and death
Yields no scrap of evidence for't.—
Keep going to your wars, you fools, as of yore;
I'm the civilization you're fighting for.

Empty Vessel

I met ayont the cairney
A lass wi' tousie hair
Singin' till a bairnie
That was nae langer there.

Wunds wi' warlds to swing
Dinna sing sae sweet.
The licht that bends owre a'thing
Is less ta'en up wi't.

O Wha's Been Here Afore Me, Lass

O wha's been here afore me, lass,
And hoo did he get in?
—A man that deed or I was born
This evil thing has din.

And left as it were on a corpse
Your maidenheid tae me?
—Nae lass, gudeman, sin' time began
'S had only mair to gi'e.

But I can gi'e ye kindness, lad,
And a pair o' willing' hands,
And you sall ha'e my breists like stars,
My limbs like willow wands,
And on my lips ye'll heed nae mair,
And in my hair forget,
The seed o' a' the men that in
My virgin womb ha'e met.

Reflections in an Iron Works

Would you resembled the metal you work with,
Would the iron entered into your souls,
Would you became like steel on your own behalf!
You are still only putty that tyranny rolls
Between its fingers! You makers of bayonets and guns
For your own destruction! No wonder that those
Weapons you make turn on you and mangle and
    murder—
You fools who equip your otherwise helpless foes!

Scunner

Your body derns
In its graces again
As the dreich grun' does
In the gowden grain,
And out o' the daith
O' pride you rise
Wi' beauty yet
For a hauf-disguise.

The skinklan' stars
Are but distant dirt.
Tho' fer owre near
You are still—whiles—girt
Wi' the bonny licht
You bood hae tint
—And I lo'e Love
Wi' a scunner in't.

The Two Parents

I love my little son, and yet when he was ill
I could not confine myself to his bedside.
   was impatient of his squalid little needs,
His laboured breathing, and the fretful way he cried,
And longed for my wide range of interests again,
Whereas his mother sank without another care
To that dread level of nothing but life itself
And stayed, day and night, till he was better, there.

Women may pretend, yet they always dismiss
Everything but mere being just like this.

Herbert Read (1893–1968)

Herbert Read was born December 4 in Kirbymoorside, Yorkshire, England and was educated at the University of Leeds. After graduation he worked at the Government Treasury Office in London, was the assistant keeper at the Victoria and Albert Museum, and edited *Burlington Magazine*. He lectured on poetry and art theory at various universities, including Harvard and Liverpool. Read wrote ten books of poetry, and well over 40 books on art and literary criticism. His one novel, *The Green Child* (1935), has been hailed as a masterpiece of twentieth century prose.

Bombing Casualties in Spain

Dolls' faces are rosier but these were children
their eyes not glass but gleaming gristle
dark lenses in whose quicksilvery glances
the sunlight quivered. These blench'd lips
were warm once and bright with blood
but blood
held in a moist bleb of flesh
not split and spatter'd in tousled hair.

In these shadowy tresses
red petals did not always
thus clot and blacken to a scar.
These are dead faces.
Wasps' nests are not so wanly waxen
wood embers not so greyly ashen.

They are laid out in ranks
like paper lanterns that have fallen
after a night of riot
extinct in the dry morning air.

The Contrary Experience
I

You cry as the gull cries
dipping low where the tide has ebbed
over the vapid reaches: your impulse
died in the second summer of the war.

The years dip their wings
brokenly over the uncovered springs.
Hands wasted for love and poetry
finger the hostile gunmetal.

Called to meaningless action
you hesitate
meditating faith to a conscience
more patently noble.

II

But even as you wait
like Arjuna in his chariot
the ancient wisdom whispers:
Live in action.

I do not forget the oath
taken one frosty dawn
when the shadows stretched
from horizon to horizon:

Not to repeat the false act
Not to inflict pain
To suffer, to hope, to build
To analyse the indulgent heart.

Wounds dried like sealing-wax
upon that bond
But time has broken
the proud mind.

No resolve can defeat suffering
no desire establish joy:
Beyond joy and suffering
is the equable heart

not indifferent to glory
if it lead to death
if it lead to the only life.

III

Lybia, Egypt, Hellas
the same tide ebbing, the same gull crying
desolate shores and rocky deserts
hunger, thirst, death

the storm threatening and the air still
but other wings
librating in the ominous hush
and the ethereal voice

thrilling and clear.

Buffeted against the storm's sullen breath
the lark rises
over the grey dried grasses
rises and sings.

Sic et Non
1. The Complaint of Heloise
Elle a aussi cette chose en sextant de marine.
—Antonin Artaud

Abelard was: God is
   my love, I his
learned lass. But God is
   not near.

Abelard my lover
   was. I felt the
lusts that burnt us were
   too sweet:

I feared they could not last.
   I saw them pass
shedding brands to harass
   my life.

They went: cruelly forc'd.
   That he should know
doom of flesh, unique loss!
   Dear me!

I could show a white face,
   a pious dress;
but very flowers in my breast
   all fresh.

Pluck them. God pluck them. I
   plucked them madly.
But ever burgeon'd rose,
   lily:

All the emblems
   of my distress.
God help me to hide them
   now.

II. The Portrait of Abelard

The wild boars are grubbing for acorns
Among the moist fallen leaves,
And the Arudzon disperses
Mist along its course.
The Paraclete is cold;
   the cloisters comfortless.

The eunuch is contrite;
His genitals are gone to dust—
Like amputated limbs are burnt
These twenty years in acid earth.
The river runs
   along the horizontal light.

His mind is foster'd on the infinite;
His voice is gentle, animate
With intellectual faith.
The flowers toss
   against his moving feet.

The body when depriv'd of lust
Offers to an outer God
Its forced immaculation.
The scaly sky
   hath cast its glittering sheath.

And now the illumination of the stars
Visits with raw radiance
The body's hollow cave.
There bounds the fleshy sphere
More playfully
   sapp'd of seminal rheum.

A World within a War
L'espérance est le seul bien que le dégoût respecte.
                                    Vauvenargues

I

Sixteen years ago I built this house
By an oak tree on an acre of wild land
Its walls white against the beechwood
Its roof of Norfolk reed and sedge.

The mossy turf I levelled for a lawn
But for the most part left the acre wild
Knowing I could never live
From its stony soil. My work is within
Between three stacks of books. My window
Looks out on a long line of elms.

A secular and insecure retreat—
The alien world is never far away.

Over the ridge, beyond the elms
The railway runs: a passing train
Sends a faint tremor through the ground
Enough to sever a rotted picture-cord
Or rattle the teaspoon against my cup.
A dozen times a day a red bus
Trundles down the lane: there is the screech and scuttle
Of minor traffic: voices rise
Suddenly from silent wheels.
But such dusty veins drain the land
And leave an interstitial stillness.

The hedgehog and the grass-snake
Still haunt my wood. Winter
Brings the starved wildings nearer: once
We woke to find a fox's tracks
Printed on the crisp film of snow.
It was the first year of my second war
When every night a maddened yaffle
Thrummed on the icicled thatch.
Another day a reckless kestrel
Dashed against a gable and fell
Dead at my feet: the children
Watched its dying flutter and the fiery eye
Slowly eclipsed under a dim grey lid.

For years the city like a stream of lava
Crept towards us: now its flow
Is frozen in fear. To the sere earth
The ancient ritual returns: the months
Have their heraldic labours once again.
A tractor chugs through frozen clods
And gold buds bead the gorse
In coppices where besom-heads are cut.
Hedges are trimmed again and primroses
Bunch in splendour on the open banks.
The sparring rooks pick twigs
For shockhead nests built high
In the dark tracery of the elms.
April and the nightingales will come

From an alien world. The squirrels
Chatter in the green hazel-trees.
The nuthatch inspects the oak's ribbed bark
While the robin jumps round his own domain.
The hay is mown in June. With summer
Comes all ripeness, rusty, red and gold
To die in September. The reaper
Spirals round the blanched fields
The corn diminishing until at last
The expected moment comes and rabbits
Zigzag across the glistening stubble
Pursued by yelping dogs and sudden guns.
In December the corn is thrashed:
In the frosty evening the engine's smoke
Trails slowly above the berried twigs
And meets the rising mist.

II

Sedate within this palisade
Which unforethinking I have made

Of brittle leaves and velvet flowers,
I re-indite a Book of Hours—

Would emulate the Lombard School
(Crisp as medals, bright but cool)

Talk mainly of the Human Passion
That made us in a conscious fashion

Strive to control our human fate:
But in the margins interpolate

Apes and angels playing tunes
On harpsichords or saxophones

Throughout the story thus maintain
Under a sacred melody the bass profane.

My saints were often silly men
Fond of wine and loose with women.

When they rose to holy stature
They kept the whims of human nature

Were mystics in their London gardens
Or wore instead of hairshirts burdens

Of a mild domestic sort: but so devout
That suddenly they would go out

And die for freedom in the street
Or fall like partridges before a butt

Of ambushed tyranny and hate.
Other legends will relate

The tale of men whose only love
Was simple work: whose usual lives

Were formed in mirth and music, or in words
Whose golden echoes are wild rewards

For all our suffering, unto death . . .

On the last page a colophon
Would conclude the liberal plan

Showing Man within a frame
Of trophies stolen from a dream.

III

The busy routine kills the flowers
That blossom only on the casual path.
The gift is sacrificed to gain: the gain
Is ploughed into the hungry ground.
The best of life is sparely spent

In contemplation of those laws
Illustrious in leaves, in tiny webs
Spun by the ground-spider: in snailshells
And mushroom gills: in acorns and gourds—
The design everywhere evident
The purpose still obscure.

                    In a free hour
I walk through the woods with God
When the air is calm and the midges
Hover in the netted sun and stillness.
Deep then I sink in reverie. There is rest
Above the beating heart: the body
Settles round its axis: mind simulates
The crystal in the cooling rock
The theorem in the beetle's eye—
After the day's mutations
Finds the silver node of sleep. . . .

In that peace
Mind looks into a mirror poised
Above body: sees in perspective
Guts, bones and glands: the make of a man.

Out of that labyrinth
The man emerges: becomes
What he is: by no grace
Can become other: can only seize
The pattern in the bone, in branching veins
In clever vesicles and valves
And imitate in acts that beauty.

His nature is God's nature: but torn
How torn and fretted by vain energies
The darting images of eye and ear
Veiled in the web of memory
Drifts of words that deaden
The subtle manuals of sense.

But the pattern once perceived and held
Is then viable: in good gait and going
In fine song and singular sign: in all
God's festival of perfect form.

IV

Here is my cell: here my houselings
Gentle in love, excelling hate, extending
Tokens of friendship to free hearts.

But well we know there is a world without
Of alarm and horror and extreme distress
Where pity is a bond of fear
And only the still heart has grace.

An ancient road winds through the wood
The wood is dark: a chancel where the mind
Sways in terror of the formal foe.

Their feet upon the peat and sand
Made no sound. But sounds were everywhere around
Life rustled under fallen leaves, rotted twigs
Snapped like rafters above the heads
Of those friars preachers, constant and firm,
Who in charity advanced against the Arian hate
Ambushed against them. See now
The falchion falls: the martyred limbs
Lie like trimmed branches on the ground.

   The ancient road winds through the wood
   A path obscure and frail.

   The martyr takes it and the man
   Who makes the martyr by his deed.

Death waits on evil and on holiness.
Death waits in the leafy labyrinth.

There is a grace to still the blood
Of those who take the daring path:

There is a grace that fills the dying eye
With pity for the wielder of the axe.

There is a grace that nulls the pain
Of martyrs in their hour of death.

Death is no pain to desperate men.

Vision itself is desperate: the act
Is born of the ideal: the hand
Must seize the hovering grail.
Out of its stillness: a white light
Is in the hills and the thin cry
The sense of glory stirs the heart
Of a hunter's horn. We shall act: we shall build
A crystal city in the age of peace
Setting out from an island of calm
A limpid source of love.

V

The branches break. The beaters
Are moving in: lie still my loves
Like deer: let the lynx
Glide through the dappled underwoods
Lie still: he cannot hear: he may not see.

Should the ravening death descend
We will be calm: die like the mouse
Terrified but tender. The claw
Will meet no satisfaction in our sweet flesh
And we shall have known peace

In a house beneath a beechwood
In an acre of wild land.

Edmund Blunden (1896–1974)

Born November 1, Edmund Blunden's parents were joint headmasters of a London school. As the family grew, the Blundens moved to the small village of Yalding in Kent. Here Blunden developed his love for rural England. He was a good student and won the senior classics scholarship at Queen's College, Oxford. In 1916 he enlisted in the Royal Sussex Regiment and fought in France and Britain, a shattering experience which he recorded in *Undertones of War* (1928). After the war, Blunden worked as Middleton Murray's assistant on the *Athenaeum* where he eventually became a regular contributor. He held the English chair at Tokyo University from 1924 to 1927, and returned to England to teach at Merton College, Oxford. Blunden went back to the Orient in 1953 to serve as the chairman of English Literature at the University of Hong Kong. He received the Queen's Gold Medal for Poetry in 1956 and was inducted into the Order of the Rising Sun, Third Class, in Japan in 1963.

Edmund Blunden published over sixteen separate works of verse, and numerous books and articles on English history and literature. His poetry is steeped in the pastoral past of England; indeed Blunden is considered the greatest and most prolific of the First World War poets who were influenced by Thomas Hardy. Though young poets criticized Blunden for disregarding the innovations of contemporary poetry, he is most notable as the keeper of the legacy of English literature.

The Giant Puffball

From what proud star I know not, but I found
Myself newborn below the coppice rail,
No bigger than the dewdrops and as round,
In a soft sward, no cattle might assail.

And here I gathered mightiness and grew
With this one dream kindling in me: that I
Should never cease from conquering light and dew
Till my white splendour touched the trembling sky.

A century of blue and stilly light
Bowed down before me, the dew came agen,
The moon my sibyl worshipped through the night,
The sun returned and long revered: but then

Hoarse drooping darkness hung me with a shroud
And switched at me with shrivelled leaves in scorn:
Red morning stole beneath a grinning cloud,
And suddenly clambering over dike and thorn

A half-moon host of churls with flags and sticks
Hallooed and hurtled up the partridge brood,
And Death clapped hands from all the echoing thicks,
And trampling envy spied me where I stood:

Who haled me tired and quaking, hid me by,
And came agen after an age of cold,
And hung me in the prison-house a-dry
From the great crossbeam. Here defiled and old

I perish through unnumbered hours, I swoon,
Hacked with harsh knives to staunch a child's torn
    hand;
And all my hopes must with my body soon
Be but as crouching dust and wind-blown sand.

The Midnight Skaters

The hop-poles stand in cones,
The icy pond lurks under,
The pole-tops steeple to the thrones
Of stars, sound gulfs of wonder;
But not the tallest there, 'tis said,
Could fathom to this pond's black bed.

Then is not death at watch
Within those secret waters?
What wants he but to catch
Earth's heedless sons and daughters?
With but a crystal parapet
Between, he has his engines set.

Then on, blood shouts, on, on,
Twirl, wheel whip above him,
Dance on this ball-floor thin and wan,
Use him as though you love him;
Court him, elude him, reel and pass,
And let him hate you through the glass.

Report on Experience

I have been young, and now am not too old;
And I have seen the righteous forsaken,
His health, his honour and his quality taken.
   This is not what we were formerly told.
I have seen a green country, useful to the race,
Knocked silly with guns and mines, its villages
      vanished,
Even the last rat and the last kestrel banished—
   God bless us all, this was peculiar grace.

I knew Seraphina; Nature gave her hue,
Glance, sympathy, note, like one from Eden.
I saw her smile warp, heard her lyric deaden;
   She turned to harlotry;—this I took to be new.

Say what you will, our God sees how they run.
These disillusions are His curious proving
That He loves humanity and will go on loving;
   Over there are faith, life, virtue in the sun.

Solutions

The swallow flew like lightning over the green
And through the gate-bars (a hand's breadth
      between);
He hurled his blackness at that chink and won;
The problem scarcely rose and it was done.

The spider, chance-confronted with starvation,
Took up another airy situation;
His working legs, as it appeared to me,
Had mastered practical geometry.

The old dog dreaming in his frowsy cask
Enjoyed his rest and did not drop his task;
He knew the person of 'no fixed abode',
And challenged as he shuffled down the road.

These creatures which (Buffon and I agree)
Lag far behind the human faculty
Worked out the question set with satisfaction
And promptly took the necessary action.

By this successful sang-froid I, employed
On 'Who wrote Shakespeare?' justly felt annoyed,
And seeing an evening primrose by the fence
Beheaded it for blooming insolence.

Ruth Pitter (Born 1897)

Ruth Pitter was born November 7 in Ilford, Essex. After her education at the Coborn School for Girls she worked at odd jobs until 1930 when she became a working partner at Deane and Forester in London. She stayed at this job until her retirement. Though Pitter has written 16 books of verse, she does not consider herself a professional writer, but a craftsman who happens to write poetry. A dedicated Christian, her poetry is deeply entrenched in the tradition of Milton and Spenser. Pitter has largely ignored her contemporaries, preferring to muse quietly on religious and metaphysical subjects. In 1937 she won the Hawthornden Prize and in 1955 she was awarded the Queen's Gold Medal for Poetry.

But for Lust

But for lust we could be friends,
   On each other's necks could weep:
In each other's arms could sleep
   In the calm the cradle lends:

Lends awhile, and takes away.
   But for hunger, but for fear,
Calm could be our day and year
   From the yellow to the grey:

From the gold to the grey hair,
   But for passion we could rest,
But for passion we could feast
   On compassion everywhere.

Even in this night I know
   By the awful living dead,
By this craving tear I shed,
   Somewhere, somewhere it is so.

The Military Harpist

Strangely assorted, the shape of song and the bloody
   man.

Under the harp's gilt shoulder and rainlike strings,
Prawn-eyed, with prawnlike bristle, well-waxed
 moustache,
With long tight cavalry legs, and the spurred boot
Ready upon the swell, the Old Sweat waits.

Now dies, and dies hard, the stupid, well-relished
 fortissimo,
Wood-wind alone inviting the liquid tone,
The voice of the holy and uncontending, the harp.

Ceasing to ruminate interracial fornications,
He raises his hands, and his wicked old mug is
 David's,
Pastoral, rapt, the king and the poet in innocence,
Singing Saul in himself asleep, and the ancient
 Devil
Clean out of countenance, as with an army of
 angels.

He is now where his bunion has no existence.
Breathing an atmosphere free of pipeclay and
 swearing,
He wears the starched nightshirt of the hereafter, his
 halo
Is plain manly brass with a permanent polish,
Requiring no oily rag and no Soldier's Friend.

His place is with the beloved poet of Israel,
With the wandering minnesinger and the loves of
 Provence,
With Blondel footsore and heartsore, the voice in the
 darkness
Crying like beauty bereaved beneath many a donjon,
O Richard! O king! where is the lion of England!

With Howell, Llewellyn, and far in the feral north
With the savage fame of the hero in glen and in ben,
At the morning discourse of saints in the island Eire,
And at nameless doings in the stone-circle, the
 dreadful grove.

Thus far into the dark do I delve for his likeness:
He harps at the Druid sacrifice, where the golden string
Sings to the golden knife and the victim's shriek.

Strangely assorted, the shape of song and the bloody man.

The Tigress

The raging and the ravenous,
The nocturnal terror in gold,
Red-fire-coated, green-fire-eyed.
The fanged, the clawed, the frightful leaper.
Great-sinewed, silent walker,
Tyrant of all the timid, the implacable
Devil of slaughter, the she-demon
Matchless in fury, matchless love
Gives her whelps in the wilderness.
Clearing the stains of slaughter
From her jaws with tongue and forearm,

She licks her young and suckles them
Delicately as a doe:
She blood-gutted is the angel
To their blindness, she is minister
Between life and these feeble young
In barren places, where no help is.

Or man-imprisoned often disdaining
To rear her royal brood, though cheated
Into bearing, she abandons
All at birth, and bids them die.
Utter love and utter hatred
Cannot compromise; she gives
Her whole being to their being
Or rejects them into death.

No thought intervenes; her justice
Is not mind-perverted: O tigress,
Royal mother without pity,
Could but one thought arise within
That greatly-sculptured skull, behind
The phosphorus-eyes compunction burn,
Well might it be for all these millions
Mind-infected, mother-betrayed:
No beast so hapless as a man.

The Viper

Barefoot I went and made no sound;
The earth was hot beneath:
The air was quivering around,
The circling kestrel eyed the ground
And hung above the heath.

There in the pathway stretched along
The lovely serpent lay:
She reared not up the heath among,
She bowed her head, she sheathed her tongue,
And shining stole away.

Fair was the brave embroidered dress,
Fairer the gold eyes shone:
Loving her not, yet did I bless
The fallen angel's comeliness;
And gazed when she had gone.

John Wheelwright (1897–1940)

Born in Massachusetts, John Wheelwright was tenth in descent from the Reverend John Wheelwright, an important figure in the great Christian debate over the nature of salvation, the Antinomian controversy. Wheelwright was also a descendent of Boston's first multimillionaire, Peter Chardon Brooks. In the 1930's, Wheelwright rebelled against his family heritage and became a socialist and later a Trotskyite. He completed three poetry collections during his short life: *Rock and Shell* (1933), *Mirror of Venus* (1938), *Political Self—Portrait* (1940). The *Collected Poems of John Wheelwright* contains most of the verse he was working on at the time of his death.

Ave Eva

Wild strawberries, gooseberries, trampled;
sweet single roses torn; I hoofed to a ground
where a woman sat, weeping over a wounded bird.
"O silent woman, weeping without tears;
"O weeping woman, silent on this ground
"more withered than the barren; may I not help you heal
"the suffering of this wounded bird?" I said.

"But let your hand first mend the axle of this wheel,
"O scarlet-handed, azure-eyed," she answered.
"Let your eyes find the balance of these scales
"fashioned from two of my sons' brain-pans."

"Woman with scale and wheel and wounded bird
"more disconsolate than a child with broken toys;
"first, I beseech you, uncripple this wounded bird
"whose sufferings give to the mute universe
"measure of its own pain." With no reply
the frightened woman, more frightened, for an answer
dropped her frightened eyes to the unanswering
eyes of a third skull between her feet. Then I commanded:

"Get up. There are more skulls hid than the three
"skulls seen. Get going on your business!"
"You flaxen-faced and purple-lipped!" she cried,
"My business is to gather up my strength;
"my purpose is to mend the axle and the hub;
"and my intent, to find the balance of the scale."

"And . . . were the balance trued, were Adam's
"dust, which was your dearest flesh and blood,
"sifted over Abel's hunger-murdered eyes,—
"should the scale tip; my apposite pan
"I would then load with the bones of the warring hordes
"of goodly Abel's brothers, Cain and Seth . . .
"Leave your gray ground, Eve, go along with me."

"Satan," she said, "when my car moves I move.
"And the bird will fly. Its flight will heal its wing.
"I, and my best sons, Cain and Seth, require
"them who wish the bird healed mend my car.
"The bird cannot be healed except by flight.
"And when I move and my car mows the roses,
"let dust and bone mold and slowly close
"Abel's insatiate, unanswering eyes,—
"you azure-eyed, you flaxen-faced, purple-lipped and scarlet-handed!
"The bird will fly. Its flight will heal its wing."

Then I departed as I came, tearing roses
and trampling the gooseberries and the strawberries.

Bread-Word Giver
For John, Unborn

John, founder of towns,—dweller in none;
Wheelwright, schismatic,—schismatic from schismatics;
friend of great men whom these great feared greatly;
Saint, whose name and business I bear with me;
rebel New England's rebel against dominion;
who made bread-giving words for bread makers;
whose blood floods me with purgatorial fire;
I, and my unliving son, adjure you:
keep us alive with your ghostly disputation
make our renunciation of dominion
mark not the escape, but the permanent of rebellion.

Speak! immigrant ancestor in blood; brain
ancestor of all immigrants I like. Speak,
who unsealed sealed wells with a flame and sword:
> 'The springs that we dug clean must be kept flowing.
> If Philistines choke wells with dirt,—open
> 'em up clear. And we have a flaming flare
> whose light is the flare that flames up in the people.

> 'The way we take (who will not fire and water
> taken away) is this: prepare to fight. If we
> fight not for fear in the night, we shall be surprised.
> Wherever we live, who want present abundance
> take care to show ourselves brave. If *we* do not try
> *they* prevail. Come out,—get ready for war;
> stalwart men, out and fight. Cursed
> are all who'll come not against strong wrong.
> First steel your swordarm and first sword.
> But the second way to go? and deed to do?

> 'That is this: Take hold upon our foes and kill.
> We are they whose power underneath a nation
> breaks it in bits as shivered by iron bars.
> What iron bars are these but working wills?
> Toothed as spiked threshing flails we beat
> hills into chaff. Wherefore, handle our second
> swords with awe. They are two-edged. They cut their
> wielders' hearts.'

In Poets' Defence
For Van Wyck Brooks

Rebel poets, who've given vicar aid
to murdered agitator and starved miner,
starve in your mind and murder in your thought
indignant will-to-help unfused with Revolution.
Nurture the calm of wrath. Though Labor fumble
a second Civil War, prevent a memory
like its first forged golden chain

to bind white peon and black serf apart.
    While labor power'd come too nearly free
in the open market of free trade for jobs,
choose from Concord conspirators their thoughts
which still remain Sedition; forget braggarts
after victory whose rage contrived defeat.
Not by old images of grief and joy,
nor mummied memory of the Civil War,
nor Mayflower Compact, nor by rebel oaths
which made the Thirteen States palladium
and shield and shibboleth, adjure ourselves.
    Now boom the double guns of Word and Deed
while liberal persons fall in love with ice men
and Wilson's ghost'll vampire Lenin's mummy.
Every memory of hope, every thought,
passions and nerves our stern philanthropy
with cheer, with eager patience for laborers' slow
smoldering of hate to crack down pedestals,
compact from bones and gold, of Quirinus and Mars.

Titanic Litany
For Leon Trotsky

Prometheus!
Prototypal Christ, pre-crucified
pushing the invisible
advance upon our pushes upon chaos.
Discoverer and inventor, never let 'em say:
"Human nature cannot change."
Institutor of fire's Sacrament
and outward forms of conscious inner will;
Prometheus!
Forethought of freedom (freedom
for her and him; concrete, in that and this)
Titan, tortured by the tyrant vulture
whom Vulcan riveted as firmly as machines
can rivet laborers to capital;
Prometheus!

O, let it never be said that the human of nature cannot
change. Saul changed to Paul. All saints change
man's nature, as men change nature's change.
Show us in our own acts that we hear our supplication.
Never a Saint is revered who was not reviled
as a rebel. Every rebel, in so far prophet
breeds holy doubt and skeptic faith in deeds'
Melchizedekian Succession.
While boom the double guns of Act and Word,
mutating fire swims through the protestant
blood of Christ, erect above your shadowed rock
Prometheus!
Our supine Crucifixion.

Train Ride

After rain, through afterglow, the unfolding fan
of railway landscape sidled on the pivot
of a larger arc into the green of evening;
I remembered that noon I saw a gradual bud
still white; though dead in its warm bloom;
always the enemy is the foe at home.
   And I wondered what surgery could recover
our lost, long stride of indolence and leisure
which is labor in reverse; what physic recalls the smile
not of lips, but of eyes as of the sea bemused.
   We, when we disperse from common sleep to several
tasks, we gather to despair; we, who assembled
once for hopes from common toil to dreams
or sickish and hurting or triumphal rapture;
always the enemy is our foe at home.
   We, deafened with far scattered city rattles
to the hubbub of forest birds (never having
"had time" to grieve or to hear through vivid sleep
the sea knock on its cracked and hollow stones)
so that the stars, almost, and birds comply,
and the garden-wet; the trees retire; We are
a scared patrol, fearing the guns behind;

always the enemy is the foe at home.
   What wonder that we fear our own eyes' look
and fidget to be at home alone, and pitifully
put off age by some change in brushing the hair
and stumble to our ends like smothered runners at their tape;
   Then (as while the stars herd to the great trough
the blind, in the always-only-outward of their dismantled
archways, awake at the smell of warmed stone
or to the sound of reeds, lifting from the dim
into their segment of green dawn) *always
our enemy is our foe at home*, more
certainly than through spoken words or from grief-
twisted writing on paper, unblotted by tears
the thought came:
                  There is no physic
for the world's ill, nor surgery; it must
(hot smell of tar on wet salt air)
burn in a fever forever, an incense pierced
with arrows, whose name is Love and another name
Rebellion (the twinge, the gulf, split seconds,
the very raindrop, render, and instancy
of Love).
   All Poetry to this not-to-be-looked-upon sun
of Passion is the moon's cupped light; all
Politics to this moon, a moon's reflected
cupped light, like the moon of Rome, after
the deep wells of Grecian light sank low;
always the enemy is the foe at home.
   But these three are friends whose arms twine
without words; as, in a still air,
the great grove leans to wind, past and to come.

The Word is Deed
For Kenneth Burke

John begins like *Genesis:*
In the Beginning was the Word;
Engels misread: *Was the Deed.*

But, before ever any Deed came
the sound of the last of the Deed, coming
came with the coming Word
(which answers everything with dancing).

In our Beginning our Word:
'Make a tool to make a tool'
distinguished Man from Brute.
(Men who dance know what was done.)
Good and Evil took root
in this, the cause of Destinies
whence every Revolution rose and stirred.

Jubal Cain and Tubal Cain
made the plow and jubilee
to protest, in ranks hostile to Seth
Seth's all-too-loyal mutiny.

Ways to work determinate
moulds for intelligence.
Discoveries follow thence
obscured by fallibilities'
compensating philosophies
doubted soon as heard.
(Who dance not know not what they do).

But when, against Fate, error wards:
"Frustrate while ye mirror kind
Disaster, blind
Chance, enemies at once and guards . . ."
muscles of thought comply:
"Think, act in answer to desire;
from the will springs Promethean fire."

Deeds make us. May, therefore, when our Last
Judgment find our work be just:
all tools, from foot rules to flutes
praise us; and our deeds' praise find
the Second Coming of the Word.
(Dance, each whose nature is to dance;
dance all, for each would dare the tune.)

Malcolm Cowley (Born 1898)

Malcolm Cowley was born August 24 in Belsano, Pennsylvania. He attended Peabody High School in Pittsburgh and went to Harvard in 1920, where he edited the *Advocate*. He was the associate editor of *Broom* magazine in 1923 and served as literary editor of the *New Republic* from 1929 to 1944. In 1948 he became the literary advisor to Viking Press, where he still works as a consulting editor. In 1929 he published his first book of poems, *Blue Juniata*, about the travels of a young man who feels himself to be a member of a "landless, uprooted generation." He has only published two other books of verse, *The Dry Season* (1941) and *Blue Juniata: Collected Poems* (1968). Cowley has written numerous prose works, and edited several of the Viking portable books, including *The Portable Faulkner, The Portable Hemingway,* and *The Portable Hawthorne*.

Though not a prolific poet, Cowley is nevertheless very talented and a master at his craft. Most of his poems trace his intellectual development and celebrate his country childhood. Several others document important moments in history, for instance World War I, the Spanish Civil War, and more recently, the Vietnam War.

For St. Bartholomew's Eve
(August 23, 1927)

Then die!
                Outside the prison gawk
the crowds that you will see no more.
A door slams shut behind you. Walk
with turnkeys down a corridor
smelling of lysol, through the gates
to where a drunken sheriff waits.

St. Nicholas who blessed your birth,
whose hands are rich with gifts, will bear
no further gifts to you on earth,
Sacco, whose heart abounds in prayer
neither to Pilate nor a saint
whose earthly sons die innocent.

And you that would not bow your knee
to God, swarthy Bartholomew,
no God will grant you liberty,
nor Virgin intercede for you,
nor bones of yours make sweet the plot
where governors and judges rot.

A doctor sneezes. A chaplain maps
the routes to heaven. You mount the chair.
A jailor buckles tight the straps
like those which aviators wear.
The surgeon makes a signal.
                              Die!
lost symbols of our liberty.

Beyond the chair, beyond the bars
of day and night, your path lies free;
yours is an avenue of stars:
march on, O dago Christs, while we
march on to spread your name abroad
like ashes in the winds of God.

The Hill above the Mine

Nobody comes to the graveyard on the hill,
lost on the blackened slope above the mine,
where coke-oven fumes drift heavily by day
and creeping fires at night; nobody stirs
here by the crumbling wall, where headstones loom
among the blackberry vines; nobody walks
in the blue starlight under the cedar branches
twisted and black against the moon, nor speaks
except the unquiet company of the dead,

and one who calls the roll:
                    "Ezekiel Cowley?"
Dead.
        "Laban and Uriah Evans?"
                              Dead.
"Jasper McCullough, your three wives, your thirty
children, of whom four bastards?"
                              Dead, all dead.
"Simon Eliot? Sergeant Danny George?
Judge Peter and Sarah Ellen Farbaugh?"
                              Dead,

sleeping under the brambles in the starlight
above the unpainted cabins and the mine.

What have you seen, O dead?
                              "We saw our woods
butchered, flames curling in the maple tops,
white ashes drifting, a railroad in the valley
bridging the creek, and mines under the hill.
We saw our farms lie fallow and houses grow
all summer in the flowerless meadows. Rats
all winter gnawed the last husks in the barn.
In spring the waters rose, crept through the fields
and stripped them bare of soil, while on the hill
we waited and stood firm."

                        Wait on, O dead!
The waters still shall rise, the hills fold in,
the tombs open to heaven, and you shall ride
eastward on a rain-wind, spurring the thunder,
your white bones drifting like herons across the moon.

Horace Gregory (1898–1982)

Horace Gregory was born in Milwaukee, Wisconsin on April 10. He was educated at the German-English Academy in Milwaukee and later went to the University of Wisconsin where he took his B.A. in 1923. After various teaching posts he settled down at Sarah Lawrence College in 1934, staying there until 1960 when he became a professor emeritus. Gregory was a Guggenheim Fellow in 1951 and won the Bollingen Prize for his 1965 *Collected Poems*. Other notable verse collections include *Chelsea Rooming House* (1930), *No Retreat* (1933), *Chorus for Survival* (1935), and *Medusa in Grammercy Park* (1961). Gregory is also well known as a teacher, critic, biographer, and editor, and was married to the famous poet and critic, Marya Zaturenska.

Dempsey, Dempsey

Everybody give the big boy a hand,
a big hand for the big boy, Dempsey,
failure king of the U.S.A.

Maybe the big boy's coming back,
there're a million boys that want to come back
with hell in their eyes and a terrible sock
that almost connects.
They've got to come back, out of the street,
out of some lowdown, lousy job
or take the count with Dempsey.

When he's on his knees for the count
and a million dollars cold,
a million boys go down with him
yelling:
       Hit him again Dempsey,
kill him for me Dempsey,
Christ's sake Dempsey,
my God they're killing Dempsey,
It's Dempsey down, Dempsey, Dempsey.

The million men and a million boys,
come out of hell and crawling back,
maybe they don't know what they're saying,
maybe they don't dare,
but they know what they mean:
knock down the big boss,

O, my little Dempsey,
my beautiful Dempsey
with that Godinheaven smile
and quick, god's body leaping,
not afraid, leaping, rising—
hit him again, he cut my pay check, Dempsey.
My God, Dempsey's down—
he cut my pay check—
Dempsey's down, down,
the bastards are killing Dempsey.
Listen, they made me go to war
and somebody did something wrong to my wife
while I was gone.
Hit him again Dempsey, don't be a quitter
like I am Dempsey,
O, for Jesus Christ, I'm out.
I can't get up, I'm dead, my legs
are dead, see, I'm no good,
down for the count.
They got me and I'm out,
I've quit, quit again,
only God save Dempsey, make him get up again,
Dempsey, Dempsey.

Hagen

Hagen is dead.
His girl remembers
his quick, bright head,
his well-washed hands
and his lean fingers
and how his cough stained
her bedroom floor.

He'd cough the moon
and a gallon of stars
red as fire torn
from a hundred wars.

All that could cure him
was "faith, hope and charity"—
she couldn't pay his
doctor bills
(and he wouldn't take pity
from her, nor tears).
There'd be no money
in the wills
he'd leave if he lived
a thousand years.

Hagen is dead.
All you can do with him
is dig up his coffin and
look at him there:
he wouldn't be changed much—
he looked like that anyway
and he'd still have
neat, red hair
and a quick, bright head.
That's all you can do.
Hagen is dead.

Hellbabies

Hellbabies sitting in speakeasies
trying to make a million dollars come to life
out of a shot of gin,
trying to make love again
to a new girl,
trying to get out of the way
of sleep and death.

Hellbabies (another brood)
walking through rain,
electric signboards,
in subways,
at shop windows,

their brains filled with tears,
trying to get out of the way
of wives and children
because there are
               NO JOBS, NO JOBS
no work, only walking.

Maybe God is waiting for
these hellbabies,
surely, hell is waiting
for them to come home:

come home, there will be sweet hell tonight,
always ready.

Salvos for Randolph Bourne

O bitterness never spoken, the death mask etched in
    silver,
the dark limbs rolled in lead where the shallow grave
    conceals
despair: the image of a large head, forward, devouring
the collarbone. No general in brass over it and no
conquering angel kneels.

II

This was the end:
               There were no firing squads
No City Hall Nathan Hale with a bronze cord at his
    throat
Speaking of lives and his country where a hundred
    million lives
rose, wavered, shattered like an invisible sea coiling
against a rock (no longer there) but sunken
into a shore line of weeds and sand.

Only a small room and a million words to be written
    before midnight
against poverty and idiot death like the gray face of
    Emerson
fading in New England winter twilight; the hard face
    vanishing
in snow, the passionately soft words issuing from the
    mouth—
O listen to the rock, the oracle no longer there!

III

To be the last American, an embryo coiled in a test tube,
To be a fixed and paralytic smile cocked upward to the
    clouds,
To see friends and enemies depart (around the corner)
Their sticks and smart fedoras bright in sunlight,
To be or not to be Hamlet, the Prince of Wales,
or last week's *New Republic;*
to be death delicately walking between chimney pots on
    Eighth Street,
possibly this is best to be
                            or not to be.

Tombstone with Cherubim

No notice in the papers,
                    only a voice over the telephone
Saying she was dead, casually,
remarkably definite.
                    Somebody whispered syphilis—
a sentimental lie.
                Somebody spoke of her
(rococo) a Florentine olive tree
that should have twined (O unmistakably!)
around the person of a football-captain stock-broker
    asleep

Upon Miami sands.
                    She shrieked at poverty.
divorced from silks, furs, and patented nickel-plated
    limousines.
                She loved relaxed security,
sleeping with men occasionally
as it were exotic dreams
                        and rich meaningless words
draping the tender portions of her body:
                            Hello, Marie!
you should have gone out like a row of mazda lamps
smashed with a crowbar.
                Even this epitaph,
true enough for a beautiful girl
pacing with unforgettable ease
down Michigan Boulevard one April morning,
does not contain the facts.
                      The facts were these:
She died in Lesbian serenity
                      neither hot nor cold
until the chaste limbs stiffened.
                      Disconnect the telephone;
cut the wires.

The Woman Who Disapproved of Music at the Bar

We heard her speaking of Chinese musicians,
And of the house she sold in Westchester;
She said that she could not live there forever
Waiting for things to happen in her mind
Until Martinis entered on a tray,
Or the door-bell rang, or footsteps on the stair
When one was sure the musicians had returned—
Better to live without doctors, lawyers, friends,
Even relatives might ask too many questions,
Better to sell everything and move away.
"If I could have said, 'Musicians are gentlemen:
They have asked permission

To rehearse *Persephone* on the front lawn,
Their viols and brasses
Are heard discreetly as the cries, the laughter,
Bird-song and weeping
Of a lonely child who wanders underground,
Her grief, the shadowy spray of maidenhair,
Her joy, the violet in April grasses,'
I could have hired them to play for guests at dinner,
Their music served with sherbets, iced Chianti,
Tinkling behind a plaster cast of Dante,
Echoes, farewells, Stravinsky quieted
Among white roses in a vase,
Trembling between the stems of stained wine glasses."

"It would have been difficult for me to prove
That they were Chinese;
They had come at night, I turned my face away
To the darkness of the wall beside my bed.
I knew that they were there, quiet as one knows
That death is in a room, or birth, or love,
Wailing and sighing;
I heard them play
Such music that is heard among the trees,
The sightless music, gong and waterfall,
And I knew that there were faces in the room,
The stone-carved smiling lips and empty eyes
Until I said like someone in a dream,
'I have locked the door: you cannot use my body
As though it were a room in a hotel—
You must let me sleep—
Even if you kill me, the police will come:
There will be blood upon the floor,
A broken chair, torn sheets and foot-prints in the garden,
And no one shall escape.'"

"If they had promised
Not to return, I would have stayed,
Have looked each neighbor in the eye and said,
'I have not lied:
There were twenty men among the hollyhocks,

Among sweet peas and oleanders,
And at twelve o'clock they came into my room,
Bare-footed, in rags and smelling of the East
As though the earth had opened where they walked.
I was careful not to let them know my name;
I am not responsible for what you may have heard.'"

When the woman left us, one could not have known
That two weeks later
She would actually disappear,
The phone disconnected, the top-flight suite for rent,
That perhaps the musicians had returned,
Even in the city:
One could not prove that they had followed her.

Leonie Adams (Born 1899)

Leonie Adams was born December 9 to Charles (a lawyer) and Henrietta Adams. She graduated Phi Beta Kappa from Barnard College in 1922 and worked, at different times, as a bookshop assistant, an assistant editor, and a research secretary. In 1924 she became the editor of *Measure*. Her 1925 collection of poems, *Those Not Elect*, met with critical acclaim as did her 1929 *High Falcon and Other Poems*. But after *Midsummer* (1929), Adams published only one more poem, *This Measure* (1933), for in her own words: "I have been silent a long time because I am now grappling with the limitations of the lyric."

Leonie Adams has taught at Sarah Lawrence and Bennington, and from 1947 to 1968 was professor at Columbia University. She is a recipient of the Bollingen Prize (1955) and the Guggenheim Fellowship (1928 and 1929). Her poetry is a fusion of the metaphysical and the romantic; though her poems evoke images of nature, her work is not purely descriptive but contemplates the meaning of those images. Adams is at her best when she juxtaposes traditional pictures of nature with a contemporary vision of the world.

Country Summer

Now the rich cherry, whose sleek wood
And top with silver petals traced,
Like a strict box its gems encased,
Has spilt from out that cunning lid,
All in an innocent green round,
Those melting rubies which it hid;
With moss ripe-strawberry-encrusted,
So birds get half, and minds lapse merry
To taste that deep-red, lark's-bite berry,
And blackcap bloom is yellow-dusted.

The wren that thieved it in the eaves
A trailer of the rose could catch
To her poor droopy sloven thatch,
And side by side with the wren's brood—
O lovely time of beggar's luck—
Opens the quaint and hairy bud;
And full and golden is the yield
Of cows that never have to house,
But all night nibble under boughs,
Or cool their sides in the moist field.

Into the rooms flow meadow airs,
The warm farm baking smell's blown round,
Inside and out, and sky and ground
Are much the same, the wishing star,
Hesperus, kind and early born,
Is risen only finger-far;
All stars stand close in summer air,
And tremble, and look mild as amber,
When wicks are lighted in the chamber,
You might say, stars were settling there.

Now straightening from the flowery hay,
Down the still light the mowers look,
Or turn, because their dreaming shook,
And they waked half to other days,
When left alone in the yellow stubble
The rusty-coated mare would graze.
Yet thick the lazy dreams are born,
Another thought can come to mind,
But like the shivering of the wind,
Morning and evening in the corn.

The Runner with the Lots

We listen, wind from where,
And two have heard
The step across the field
That went from us unseen,
The word that scarcely stirred
Along the corn's stiff green,
Or in their hair who bend among the corn.

And two have understood:
Though the great sails untorn
Of high September bear,
Toward harbour earth and yield,
The amber-dwindled mood
Is come, the bronze, the blue,
And every hue entering its solitude.

And all about we seize,
Of all that summers knew
Or autumns reconciled,
Sense of some utmost thing,
Some clasp unransoming,
Proffered the destinies,
And on the face recalled to its grave love,

Piercing on each, one air
Has touched them, earth and child;
And fairest here,
Fair now, whom love has sealed;
But fair unseen there move
Before us unbeguiled
The equal feet of love,
And the blind hands bearing the luck of the year.

Allen Tate (1899–1979)

Allen Tate was born November 19 in Clark County, Kentucky. While at Vanderbilt he studied under John Crowe Ransom and roomed with Robert Penn Warren. Tate contributed two poems to the first issue of the short-lived but famous magazine, *The Fugitive*. After spending time as a free lance writer in New York, he traveled to England and France on a Guggenheim Fellowship in 1928. Tate taught at the University of Minnesota from 1951 to 1968. His numerous collections of poetry won many awards, including the Bollingen Prize in 1956. Tate also published two biographies, one on Stonewall Jackson and the other on Jefferson Davis. His only novel, *The Fathers* is considered one of the finest American novels to be written in the twentieth century.

Ode to the Confederate Dead

Row after row with strict impunity
The headstones yield their names to the element,
The wind whirrs without recollection;
In the riven troughs the splayed leaves
Pile up, of nature the casual sacrament
To the seasonal eternity of death,
Then driven by the fierce scrutiny
Of heaven to their business in the vast breath,
They sough the rumour of mortality.
Autumn is desolation in the plot
Of a thousand acres, where these memories grow
From the inexhaustible bodies that are not
Dead, but feed the grass row after rich row:
Remember now the autumns that have gone—
Ambitious November with the humors of the year,
With a particular zeal for every slab,
Staining the uncomfortable angels that rot
On the slabs, a wing chipped here, an arm there:
The brute curiosity of an angel's stare
Turns you like them to stone,
Transforms the heaving air,
Till plunged to a heavier world below
You shift your sea-space blindly,
Heaving, turning like the blind crab.

  Dazed by the wind, only the wind
  The leaves flying, plunge

You know who have waited by the wall
The twilit certainty of an animal;
Those midnight restitutions of the blood
You know—the immitigable pines, the smoky frieze
Of the sky, the sudden call; you know the rage—
The cold pool left by the mounting flood—
The rage of Zeno and Parmenides.
You who have waited for the angry resolution
Of those desires that should be yours tomorrow,
You know the unimportant shrift of death
And praise the vision
And praise the arrogant circumstance
Of those who fall
Rank upon rank, hurried beyond decision—
Here by the sagging gate, stopped by the wall.

    Seeing, seeing only the leaves
    Flying, plunge and expire

Turn your eyes to the immoderate past
Turn to the inscrutable infantry rising
Demons out of the earth—they will not last.
Stonewall, Stonewall—and the sunken fields of hemp
Shiloh, Antietam, Malvern Hill, Bull Run.
Lost in that orient of the thick and fast
You will curse the setting sun.

    Cursing only the leaves crying
    Like an old man in a storm

You hear the shout—the crazy hemlocks point
With troubled fingers to the silence which
Smothers you, a mummy, in time. The hound bitch
Toothless and dying, in a musty cellar
Hears the wind only.

    Now that the salt of their blood
Stiffens the saltier oblivion of the sea,
Seals the malignant purity of the flood,
What shall we, who count our days and bow

Our heads with a commemorial woe,
In the ribboned coats of grim felicity,
What shall we say of the bones, unclean—
Their verdurous anonymity will grow—
The ragged arms, the ragged heads and eyes
Lost in these acres of the insane green?
The grey lean spiders come; they come and go;
In a tangle of willows without light
The singular screech-owl's bright
Invisible lyric seeds the mind
With the furious murmur of their chivalry.

      We shall say only, the leaves
      Flying, plunge and expire

We shall say only, the leaves whispering
In the improbable mist of nightfall
That flies on multiple wing:
Night is the beginning and the end,
And in between the ends of distraction
Waits mute speculation, the patient curse
That stones the eyes, or like the jaguar leaps
For his own image in a jungle pool, his victim.

What shall we say who have knowledge
Carried to the heart? Shall we take the act
To the grave? Shall we, more hopeful, set up the grave
In the house? The ravenous grave?

                              Leave now
The turnstile and the old stone wall:
The gentle serpent, green in the mulberry bush,
Riots with his tongue through the hush—
Sentinel of the grave who counts us all!

The Trout Map

The Management Area of Cherokee
National Forest, interested in fish,
Has mapped Tellico and Bald rivers
And North River, with the tributaries
Brookshire Branch and Sugar Cove Creek:
A fishy map for facile fishery

In Marvel's kind Ocean: drawn in two
Colours, blue and red—blue for the hue
Of Europe (Tennessee water is green),
Red lines by blue streams to warn
The fancy-fishmen from protected fish;
Black borders hold the Area in a cracked dish

While other blacks, the dots and dashes, wire
The fisher's will through classic laurel
Over boar tracks to creamy pot-holes lying
Under Bald falls that thump the shying
Trout: we flew Professor, the Hackles, and Worms.
(Tom Bagley and I were dotted and dashed wills.)

Up Green Cove gap from Preacher Millsap's cabin
We walked a confident hour of victory,
Sloped to the west on a trail that led us
To Bald River where map and scene were one
In seen-identity. Eight trout is the story
In three miles. We came to a rock-bridge

On which the road went left around a hill,
The river, right, tumbled into a cove;
But the map dashed the road along the stream
And we dotted man's fishiest enthymeme
With jellied feet upon understanding love
Of what eyes see not, that nourishes the will:

We were fishers, weren't we? And tried to fish
The egoed belly's dry cartograph—
Which made the government fish lie down and laugh.
(Tommy and I listened, we heard them shake
Mountain and cove because the map was fake.)
After eighteen miles our feet were clownish,

Then darkness took us into wheezing straits
Where coarse Magellan idling with his fates
Ran with the gulls for map around the Horn,
Or wheresoever the mind with tidy scorn
Revisits the world upon a dry sunbeam.
Now mapless the mountains were a dream.

Oscar Williams (1900–1964)

Oscar Williams was born in Brooklyn, New York. His first book, *The Golden Darkness*, received the Yale Younger Poets Award in 1921. Though *The Golden Darkness* was a great success, Williams opted to go into the advertising business. In 1937, after deciding that poetry was his true vocation, he quit advertising to devote his energies to writing. Williams is probably best known for his poetry anthologies which have sold millions of copies and continue to be widely used as text books in colleges and universities.

The Elements

Above the hemispheres there floats
A melody both strange and rare
Where aeroplanes like molten notes
Fall on the mammoth ear of air.

Over the seven vibrant seas
The giant hand of commerce dips
Touching the morrow's harmonies
With steamships for its fingertips.

With forges in its throat, fire clangs
And bellows paean to the light;
Then chasing setting suns, it hangs
Its neon necklaces on night.

And through the ancient earth there moves
Amazing music, canyon-deep,
Where under the momentous hooves
The ivory flames of granite leap,

As down this morning of mankind
Through winding valleys of events,
Man blows the golden horn of mind
And hunts beside his elements.

Milk at the Bottom of the Sea

In the bowl of buildings *alias* the back yard
The milk of snow endlessly pours, but the bowl never
Fills. The century's live inhabitant caught behind
The window pane watches the single rakish tree
Blaze forth in ponderously immaculate italics.
The snowflakes pour everywhere in a panic, dizzyingly,
Or whirl to re-organize in the mid-air and float
Undecided; the sky tilts its ominous mountain, insuring
Another waterfall of snowflakes with all feathery speed.
Such activity should be noisy, a school's-out! of sounds,
But the silence is reverberating on the window glass
Exploring the deep-sea life of waywardness.

I am the traveller in the middle of the winter
In a wood-and-glass ship on the deeps of the age.
From peril's hold I watch the white germs from heaven
And blithe nothingness, the delicate roe of purity
Splurging to fill the air with their multipleness,
Making not even the sound of rain against rock.
I am an eye, I know, frozen in an undersea facade,
And have lost my hearing in such fantastic depths
Where the pressures cave in the senses, but still
My eye kindles to all this whiteness bearing down
In a dance of spiritual blindspots on our town.

In the end the wandering snowflakes are driven
Together, foam fat in the bottom of time, and I
Assuage through the mouth of the mind my entity;
The army of my veins, blood-drops, pores, thoughts
Crowds to my bones in one supreme act of gravity,
Closer than earth to a hill, than leaves to a tree,
Till I am the very body of oneness and cannot go
Pure, cold, diffuse and wayward like the snow.

The Road from Election to Christmas

The hurdy-gurdy, public piano of the past
Grinds out a thousand lithe cats on the autumn street;
The heart trembles like a lower lip
And memories crowd the doorway:
Out of the skyline, above the façades and the clocks,
The music box of the giant years
Drips its tinkling agonies about our ears:
The young, the newer moments steadily arrive:
The famous painting on the wall listens politely
But refuses to come alive . . .

Out of the belly of the public address system
Arises the speaker to people the evening air:
All wandering ears are now conscripted
On a dreadful march into the annals of winter:
You are now to hear pouring from all the crevices
Of the cracked voice, the revelations of despair—
From the water-tank perched on civilization's horizon
Flow the melted down, long overdue, fluid haloes
For the despoiled, the cheated and the badly bruised:
Fellow citizens, in what part of your anatomy
Do you hide your vote? Little bird inside the human
  skin
Come forth: we have a worm for your beak:
It's a long unending worm, designed to choke you in
  the end . . .

The ocean slobbers on the shore, flapping slattern
  breakers,
But cannot confuse the issue
Nor wash away the brazen voice that hammers in the
  brain:
The election auctions off
The ornate sentiments, the burled thighs of the furniture;
The wooden pillars of society are taken from the files;
The evening becomes a lamp in the throat of silence,
And everywhere one can see on the streets

The black baleful cocked eyes of the loudspeakers
Like spies out of the subconscious surveying the age:
Mr. Voter, the bread you have been eating is wormy
With blackguards: look at his record: our worthy op-
 ponent
Is handing out alphabet soup in the kitchens of his mind:
Don't be fooled any longer: salvation has both
Her arms around your neck: we appeal to the highest
In your lower instincts . . .

The radio cracks its whip, the election shifts,
The glacier moves, elbowing into the foaming forest:
The brain splits open: the victor crams the headlines
Hurriedly into his mouth, and a sound of eating
Disturbs the polite conversation: the loser
Sits on an ice floe, his friends scampering in the horizon:
The rock of ages falls and spreads the citizen
Into his three dimensions: the election is over:
That bear, the people, eats honey in the dark:
Time now to clean the ticker-tape from the clover,
The pamphlets and buttons from the violated park:
No need to fear the fear of fear,
The road to Christmas is clear.

Sterling A. Brown (Born 1901)

Sterling A. Browns's father, Sterling Nelson Brown, a minister and professor of religion at Howard University, was born a slave in eastern Tennessee. Unlike many former slaves, Sterling Brown Senior was not ashamed of his heritage and celebrated Black-American history and culture. Growing up in such an environment probably had as much influence on Sterling A. Brown's poetry as did his later experiences with Black folk culture in the South.

Sterling A. Brown was born in 1901 in Washington D.C. He attended Dunbar High School where he edited a magazine and began to write poetry. In 1918 he went to Williams College and was influenced by the poets of the New Poetry Movement: Amy Lowell, Edgar Lee Masters, Robert Frost, and Carl Sandburg. Brown was particularly attracted to their rejection of Romanticism and sentimentality. He received his M.A. from Harvard University in 1923.

Brown traveled to the South to begin a teaching career. Between 1926 and 1928 he taught at The Virginia Seminary and College, Lincoln University in Missouri, and Atlanta University. He was profoundly affected by the climate of political and social change that pervaded the South just after World War I. In 1929 he joined the faculty of Howard University where he has resided ever since. During the late twenties Brown began to explore the Southern Negro experience. His poems revealed the serious nature of Black culture, portraying Blacks as three-dimensional human beings with deep and meaningful interior lives, thus challenging popular misconceptions and making accessible this rich and vital part of the American heritage. The result was Brown's landmark first book of poems, *Southern Road*, published in 1932. Though it takes as its subject matter American Negro folklore, it is universally appealing as a meditation on the nature of man. Even though *Southern Road* was a great critical success, the intervening lack of interest in Black poetry deterred the publication of another book of his verse until 1975. From 1936 to 1939 he was the editor on Negro affairs for the Federal Writer's Project. Brown was awarded a Guggenheim Fellowship in 1937. In 1938 he came out with two of his most important contributions to Black American studies: *The Negro in American Fiction* and *Negro Poetry and Drama*. His *Collected Poems* was published in 1980. In addition to composing poetry and essays throughout his life, Brown became a renowned and legendary teacher at Howard University.

After Winter

He snuggles his fingers
In the blacker loam
The lean months are done with,
The fat to come.

His eyes are set
On a brushwood-fire
But his heart is soaring
Higher and higher.

Though he stands ragged
An old scarecrow,
This is the way
His swift thoughts go,

> "Butter beans fo' Clara
> Sugar corn fo' Grace
> An' fo' de little feller
> Runnin' space.

"Radishes and lettuce
Eggplants and beets
Turnips fo' de winter
An' candied sweets.

> "Homespun tobacco
> Apples in de bin
> Fo' smokin' an' fo' cider
> When de folks draps in."

He thinks with the winter
His troubles are gone;
Ten acres unplanted
To raise dreams on.

> The lean months are done with,
> The fat to come.
> His hopes, winter wanderers,
> Hasten home.

"Butterbeans fo' Clara
Sugar corn fo' Grace
An' fo' de little feller
Runnin' space . . ."

Foreclosure

Father Missouri takes his own.
These are the fields he loaned them,
Out of hearts' fullness; gratuitously;
Here are the banks he built up for his children—
Here are the fields; rich, fertile silt.

Father Missouri, in his dotage
Whimsical and drunkenly turbulent,
Cuts away the banks; steals away the loam;
Washes the ground from under wire fences,
Leaves fenceposts grotesquely dangling in the air;
And with doddering steps approaches the shanties.

Father Missouri; far too old to be so evil.

Uncle Dan, seeing his garden lopped away,
Seeing his manured earth topple slowly in the stream,
Seeing his cows knee-deep in yellow water,
His pig-sties flooded, his flower beds drowned,
Seeing his white leghorns swept down the stream—

Curses Father Missouri, impotently shakes
His fist at the forecloser, the treacherous skinflint;
Who takes what was loaned so very long ago,
And leaves puddles in his parlor, and useless lakes
In his fine pasture land.

Sees years of work turned to nothing—
Curses, and shouts in his hoarse old voice,
"Ain't got no right to act dat way at all"
And the old river rolls on, slowly to the gulf.

Old Lem

I talked to old Lem
And old Lem said:
   "They weigh the cotton
   They store the corn
      We only good enough
      To work the rows;
   They run the commissary
   They keep the books
      We gotta be grateful
      For being cheated;
   Whippersnapper clerks
   Call us out of our name
      We got to say mister
      To spindling boys
   They make our figgers
   Turn somersets
   We buck in the middle
      Say, 'Thankyuh, sah.'
         They don't come by ones
         They don't come by twos
         But they come by tens.

   "They got the judges
   They got the lawyers
   They got the jury-rolls
   They got the law
      They don't come by ones
   They got the sheriffs
   They got the deputies
      They don't come by twos
   They got the shotguns
   They got the rope
     We git the justice
     In the end
      And they come by tens.
   "Their fists stay closed
   Their eyes look straight
     Our hands stay open

Our eyes must fall
    They don't come by ones
They got the manhood
They got the courage
    They don't come by twos
  We got to slink around,
  Hangtailed hounds.
They burn us when we dogs
They burn us when we men
    They come by tens. . . .

"I had a buddy
Six foot of man
Muscled up perfect
Game to the heart
    They don't come by ones
Outworked and outfought
Any man or two men
    They don't come by twos
He spoke out of turn
At the commissary
They gave him a day
To git out the county.
He didn't take it.
He said 'Come and get me.'
They came and got him.
    And they came by tens.
He stayed in the county—
He lays there dead.

    They don't come by ones
    They don't come by twos
    But they come by tens."

Remembering Nat Turner

We saw a bloody sunset over Courtland, once Jerusalem,
As we followed the trail that old Nat took
When he came out of Cross Keys down upon Jerusalem,
In his angry stab for freedom a hundred years ago.
The land was quiet, and the mist was rising,
Out of the woods and the Nottaway swamp,
Over Southampton the still night fell,
As we rode down to Cross Keys where the march began.

When we got to Cross Keys, they could tell us little of him.
The Negroes had only the faintest recollections:
   "I ain't been here so long, I come from up roun' Newsome;
   Yassah, a town a few miles up de road,
   The old folks who coulda told you is all dead an' gone.
   I heard something, sometime; I doan jis remember what.
   'Pears lak I heard that name somewheres or other.
   So he fought to be free. Well. You doan say."

An old white woman recalled exactly
How Nat crept down the steps, axe in his hand,
After murdering a woman and child in bed,
"Right in this house at the head of these stairs."
(In a house built long after Nat was dead.)
She pointed to a brick store where Nat was captured,
(Nat was taken in a swamp, three miles away)
With his men around him, shooting from the windows
(She was thinking of Harper's Ferry and old John Brown.)
She cackled as she told how they riddled Nat with bullets
(Nat was tried and hanged at Courtland, ten miles away)
She wanted to know why folks would come miles
Just to ask about an old nigger fool.
   "Ain't no slavery no more, things is going all right,
   Pervided thar's a good goober market this year.
   We had a sign post here with printing on it,
   But it rotted in the hole and thar it lays;
   And the nigger tenants split the marker for kindling.
   Things is all right, naow, ain't no trouble with the niggers.
   Why they make this big to-do over Nat?"

As we drove from Cross Keys back to Courtland,
Along the way that Nat came down from Jerusalem,
A watery moon was high in the cloud-filled heavens,
The same moon he dreaded a hundred years ago.
The tree they hanged Nat on is long gone to ashes,
The trees he dodged behind have rotted in the swamps.

The bus for Miami and the trucks boomed by,
And touring cars, their heavy tires snarling on the pavement.
Frogs piped in the marshes, and a hound bayed long,
And yellow lights glowed from the cabin windows.

As we came back the way that Nat led his army,
Down from Cross Keys, down to Jerusalem,
We wondered if his troubled spirit still roamed the Nottaway,
Or if it fled with the cock-crow at daylight,
Or lay at peace with the bones in Jerusalem,
Its restlessness stifled by Southampton clay.

We remembered the poster rotted through and falling,
The marker split for kindling a kitchen fire.

Sister Lou

Honey
When de man
Calls out de las' train
You're gonna ride,
Tell him howdy.

Gather up yo' basket
An' yo knittin' an' yo' things,
An' go on up an' visit
Wid frien' Jesus fo' a spell.

Show Marfa
How to make yo' greengrape jellies,
An' give po' Lazarus
A passel of them Golden Biscuits.

Scald some meal
Fo' some rightdown good spoonbread
Fo' li'l box-plunkin' David.

An' sit aroun'
An' tell them Hebrew Chillen
All yo' stories . . .

Honey
Don't be feared of them pearly gates,
Don't go 'round to de back,
No mo' dataway
Not evah no mo'.

Let Michael tote yo' burden
An' yo' pocketbook an' evah thing
'Cept yo' Bible,
While Gabriel blows somp'n
Solemn but loudsome
On dat horn of his'n.

Honey
Go Straight on the de Big House,
An' speak to yo' God
Widout no fear an' tremblin'.

Then sit down
An' pass de time of day awhile.

Give a good talkin' to
To yo' favorite 'postle Peter,
An' rub the po' head
Of mixed-up Judas,
An' joke awhile wid Jonah.

Then, when you gits de chance,
Always rememberin' yo' raisin',
Let 'em know youse tired
Jest a mite tired.

Jesus will find yo' bed fo' you
Won't no servant evah bother wid yo' room.
Jesus will lead you
To a room wid windows
Openin' on cherry trees an' plum trees
Bloomin' everlastin'.
An' dat will be yours
Fo' keeps.

Den take yo' time . . .
Honey, take yo' bressed time.

Roy Campbell (1901–1957)

Roy Campbell was born and raised in the developing colonial port of Dunbar, South Africa. His father, Samuel Campbell, was a well known doctor who founded the major technical college of Dunbar. Roy Campbell's high school years were difficult because of the headmaster's antagonism toward his family. Campbell stood up to the headmaster though and credited his later insensitivity to critical attacks to this early experience. Campbell worked his way to England on a freighter in 1918 and incorporated the events of the voyage into his 1924 poem *The Flaming Terrapin*.

In 1919 Campbell appeared in Oxford, and though never formally matriculated he made quite a number of important and influential friends—among others Edith Sitwell and Wyndham Lewis—who would support his literary efforts for the rest of his life. After a trip to Provence and Iberia, Campbell married Mary Garman in 1922. The couple moved to Wales where Campbell began to work on *The Flaming Terrapin*. Its publication delighted some critics but horrified others for what was considered its vulgarity and extravagant energy. Nevertheless, it was a financial success and in 1924 Campbell moved his family to South Africa. He tried to import English culture by founding a literary magazine, *Voorslag* (Whiplash), but it outraged the public because of its liberal views on apartheid and Campbell's family had to leave the country.

Humiliated and impoverished, the Campbells began an odyssey which took them to England, Provence, Spain, and Portugal. In turn Campbell worked as a farmer, a fisherman, a horsetrader, and a bullfighter. In 1930 T.S. Eliot, literary editor at Faber and Faber, accepted Campbell's first collection of poems, *Adamastor*.

During World War II Campbell fought in the King's African Rifles, serving primarily in Kenya and reportedly participating in the Tobruck campaign. After the war he published *Talking Bronco*. His creative abilities were in decline (some say because of his extended absence from his beloved South Africa), and he settled down in London to work as a producer for the BBC. He bought a farm near Lisbon in 1952, and published the prose work *Portugal* in 1956. On April 23, 1957 Roy Campbell died in an automobile accident.

Critics are deeply divided over the merits of Campbell's poetry—most fail to separate his dynamic and over-bearing personality from the work itself. When one concentrates on the poetry one finds some of the best and most passionate lyric verse of the twentieth century. In the words of his old Oxford friend, Edith Sitwell: "(Roy Campbell is) a poet whose every line conveyed vigor and fire . . ."

Death of the Bull

Those horns, the envy of the moon,
now, targeting the sun, have set:
the eyes are cinders of regret
that were the tinder of the noon.
But from the hornèd Alp that kneels,
as if the Rhône should sluice its flood,
out of a Wound that never heals
rills forth the lily-scented blood,

the snow-fed wine of scarlet stain,
that widens, flowering through the plains,
and from the Wound its anguish drains—
as you may hear from one who drank,
down on his knees, beside the bank,
and lost the memory of pain.

Choosing a Mast

This mast, new-shaved, through whom I rive the ropes,
Says she was once an oread of the slopes,
Graceful and tall upon the rocky highlands,
A slender tree as vertical as noon,
And her low voice was lovely as the silence
Through which a fountain whistles to the moon,
Who now of the white spray must take the veil
And, for her songs, the thunder of the sail.

I chose her for her fragrance, when the spring
With sweetest resins swelled her fourteenth ring
And with live amber welded her young thews:
I chose her for the glory of the Muse,
Smoother of forms, that her hard-knotted grain,
Grazed by the chisel, shaven by the plane,
Might from the steel as cool a burnish take
As from the bladed moon a windless lake.

I chose her for her eagerness of flight
Where she stood tiptoe on the rocky height
Lifted by her own perfume to the sun,
While through her rustling plumes with eager
    sound
Her eagle spirit, with the gale at one,
Spreading wide pinions, would have spurned the
    ground
And her own sleeping shadow, had they not
With thymy fragrance charmed her to the spot.

Lover of song, I chose this mountain pine
Not only for the straightness of her spine
But for her songs: for there she loved to sing
Through a long noon's repose of wave and wing,
The fluvial swirling of her scented hair
Sole rill of song in all that windless air,
And her slim form the naiad of the stream
Afloat upon the languor of its theme;

And for the soldier's fare on which she fed:
Her wine the azure, and the snow her bread;
And for her stormy watches on the height,
For only out of solitude or strife
Are born the sons of valour and delight;
And lastly for her rich exulting life,
That with the wind stopped not its singing breath
But carolled on, the louder for its death.

Under a pine, when summer days were deep,
We loved the most to lie in love or sleep:
And when in long hexameters the west
Rolled his grey surge, the forest for his lyre,
It was the pines that sang us to our rest,
Loud in the wind and fragrant in the fire,
With legioned voices swelling all night long,
From Pelion to Provence, their storm of song.

It was the pines that fanned us in the heat,
The pines, that cheered us in the time of sleet,
For which sweet gifts I set one dryad free;
No longer to the wind a rooted foe,
This nymph shall wander where she longs to be
And with the blue north wind arise and go,
A silver huntress with the moon to run
And fly through rainbows with the rising sun;

And when to pasture in the glittering shoals
The guardian mistral drives his thundering foals,
And when like Tartar horsemen racing free

We ride the snorting fillies of the sea,
My pine shall be the archer of the gale
While on the bending willow curves the sail
From whose great bow the long keel shooting home
Shall fly, the feathered arrow of the foam.

Luis De Camões

Camões, alone, of all the lyric race,
Born in the black aurora of disaster,
Can look a common soldier in the face:
I find a comrade where I sought a master:
For daily, while the stinking crocodiles
Glide from the mangroves on the swampy shore,
He shares my awning on the dhow, he smiles,
And tells me that he lived it all before.
Through fire and shipwreck, pestilence and loss,
Led by the ignis fatuus of duty
To a dog's death—yet of his sorrows king—
He shouldered high his voluntary Cross,
Wrestled his hardships into forms of beauty,
And taught his gorgon destinies to sing.

The Serf

His naked skin clothed in the torrid mist
That puffs in smoke around the patient hooves,
The ploughman drives, a slow somnambulist,
And through the green his crimson furrow grooves.
His heart, more deeply than he wounds the plain,
Long by the rasping share of insult torn,
Red clod, to which the war-cry once was rain
And tribal spears the fatal sheaves of corn,
Lies fallow now. But as the turf divides
I see in the slow progress of his strides
Over the toppled clods and falling flowers,
The timeless, surly patience of the serf
That moves the nearest to the naked earth
And ploughs down palaces, and thrones, and towers.

The Sisters

After hot loveless nights, when cold winds stream
Sprinkling the frost and dew, before the light,
Bored with the foolish things that girls must dream
Because their beds are empty of delight,

Two sisters rise and strip. Out from the night
Their horses run to their low-whistled pleas—
Vast phantom shapes with eyeballs rolling white
That sneeze a fiery steam about their knees:

Through the crisp manes their stealthy prowling
   hands,
Stronger than curbs, in slow caresses rove,
They gallop down across the milk-white sands
And wade far out into the sleeping cove:

The frost stings sweetly with a burning kiss
As intimate as love, as cold as death:
Their lips, whereon delicious tremors hiss,
Fume with the ghostly pollen of their breath.

Far out on the grey silence of the flood
They watch the dawn in smouldering gyres expand
Beyond them: and the day burns through their blood
Like a white candle through a shuttered hand.

Toledo, July 1936

Toledo, when I saw you die
And heard the roof of Carmel crash,
A spread-winged phoenix from its ash
The Cross remained against the sky!
With horns of flame and haggard eye
The mountain vomited with blood,
A thousand corpses down the flood
Were rolled gesticulating by,
And high above the roaring shells

I heard the silence of your bells
Who've left these broken stones behind
Above the years to make your home,
And burn, with Athens and with Rome,
A sacred city of the mind.

Kenneth Fearing (1902–1961)

Kenneth Fearing was born July 28 in Oak Park, Illinois. He graduated from the University of Wisconsin in 1924 and worked at a series of odd jobs: salesman, millhand, clerk, etc. In 1927, Fearing decided to become a free lance writer. His first book of poetry, *Angel Arms*, appeared in 1929. Other verse works included *Poems* (1935), *Dead Reckoning* (1938), *Afternoon of a Pawnbroker and Other Poems* (1943), and *Stranger at Coney Island and Other Poems* (1948). Fearing's poetry deals with the urban landscape and the loss of love and meaning in industrial society.

C Stands for Civilization

They are able, with science, to measure the millionth of a millionth of an electron-volt,
THE TWENTIETY CENTURY COMES BUT ONCE
The natives can take to caves in the hills, said the British M.P., when we bomb their huts,
THE TWENTIETH CENTURY COMES BUT ONCE

Electric razors;
I am the law, said Mayor Hague;
The lynching was televised, we saw the whole thing from beginning to end, we heard the screams and the crackle of flames in a soundproof room,
THE TWENTIETH CENTURY COMES BUT ONCE

You are born but once,
You have your chance to live but once,
You go mad and put a bullet through your head but once,

THE TWENTIETH CENTURY COMES BUT ONCE
Once too soon, or a little too late, just once too often,

But zooming through the night in Lockheed monoplanes the witches bring accurate pictures of the latest disaster exactly on time,
THE TWENTIETH CENTURY COMES BUT ONCE

ONLY ONCE, AND STAYS FOR BUT ONE HUNDRED YEARS.

Devil's Dream

But it could never be true;
How could it ever happen, if it never did before, and it's not so now?

But suppose that the face behind those steel prison bars—
Why do you dream abour a face lying cold in the trenches streaked
 with rain and dirt and blood?
Is it the very same face seen so often in the mirror?
Just as though it could be true—

But what if it is, what if it is, what if it is, what if the thing that cannot
 happen really happens just the same,
Suppose the fever goes a hundred, then a hundred and one,
What if Holy Savings Trust goes from 98 to 88 to 78 to 68, then
 drops down to 28 and 8 and out of sight,
And the fever shoots a hundred two, a hundred three, a hundred
 four, then a hundred five and out?

But now there's only the wind and the sky and sunlight and the
 clouds,
With everyday people walking and talking as they always have before
 along the everyday street,
Doing ordinary things with ordinary faces and ordinary voices in the
 ordinary way,
Just as they always will—

Then why does it feel like a bomb, why does it feel like a target,
Like standing on the gallows with the trap about to drop,
Why does it feel like a thunderbolt the second before it strikes,
 why does it feel like a tight-rope walk high over hell?

Because it is not, will not, never could be true
That the whole wide, bright, green, warm, calm world goes:
CRASH.

Dirge

1-2-3 was the number he played but today the number came 3-2-1;
Bought his Carbide at 30 and it went to 29; had the favorite at Bowie
    but the track was slow—

O executive type, would you like to drive a floating-power,
    knee-action, silk-upholstered six? Wed a Hollywood star?
    Shoot the course in 58? Draw to the ace, king, jack?
O fellow with a will who won't take no, watch out for three cigarettes
    on the same, single match; O democratic voter born in August
    under Mars, beware of liquidated rails—

Denouement to denouement, he took a personal pride in the certain,
    certain way he lived his own, private life,
But nevertheless, they shut off his gas; nevertheless, the bank
    foreclosed; nevertheless, the landlord called; nevertheless, the
    radio broke,

And twelve o'clock arrived just once too often,
Just the same he wore one gray tweed suit, bought one straw hat,
    drank one straight Scotch, walked one short step, took one
    long look, drew one deep breath,
Just one too many,

And wow he died as wow he lived,
Going whop to the office and blooie home to sleep and biff got
    married and bam had children and oof got fired,
Zowie did he live and zowie did he die,

With who the hell are you at the corner of his casket, and where the
    hell're we going on the right-hand silver knob, and who the
    hell cares walking second from the end with an American
    Beauty wreath from why the hell not,

Very much missed by the circulation staff of the New York Evening
    Post; deeply, deeply mourned by the B.M.T.
Wham, Mr. Roosevelt; pow, Sears Roebuck; awk, big dipper; bop,
    summer rain;
Bong, Mr., bong, Mr., bong, Mr., bong.

Dividends

This advantage to be seized; and here, an escape prepared against an
 evil day.
 So it is arranged, consummately, to meet the issues. Convenience
 and order. Necessary murder and divorce. A decent repute.
Such are the plans, in clear detail.
 She thought it was too soon but they said no, it was too late. They
 didn't trust the other people.
 Sell now.
 He was a fool to ignore the market. It could be explained, he said.
 With the woman, and after the theater she made a scene.
 None of them felt the crash for a long time.
 What is swifter than time?
So it is resolved, upon awakening. This way it is devised, preparing
 for sleep. So it is revealed, uneasily, in strange dreams.
 A defense against grey, hungry, envious millions. A veiled watch
 to be kept upon this friend.
 Dread that handclasp. Seek this. Smile.
 They didn't trust the others. They were wary. It looked suspi-
 cious. They preferred to wait, they said.
Gentlemen, here is a statement for the third month,
 And here, Mildred, is the easiest way.
 Such is the evidence, convertible to profit; these are the
 dividends; waiting to be used;
 waiting to be used;
 here are the demands again, considered again, and again the end-
 less issues are all secure.
 Such are the facts. Such are the details. Such are the proofs.
Almighty God, these are the plans,
 these are the plans until the last moment of the last hour of the
 last day,
 and then the end. By error or accident.
 Burke of cancer. Jackson out at the seret meeting of the board.
 Hendricks through the window of the nineteenth floor.
 Maggots and darkness will attend the alibi.
 Peace on earth. And the finer things.
 So it is all arranged.
 Thomas, the car.

No Credit

Whether dinner was pleasant, with the windows lit by gunfire, and no one disagreed; or whether, later, we argued in the park, and there was a touch of vomit-gas in the evening air;
Whether we found a greater, deeper, more perfect love, by courtesy of Camels, over NBC; whether the comics amused us, or the newspapers carried a hunger death and a White House prayer for Mother's Day;
Whether the bills were paid or not, whether or not we had our doubts, whether we spoke our minds at Joe's, and the receipt said "Not Returnable," and the cash-register rang up "No Sale,"
Whether the truth was then, or later, or whether the best had already gone—

Nevertheless, we know; as every turn is measured; as every unavoidable risk is known;
As nevertheless, the flesh grows old, dies, dies in its only life, is gone;
The reflection goes from the mirror; as the shadow, of even a rebel, is gone from the wall;
As nevertheless, the current is thrown and the wheels revolve; and nevertheless, as the word is spoken and the wheat grows tall and the ships sail on—

None but the fool is paid in full; none but the broker, none but the scab is certain of profit;
The sheriff alone may attend the third degree in formal attire; alone, the academy artists multiply in dignity as trooper's bayonet guards the door;

Only Steve, the side-show robot, knows content; only Steve, the mechanical man in love with a photo-electric beam, remains aloof; only Steve, who sits and smokes or stands in salute, is secure;
Steve, whose shoebutton eyes are blind to terror, whose painted ears are deaf to appeal, whose welded breast will never be slashed by bullets, whose armature soul can hold no fear.

Stevie Smith (1902–1971)

Florence Margaret Smith was born in Hull, England, but moved with her parents and sister to Palmers Green, a northern suburb of London, when she was three, where she resided for over sixty years. Her father went to sea when she was very young and her mother died when she was sixteen. Smith acquired her nickname "Stevie" in her late teens, and it stuck. Never marrying, she lived with her "Lion Aunt" for most of her life.

Smith's first novel, *Novel on Yellow Paper* (1936) and first volume of poems, *A Good Time Was Had by All* (1937) established her literary reputation. Seven more collections of verse followed; her unique poetic talents were widely recognized. Smith was a popular reciter of her poetry on the radio and at readings, and her fame broadened with the highly acclaimed stage and motion picture play "Stevie." She won the Cholmomndeley Poetry Award in 1966 and was in 1969 awarded the Queen' Gold Medal for Poetry.

The Bereaved Swan

Wan
Swan
On the lake
Like a cake
Of soap
Why is the swan
Wan
On the lake?
He has abandoned hope.

>   Wan
>   Swan
>   On the lake afloat
>   Bows his head:
>   O would that I were dead
>   For her sake that lies
>   Wrapped from my eyes
>   In a mantle of death,
>   The swan saith.

The Heavenly City

I sigh for the heavenly country,
Where the heavenly people pass,
And the sea is as quiet as a mirror
Of beautiful glass.

I walk in the heavenly field,
With lilies and poppies bright,
I am dressed in a heavenly coat
Of polished white.

When I walk in the heavenly parkland
My feet on the pastures are bare,
Tall waves the grass, but no harmful
Creature is there.

At night I fly over the housetops,
And stand on the bright moony beams;
Gold are all heaven's rivers.
And silver her streams.

The Little Boy Lost

The wood was rather old and dark
The witch was very ugly
And if it hadn't been for father
Walking there so smugly
I never should have followed
The beckoning of her finger.
Ah me how long ago it was
And still I linger
Under the ever interlacing beeches
Over a carpet of moss
I lift my hand but it never reaches
To where the breezes toss
The sun-kissed leaves above.
The sun?
Beware.

The sun never comes here.
Round about and round I go
Up and down and to and fro
The woodlouse hops upon the tree
Or should do but I really cannot see.
Happy fellow. Why can't I be
Happy as he?
The wood grows darker every day
It's not a bad place in a way
But I lost the way
Last Tuesday
Did I love father, mother, home?
Not very much; but now they're gone
I think of them with kindly toleration
Bred inevitability of separation.
Really if I could find some food
I should be happy enough in this wood
But darker days and hungrier I must spend
Till hunger and darkness make an end.

The River God
Of the River Mimram in Hertfordshire.

I may be smelly and I may be old,
Rough in my pebbles, reedy in my pools,
But where my fish float by I bless their swimming
And I like the people to bathe in me, especially
    women.
But I can drown the fools
Who bathe too close to the weir, contrary to rules.
And they take a long time drowning
As I throw them up now and then in a spirit of
    clowning.
Hi yih, yippity-yap, merrily I flow,
O I may be an old foul river but I have plenty of go.
Once there was a lady who was too bold
She bathed in me by the tall black cliff where the
    water runs cold,
So I brought her down here

To be my beautiful dear.
Oh will she stay with me will she stay
This beautiful lady, or will she go away?
She lies in my beautiful deep river bed with many a
　　weed
To hold her, and many a waving reed.
Oh who would guess what a beautiful white face lies
　　there
Waiting for me to smooth and wash away the fear
She looks at me with. Hi yih, do not let her
Go. There is no one on earth who does not forget
　　her
Now. They say I am a foolish old smelly river
But they do not know of my wide original bed
Where the lady waits, with her golden sleepy head.
If she wishes to go I will not forgive her.

To the Tune of the Coventry Carol

The nearly right
And yet not quite
In love is wholly evil
And every heart
That loves in part
Is mortagaged to the devil.

I loved or thought
I loved in sort
Was this to love akin
To take the best
And leave the rest
And let the devil in?

O lovers true
And others too
Whose best is only better
Take my advice
Shun compromise
Forget him and forget her.

The Weak Monk

The monk sat in his den,
He took the mighty pen
And wrote 'Of God and Men'.

One day the thought struck him
It was not according to Catholic doctrine;
His blood ran dim.

He wrote till he was ninety years old,
Then he shut the book with a clasp of gold
And buried it under the sheep fold.

He'd enjoyed it so much, he loved to plod,
And he thought he'd a right to expect that God
Would rescue his book alive from the sod.

Of course it rotted in the snow and rain;
No one will ever know now what he wrote of God
    and men.
For this the monk is to blame.

Richard Palmer Blackmur (1904–1965)

R.P. Blackmur was born January 21 to George Edward and Helen Palmer Blackmur, in Springfield, Massachusetts. Self-educated, Blackmur worked as a free-lance poet and critic from 1928–1940. From 1940–1943 he was a resident fellow at Princeton, and became professor of English at Cambridge in 1951. His books of poetry include: *From Jordan's Delight* (1937), *The Second World* (1942), and *The Good European and other Poems* (1947). A distinguished critic, Blackmur constantly affirmed the social responsibility of the poet and the importance of art and criticism in society.

The Dead Ride Fast

Nobody ever galloped on this road
without probable cause. Nobody wants
false wind in the face at a dead end.
Nobody wants, this day, his hair to grow.
No one would disagree about that, unless
to cover up deeper agreement, hide
the robber's sense, the pounding, the vertigo,
the confusion under expert discernment:
all we leave out to make a faith of hope.

And if you think I am not talking about anything
it is because you have not looked out the window
where I wash and shave and sometimes trim my hair,
and I have not seen the inviolable standstill
everything comes to, people, horses, cars,
beyond the little rise above the culvert.
It is that standstill finds all coming things
between the woods they come from and the rise
where, recognised, they seem already here.
With me it is no longer a matter of not looking
or whether this day everything comes at once;
because of that eddying standstill I am,
expectant, reverent, or suddenly degenerate,
always deliberately unprepared.

Perhaps you don't catch what I mean. Look here.
There have been bats in this house, variously
crawling and flitting, not easy to get out,

but always bats whether you knew them or not;
there have been seabirds beat against the window,
bill on, some die, but mostly only stun;
ducks in the marsh, with their known unknowable voices;
also telegrams delivered at night;
all these are wholesome until you stiffen to meet them.

You understand: I will not make of politics
a superstition, of religion a distrust,
of thought a mania. I will not look under beds
with stiffened eyes, knowing what I shall see.
I will look at horses, people, cars, look up
from shaving, and the hurried dead, look up
through the light-sodden, reverberating air—

until that day, hopeful, thoroughly prepared,
in my own glass I trim my snakey locks.

Cecil Day Lewis (1904–1972)

Cecil Day Lewis was born April 27 in Ballintupper, Ireland, an only child. In 1923 he attended Wadham College, Oxford where he came under the influence of W.H. Auden. In 1927 he and Auden published an anthology of poetry, *Oxford Poetry, 1927,* in which they composed a poetic manifesto in the preface declaring their independence from Eliot and forging a blueprint for a new and truly twentieth century school of verse. The period 1929–1938 was especially fertile for Day Lewis when the Auden group—Day Lewis, Auden, and Stephen Spender—dominated the English poetic scene. In 1929 Day Lewis published his first substantial poem, *Transitional Poem*, and in 1931 and 1933 published his two major poems: *From Feathers To Iron* (1931) and *The Magnetic Mountain* (1933). In 1935 his first collection, *Collected Poems*, appeared. His reputation declined significantly after the thirties and he supported himself by lecturing, and writing novels, plays, and books of criticism. He has published twenty detective novels under the nom de plume of Nicholas Blake. Day Lewis' greatest honor came four years before his death when Queen Elizabeth II appointed him Poet Laureate of England in 1968.

All Gone

The sea drained off, my poverty's uncovered—
Sand, sand, a rusted anchor, broken glass,
The listless sediment of sparkling days
When through a paradise of weed joy wavered.

The sea rolled up like a blind, oh pitiless light
Revealing, shrivelling all! Lacklustre weeds
My hours, my truth a salt-lick. Love recedes
From rippled flesh bared without appetite.

A stranded time, neap and annihilation
Of spirit. Gasping on the inglorious rock,
I pray the sea return, even though its calm
Be treachery, its virtue a delusion.

Put forth upon my sands, whether to mock,
Revive or drown, a liberating arm!

'As One Who Wanders into Old Workings'

As one who wanders into old workings
Dazed by the noonday, desiring coolness,
Has found retreat barred by fall of rockface;
Gropes through galleries where granite bruises
Taut palm and panic patters close at heel;
Must move forward as tide to the moon's nod,
As mouth to breast in blindness is beckoned.
Nightmare nags at his elbow and narrows
Horizon to pinpoint, hope to hand's breadth.
Slow drip the seconds, time is stalactite,
For nothing intrudes here to tell the time,
Sun marches not, nor moon with muffled step.
He wants an opening,—only to break out,
To see the dark glass cut by day's diamond,
To relax again in the lap of light.

But we seek a new world through old workings,
Whose hope lies like seed in the loins of earth,
Whose dawn draws gold from the roots of darkness.
Not shy of light nor shrinking from shadow
Like Jesuits in jungle we journey
Deliberately bearing to brutish tribes
Christ's assurance, arts of agriculture.
As a train that travels underground track
Feels current flashed from far-off dynamos,
Our wheels whirling with impetus elsewhere
Generated we run, are ruled by rails.
Train shall spring from tunnel to terminus,
Out on to plain shall the pioneer plunge,
Earth reveal what veins fed, what hill covered.
Lovely the leap, explosion into light.

Birthday Poem for Thomas Hardy

Is it birthday weather for you, dear soul?
Is it fine your way,
With tall moon-daisies alight, and the mole
Busy, and elegant hares at play
By meadow paths where once you would stroll
In the flush of day?

I fancy the beasts and flowers there beguiled
By a visitation
That casts no shadow, a friend whose mild
Inquisitive glance lights with compassion,
Beyond the tomb, on all of this wild
And humbled creation.

It's hard to believe a spirit could die
Of such generous glow,
Or to doubt that somewhere a bird-sharp eye
Still broods on the capers of men below,
A stern voice asks the Immortals why
They should plague us so.

Dear poet, wherever you are, I greet you.
Much irony, wrong,
Innocence you'd find here to tease or entreat you,
And many the fate-fires have tempered strong,
But none that in ripeness of soul could meet you
Or magic of song.

Great brow, frail frame—gone. Yet you abide
In the shadow and sheen,
All the mellowing traits of a countryside
That nursed your tragic-comical scene;
And in us, warmer-hearted and brisker-eyed
Since you have been.

Come, Live with Me and Be My Love

Come, live with me and be my love,
And we will all the pleasures prove
Of peace and plenty, bed and board,
That chance employment may afford.

I'll handle dainties on the docks
And thou shalt read of summer frocks:
At evening by the sour canals
We'll hope to hear some madrigals.

Care on thy maiden brow shall put
A wreath of wrinkles, and thy foot
Be shod with pain: not silken dress
But toil shall tire thy loveliness.

Hunger shall make thy modest zone
And cheat fond death of all but bone—
If these delights thy mind may move,
Then live with me and be my love.

The Conflict

I sang as one
Who on a tilting deck sings
To keep their courage up, though the wave hangs
That shall cut off their sun.

As storm-cocks sing,
Flinging their natural answer in the wind's teeth,
And care not if it is waste of breath
Or birth-carol of spring.

As ocean-flyer clings
To height, to the last drop of spirit driving on
While yet ahead is land to be won
And work for wings.

Singing I was at peace,
Above the clouds, outside the ring:
For sorrow finds a swift release in song
And pride its poise.

Yet living here,
As one between two massing powers I live
Whom neutrality cannot save
Nor occupation cheer.

None such shall be left alive:
The innocent wing is soon shot down,
And private stars fade in the blood-red dawn
Where two worlds strive.

The red advance of life
Contracts pride, calls out the common blood,
Beats song into a single blade,
Makes a depth-charge of grief.

Move then with new desires,
For where we used to build and love
Is no man's land, and only ghosts can live
Between two fires.

Departure in the Dark

Nothing so sharply reminds a man he is mortal
As leaving a place
In a winter morning's dark, the air on his face
Unkind as the touch of sweating metal:
Simple goodbyes to children or friends become
A felon's numb
Farewell, and love that was a warm, a meeting place—
Love is the suicide's grave under the nettles.

Gloomed and clemmed as if by an imminent ice-age
Lies the dear world
Of your street-strolling, field-faring. The senses, curled
At the dead end of a shrinking passage,

Care not if close the inveterate hunters creep,
And memories sleep
Like mammoths in lost caves. Drear, extinct is the world,
And has no voice for consolation or presage.

There is always something at such times of the passover,
When the dazed heart
Beats for it knows not what, whether you part
From home or prison, acquaintance or lover—
Something wrong with the time-table, something unreal
In the scrambled meal
And the bag ready packed by the door, as though the heart
Has gone ahead, or is staying here for ever.

No doubt for the Israelites that early morning
It was hard to be sure
If home were prison or prison home: the desire
Going forth meets the desire returning.
This land, that had cut their pride down to the bone
Was now their own
By ancient deeds of sorrow. Beyond, there was nothing sure
But a desert of freedom to quench their fugitive yearnings.

At this blind hour the heart is informed of nature's
Ruling that man
Should be nowhere a more tenacious settler than
Among wry thorns and ruins, yet nurture
A seed of discontent in his ripest ease.
There's a kind of release
And a kind of torment in every goodbye for every man—
And will be, even to the last of his dark departures.

In the Heart of Contemplation

In the heart of contemplation—
Admiring, say, the frost-flowers of the white lilac,
Or lark's song busily sifting like sand-crystals
Through the pleased hourglass an afternoon of summer,
Or your beauty, dearer to me than these—
Descretly a whisper in the ear,
The glance of one passing my window recall me
From lark, lilac, you, grown suddenly strangers.

In the plump and pastoral valley
Of a leisure time, among the trees like seabirds
Asleep on a glass calm, one shadow moves—
The sly reminder of the forgotten appointment.
All the shining pleasures, born to be innocent,
Grow dark with a truant's guilt:
The day's high heart falls flat, the oaks tremble,
And the shadow sliding over your face divides us.

In the act of decision only,
In the hearts cleared for action like lovers naked
For love, this shadow vanishes: there alone
There is nothing between our lives for it to thrive on.
You and I with lilac, lark and oak-leafed
Valley are bound together
As in the astounded clarity before death.
Nothing is innocent now but to act for life's sake.

In Heaven, I Suppose, Lie Down Together

In heaven, I suppose, lie down together
Agonised Pilate and the boa-constrictor
That swallows anything: but we must seize
One horn or other of our antitheses.
When I consider each independent star
Wearing its world of darkness like a fur
And rubbing shoulders with infinity,

I am content experience should be
More discontinuous than the points pricked
Out by the mazy course of a derelict,
Iceberg, or Flying Dutchman, and the heart
Stationary and passive as a chart.
In such star-frenzy I could boast, betwixt
My yester and my morrow self are fixed
All the birds carolling and all the seas
Groaning from Greenwich to the Antipodes.

But an eccentric hour may come, when systems
Not stars divide the dark; and then life's pistons
Pounding into their secret cylinder
Begin to tickle the most anchorite ear
With hints of mechanisms that include
The man. And once that rhythm arrests the blood,
Who would be satisfied his mind is no
Continent but an archipelago?
They are preposterous paladins and prance
From myth to myth, who take an Agag stance
Upon the needle points of here and now,
Where only angels ought to tread. Allow
One jointure feasible to man, one state
Squared with another—then he can integrate
A million selves and where disorder ruled
Straddle a chaos and beget a world.

Peals of the New Year once for me came tumbling
Out of the narrow night like clusters of humming-
Birds loosed from a black bag, and rose again
Irresponsibly to silence: but now I strain
To follow them and see for miles around
Men square or shrug their shoulders at the sound.
Then I remember the pure and granite hills
Where first I caught an ideal tone that stills,
Like the beloved's breath asleep, all din
Of earth at traffic: silence's first-born,
Carrying over each sensual ravine
To inform the seer and uniform the seen.

So from this ark, this closet of the brain,
The dove emerges and flies back again
With a Messiah sprig of certitude—
Promise of ground below the sprawling flood.

Maple and Sumach

Maple and sumach down this autumn ride—
Look, in what scarlet character they speak!
For this their russet and rejoicing week
Trees spend a year of sunsets on their pride.
You leaves drenched with the lifeblood of the year—
What flamingo dawns have wavered from the east,
What eves have crimsoned to their toppling crest
To give the fame and transience that you wear!
Leaf-low he shall lie soon: but no such blaze
Briefly can cheer man's ashen, harsh decline;
His fall is short of pride, he bleeds within
And paler creeps to the dead end of his days.
O light's abandon and the fire-crest sky
Speak in me now for all who are to die!

Nearing Again the Legendary Isle

Nearing again the legendary isle
Where sirens sang and mariners were skinned,
We wonder now what was there to beguile
That such stout fellows left their bones behind.

Those chorus-girls are surely past their prime,
Voices grow shrill and paint is wearing thin,
Lips that sealed up the sense from gnawing time
Now beg the favour with a graveyard grin.

We have no flesh to spare and they can't bite,
Hunger and sweat have stripped us to the bone;
A skeleton crew we toil upon the tide
And mock the theme-song meant to lure us on:

No need to stop the ears, avert the eyes
From purple rhetoric of evening skies.

O Dreams, O Destinations

I

For infants time is like a humming shell
Heard between sleep and sleep, wherein the shores
Foam-fringed, wind-fluted of the strange earth dwell
And the sea's cavernous hunger faintly roars.
It is the humming pole of summer lanes
Whose sound quivers like heat-haze endlessly
Over the corn, over the poppied plains—
An emanation from the earth or sky.
Faintly they hear, through the womb's lingering haze,
A rumour of that sea to which they are born:
They hear the ringing pole of summer days,
But need not know what hungers for the corn.
They are the lisping rushes in a stream—
Grace-notes of a profound, legato dream.

II

Children look down upon the morning-grey
Tissue of mist that veils a valley's lap:
Their fingers itch to tear it and unwrap
The flags, the roundabouts, the gala day.
They watch the spring rise inexhaustibly—
A breathing thread out of the eddied sand,
Sufficient to their day: but half their mind
Is on the sailed and glittering estuary.
Fondly we wish their mist might never break,
Knowing it hides so much that best were hidden:
We'd chain them by the spring, lest it should broaden
For them into a quicksand and a wreck.
But they slip through our fingers like the source,
Like mist, like time that has flagged out their course.

III

That was the fatal move, the ruination
Of innocence so innocently begun,
When in the lawless orchard of creation
The child left this fruit for that rosier one.
Reaching towards the far thing, we begin it;
Looking beyond, or backward, more and more
We grow unfaithful to the unique minute
Till, from neglect, its features stale and blur.
Fish, bird or beast was never thus unfaithful—
Man only casts the image of his joys
Beyond his senses' reach; and by this fateful
Act, he confirms the ambiguous power of choice.
Innocence made that first choice. It is she
Who weeps, a child chained to the outraged tree.

IV

Our youthtime passes down a colonnade
Shafted with alternating light and shade.
All's dark or dazzle there. Half in a dream
Rapturously we move, yet half afraid
Never to wake, That diamond-point, extreme
Brilliance engraved on us a classic theme:
The shaft of darkness had its lustre too,
Rising where earth's concentric mysteries gleam.
Oh youth-charmed hours, that made an avenue
Of fountains playing us on to love's full view,
A cypress walk to some romantic grave—
Waking, how false in outline and in hue
We find the dreams that flickered on our cave:
Only your fire, which cast them, still seems true.

V

All that time there was thunder in the air:
Our nerves branched and flickered with summer lightning.

The taut crab-apple, the pampas quivering, the glare
On the roses seemed irrelevant, or a heightening
At most of the sealed-up hour wherein we awaited
What?—some explosive oracle to abash
The platitudes on the lawn? heaven's delegated
Angel—the golden rod, our burning bush?
No storm broke. Yet in retrospect the rose
Mounting vermilion, fading, glowing again
Like a fire's heart, that breathless inspiration
Of pampas grass, crab-tree's attentive pose
Never were so divinely charged as then—
The veiled Word's flesh, a near annunciation.

VI

Symbols of gross experience!—our grief
Flowed, like a sacred river, underground:
Desire bred fierce abstractions on the mind,
Then like an eagle soared beyond belief.
Often we tried our breast against the thorn,
Our paces on the turf: whither we flew,
Why we should agonize, we hardly knew—
Nor what ached in us, asking to be born.
Ennui of youth!—thin air above the clouds,
Vain divination of the sunless stream
Mirror that impotence, till we redeem
Our birthright, and the shadowplay concludes.
Ah, not in dreams, but when our souls engage
With the common mesh and moil, we come of age.

VII

Older, we build a road where once our active
Heat threw up mountains and the deep dales veined:
We're glad to gain the limited objective,
Knowing the war we fight in has no end.
The road must needs follow each contour moulded
By that fire in its losing fight with earth:

We march over our past, we may behold it
Dreaming a slave's dream on our bivouac hearth.
Lost the archaic dawn wherein we started,
The appetite for wholeness: now we prize
Half-loaves, half-truths—enough for the half-hearted,
The gleam snatched from corruption satisfies.
Dead youth, forgive us if, all but defeated,
We raise a trophy where your honour lies.

VIII

But look, the old illusion still returns,
Walking a field-path where the succory burns
Like summer's eye, blue lustre-drops of noon,
And the heart follows it and freshly yearns:
Yearns to the sighing distances beyond
Each height of happiness, the vista drowned
In gold-dust haze, and dreams itself immune
From change and night to which all else is bound.
Love, we have caught perfection for a day
As succory holds a gem of halcyon ray:
Summer burns out, its flower will tarnish soon—
Deathless illusion, that could so relay
The truth of flesh and spirit, sun and clay
Singing for once together all in tune!

IX

To travel like a bird, lightly to view
Deserts where stone gods founder in the sand,
Ocean embraced in a white sleep with land;
To escape time, always to start anew.
To settle like a bird, make one devoted
Gesture of permanence upon the spray
Of shaken stars and autumns; in a bay
Beyond the crestfallen surges to have floated.
Each is our wish. Alas, the bird flies blind,
Hooded by a dark sense of destination:

Her weight on the glass calm leaves no impression,
Her home is soon a basketful of wind.
Travellers, we're fabric of the road we go;
We settle, but like feathers on time's flow.

Rest from Loving and Be Living

Rest from loving and be living.
Fallen is fallen past retrieving
The unique flyer dawn's dove
Arrowing down feathered with fire.

Cease denying, begin knowing.
Comes peace this way here comes renewing
With dower of bird and bud knocks
Loud on winter wall on death's door.

Here's no meaning but of morning.
Naught soon of night but stars remaining,
Sink lower, fade, as dark womb
Recedes creation will step clear.

The Sitting
For Laurence Gowing

So like a god I sit here,
One of those stone dreamers quarried from solitude,
A genius—if ever there was one—of the place:
The mountain's only child, lips aloof as a snow line,
Forearms impassive along the cloud-base of aeons,
Eyes heavy on distance—
Graven eyes that flinch not, flash not, if eagles
Clap their wings in my face.

With hieratic gestures
He the suppliant, priest, interpreter, subtly
Wooing my virtue, officiates by the throne.

I know the curious hands are shaping, reshaping the
      image
Of what is only an image of things impalpable.
I feel how the eyes strain
To catch a truth behind the oracular presence—
Eyes that augur through stone.

And the god asks, 'What have I for you
But the lichenous shadow of thought veiling my
      temple,
The runnels a million time-drops have chased on my
      cheek?'
And the man replies, 'I will show you the creed of
      your bone, I'll draw you
The shape of solitude to which you were born.'
And the god cries, 'I am meek,
Brushed by an eagle's wind; and a voice bids me
Speak. But I cannot speak.'

The god thinks, Let him project, if
He must, his passionate shapings on my stone heart,
Wrestle over my body with his sprite,
Through these blind eyes imagine a skin-deep world
      in perspective:
Let him make, if he will, the crypt of my holy
      mountain
His own: let even the light
That bathes my temple become as it were an active
Property of his sight.

O man, O innocent artist
Who paint me with green of your fields, with
   amber or yellow
Of love's hair, red of the heart's blood, eyebright
      blue,
Conjuring forms and rainbows out of an empty mist—
Your hand is upon me, as even now you follow
Up the immortal clue
Threading my veins of emerald, topaz, amethyst,
And know not it ends in you.

A Time to Dance

For those had the power
  of the forest fires that burn
Leaving their source in ashes
  to flush the sky with fire:
Those whom a famous urn
  could not contain, whose passion
Brimmed over the deep grave
  and dazzled epitaphs:
For all that have won us wings
  to clear the tops of grief,
My friend who within me laughs
  bids you dance and sing.

Some set out to explore
  earth's limit, and little they recked if
Never their feet came near it
  outgrowing the need for glory:
Some aimed at a small objective
  but the fierce updraught of their spirit
Forced them to the stars.
  Are honoured in public who built
The dam that tamed a river;
  or holding the salient for hours
Against odds, cut off and killed,
  are remembered by one survivor.

All these. But most for those
  whom accident made great,
As a radiant chance encounter
  of cloud and sunlight grows
Immortal on the heart:
  whose gift was the sudden bounty
Of a passing moment, enriches
  The fulfilled eye for ever.
Their spirits float serene
  above time's roughest reaches,
But their seed is in us and over
  our lives they are evergreen.

You That Love England

You that love England, who have an ear for her music,
The slow movement of clouds in benediction,
Clear arias of light thrilling over her uplands,
Over the chords of summer sustained peacefully;
Ceaseless the leaves' counterpoint in a west wind lively,
Blossom and river rippling loveliest allegro,
And the storms of wood strings brass at year's finale:
Listen. Can you not hear the entrance of a new theme?

You who go out alone, on tandem or on pillion,
Down arterial roads riding in April,
Or sad beside lakes where hill-slopes are reflected
Making fires of leaves, your high hopes fallen:
Cyclists and hikers in company, day excursionists,
Refugees from cursed towns and devastated areas;
Know you seek a new world, a saviour to establish
Long-lost kinship and restore the bloods fulfilment.

You who like peace, good sticks, happy in a small way
Watching birds or playing cricket with schoolboys,
Who pay for drinks all round, whom disaster chose
   not;
Yet passing derelict mills and barns roof-rent
Where despair has burnt itself out—hearts at a stand-
   still,
Who suffer loss, aware of lowered vitality;
We can tell you a secret, offer a tonic; only
Submit to the visiting angel, the strange new healer.

You above all who have come to the far end, victims
Of a run-down machine, who can bear it no longer;
Whether in easy chairs chafing at impotence
Or against hunger, bullies and spies preserving
The nerve for action, the spark of indignation—
Need fight in the dark no more, you know your
   enemies.
You shall be leaders when zero hour is signalled,
Wielders of power and welders of a new world.

Richard Eberhart (Born 1904)

Richard Eberhart was born April 15 in Austin, Minnesota. When he was 18 he witnessed the protracted death of his mother from cancer, an event which he marks as the turning point in his life, and the probable cause for his decision to become a poet. Eberhart took his B.A. from Harvard in 1926 and his M.A. from St. John's College, Cambridge in 1929. While at St. John's he was exposed to the modernist poets of the day—T.S. Elliot, Gerard Hopkins, and D.H. Lawrence—and his first book of poems, *A Bravery of Earth*, shows this influence. After spending a year as tutor to the son of the King of Siam, Eberhart returned to America to begin a teaching career. From 1942–1946 he was a Lieutenant Commander in the U.S. Naval Reserve. He has written over 28 books of poetry, as well as numerous plays and critical essays, and is the recipient of the 1966 Pulitzer Prize.

Eberhart's basic theme is man's fallen state, and his subsequent search for unity. Eberhart often takes a moral stance, condemning man's cruel and self-destructive tendencies, and urging his readers to respect and celebrate the value of human life.

The Goal of Intellectual Man

The goal of intellectual man
Striving to do what he can
To bring down out of uncreated light
Illumination to our night

Is not possession of the fire
Annihilation of his own desire
To the source a secret soaring
And all his self outpouring

Nor is it an imageless place
Wherein there is no human face
Nor laws, nor hierarchies, nor dooms
And only the cold weight of the tomb

But it is human love, love
Concrete, specific, in a natural move
Gathering goodness, it is free
In the blood as in the mind's harmony,

It is love discoverable here
Difficult, dangerous, pure, clear,
The truth of the positive hour
Composing all of human power.

The Groundhog

In June, amid the golden fields,
I saw a groundhog lying dead.
Dead lay he; my senses shook,
And mind outshot our naked frailty.
There lowly in the vigorous summer
His form began its senseless change,
And made my senses waver dim
Seeing nature ferocious in him.
Inspecting close his maggots' might
And seething cauldron of his being,
Half with loathing, half with a strange love,
I poked him with an angry stick.
The fever arose, became a flame
And Vigour circumscribed the skies,
Immense energy in the sun,
And through my frame a sunless trembling.
My stick had done nor good nor harm.
Then stood I silent in the day
Watching the object, as before;
And kept my reverence for knowledge
Trying for control, to be still,
To quell the passion of the blood;
Until I had bent down on my knees
Praying for joy in the sight of decay.
And so I left; and I returned
In Autumn strict of eye, to see
The sap gone out of the groundhog,
But the bony sodden hulk remained.
But the year had lost its meaning,
And in intellectual chains
I lost both love and loathing,
Mured up in the wall of wisdom.
Another summer took the fields again
Massive and burning, full of life,
But when I chanced upon the spot
There was only a little hair left,
And bones bleaching in the sunlight
Beautiful as architecture;

I watched them like a geometer,
And cut a walking stick from a birch.
It has been three years, now.
There is no sign of the groundhog.
I stood there in the whirling summer,
My hand capped a withered heart,
And thought of China and of Greece,
Of Alexander in his tent;
Of Montaigne in his tower,
Of Saint Theresa in her wild lament.

I Walked Out to the Graveyard To See the Dead

I walked out to the graveyard to see the dead
The iron gates were locked, I couldn't get in.
A golden pheasant on the dark fir boughs
Looked with fearful method at the sunset,

Said I, Sir bird, wink no more at me
I have had enough of my dark eye-smarting.
I cannot adore you, nor do I praise you,
But assign you to the rafters of Montaigne.

Who talks with the Absolute salutes a Shadow,
Who seeks himself shall lose himself;
And the golden pheasants are no help
And action must be learned from love of man.

Mysticism Has Not the Patience to Wait for God's Revelation
Kierkegaard

But to reach the archimedean point
Was all my steadfastness;
The disjointed times to teach
Courage from what is dreadful.

It was the glimpses in the lightning
Made me a sage, but made me say
No word to make another fight,
My own fighting heart full of dismay.

Spirit, soul, and fire are reached!
And springs of the mind, like springs of the feet
Tell all, all know, nothing wavers there!
All the flowers of my heart turned to ice-flowers,

Heaviness of the world prevailing,
("The higher we go the more terrible it is,")
Duplicity of man, heart-hate,
The hypocrite, the vain, the whipper, the cheat,

The eternal ape on the leash,
Drawing us down to faith,
Which the Greeks call divine folly,
The tug of laughter and of irony.

Robert Penn Warren (Born 1905)

Robert Penn Warren was born April 25 in Guthrie, Kentucky. His father, Robert Franklin Warren, was a self-educated man who had had a few poems anthologized. The Warren household was full of books of all kinds, and young Robert Penn grew up with a fondness for reading and learning. He graduated at the age of fifteen from high school and enrolled in Vanderbilt University with the intention of becoming a scientist. But like most students who came under the influence of John Crowe Ransom, the eminent teacher and critic, Warren quickly abandoned his original ambitions in favor of the study of literature, and the craft of poetry. He became involved with the literary circle known as the "fugitives" and published many poems in their magazine, *The Fugitive*. At 16, Warren was considered the most brilliant of Ransom's protégés, causing Allen Tate to state: "That boy's a wonder-he has more sheer genius than any of us; watch him: his work from now on will have what none of us can achieve-power."

Warren graduated *summa cum laude* from Vanderbilt and received his M.A. from the University of California at Berkeley in 1927. He secured a commission to write a biography of John Brown. The result, the 1929 *John Brown: The Making of a Martyr*, was a critical, but not a financial, success. Nevertheless, on the strength of his first book Warren was awarded a Rhodes Scholarship and received a B.Litt. from Oxford in 1930. He returned to America to teach at Vanderbilt and Louisiana State University. He and two other Vanderbilt graduates, Cleanth Brooks and Charles Pipkin founded the now prestigious literary journal *Southern Review* in 1935. In that same year, Warren published his first collection of verse, *Thirty-Six Poems*. This first book of poetry extablished what turned out to be many of Warren's recurrent themes: the eternal cycle of rejection and return, the ambivalence of the mother-son relationship, and familial obligations. He reworked these basic ideas in his 1942 *Eleven Poems On The Same Theme*. The "same theme" was loss of innocence and redemption through knowledge.

In 1943 Warren was selected to occupy the Chair of Poetry of the Library of Congress. He used the time to complete a long planned novel, *All The King's Men* (1946), which became an immediate popular and critical success. The novel won the Pulitzer Prize and the movie version won the Academy Award. After the success of *All The King's Men*, Warren went on the teach playwright at Yale from 1950 to 1956. He did not produce another collection of verse until his 1958 *Promise Poems, 1954–1956*, for which he was awarded his second Pulitzer Prize. *Promises* also won the National Book Award and the Edna St. Vincent Millay Prize of Poetry Society of America. Yet Warren refused to rest on his laurels. His 1966 *Selected Poems: New and Old 1923–1966*, received the Bollingen Prize. Warren was awarded his third Pulitzer Prize for *Now and Then, Poems 1976 1978*. To date, Warren has published over 13 books of poetry, 10 novels, one biography, one play two children's books, eight collections of essays, and several textbooks. Warren continues to contribute poetry to literary journals. He has recently completed a long poem on Chief Joseph of the Nez Percé.

Robert Penn Warren is a master of almost every form of traditional verse-sonnets, lullabies, lyric tall tales, etc. But he uses these structures to express distinctly twentieth century themes. The themes are usually either abstract philosophical problems or anecdotes-more commonly one feeds of the other. Though his subjects are culled from his southern roots, his larger concerns rest regionalism, thus his almost universal appeal. Tate's prediction has come true-it is the power Warren's lyrics which enables him to be so prolific and original. As the critic Charles Bohner say ". . . there is a gusto and masculine force, a willingness to risk bathos and absurdity, reminiscent the writer who, Warren has said, has had the greatest influence on his life-Shakespeare."

Revelation

Because he had spoken harshly to his mother,
The day became astonishingly bright,
The enormity of distance crept to him like a dog now,
And earth's own luminescence seemed to repel the night.

Roof was rent like loud paper tearing to admit
Sun-sulphurous splendor where had been before
But the submarine glimmer by kindly counterances lit.
As slow, phosphorescent dignities light the ocean floor.

By walls, by walks, chrysanthemum and aster,
All hairy, fat-petalled species, lean, confer,
And his ears, and heart, should burn at that insidious whisper
Which concerns him so, he knows; but he cannot make out the
    words.

The peacock screamed, and his feathered fury made
Legend shake, all day, while the sky ran pale as milk;
That night, all night, the buck rabbit stamped in the moonlit glade,
And the owl's brain glowed like a coal in the grove's combustible
    dark.

When Sulla smote and Rome was rent, Augustine
Recalled how Nature, shuddering, tore her gown,
And kind changed kind, and the blunt herbivorous tooth dripped
    blood;
At Duncan's death, at Dunsinane, chimneys blew down.

But, oh! his mother was kinder than ever Rome,
Dearer than Duncan—no wonder, then, Nature's frame
Thrilled in voluptuous hemispheres far off from his home;
But not in terror: only as the bride, as the bride.

In separateness only does love learn definition,
Though Brahma smiles beneath the dappled shade,
Though tears, that night, wet pillow where the boy's head was
    laid
Dreamless of splendid antipodal agitation;

And though across what tide and tooth Time is,
He was to lean back toward that recalcitrant face,
He would think, than Sulla more fortunate, how once he had learned
Something important above love, and about love's grace.

Pursuit

The hunchback on the corner, with gum and shoelaces,
Has his own wisdom and pleasures, and may not be lured
To divulge them to you, for he has merely endured
Your appeal for his sympathy and your kind purchases;
And wears infirmity but as the general who turns
Apart, in his famous old greatcoat here on the hill
At dusk when the rapture and cannonade are still,
To muse withdrawn from the dead, from his gorgeous subalterns;
Or stares from the thicket of his familiar pain, like a fawn
That meets you a moment, wheels in imperious innocence is gone.

Go to the clinic. Wait in the outer room
Where like an old possum the snag-nailed hand will hump
On its knee in murderous patience, and the pomp
Of pain swells like the Indies, or a plum.
And there you will stand, as on the Roman hill,
Stunned by each withdrawn gaze and severe shape,
The first barbarian victor stood to gape
At the sacrificial fathers, white-robed, still;
And even the feverish old Jew stares stern with authority
Till you feel like one who has come too late, or improperly clothed, to a party

The doctor will take you now. He is burly and clean;
Listening, like lover or worshiper, bends at your heart;
But cannot make out just what it tries to impart;
So smiles; says you simply need a change of scene.
Of scene, of solace: therefore Flordia,
Where Ponce de Leon clanked among the lilies,
Where white sails skit on blue and cavort like fillies,
And the shoulder gleams in the moonlit corridor.
A change of love: if love is a groping Godward, though blind,
No matter what crevice, cranny, chink, bright in dark, the pale tentacle fin

In Florida consider the flamingo
Its color passion but its neck a question;
Consider even that girl the other guests shun
On beach, at bar, in bed, for she may know
The secret you are seeking, after all;
Or the child you humbly sit by, excited and curly,
That screams on the shore at the sea's sunlit hurlyburly,
Till the mother calls its name, toward nightfall.
Till you sit alone: in the dire meridians, off Ireland, in fury
Of spume-tooth and dawnless sea-heave, salt rimes the lookout's devout eye.

Till you sit alone—which is the beginning of error—
Behind you the music and lights of the great hotel:
Solution, perhaps, is public, despair personal,
But history held to your breath clouds like a mirror.
There are many states, and towns in them, and faces,
But meanwhile, the little old lady in black, by the wall,
Who admires all the dancers, and tells you how just last fall
Her husband died in Ohio, and damp mists her glasses;
She blinks and croaks, like a toad or a Norn, in the horrible light,
And rattles her crutch, which may put forth a small bloom, perhaps white.

Terror

I Volontari Americani Presso Eserciti Stranieri Non Perdono La Cittadinaza. IL MESSAGGERO, Roma, Sabato, 27 Gennaio, 1940.

Not picnics or pageants or the improbable
Powers of air whose tongues ecxlaim dominion
And gull the great man to follow his terrible
Star, suffice; not the window-box, or the bird on
The ledge, which means so much to the invalid,
Nor the joy you learned after, as by the tracks the grass
In the emptiness after the lighted Pullmans fled,
Suffices; nor faces, which, like disctaction, pass
Under the street-lamps, teasing to faith or pleasure,
Suffice you, born to no adequate definition of terror.

For yours, like a puppy, is darling and inept,
Though his cold nose brush your hand while you laugh at his clowning;
Or the kitten you sleep with, though once or twice while you slept
It tried to suck your breath, and you dreamed of drowning,
Perjured like Clarence, sluiced from the perilous hatches;
But never of lunar wolf-wasted or the arboreal
Malignancy, with the privy breath, which watches
And humps in the dark; but only a dream, after all.
At the worst, you think, with a little twinge of distress,
That contagion may nook in the comforting fur you love to caress.

Though some, unsatisfied and sick, have sought
That immitigable face, whose smile is ice,
And fired their hears like pitch-pine, for they thought
Rather flame than the damp worm-toothe of compromise:
So Harry L. I knew, whose whores and gin
Had dwindled to a slick smile in the drug store
But for the absurd contraption of a plane,
Which flung on air the unformulable endeavor
While hear bled speed to lave the applauded name.
The crash was in an old cornfield; not even flame.

So some, whose passionate emptiness and tital
Lust swayed toward the debris of Madrid,
And left New York to loll in their fierce idyll
Among the olives, where the snipers hid;
And now the North, to seek the visioned face
And polarize their iron of despair,
Who praise no beauty like the boreal grace
Which greens the dead eye under the rocket's flare.
They fight old friends, for their obsession knows
Only the immaculate itch, not human friends or foes.

They sought a secret which fat Franco's Moor,
Hieratic, white-robed, pitiless, might teach,
Who duped and dying but for pride, therefore
Hugged truth which cause or conscience scarcely reach.
As Jacob all night with the angelic foe,
They wrestled him who did not speak, but died,
And wrestle now, by frozen fen and floe,

New Courier, in fury sanctified;
And seek that face which, greasy, frost-breathed, in furs,
Bends to the bomb-sight over bitter Helsingfors.

Blood splashed on the terrorless intellect creates
Corrosive fizzle like the spattered lime,
And its enseamed stew but satiates
Itself, in that lewd and faceless pantomime.
You know, by radio, how hotly the world repeats,
When the brute crowd roars or the blunt boot-heels resound
In the Piazza or the Wilhelmplatz,
The crime of Onan, spilled upon the ground;
You know, whose dear hope Alexis Carrel kept
Alive in a test tube, where it monstrously grew, and slept.

But it is dead, and you now, guiltless, sink
To rest in lobbies, or pace gardens where
The slow god crumbles and the fountains prink,
Nor heed the criminal king, who paints the air
With discoursed madness and protruding eye,
Nor give the alarm, nor ask tonight where sleeps
That head which hooped the jewel Fidelity,
But like an old melon now, in the dank ditch, seeps;
But you crack nuts, while the conscience-stricken stare
Kisses the terror; for you see an empty chair

John Betjeman (1906-1984)

John Betjeman, an only child, was born August 28th to Ernest Edward and Mabel Bessie Betjeman. His father was a furniture, glassware, and silver designer. Betjeman decided at an early age to become a poet. while still in secondary school he bound his poems into a book, titled them "The Best of Betjeman," and submitted his project to T. S. Eliot, one of his schoolmasters. He also, at an early age, developed a passion for architecture, which he began to study and write about in preparatory school.

In 1925 Betjeman went to Magdalen College, Oxford and studies under C. S. Lewis. Betjeman also edited the literary magazine *Cherwell*. His days at Oxford were very happy and busy; Betjeman counted among his friends W. H. Auden and Evelyn Waugh. Despite his social success Betjeman left Oxford in 1928 without taking a degree, having failed his examination in divinity.

After his disappointed father cut off his allowance, Betjeman became in turn a schoolmaster and an insurance broker. Not happy with these occupations, he worked as assistant editor of *The Architectural Review* and film critic for the *Evening Standard*, all the while writing poetry. In 1931 his first book of verse, *Mount Zion, or, In Touch with the Infinite* came out and he followed in 1937 with *Continual Den: A Little Book of Bourgeois Verse*. He also produced books on architecture and series of guide books to England for the Shell company. In 1933 Betjeman married Penelope Valentine Hester, the daughter of the English commander-in-chief of India.

During the Second World War Betjeman served in the Ministry of Information, but still found time to produce two more books of poetry: *Old Lights for New Chancels* (1940) and *New Bats in Old Belfries* (1945). In 1958 he published his most popular work, *Collected Poems*, which sold at the rate of 1,000 copies per day. Queen Elizabeth II knighted Betjeman in 1969, and appointed him Poet Laureate in 1972.

One of the few major poets of the twentieth century not influenced by Pound or Eliot, Betjeman modeled himself after certain poets of the nineteenth century. He uses conventional rhyme and meter patterns and writes about familiar concerns. Despite his reluctance to incorporate the innovations of modern poetry, and his mass popularity, Betjeman is respected by many poets and critics for his gift for dialogue, his mastery of the English language, and his metrical skill.

Parliament Hill Fields

Rumbling under blackened girders, Midland, bound
    for Cricklewood,
Puffed its sulphur to the sunset where that Land of
    Laundries stood.
Rumble under, thunder over, train and tram alternate
    go,
Shake the floor and smudge the ledger, Charrington,
    Sells, Dale and Co.,
Nuts and nuggets in the window, trucks along the
    lines below.

When the Bon Marché was shuttered, when the feet
    were hot and tired,
Outside Charrington's we waited, by the STOP
    HERE IF REQUIRED,
Launched aboard the shopping basket, sat
    precipitately down,
Rocked past Zwanziger the Baker's, and the terrace
    blackish brown,
And the Anglo, Anglo-Norman Parish Church of
    Kentish Town.

Till the tram went over thirty, sighting terminus
    again,
Past the municipal lawn tennis and the bobble-
    hanging plane;
Soft the light suburban evening caught our ashlar-
    speckled spire,
Eighteen-sixty Early English, as the mighty elms
    retire,
Either side of Brookfield Mansions flashing fine
    French-window fire.

Oh, the after tram ride quiet, when we heard a mile
    beyond,
Silver music from the bandstand, barking dogs by
    Highgate Pond;
Up the hill where stucco houses in Virginia creeper
    drown;
And my childish wave of pity, seeing children
    carrying down
Sheaves of drooping dandelions to the courts of
    Kentish Town.

Upper Lambourne

Up the ash tree climbs the ivy,
   Up the ivy climbs the sun.
With a twenty thousand pattering
   Has a valley breeze begun,
Feathery ash, neglected elder,
   Shift the shade and make it run—

Shift the shade towards the nettles,
   And the nettles set it free
To streak the stained Cararra headstone
   Where, in nineteen-twenty-three,
He who trained a hundred winners
   Paid the Final Entrance Fee.

Leathery limbs of Upper Lambourne,
   Leathery skin from sun and wind,
Leathery breeches, spreading stables,
   Shining saddles left behind,
To the down the string of horses
   Moving out of sight and mind.

Feathery ash in leathery Lamborune
   Waves above the sarsen stone,
And Edwardian plantations
   So coniferously moan
As to make the swelling downland,
   Far surrounding, seem their own.

Youth and Age on Beaulieu River, Hants

Early sun on beaulieu water
   Lights the undersides of oaks,
Clumps of leaves it floods and blanches
All transparent glow the branches
   Which the double sunlight soaks;
And to her craft on Beaulieu water
Clemency the General's daughter
   Pulls across with even strokes.

Schoolboy sure she is this morning;
   Soon her sharpie's rigg'd and free.
Coll beneath a garden awning
   Mrs Fairclough sipping tea
And raising large long-distance glasses
As the little sharpie passes,
   Sighs our sailor girl to see:

Tulip figure, so appealing,
   Oval face, so serious-eyed,
Tree-roots pass'd and muddy beaches,
On to huge and lake-like reaches,
   Soft and sun-warm, see her glide,
Slacks the slim young limbs revealing,
Sun-brown arm the tiller feeling,
   Before the wind and tide.

Evening light will bring the water,
   Day-long sun will burst the bud,
Clemency, the General's daughter,
   Will return upon the flood.
But the older woman only
knows the ebb tide leaves her lonely
   With the shining fields of mud.

William Empson (1906–1984)

Born at Yokefleet Hall, Howden, Yorkshire, Empson was educated at Cambridge where he studied mathematics and English. At the age of 24 he published his most famous work, *Seven Types of Ambiguity*, a book of literary criticism demonstrating Empson's remarkable method of verbal analysis in the interpretation of literature. In 1935 he published his first book of poetry, *Poems*. Unlike most poetry of the thirties, Empson's verse did not deal with political or social problems, but was concerned with philosophical and metaphysical matters. He has taught at the Bunrika Daigaku University in Tokyo and the Peking National University of China. After these experiences he was made Chinese editor for the B.B.C. He joined the faculty of Sheffield University in 1953. William Empson died in April of 1984. In a recent tribute, the editor John Gross said: ". . . (Empson) is someone who is going to go on fascinating readers long after many a more widely acclaimed and noisily touted name has been consigned to the scrapheap."

Camping Out

And now she cleans her teeth into the lake:
Gives it (God's grace) for her own bounty's sake
What morning's pale and the crisp mist debars:
Its glass of the divine (that Will could break)
Restores, beyond Nature: or lets Heaven take
(Itself being dimmed) her pattern, who half awake
Milks between rocks a straddled sky of stars.

Soap tension the star pattern magnifies.
Smoothly Madonna through-assumes the skies
Whose vaults are opened to achieve the Lord.
No, it is we soaring explore galaxies,
Our bullet boat light's speed by thousands flies.
Who moves so among stars their frame unties;
See where they blur, and die, and are outsoared.

Homage to the British Museum

There is a supreme God in the ethnological section;
A hollow toad shape, faced with a blank shield.
He needs his belly to include the Pantheon,
Which is inserted through a hole behind.
At the navel, at the points formally stressed, at the
    organs of sense,
Lice glue themselves, dolls, local deities,
His smooth wood creeps with all the creeds of the
    world.

Attending there let us absorb the cultures of nations
And dissolve into our judgement all their codes.
Then, being clogged with a natural hesitation
(People are continually asking one the way out),
Let us stand here and admit that we have no road.
Being everything, let us admit that is to be something,
Or give ourselves the benefit of the doubt;
Let us offer our pinch of dust all to this God,
And grant his reign over the entire building.

Invitation to Juno

Lucretius could not credit centaurs;
Such bicycle he deemed asynchronous.
'Man superannuates the horse;
Horse pulses will not gear with ours.'

Johnson could see no bicycle would go;
'You bear yourself, and the machine as well.'
Gennets for germans sprang not from Othello,
And Ixion rides upon a single wheel.

Courage. Weren't strips of heart culture seen
Of late mating two periodicities?
Could not Professor Charles Darwin
Graft annual upon perennial trees?

Flighting for Duck

Egyptian banks, an avenue of clay,
Define the drain between constructed marshes
(Two silted lakes, silver and brown, with grass,
Without background, far from hills, at evening).
Its pomp makes a high road between their sheets
(Mud shoals, a new alluvium, dabbled water,
Shallow, and specked with thistles, not yet mastered)
At the subdued triumph of whose end
Two transept banks, the castle guard, meet it,
Screening the deeper water they surround
With even line of low but commanding pinetrees
Dark but distinguished as a row of peacocks.
The darker silhouette is where a barn
Straddling two banks over a lesser channel
Stands pillared upon treetrunks like a guildhall
Empty, mudheaped, through which the alluvial scheme
Flows temporary as the modern world.
The mud's tough glue is drying our still feet.
A mild but powerful flow moves through the flats
Laden with soil to feed the further warping.

"What was that drumming in the sky? What cry
Squawked from the rustled rushes a reply?
Was it near? Are they coming?
Could you hear?" Sound travels a good way by night.
That farm dog barking's half a mile away.

But when the swarms gathering for food repay us
This hint of anti-aircraft is disarmed
And as the fleets at a shot reascend
The eye orders their unreachable chaos
(The stars are moving like these duck, but slower,
Sublime, their tails absurd, their voices harsh)
And analyses into groups the crowds.
Two surfaces of birds, higher and lower,
Rise up and cross each other and distend
As one flight to the river turns, alarmed.
They are out of shot, and like the turning clouds

From meditative cigarettes amuse,
Manure in smoke over the fructuant marsh,
Curled vapour, incense from the cult of Ouse.

Bang. Bang. Two duck blur 'mid the social crew;
For man created, to man's larder due.
With plump or splash on the new-nurtured field
To Reason's arm they proper homage yield.
The well-taught dogs wait but the voice to run,
Eager, and conscious of the murd'ring gun.

Starlit, mistcircled, one whole pearl embrowned,
An even dusked silver of earth and sky
Held me, dazzled with cobwebs, staring round.
The black band of my hat lept to my eye.
Alone in sight not coloured like the ground
It lit, like a struck match, everything by.

Four Legs, Three Legs, Two Legs

Delphic and Theban and Corinthian,
Three lines, by the odd chance, met at a point,
The delta zero, the case trivial.

A young man's cross-road but a shady one.
Killing a mistaken black cat in the dark
He had no other metaphysical trait.

God walks in a mysterious way
Neither delighteth he in any man's legs.

The wrecked girl, still raddled with Napoleon's paint,
Nose eaten by a less clear conqueror,
Still orientated to the average dawn,
Behind, Sahara, before, Nile and man
A toy abandoned, sure, after so many,
That the next sun will take her for a walk,
Still lifts a touching dog's face eager for a sign.
Not one for generalising his solutions

Oedipus placed the riddle with a name.
Another triumph for the commonplace.
While too much to pretend she fell and burst
It is a comfort that the Sphinx took such an answer.

Legal Fiction

Law makes long spokes of the short stakes of men.
Your well fenced out real estate of mind
No high flat of the nomad citizen
Looks over, or train leaves behind.

Your rights extend under and above your claim
Without bound; you own land in Heaven and Hell;
Your part of earth's surface and mass the same,
Of all cosmos' volume, and all stars as well.

Your rights reach down where all owners meet, in
    Hell's
Pointed exclusive conclave, at earth's centre
(Your spun farm's root still on that axis dwells);
And up, through galaxies, a growing sector.

You are nomad yet; the lighthouse beam you own
Flashes, like Lucifer, through the firmament.
Earth's axis varies; your dark central cone
Wavers, a candle's shadow, at the end.

Missing Dates

Slowly the poison the whole blood stream fills.
It is not the effort nor the failure tires.
The waste remains, the waste remains and kills.

It is not your system or clear sight that mills
Down small to the consequence a life requires;
Slowly the poison the whole blood stream fills.

They bled an old dog dry yet the exchange rills
Of young dog blood gave but a month's desires;
The waste remains, the waste remains and kills.

It is the Chinese tombs and the slag hills
Usurp the soil, and not the soil retires.
Slowly the poison the whole blood stream fills.

Not to have fire is to be a skin that shrills.
The complete fire is death. From partial fires
The waste remains, the waste remains and kills.

It is the poems you have lost, the ills
From missing dates, at which the heart expires.
Slowly the poison the whole blood stream fills.
The waste remains, the waste remains and kills.

Note on Local Flora

There is a tree native in Turkestan,
Or further east towards the Tree of Heaven,
Whose hard cold cones, not being wards to time,
Will leave their mother only for good cause;
Will ripen only in a forest fire;
Wait, to be fathered as was Bacchus once,
Through men's long lives, that image of time's end.
I knew the Phoenix was a vegetable.
So Semele desired her deity
As this in Kew thirsts for the Red Dawn.

This Last Pain

This last pain for the damned the Fathers found:
'They knew the bliss with which they were not crowned.'
   Such, but on earth, let me foretell,
     Is all, of heaven or of hell.

Man, as the prying housemaid of the soul,
May know her happiness by eye to hole:
   He's safe; the key is lost; he knows
   Door will not open, nor hole close.

'What is conceivable can happen too,'
Said Wittgenstein, who had not dreamt of you;
   But wisely; if we worked it long
   We should forget where it was wrong:

Those thorns are crowns which, woven into knots,
Crackle under and soon boil fools' pots;
   And no man's watching, wise and long,
   Would ever stare them into song.

Thorns burn to a consistent ash, like man;
A splendid cleanser for the frying-pan:
   And those who leap from pan to fire
   Should this brave opposite admire.

All those large dreams by which men long live well
Are magic-lanterned on the smoke of hell;
   This then is real, I have implied,
   A painted, small, transparent slide.

These the inventive can hand-paint at leisure,
Or most emporia would stock our measure;
   And feasting in their dappled shade
   We should forget how they were made.

Feign then what's by a decent tact believed
And act that state is only so conceived,
   And build an edifice of form
   For house where phantoms may keep warm.

Imagine, then, by miracle, with me,
(Ambiguous gifts, as what gods give must be)
   What could not possibly be there,
   And learn a style from a despair.

W. H. Auden (1907–1973)

Wystan Hugh Auden was born February 21 in York, England, the youngest of three children. His father, a doctor, moved the family to a suburb of Birmingham when Auden was one and a half. It was here that Auden spent his formative years and developed an intense interest in mining and machinery—two subjects which were to pervade his later poetry. He was educated at a series of preparatory schools whose austere and rigid behavior codes had a life-long effect on Auden. He sought, in his work and in his personal life, to liberate himself from the strict social mores of his upbringing. It was at one of these schools, Gresham's, that a friend, after an argument over the nature of organized religion, suggested that Auden write poetry, which he began to do at the age of 15.

In 1928 Auden received his degree from Christ Church, Oxford in English Language and Literature. After spending some time in Berlin, the allowance Auden received from his family was terminated and he returned to England to become a school teacher. In 1930 he took up a teaching post vacated by Cecil Day Lewis at the Larchfield Academy. Soon after, Auden's first book entitled simply *Poems*, was accepted for publication by the poetry editor at Faber and Faber: T. S. Eliot.

After teaching school and writing commentaries for documentaries, Auden began a travel phase. With Louis MacNeice he set out for Iceland to write a travel book entitled *Letters From Iceland*. In 1937 Auden went to Spain to drive an ambulance for the Republican army; this experience spawned one of his most famous poems, "Spain," published in the spring of 1937. In 1938 Auden and Christopher Isherwood went to China to write another travel book, *Journey To A War*. They returned to England via New York City where they were introduced to the cultural scene by George Davis, the fiction editor of *Harper's Bazaar*. Both Isherwood and Auden were fascinated by New York and a few months after their return to England decided to emigrate to America.

In January of 1939, Auden and Isherwood arrived in the United States. Isherwood eventually moved on to California, but Auden settled in New York, and in 1946 became a U. S. citizen. Though he was a guest lecturer and teacher at various colleges throughout the country, Auden concentrated on writing and earned his living from his poems, critical essays, and plays. Auden received the Pulitzer Prize in 1948 for his long poem *The Age of Anxiety*, which inspired Jerome Robbins' 1950 ballet of the same name and Leonard Bernstein's Second Symphony. In 1956 Auden was named Professor of Poetry at Oxford. Shortly thereafter Auden won an Italian literary prize which carried with it a substantial monetary reward. With this award he bought a cottage in Kirchstetten, Austria near Vienna. From 1957 until his death Auden divided his time between New York, Oxford, and Austria.

Oxford University offered Auden a permanent residence at Christ Church and in 1972 he moved to England. On September 28th, 1973, after giving a poetry reading in the Palais Palffy in Josefplatz, Austria, Auden died of a heart attack, alone in his hotel room.

W. H. Auden was the most gifted and honored poet of his era, having a great influence on younger poets and artists from all fields—an influence which is still felt today. His accomplishments in poetry have been compared to those of Picasso's in painting and Stravinsky's in music. In the words of a fellow poet, Geoffery Grigson: "If we follow him round, as he celebrates, investigates, discards, adds, re-attempts, we find in him explicit recipes for being human."

The Airman's Alphabet

ACE—
    Pride of parents
    and photographed person
    and laughter in leather.

BOMB—
    Curse from cloud
    and coming to crook
    and saddest to steeple.

COCKPIT—
    Soft seat
    and support of solider
    and hold for hero.

DEATH—
    Award for wildness
    and worst in the west
    and painful to pilots.

ENGINE—
    Darling of designers
    and dirty dragon
    and revolving roarer.

FLYING—
    Habit of hawks
    and unholy hunting
    and ghostly journey.

GAUGE—
    Informer about oil
    and important to eye
    and graduated glass.

HANGAR—
    Mansion of machine
    and motherly to metal
    and house of handshaking.

INSTRUMENT—
    Dial on dashboard
    and destroyer of doubt
    and father of fact.

JOYSTICK—
    Pivot of power
    and responder to pressure
    and grip for the glove.

KISS—   Touch taking off
             and tenderness in time
             and firmness on flesh.

LOOPING—   Flying folly
             and feat at fairs
             and brave to boys.

MECHANIC—   Owner of overalls
             and interested in iron
             and trusted with tools.

NOSE-DIVE—   Nightmare to nerves
             and needed by no one
             and dash toward death.

OBSERVER—   Peeper through periscope
             and peerer at pasture
             and eye in the air.

PROPELLER—   Wooden wind-oar
             and twisted whirler
             and lifter of load.

QUIET—   Absent from airmen
             and easy to horses
             and got in the grave.

RUDDER—   Deflector of flight
             and flexible fin
             and pointer of path.

STORM—   Night from the north
             and numbness nearing
             and hail ahead.

TIME—   Expression of alarm
             and used by the ill
             and personal space.

UNDERCARRIAGE—   Softener of shock
                 and seat on the soil
                 and easy to injure.

VICTIM—   Corpse after crash
                 and carried through country
                 and atonement for aircraft.

WIRELESS—   Sender of signal
                 and speaker of sorrow
                 and news from nowhere

X—   Mark upon map
                 and meaning mischief
                 and lover's lingo.

YOUTH—   Daydream of devils
                 and dear to the damned
                 and always to us.

ZERO—   Love before leaving
                 and touch of terror
                 and time of attack.

At the Grave of Henry James

The snow, less intransigeant than their marble,
Has left the defense of whiteness to these tombs;
   For all the pools at my feet
Accommodate blue now, and echo such clouds as occur
To the sky, and whatever bird or mourner the passing
   Moment remarks they repeat.

While the rocks, named after singular spaces
Within which images wandered once that caused
   All to tremble and offend,
Stand here in an innocent stillness, each marking the spot
Where one more series of errors lost its uniqueness
   And novelty came to an end.

To whose real advantage were such transactions
When words of reflection were exchanged for trees?
    What living occasion can
Be just to the absent? O noon but reflects on itself,
And the small taciturn stone that is the only witness
    To a great and talkative man

Has no more judgement than my ignorant shadow
Of odious comparisons or distant clocks
    Which challenge and interfere
With the heart's instantaneous reading of time, time that is
A warm enigma no longer in you for whom I
Surrender my private cheer

Startling the awkward footsteps of my apprehension,
The flushed assault of your recognition is
    The *donnée* of this doubtful hour:
O stern proconsul of intractable provinces,
O poet of the difficult, dear addicted artist,
    Assent to my soil and flower.

As I stand awake on our solar fabric,
That primary machine, the earth, which gendarmes, banks,
    And aspirin pre-suppose.
On which the clumsy and sad may all sit down, and any who will
Say their a-ha to the beautiful, the common locus
    Of the master and the rose.

Our theatre, scaffold, and erotic city
Where all the infirm species are partners in the act
    Of encroachment bodies crave,
Though solitude in death is *de rigueur* for their flesh
And the self-denying hermit flies as it approaches
    Like the carnivore to a cave.

That its plural numbers may unite in meaning,
Its vulgar tongues unravel the knotted mass
    Of the improperly conjunct,
Open my eyes now to all its hinted significant forms,
Sharpen my ears to detect amid its brilliant uproar
    The low thud of the defunct.

O dwell, ironic at my living centre,
Half ancestor, half child; because the actual self
   Round whom time revolves so fast
Is so afraid of what its motions might possibly do
That the actor is never there when his really important
   Acts happen. Only the past

Is present, no one about but the dead as,
Equipped with a few inherited odds and ends,
   One after another we are
Fired into life to seek that unseen target where all
Our equivocal judgments are judged and resolved in
   One whole Alas or Hurrah.

And only the unborn remark the disaster
When, though it makes no difference to the pretty airs
   The bird of Appetite sings,
And Amour Propre is his usual amusing self,
Out from the jungle of an undistinguished moment
   The flexible shadow springs.

Now more than ever, when torches and snare-drums
Excite the squat women of the saurian brain
   Till a milling mob of fears
Breaks in insultingly on anywhere, when in our dreams
Pigs play on the organs and the blue sky runs shrieking
   As the Crack of Doom appears,

Are the good ghosts needed with the white magic
Of their subtle loves. War has no ambiguities
   Like a marriage; the result
Required of its *affaire fatale* is simple and sad,
The physical removal of all human objects
   That conceal the Difficult.

Then remember me that I may remember
The test we have to learn to shudder for is not
   An historical event,
That neither the low democracy of a nightmare nor
An army's primitive tidiness may deceive me
   About our predicament.

That catastrophic situation which neither
Victory nor defeat can annul; to be
    Deaf yet determined to sing,
To be lame and blind yet burning for the Great Good Place,
To be radically corrupt yet mournfully attracted
    By the Real Distinguished Thing.

And shall I not specially bless you as, vexed with
My little inferior questions, today I stand
    Beside the bed where you rest
Who opened such passionate arms to your *Bon* when It ran
Toward you with its overwhelming reasons pleading
    All beautifully in Its breast?

O with what innocence your hand submitted
To these formal rules that help a child to play,
    While your heart, fastidious as
A delicate nun, remained true to the rare noblesse
Of your lucid gift and, for its own sake, ignored the
    Resentful muttering Mass.

Whose ruminant hatred of all which cannot
Be simplified or stolen is still at large;
    No death can assuage its lust
To vilify the landscape of Distinction and see
The heart of the Personal brought to a systolic standstill,
    The Tall to diminished dust.

Preserve me, Master, from its vague incitement;
Yours be the disciplinary image that holds
    Me back from agreeable wrong.
And the clutch of eddying muddle, lest Proportion shed
The alpine chill of her shrugging editorial shoulder
    On my loose impromptu song,

Suggest; so may I segregate my disorder
Into districts of prospective value: approve;
    Lightly, lightly, then, may I dance
Over the frontier of the obvious and fumble no more
In the old limp pocket of the minor exhibition,
    Nor riot with irrelevance.

And no longer shoe geese or water stakes, but
Bolt in my day my grain of truth to the barn
   Where tribulations may leap
With their long-lost brothers at last in the festival
Of which not one had a dissenting image, and the
   Flushed immediacy sleep.

Into this city from the shining lowlands
Blows a wind that whispers of uncovered skulls
   And fresh ruins under the moon,
Of hopes that will not survive the *secousse* of this spring
Of blood and flames, of the terror that walks by night and
   The sickness that strikes at noon.

All will be judged. Master of nuance and scruple,
Pray for me and for all writers living or dead;
   Because there are many whose works
Are in better taste than their lives; because there is no end
To the vanity of our calling: make intercession
   For the treason of all clerks.

Because the darkness is never so distant,
And there is never much time for the arrogant
   Spirit to flutter its wings,
Or the broken bone to rejoice, or the cruel to cry
For Him whose property is always to have mercy, the author
   And giver of all good things.

A Bride in the '30'S
For Madame Mangeot

Easily, my dear, you move, easily your head
And easily as through leaves of a photograph album I'm
   led
Through the night's delights and the day's impressions
Past the tall tenements and the trees in the wood
Though sombre the sixteen skies of Europe
      And the Danube flood.

Looking and loving our behaviours pass
The stones the steels and the polished glass;
Lucky to love the new pansy railway
The sterile farms where his looks are fed,
And in the policed unlucky city
      Lucky his bed.

He from these lands of terrifying mottoes
Makes worlds as innocent as Beatrix Potter's;
Through bankrupt countries where they mend the
   roads
Along the endless plains his will is
Intent as a collector to pursue
      His greens and lilies.

Easy for him to find in your face
The pool of silence and the tower of grace
To conjure a camera into a wishing rose
Simple to excite in the air from a glance
The horses, the fountains, the sidedrum, the trombone
      And the dance, the dance.

Summoned by such a music from our time
Such images to audience come
As vanity cannot dispel nor bless:
Hunger and love in their variations
Grouped invalids watching the flight of the birds
      And single assassins.

Ten thousand of the desperate marching by
Five feet, six feet, seven feet high:
Hitler and Mussolini in their wooing poses
Churchill acknowledging the voter's greeting
Roosevelt at the microphone, Van Lubbe laughing
      And our first meeting.

But love except at our proposal
Will do no trick at his disposal;
Without opinions of his own performs

The programme that we think of merit,
And through our private stuff must work
      His public spirit.

Certain it became while we were still incomplete
There were certain prizes for which we would never
    compete;
A choice was killed by every childish illness,
The boiling tears among the hothouse plants,
The rigid promise fractured in the garden,
      And the long aunts.

And every day there bolted from the field
Desires to which we could not yield;
Fewer and clearer grew the plans,
Schemes for a life and sketches for a hatred,
And early among my interesting scrawls
      Appeared your portrait.

You stand now before me, flesh and bone
These ghosts would like to make their own.
Are they your choices? O, be deaf
To hatred proffering immediate pleasure
Glory to swap her fascinating rubbish
      For your one treasure.

Be deaf too standing uncertain now,
A pine tree shadow across your brow,
To what I hear and wish I did not,
The voice of love saying lightly, brightly
'Be Lubbe, Be Hitler, but be my good
      Daily, nightly'.

The power which corrupts, that power to excess
The beautiful quite naturally possess:
To them the fathers and the children turn
And all who long for their destruction
The arrogant and self-insulted wait
      The looked instruction.

Shall idleness ring then your eyes like the pest?
O will you unnoticed and mildly like the rest,
Will you join the lost in their sneering circles,
Forfeit the beautiful interest and fall
Where the engaging face is the face of the betrayer
    And the pang is all?

Wind shakes the tree; the mountains darken:
And the heart repeats though we would not hearken;
'Yours the choice to whom the gods awarded
The language of learning and the language of love
Crooked to move as a moneybug or a cancer
    Or straight as a dove'.

Carry Her over the Water

Carry her over the water,
    And set her down under the tree,
Where the culvers white all day and all night,
    And the winds from every quarter
Sing agreeably, agreeably, agreeably of love.

Put a gold ring on her finger,
    And press her close to your heart,
While the fish in the lake their snapshots take,
    And the frog, that sanguine singer,
Sings agreeably, agreeably, agreeably of love.

The streets shall all flock to your marriage,
    The houses turn round to look,
The tables and chairs say suitable prayers,
    And the horses drawing your carriage
Sing agreeably, agreeably, agreeably of love.

Casino

Only the hands are living; to the wheel attracted,
Are moved as deer trek desperately towards a creek
   Through the dust and scrub of the desert, or gently
   As sunflowers turn to the light,

And, as the night takes up the cries of feverish children,
The cravings of lions in dens, the loves of dons,
   Gathers them all and remains the night, the
   Great room is full of their prayers.

To the last feast of isolation self-invited
They flock, and in the rite of disbelief are joined;
   From numbers all their stars are recreated,
   The enchanted, the world, the sad.

Without, the rivers flow among the wholly living,
Quite near their trysts; and the mountains part them; and the bird
   Deep in the greens and moistures of summer
   Sings towards their work.

But here no nymph comes naked to the youngest shepherd;
The fountain is deserted; the laurel will not grow;
   The labyrinth is safe but endless, and broken
   As Ariadne's thread.

As deeper in these hands is grooved their fortune: 'Lucky
Were few, and it is possible that none was loved;
   And what was godlike in this generation
   Was never to be born.'

In Memory of Sigmund Freud
(*d. September* 1939)

When there are so many we shall have to mourn,
When grief has been made so public, and exposed
   To the critique of a whole epoch
   The frailty of our conscience and anguish,

Of whom shall we speak? For every day they die
Among us, those who were doing us some good,
   And knew it was never enough but
   Hoped to improve a little by living.

Such was this doctor: still at eighty he wished
To think of our life, from whose unruliness
   So many plausible young futures
   With threats or flattery ask obedience.

But his wish was denied him; he closed his eyes
Upon that last picture common to us all,
   Of problems like relatives standing
   Puzzled and jealous about our dying.

For about him at the very end were still
Those he had studied, the nervous and the nights,
   And shades that still waited to enter
   The bright circle of his recognition

Turned elsewhere with their disappointment as he
Was taken away from his old interest
   To go back to the earth in London
   An important Jew who died in exile.

Only Hate was happy, hoping to augment
His practice now, and his shabby clientèle
   Who think they can be cured by killing
   And covering the gardens with ashes.

They are still alive but in a world he changed
Simply by looking back with no false regrets;
   All that he did was to remember
   Like the old and be honest like children.

He wasn't clever at all: he merely told
The unhappy Present to recite the Past
   Like a poetry lesson till sooner
   Or later it faltered at the line where

Long ago the accusations had begun,
And suddenly knew by whom it had been judged,
   How rich life had been and how silly,
   And was life-forgiven and more humble.

Able to approach the Future as a friend
Without a wardrobe of excuses, without
   A set mask of rectitude or an
   Embarrassing over-familiar gesture.

No wonder the ancient cultures of conceit
In his technique of unsettlement foresaw
   The fall of princes, the collapse of
   Their lucrative patterns of frustration.

If he succeeded, why, the Generalized Life
Would become impossible, the monolith
   Of State be broken and prevented
   The co-operation of avengers.

Of course they called on God: but he went his way,
Down among the Lost People like Dante, down
   To the stinking fosse where the injured
   Lead the ugly life of the rejected.

And showed us what evil is: not as we thought
Deeds that must be punished, but our lack of faith,
   Our dishonest mood of denial,
   The concupiscence of the oppressor.

And if something of the autocratic pose,
The paternal strictness he distrusted, still
   Clung to his utterance and features,
   It was a protective imitation

For one who lived among enemies so long;
If often he was wrong and at times absurd,
   To us he is no more a person
   Now but a whole climate of opinion,

Under whom we conduct our differing lives:
Like weather he can only hinder or help,
    The proud can still be proud but find it
    A little harder, and the tyrant tries

To make him do but doesn't care for him much.
He quietly surrounds all our habits of growth;
    He extends, till the tired in even
    The remotest most miserably duchy

Have felt the change in their bones and are cheered,
And the child unlucky in his little State,
    Some hearth where freedom is excluded,
    A hive whose honey is fear and worry,

Feels calmer now and somehow assured of escape;
While as they lie in the grass of our neglect,
    So many long-forgotten objects
    Revealed by his undiscouraged shining

Are returned to us and made precious again;
Games we had thought we must drop as we grew up,
    Little noises we dared not laugh at,
    Faces we made when no one was looking.

But he wishes us more than this: to be free
Is often to be lonely; he would unite
    The unequal moieties fractured
    By our own well-meaning sense of justice.

Would restore to the larger the wit and will
The smaller possesses but can only use
    For arid disputes, would give back to
    The son the mother's richness of feeling.

But he would have us remember most of all
To be enthusiastic over the night
    Not only for the sense of wonder
    It alone has to offer, but also

Because it needs our love: for with sad eyes
Its delectable creatures look up and beg
   Us dumbly to ask them to follow;
   They are exiles who long for the future

That lies in our power. They too would rejoice
If allowed to serve enlightenment like him,
   Even to bear our cry of 'Judas',
   As he did and all must bear who serve it.

One rational voice is dumb: over a grave
The household of Impulse mourns one dearly loved.
   Sad is Eros, builder of cities,
   And weeping anarchic Aphrodite.

The Lesson

The first time that I dreamed, we were in flight,
And fagged with running; there was civil war,
A valley full of thieves and wounded bears.

Farms blazed behind us; turning to the right,
We came at once to a tall house, its door
Wide open, waiting for its long-lost heirs.

An elderly clerk sat on the bedroom stairs
Writing; but we had tiptoed past him when
He raised his head and stuttered—'Go away'.
We wept and begged to stay:
He wiped his pince-nez, hesitated, then
Said no, he had no power to give us leave;
Our lives were not in order; we must leave.

      * * *

The second dream began in a May wood;
We had been laughing; your blue eyes were kind,
Your excellent nakedness without disdain.
Our lips met, wishing universal good;

But on their impact sudden flame and wind
Fetched you away and turned me loose again

To make a focus for a wide wild plain,
Dead level and dead silent and bone dry,
Where nothing could have suffered, sinned, or grown.
On a high chair alone
I sat, my little master, asking why
The cold and solid object in my hands
Should be a human hand, one of your hands.

* * *

And the last dream was this: we were to go
To a great banquet and a Victory Ball
After some tournament or dangerous test.

Only our seats had velvet cushions, so
We must have won; though there were crowns for all,
Ours were of gold, of paper all the rest.
O fair or funny was each famous guest.
Love smiled at Courage over priceless glass,
And rockets died in hundreds to express
Our learned carelessness.
A band struck up; all over the green grass
A sea of paper crowns rose up to dance:
Ours were too heavy; we did not dance.

* * *

I woke. You were not there. But as I dressed
Anxiety turned to shame, feeling all three
Intended one rebuke. For had not each
In its own way tried to teach
My will to love you that it cannot be,
As I think, of such consequence to want
What anyone is given, if they want?

Miranda's Song

My Dear One is mine as mirrors are lonely,
As the poor and sad are real to the good king,
And the high green hill sits always by the sea.

Up jumped the Black Man behind the elder tree,
Turned a somersault and ran away waving;
My Dear One is mine as mirrors are lonely.

The Witch gave a squawk: her venomous body
Melted into light as water leaves a spring
And the high green hill sits always by the sea.

At his crossroads, too, the Ancient prayed for me;
Down his wasted cheeks tears of joy were running:
My Dear One is mine as mirrors are lonely.

He kissed me awake, and no one was sorry;
The sun shone on sails, eyes, pebbles, anything,
And the high green hill sits always by the sea.

So, to remember our changing garden, we
Are linked as children in a circle dancing:
My Dear One is mine as mirrors are lonely,
And the high green hill sits always by the sea.

Musée des Beaux Arts

About suffering they were never wrong,
The Old Masters: how well they understood
Its human position; how it takes place
While someone else is eating or opening a window or just walking
    dully along;
How, when the aged are reverently, passionately waiting
For the miraculous birth, there always must be
Children who did not specially want it to happen, skating
On a pond at the edge of the wood:
They never forgot

That even the dreadful martyrdom must run its course
Anyhow in a corner, some untidy spot
Where the dogs go on with their doggy life and the torturer's horse
Scratches its innocent behind on a tree.

In Breughel's Icarus, for instance: how everything turns away
Quite leisurely from the disaster; the ploughman may
Have heard the splash, the forsaken cry,
But for him it was not an important failure; the sun shone
As it had to on the white legs disappearing into the green
Water; and the expensive delicate ship that must have seen
Something amazing, a boy falling out of the sky,
Had somewhere to get to and sailed calmly on.

Perhaps

O Love, the interest itself in thoughtless Heaven,
Make simpler daily the beating of man's heart; within,
There in the ring where name and image meet,

Inspire them with such a longing as will make his thought
Alive like patterns a murmuration of starlings,
Rising in joy over wolds, unwittingly weave.

Here too on our little reef display your power,
This fortress perched on the edge of the Atlantic scarp,
The mote between all Europe and the exile-crowded sea;

And make us as *Newton* was who, in his garden watching
The apple falling towards *England*, became aware
Between himself and her of an eternal tie.

For now that dream which so long had contented our will,
I mean, of uniting the dead into a splendid empire,
Under whose fertilising flood the Lancashire moss

Sprouted up chimneys, and *Glamorgan* hid a life
Grim as a tidal rock-pool's in its glove-shaped valleys,
Is already retreating into her maternal shadow;

Leaving the furnaces gasping in the impossible air,
That flotsam at which *Dumbarton* gapes and hungers;
While upon wind-loved *Rowley* no hammer shakes

The cluster of mounds like a midget golf-course, graves
Of some who created these intelligible dangerous marvels,
Affectionate people, but crude their sense of glory.

Far-sighted as falcons, they looked down another future;
For the seed in their loins were hostile though afraid of their pride,
And, tall with a shadow now, inertly wait.

In bar, in netted chicken-farm, in lighthouse,
Standing on these impoverished constricted acres,
The ladies and gentlemen apart, too much alone,

Consider the years of the measured world begun,
The barren virtuous marriage of stone and water.
Yet, O, at this very moment of a hopeless sigh,

When, inland, they are thinking their thoughts but watching these islands
As children in *Chester* look to *Moel Fammau* to decide
On picnics by the clearness or withdrawal of her treeless crown.

Some possible dream, long coiled in the ammonite's slumber
Is uncurling, prepared to lay on our talk and reflection
Its military silence its surgeon's idea of pain;

And out of the future into actual history,
As when *Merlin*, tamer of horses, and his lords to whom
Stonehenge was still a thought, the *Pillars* passed

And into the undared ocean swung north their prow,
Drives through the night and star-concealing dawn
For the virgin roadsteads of our hearts an unwavering keel.

Petition

Sir, no man's enemy, forgiving all
But will his negative inversion, be prodigal:
Send to us power and light, a sovereign touch
Curing the intolerable neural itch,
The exhaustion of weaning, the liar's quinsy,
And the distortions of ingrown virginity.
Prohibit sharply the rehearsed response

And gradually correct the coward's stance;
Cover in time with beams those in retreat
That, spotted, they turn though the reverse were great;
Publish each healer that in city lives
Or country houses at the end of drives;
Harrow the house of the dead; look shining at
New styles of architecture, a change of heart.

Song for St. Cecilia's Day

I

In a garden shady this holy lady
With reverent cadence and subtle psalm,
Like a black swan as death came on
Poured forth her song in perfect calm:
And by ocean's margin this innocent virgin
Constructed an organ to enlarge her prayer,
And notes tremendous from her great engine
Thundered out on the Roman air.

Blonde Aphrodite rose up excited,
Moved to delight by the melody,
White as an orchid she rode quite naked
In an oyster shell on top of the sea;
At sounds so entrancing the angels dancing
Came out of their trance into time again,
And around the wicked in Hell's abysses
The huge flame flickered and eased their pain.

Blessed Cecilia, appear in visions
To all musicians, appear and inspire:
Translated Daughter, come down and startle
Composing mortals with immortal fire.

II

I cannot grow:
I have no shadow
To run away from,
I only play.

I cannot err;
There is no creature
Whom I belong to,
Whom I could wrong.

I am defeat
When it knows it
Can now do nothing
By suffering.

All you lived through,
Dancing because you
No longer need it
For any deed.

I shall never be
Different. Love me.

III

O ear whose creatures cannot wish to fall,
O calm spaces unafraid of weight,
Where Sorrow is herself, forgetting all
The gaucheness of her adolescent state,

Where Hope within the altogether strange
From every outworn image is released,
And Dread born whole and normal like a beast
Into a world of truths that never change:
Restore our fallen day; O re-arrange.

O dear white children casual as birds,
Playing among the ruined languages,
So small beside their large confusion words,
So gay against the greater silences
Of dreadful things you did: O hang the head,
Impetuous child with the tremendous brain,
O weep, child, weep, O weep away the stain,
Lost innocence who wished your lover dead,
Weep for the lives your wishes never led.

O cry created as the bow of sin
Is drawn across our trembling violin.
O weep, child, weep, O weep away the stain.
O law drummed out by hearts against the still
Long winter of our intellectual will.
That what has been may never be again,
O flute that throbs with the thanksgiving breath
Of convalescents on the shores of death.
O bless the freedom that you never chose.
O trumpets that unguarded children blow
About the fortress of their inner foe.
O wear your tribulation like a rose.

Watch Any Day

Watch any day his nonchalant pauses, see
His dextrous handling of a wrap as he
Steps after into cars, the beggar's envy.

'There is a free one' many say, but err.
He is not that returning conqueror,
Nor ever the poles' circumnavigator.

But poised between shocking falls on razor-edge
Has taught himself this balancing subterfuge
Of the accosting profile, the erect carriage.

The song, the varied action of the blood
Would drown the warning from the iron wood
Would cancel the inertia of the buried:

Travelling by daylight on from house to house
The longest way to the intrinsic peace,
With love's fidelity and with love's weakness.

Louis MacNeice (1907–1963)

Louis MacNeice was born September 12 in Belfast, Ireland. His father, John Frederick MacNeice, was the rector of St. Nicholas Church at Carrickfergus. MacNeice's childhood was largely unhappy: his mother died when he was young, he had many fears, nightmares, bouts of mental illness and mental deficiency, and he was frail and shy. He was educated at Oxford, graduating with honors. While at Oxford he and Stephen Spender edited *Oxford Poetry: 1929* in which they provided ample space for their own works. In the same year MacNeice published his first collection of verse, *Blind Fireworks*. After Oxford, he was appointed lecturer in Classics at the University of Birmingham and later went to Bedford College, in London. MacNeice traveled to America in 1940 as a visiting lecturer at Cornell University, but returned to England to help out in the war effort. He was not accepted into the armed forces, so he joined the BBC as a producer and writer, a post he held until his death. While recording a feature program for the BBC in 1963, MacNeice contracted a chill as he worked with the engineers on location. The chill turned into pneumonia and he died on September 3, 1963.

Louis MacNeice is usually mentioned as an important member of the so called "Auden group" in the thirties. But a survey of his overall work reveals that MacNeice was not a static artist, but one who steadily matured. His 1935 *Poems* was a critical success and the foundation for many of the themes which MacNeice would spend the rest of his career working out. Its most famous poem, "Eclogue for Christmas," sounded the basic concerns of Eliot—the decay of modern society and the desire to escape to an idyllic past—but also introduced a new vocabulary of rough, colloquial, and non-abstract words, an emphasis on sing-song phrases, and a sense of doom that pervaded many writers of the thirties. The 1939 *Autumn Journal: A Poem* asks, on the eve of World War II, what the common man can do to stop the destruction of the world. MacNeice answers: nothing. Here he begins to doubt the communistic idealism of the thirties. *Autumn Journal* realizes that abstract dreams for a better society are worthless without a practical plan and a firm grounding in the real world. His *Holes in the Sky: Poems, 1944–1947*, completes the tone of *Autumn Journal* in that MacNeice repeats his conviction that liberalism does nothing to help mankind. *Ten Burnt Offerings* (1952) represents the mature MacNeice who has complete mastery over almost all poetic forms and techniques. The poems no longer speak of the despair of contemporary society; they are more religious and content. While he offers no final philosophical conclusions, MacNeice seems to be reconciled to the imponderables of life. Thus Louis MacNeice, as did all great poets who came to prominence in the thirties (Auden and Sender), progressed beyond the socialist and liberal dogmas of that era, and developed into a poet with a universal appeal.

Autobiography

In my childhood trees were green
And there was plenty to be seen.

Come back early or never come.

My father made the walls resound,
He wore his collar the wrong way round.

Come back early or never come.

My mother wore a yellow dress;
Gently, gently, gentleness.

Come back early or never come.

When I was five the black dreams came;
Nothing after was quite the same.

Come back early or never come.

The dark was talking to the dead;
The lamp was dark beside my bed.

Come back early or never come.

When I woke they did not care;
Nobody, nobody was there.

Come back early or never come.

When my silent terror cried,
Nobody, nobody replied.

Come back early or never come.

I got up; the chilly sun
Saw me walk away alone.

Come back early or never come.

Brother Fire

When our brother Fire was having his dog's day
Jumping the London streets with millions of tin cans
Clanking at his tail, we heard some shadow say
'Give the dog a bone'—and so we gave him ours;
Night after night we watched him slaver and crunch away
The beams of human life, the tops of topless towers.

Which gluttony of his for us was Lenten fare
Who mother-naked, suckled with sparks, were chill.

Though cotted in a grill of sizzling air
Striped like a convict—black, yellow and red;
Thus were we weaned to knowledge of the Will
That wills the natural world but wills us dead.

O delicate walker, babbler, dialectician Fire,
O enemy and image of ourselves,
Did we not on those mornings after the All Clear,
When you were looting shops in elemental joy
And singing as you swarmed up city block and spire,
Echo your thought in ours? 'Destroy! Destroy!'

Conversation

Ordinary people are peculiar too:
Watch the vagrant in their eyes
Who sneaks away while they are talking with you
Into some black wood behind the skull,
Following un-, or other, realities,
Fishing for shadows in a pool.

But sometimes the vagrant comes the other way
Out of their eyes and into yours
Having mistaken you perhaps for yesterday
Or for tomorrow night, a wood in which
He may pick up among the pine-needles and burrs
The lost purse, the dropped stitch.

Vagrancy however is forbidden; ordinary men
Soon come back to normal, look you straight
In the eyes as if to say 'It will not happen again',
Put up a barrage of common sense to baulk
Intimacy but by mistake interpolate
Swear-words like roses in their talk.

An Eclogue for Christmas

A. I meet you in an evil time.
B.   The evil bells
Put out of our heads, I think, the thought of everything else.
A. The jaded calendar revolves,
    Its nuts need oil, carbon chokes the valves,
    The excess sugar of a diabetic culture
    Rotting the nerve of life and literature;
    Therefore when we bring out the old tinsel and frills
    To announce that Christ is born among the barbarous hills
    I turn to you whom a morose routine
    Saves from the mad vertigo of being what has been.
B. Analogue of me, you are wrong to turn to me,
    My country will not yield you any sanctuary,
    There is no pinpoint in any of the ordnance maps
    To save you when your towns and town-bred thoughts collapse,
    It is better to die *in situ* as I shall,
    One place is as bad as another. Go back where your instincts call
    And listen to the crying of the town-cats and the taxis again,
    Or wind your gramophone and eavesdrop on great men.
A. Jazz-weary of years of drums and Hawaiian guitar,
    Pivoting on the parquet I seem to have moved far
    From bombs and mud and gas, have stuttered on my feet
    Clinched to the streamlined and butter-smooth trulls of the élite,
    The lights irritating and gyrating and rotating in gauze—
    Pomade-dazzle, a slick beauty of gewgaws—
    I who was Harlequin in the childhood of the century,
    Posed by Picasso beside an endless opaque sea,
    Have seen myself sifted and splintered in broken facets,
    Tentative pencillings, endless liabilities, no assets,
    Abstractions scalpelled with a palette-knife
    Without reference to this particular life.
    And so it has gone on; I have not been allowed to be
    Myself in flesh or face, but abstracting and dissecting me
    They have made of me pure form, a symbol or a pastiche,
    Stylised profile, anything but soul and flesh:
    And that is why I turn this jaded music on
    To forswear thought and became an automaton.
B. There are in the country also of whom I am afraid—

Men who put beer into a belly that is dead,
Women in the forties with terrier and setter who whistle and
   swank
Over down and plough and Roman road and daisied bank,
Half-conscious that these barriers over which they stride
Are nothing to the barbed wire that has grown round their pride.

A. And two there are, as I drive in the city, who suddenly perturb—
The one sirening me to draw up by the kerb
The other, as I lean back, my right leg stretched creating speed,
Making me catch and stamp, the brakes shrieking, pull up dead:
She wears silk stockings taunting the winter wind,
He carries a white stick to mark that he is blind.

B. In the country they are still hunting, in the heavy shires
Greyness is on the fields and sunset like a line of pyres
Of barbarous heroes smoulders through the ancient air
Hazed with factory dust and, orange opposite, the moons's glare,
Goggling yokel-stubborn through the iron trees,
Jeers at the end of us, our bland ancestral ease;
We shall go down like palaeolithic man
Before some new Ice Age or Genghiz Khan.

A. It is time for some new coinage, people have got so old,
Hacked and handled and shiny from pocketing they have made
   bold
To think that each is himself through these accidents, being
   blind
To the fact that they are merely the counters of an unknown
   Mind.

B. A Mind that does not think, if such a thing can be,
Mechanical Reason, capricious Identity.
That I could be able to face this domination nor flinch—

A. The tin toys of the hawker move on the pavement inch by inch
Not knowing that they are wound up; it is better to be so
Than to be, like us, wound up and while running down to
   know—

B. But everywhere the pretence of individuality recurs—
A. Old faces frosted with powder and choked in furs.
B. The jutlipped farmer gazing over the humpbacked wall.
A. The commercial traveller joking in the urinal.—
B. I think things draw to an end, the soil is stale.
A. And over-elaboration will nothing now avail,

    The street is up again, gas, electricity or drains,
    Ever-changing conveniences, nothing comfortable remains
    Unimproved, as flagging Rome improved villa and sewer
    (A sound-proof library and a stable temperature).
    Our street is up, red lights sullenly mark
    The long trench of pipes, iron guts in the dark,
    And not till the Goths again come swarming down the hill
    Will cease the clangour of the pneumatic drill.
    But yet there is beauty narcotic and deciduous
    In this vast organism grown out of us:
    On all the traffic-islands stand white globes like moons,
    The city's haze is clouded amber that purrs and croons,
    And tilting by the noble curve bus after tall bus comes
    With an osculation of yellow light, with a glory like
       chrysanthemums.
B. The country gentry cannot change, they will die in their shoes
    From angry circumstances and moral self-abuse,
    Dying with a paltry fizzle they will prove their lives to be
    An ever-diluted drug, a spiritual tautology.
    They cannot live once their idols are turned out,
    None of them can endure, for how could they, possibly, without
    The flotsam of private property, pekinese and polyanthus,
    The good things which in the end turn to poison and pus,
    Without the bandy chairs and the sugar in the silver tongs
    And the inter-ripple and resonance of years of dinner-gongs?
    Or if they could find no more that cumulative proof
    In the rain dripping off the conservatory roof?
    What will happen when the only sanction the country-dweller
       has—
A. What will happen to us, planked and panelled with jazz?
    Who go to the theatre where a black man dances like an eel,
    Where pink thighs flash like the spokes of a wheel, where we
       feel
    That we know in advance all the jogtrot and the cake-walk jokes,
    All the bumfun and the gags of the comedians in boaters and
       toques,
    All the tricks of the virtuosos who invert the usual—
B. What will happen to us when the State takes down the manor
       wall,
    When there is no more private shooting or fishing, when the
       trees are all cut down,

When faces are all dials and cannot smile or frown—
A. What will happen when the sniggering machine-guns in the
     hands of the young men
   Are trained on every flat and club and beauty parlour and
     Father's den?
   What will happen when our civilisation like a long pent
     balloon—
B. What will happen will happen; the whore and the buffoon
   Will come off best; no dreamers, they cannot lose their dream
   And are at least likely to be reinstated in the new régime.
   But one thing is not likely—
A.   Do not gloat over yourself
   Do not be your own vulture, high on some mountain shelf
   Huddle the pitiless abstractions bald about the neck
   Who will descend when you crumble in the plains a wreck.
   Over the randy of the theatre and cinema I hear songs
   Unlike anything—
B.   The lady of the house poises the silver tongs
   And picks a lump of sugar, 'ne plus ultra' she says
   'I cannot do otherwise, even to prolong my days'—
A. I cannot do otherwise either, to-night I will book my seat—
B. I will walk about the farm-yard which is replete
   As with the smell of dung so with memories—
A. I will gorge myself to satiety with the oddities
   Of every artiste, official or amateur,
   Who has pleased me in my rôle of hero-worshipper
   Who has pleased me in my rôle of individual man—
B. Let us lie once more, say 'What we think, we can'
   The old idealist lie—
A.   And for me before I die
   Let me go round of the garish glare—
B.   And one the bare and high
   Places of England, the Wiltshire Downs and the Long Mynd
   Let the balls of my feet bounce on the turf, my face burn in
     the wind
   My eyelashes stinging in the wind, and the sheep like grey
     stones
   Humble my human pretensions—
A.   Let the saxophones and the xylophones
   And the cult of every technical excellence, the miles of canvas
     in the galleries

    And the canvas of the rich man's yacht snapping and tacking
        on the seas
    And the perfection of a grilled steak—
B.   Let all these so ephemeral things
    Be somehow permanent like the swallow's tangent wings:
    Good-bye to you, this day remember is Christmas, this morn
    They say, interpret it your own way, Christ is born.

Explorations

The whale butting through scarps of moving marble,
The tapeworm probing the intestinal darkness,
The swallows drawn collectively to their magnet,
   These are our prototypes and yet,
Though we may envy them still, they are merely patterns
   To wonder at—and forget.

For the ocean-carver, cumbrous but unencumbered,
Who tired of land looked for his freedom and frolic in water,
Though he succeeded, has failed; it is only instinct
   That plots his graph and he,
   Though appearing to us a free and happy monster, is merely
   An appanage of the sea.

And the colourless blind worm, triumphantly self-degraded,
Who serves as an image to men of the worst adjustment—
Oxymoron of parasitical glory—
   Cannot even be cursed,
Lacking the only pride of his way of life, not knowing
   That he has chosen the worst.

So even that legion of birds who appear so gladly
Purposeful, with air in their bones, enfranchised
Citizens of the sky and never at odds with
   The season or out of line,
Can be no model to us; their imputed purpose
   Is a foregone design—

And ours is not. For we are unique, a conscious
Hoping and therefore despairing creature, the final
Anomaly of the world, we can learn no method
    From whales or birds or worms;
Our end is our own to be on by our own endeavour
    And held on our own terms.

June Thunder

The Junes were free and full, driving through tiny
Roads, the mudguards brushing the cowparsley,
Through fields of mustard and under boldly embattled
    Mays and chestnuts

Or between beeches verdurous and voluptuous
Or where broom and gorse beflagged the chalkland—
All the flare and gusto of the unenduring
    Joys of a season

Now returned but I note as more appropriate
To the maturer mood impending thunder
With an indigo sky and the garden hushed except for
    The treetops moving.

Then the curtains in my room blow suddenly inward,
The shrubbery rustles, birds fly heavily homeward,
The white flowers fade to nothing on the trees and rain comes
    Down like a dropscene.

Now there comes the catharsis, the cleansing downpour
Breaking the blossoms of our overdated fancies
Our old sentimentality and whimsicality
    Love of the morning.

Blackness at half-past eight, the night's precursor,
Clouds like falling masonry and lightning's lavish
Annunciation, the sword of the mad archangel
    Flashed from the scabbard.

If only you would come and dare the crystal
Rampart of rain and the bottomless moat of thunder,
If only now you would come I should be happy
  Now if now only.

The Mixer

With a pert moustache and a ready candid smile
He has played his way through twenty years of pubs,
Deckchairs, lounges, touchlines, junctions, homes,
And still as ever popular, he roams
Far and narrow, mimicking the style
Of other people's leisure, scattering stubs.

Colourless, when alone, and self-accused,
He is only happy in reflected light
And only real in the range of laughter;
Behind his eyes are shadows of a night
In Flanders but his mind long since refused
To let that time intrude on what came after.

So in this second war which is fearul too,
He cannot away with silence but has grown
Almost a cypher, like a Latin word
That many languages have made their own
Till it is worn and blunt and easy to construe
And often spoken but no longer heard.

Museums

Museums offer us, running from among the 'buses,
A centrally heated refuge, parquet floors and sarcopha-
  guses,
Into whose tall fake porches we hurry without a sound
Like a beetle under a brick that lies, useless on the
  ground.
Warmed and cajoled by the silence, the cowed cipher
  revives,

Mirrors himself in the cases of pots, paces himself by
  marble lives,
Makes believe it was he that was the glory that was
  Rome,
Soft on his cheek the nimbus of other people's martyr-
  dom,
And then returns to the street, his mind an arena where
  sprawls
Any number of consumptive Keatses and dying Gauls.

Neutrality

The neutral island facing the Atlantic,
The neutral island in the heart of man,
Are bitterly soft reminders of the beginnings
That ended before the end began.

Look into your heart, you will find a County Sligo,
A Knocknarea with for navel a cairn of stones,
You will find the shadow and sheen of a moleskin mountain
And a litter of chronicles and bones.

Look into your heart, you will find fermenting rivers,
Intricacies of gloom and glint,
You will find such ducats of dream and great doubloons
  of ceremony
As nobody today would mint.

But then look eastward from your heart, there bulks
A continent, close, dark, as archetypal sin,
While to the west off your own shores the mackerel
Are fat—on the flesh of your kin.

Perseus

Borrowed wings on his ankles,
Carrying a stone death,
The hero entered the hall,
All in the hall looked up,
Their breath frozen on them,
And there was no more shuffle or clatter in the hall at all.

So a friend of a man comes in
And leaves a book he is lending or flowers
And goes again, alive but as good as dead,
And you are left alive, no better than dead,
And you dare not turn the leaden pages of the book or touch the flowers,
   the hooded and arrested hours.

Close your eyes,
There are suns beneath your lids,
Or look in the looking-glass in the end room—
You will find it full of eyes,
The ancient smiles of men cut out with scissors and kept in mirrors.

Ever to meet me comes, in sun or dull,
The gay hero swinging the Gorgon's head
And I am left, with the dull drumming of the sun, suspended and dead,
Or the dumb grey-brown of the day is a leper's cloth,
And one feels the earth going round and round the globe of the blackening
   mantle, a mad moth.

Slow Movement

Waking, he found himself in a train, andante,
With wafers of early sunlight blessing the unknown
      fields
And yesterday cancelled out, except for yesterday's
      papers
   Huddling under the seat.

It is still very early, this is a slow movement;
The viola-player's hand like a fish in a glass tank
Rises, remains quivering, darts away
   To nibble invisible weeds.

Great white nebulae lurch against the window
To deploy across the valley, the children are not yet up
To wave us on—we pass without spectators,
   Braiding a voiceless creed.

And the girl opposite, name unknown, is still
Asleep and the colour of her eyes unknown
Which might be wells of sun or moons of wish
   But it is still very early.

The movement ends, the train has come to a stop
In buttercup fields, the fiddles are silent, the whole
Shoal of silver tessellates the aquarium
   Floor, not a bubble rises . . .

And what happens next on the programme we do not
     know,
If, the red line topped on the gauge, the fish will go
     mad in the tank
Accelerando con forza, the sleeper open her eyes
   And, so doing, open ours.

Stylite

The saint on the pillar stands,
The pillar is alone,
He has stood so long
That he himself is stone;
Only his eyes
Range across the sand
Where no one ever comes
And the world is banned.

Then his eyes close,
He stands in his sleep,
Round his neck there comes
The conscience of a rope,
And the hangman counting
Counting to ten—
At nine he finds
He has eyes again.

The saint on the pillar stands,
The pillars are two.
A young man opposite
Stands in the blue,
A white Greek god,
Confident, with curled
Hair above the groin
And his eyes on the world.

Sunday Morning

Down the road someone is practising scales,
The notes like little fishes vanish with a wink of tails,
Man's heart expands to tinker with his car
For this is Sunday morning, Fate's great bazaar;
Regard these means as ends, concentrate on this Now,
And you may grow to music or drive beyond Hindhead anyhow,
Take corners on two wheels until you go so fast
That you can clutch a fringe or two of the windy past,
That you can abstract this day and make it to the week of time
A small eternity, a sonnet self-contained in rhyme.

But listen, up the road, something gulps, the church spire
Opens its eight bells out, skulls' mouths which will not tire
To tell how there is no music or movement which secures
Escape from the weekday time. Which deadens and endures.

The Sunlight on the Garden

The sunlight on the garden
Hardens and grows cold,
We cannot cage the minute
Within its nets of gold,
When all is told
We cannot beg for pardon.

Our freedom as free lances
Advances towards its end;
The earth compels, upon it
Sonnets and birds descend;
And soon, my friend,
We shall have no time for dances.

The sky was good for flying
Defying the church bells
And every evil iron
Siren and what it tells:
The earth compels,
We are dying, Egypt, dying

And not expecting pardon,
Hardened in heart anew,
But glad to have sat under
Thunder and rain with you,
And grateful too
For sunlight on the garden.

Les Sylphides

Life in a day: he took his girl to the ballet;
Being shortsighted himself could hardly see it—
　The white skirts in the grey
　Glade and the swell of the music
　Lifting the white sails.

Calyx upon calyx, canterbury bells in the breeze
The flowers on the left mirror to the flowers on the right
  And the naked arms above
  The powdered faces moving
  Like seaweed in a pool.

Now, he thought, we are floating—ageless, oarless—
Now there is no separation, from now on
  You will be wearing white
  Satin and a red sash
  Under the waltzing trees.

But the music stopped, the dancers took their curtain,
The river had come to a lock—a shuffle of programmes—
  And we cannot continue down
  Stream unless we are ready
  To enter the lock and drop.

So they were married—to be the more together—
And found they were never again so much together,
  Divided by the morning tea,
  By the evening paper,
  By children and tradesmen's bills.

Waking at times in the night she found assurance
In his regular breathing but wondered whether
  It was really worth it and where
  The river had flowed away
  And where were the white flowers.

E. J. Scovell (Born 1907)

Edith Joy Scovell, born in Sheffield, Yorkshire, England, took her B.A. at Somerville College, Oxford in 1930. She married Charles Elton in 1937. Her three books of verse—*Shadows of Chrysanthemum and Other Poems* (1944), *The Midsummer Meadow and Other Poems* (1946), and *The River Steamer and Other Poems* (1956)—largely went unnoticed against the backdrop of apocalyptic poetry which was so popular in Britain during the fifties. Scovell's quiet, delicate, and mystical verse, similar to the work of Anne Ridler and Stevie Smith, is distinguished in its careful attention to the details of persons and objects.

Evening Scene

The waves lay down their trail,
On the brown water feathers of foam.
Over the dark bituminous sands
The stragglers loiter home.

Where the stream seeps to sea
And the sands are tarnished glass to the sky
They walk as if on evening light,
They run and seem to fly.

The shallow acre-wide
Waves of low tide swathe their feet like a meadow.
Surely they feel themselves unmade,
Spirits that cast no shadow.

I see them small, distinct,
Dark, and see on the sheen of what wings they fly,
The two lit wings of land and sea,
The one vane of the sky;

And see, not near nor far,
The black-brown cliffs stand with their slopes of green
Stippled with darkness. All of space
Is the sand's width between.

The First Year *(sel.)*
II

Before she first had smiled or looked with calm
Light-answering eyes and claimed to be of man
I put my finger in her shadowy palm,
And her own whispering ones from their chestnut fan
Closed again (as they must) on mine, to a bud.
Then I was where strong currents piled and slackened.
Like a pulse telling all the power of blood
This palm seemed the cavern where alone her darkened
And secret rock-roofed river showed to man
(Except when one inside half-raised the blind
Of her inky eyes, and fierce a dark beam ran
Searchlighting day). So I stayed on her mind;
And thought I trespassed in that covered land.
Her hand seemed private, still an unborn hand.

The Swan's Feet

Who is this whose feet
Close on the water,
Like muscled leaves darker than ivy
Blown back and curved by unwearying wind?
They, that thrust back the water,
Softly crumple now and close, stream in his wake.

These dank weeds are also
Part and plumage of the magnolia-flowering swan.
He puts forth these too—
Leaves of ridged and bitter ivy
Sooted in towns, coal-bright with rain.

He is not moved by winds in air
Like the vain boats on the lake.
Lest you think him too a flower of parchment,
Scentless magnolia,
See his living feet under the water fanning.
In the leaves' self blows the efficient wind
That opens and bends closed those leaves.

Vernon Watkins (1907–1967)

Vernon Watkins was born June 27 in Maesteg, South Wales. He spent one year, 1924 to 1925, at Magdalene College, Cambridge. From 1925 to 1966, Watkins worked as a clerk at Loyds Bank, Ltd. in Swansea, Wales. He was a visiting professor of poetry at the University of Washington in Seattle in 1964 and again in 1967. Watkins won the Levinson Prize in 1953 and the Guinness Poetry Prize in 1957. Though he worked as a clerk for most of his life, Watkins' immersion in the craft of poetry was complete. He had written over 1,000 poems before his first one was ever published. Watkins published over 10 volumes of verse during his career.

The Collier

When I was born on Amman hill
A dark bird crossed the sun.
Sharp on the floor the shadow fell;
I was the youngest son.

And when I went to the County School
I worked in a shaft of light.
In the wood of the desk I cut my name:
Dai for Dynamite.

The tall black hills my brothers stood;
Their lessons all were done.
From the door of the school when I ran out
They frowned to watch me run.

The slow grey bells they rung a chime
Surly with grief or age.
Clever or clumsy, lad or lout,
All would look for a wage.

I learnt the valley flowers' names
And the rough bark knew my knees.
I brought home trout from the river
And spotted eggs from the trees.

A coloured coat I was given to wear
Where the lights of the rough land shone.
Still jealous of my favour
The tall black hills looked on.

They dipped my coat in the blood of a kid
And they cast me down a pit,
And although I crossed with strangers
There was no way up from it.

Soon as I went from the Country School
I worked in a shaft. Said Jim,
'You will get your chain of gold, my lad,
But not for a likely time.'

And one said, 'Jack was not raised up
When the wind blew out the light
Though he interpreted their dreams
And guessed their fears by night.'

And Tom, he shivered his leper's lamp
For the stain that round him grew;
And I heard mouths pray in the after-damp
When the picks would not break through.

They changed words there in the darkness
And still through my head they run,
And white on my limbs is the linen sheet
And gold on my neck the sun.

Indolence

Count up those books whose pages you have read
Moulded by water. Wasps this paper made.
Come. You have taken tribute from the dead.
Your tribute to the quick must now be paid.

What lovelier tribute than to rest your head
Beneath this birchtree which is bound to fade?
And watch the branches quivering by a thread
Beyond interpretation of the shade.

The Turning of the Leaves

Not yet! Do not yet touch,
Break not this branch of silver-birch,
Nor ask the stealthy river why it laves
Black roots that feed the leaves.

Ask first the flickering wren.
He will move further. Ask the rain.
No drop, though round, through that white miracle
Will sink, to be your oracle.

Not yet! Do not yet bend
Close to that root so tightly bound
Loosened by creeping waters as they run
Along the fork's rough groin.

Ask not the water yet
Why the root's tapering tendrils eat
Parched earth away that they may be
Nearer the source those fibres must obey.

Behind the bark your hands will find
No Sycorax or flying Daphne faned
And the brown ignorant water bindweed breeds
Not caring there what brows it braids.

Light in the branches weaves.
Hard is the waiting moment while it waves,
This tree whose trunk curves upward from the stream
Where faltering ripples strum.

See how it hangs in air.
The leaves are turning now. We cannot hear
The death and birth of life. But that disguise,
Look up now, softly: break it with your eyes.

Zacchaeus in the Leaves

Silence before
Sound.
Sycamore:

A tree
Predestined to beauty.
Blown leaves. Antiquity.
Light lost. Light found.

The myth above the myth.
The imagined zenith
Of youth in youth.

Light on the leaves in wind
Flying. The silver-sequined
Goat-leaf, dark-skinned.

Sycamore leaves; coiled thick,
God-dark, Dionysaic,
The ascending trunk. Pan's music.
The sap made quick.

Wind-gathered sound. The flow
Of lives. Wood-sounds. Wood-hollow.
Hades locked below.

Sap leaps. The springing race
Threading the magic surface
Drops to one place.

A sign to us!
A tree, and then a tree
No more.
Silent Zacchaeus,
Ageless one.
The buried sun,
And the key it bore.

* * *

Light found in every age
The leaves of Spring
Fading from lineage,
The seed, the wing.

From what dark scent
Of waters breaking
In night most innocent
Of dead men waking.

From what laid bone
Rose man's belief?
What Sibyl wrote upon
The breaking leaf?

Sibylline words.
The buried lives.
Lost among nesting-birds,
The burden of the leaves.

The myth above the myth,
Pan above Zacchaeus;
Zacchaeus climbing,
Mounted above his youth,
Alone in time
Seeking the heavenly death.
The crooked he had left,
Yes, and the wise,
To climb the tree-trunk,
To sit in a cleft
And see through his eyes
Not what they saw,
Not what they heard,
No leaf, no claw,
No wing, no bird,
But light surpassing
All known green,
As if all drunk
And sober stirred
Known, unknown,
Where seen, unseen,

Were one alone;
Jesus passing,
The Nazarene.

Lovers embraced
And their eyes were solaced;
But Zacchaeus gripped fast

The tree-branch, crouching,
Watching the myth
Moving, the myth
Move to the zenith
Not found in youth:
'If His eyes see us,
If His eyes see us,

Dazzled above men,
Though we are buried then,
The myth above the truth.'

Who stilled the pipes of Pan?
What marvel weaves
Death, deathless, pagan,
Turning the Sibyl's leaves?

Firm, yet betrayed no more,
The young lie with the young.
Leaves of the sycamore,
Lifted on wind, give tongue:

'I have supported one
In my own right
Who watched the procession,
His eyes full of light.

I can fade now.
My thought heard or unheard.
Did he not leave my bough,
And said no word?'

   * * *

Slow the procession was coming. The drinkers
   remained
Sitting cross-legged, close to the dead who were
   chained,
Beggars of light. Only the man in the tree
Looked on the road, and saw where light was
   ordained.

Among the quick and the dead is the point divine,
Moving; among those talking, the drinkers of wine,
The shuffling of feet, the running of time, the gust
Of windblown leaves, no, not the Muses, the nine,

Have seen the universe race through the leaves and
   thrill
Because it has found the point of predestined will,
There where the fountain breaks from lips that
   are dust.
Stop: the great branches are moving. Now they are
   still.

Kathleen Raine (Born 1908)

At the outbreak of the First World War, Kathleen Raine was sent to a Northern England hamlet where she spent, by her own admission, the happiest years of her life. She returned to London when she was ten years old, much to her dismay. Raine took her M.A. in Natural Sciences from Girton College, Cambridge in 1929. Soon after, she went through two short-lived marriages. The second, to Charles Madge, a poet and professor, disturbed her deeply and to soothe herself she began to write poetry. She has written over 19 books, including *Stone and Flower: Poems 1935–1943* and *The Oracle in the Heart: Poems 1974–1978*. The 1968 mammouth study, *Blake and Tradition*, is her most famous work.

Though of the same generation as the Oxford poets, Auden, Spenser, and Lewis, the Cambridge poets: Kathleen Raine, William Empson, Ronald Bottrall, and Charles Madge, did not receive very much attention. This may have been due to the austere nature of the Cambridge tradition. Raine did not study literature, but natural sciences, and the rigor and exactitude of her training is reflected in her poetry. She has spurned contemporary verse, especially its tendencies towards self indulgence and emotivism—opting instead for more traditional language to express what she feels are eternal truths; indeed Raine has been described as a "Platonic" poet. Though criticized for being thin and vision less, Raine is engaged in a scientific search for the nature of the world. As Ralph J. Mills put it ". . . like Blake, Wordsworth, and Coleridge, she (Raine) is concerned with deciphering the secret hints of the larger scheme of being embodied in the visible surface of the natural world."

The Crystal Skull

At the focus of thought there is no face,
the focus of the sun is in crystal with no shadow.
Death of the victim is the power of the god.

Out of the eyes is the focus of love,
the face of love is the sun, that all see,
the skull of the victim is the temple of sight.

The eyes of the victim are the crystal of divination.
Sun clears the colours of life.
The crystal of the skull is the work of the sun.

The stone of my destruction casts no shadow.
The sun kills perfectly with the stroke of noon.
The clarity of the crystal is the atonement of the god.

The perfection of man is the pride of death,
the crystal skull is the perpetuity of life.
The power of the god is the taking of love.

The perfection of light is the destruction of the world,
death and love turn the faces of day and night.
The illumination of the skull is the joy of the god.

Desire

I did not make the conditions of my life whereby
the laws of stars will never change, though I
say "Give me to a god, or I will die."

I am not wise, why must I know so much
that teaches me what I can never learn,
that I can put my trust in house or home.

The solid earth and the extensive sky
are flimsy and impermanent as I—
my earth, my love, my thought will die with me.

Oh lovely earth, with richer life than mine,
whose teeming seas and blooming fields decline
slowly toward stillness, yet remain!

For animals shall fly the secret plains,
and human greatness suffer greater pangs
while engines dance beneath revolving suns.

Your shrinking form, broken forgetful face,
your bursting entrails, and your cooling heart
shall all lie lifeless, cold and motionless.

The hot blood and the conscious grief shall cool,
and forests burn in their own funeral.

The Fall

It is the fall, the eternal fall of water,
of rock, of wounded birds, and the wounded heart,
the waterfall of freedom. Angels fall
like lovers from the azure, separate,
and die by that same death that ends us all.

Falling ten million years, we fling ourselves
again into the inviting arms of time;
our nuptial flight must end again in death
that serves for freedom time and time again
while the hard labouring mystic holds his breath.

The watching surface of the living sea
ever intact, smiles with the face of love,
where living blood drowns in its ecstasy,
impelled by nature that can mountains move,
feeling most freedom when it least is free.

Shall we go down, shall we go down together?
here on the mountain top, the wind and snow
urge us to fall, and go the way they go.
The way is clear, the end we shall not know,
the sea will carry us where tides run and currents flow.

The Goddess

She goes by many names; Diana of the sacred wood
With manifold breasts like acorns on an oak
And primitive features, image of the joy men take
In her, all powerful where in caves and shadows lie
These mortal beasts, her offspring and her prey.

We have known her as archaic mother Eve.
The earth is all her cradle
Where we awake from our first sleep to see
Her flower-face bending over us
The sky, the rowan, and the elder-tree.

Some worship her as queen of angels, Venus of the sea,
House of gold, palace of ivory,
Gate of heaven and rose of mystery,
Inviolate and ever-virgin earth,
Daughter of time and mother of eternity.

Lover, in your true love's body lies
The sacred darkness of Diana's grove,
Hers are the careful arms that Adams's children hold,
And in her heart the cause of joy, the house of gold,
The gate of Heaven, the ever-virgin rose.

Isis Wanderer

This too is an experience of the soul
The dismembered world that once was the whole god
Whose broken fragments now lie dead.
This passing of reality itself is real.

Gathering under my black cloak the remnants of life
That lie dishonoured among people and places
I search the twofold desert of my solitude,
The outward perished world, and the barren mind.

Once he was present, numinous, in the house of the
   world,
Wearing day like a garment, his beauty manifest
In corn and man as he journeyed down the fertile
   river
With love he filled my distances of night.

I trace the contour of his hand fading upon a cloud,
And this his blood flows from a dying soldier's wound.
In broken fields his body is scattered and his limbs lie
Spreadeagled like wrecked fuselage in the sand.

His skull is a dead cathedral, and his crown's rays
Glitter from worthless tins and broken glass.
His blue eyes are reflected from pools in the gutter,
And his strength is the desolate stone of fallen cities.

Oh in the kitchen-midden of my dreams
Turning over the potsherds of past days
Shall I uncover his loved desecrated face?
Are the unfathomed depths of sleep his grave?

Beyond the looming dangerous end of night
Beneath the vaults of fear do his bones lie,
And does the maze of nightmare lead to the power
    within?
Do menacing nether waters cover the fish king?

I piece the divine fragments into the mandala
Whose centre is the lost creative power,
The sun, the heart of God, the lotus, the electron
That pulses world upon world, ray upon ray
That he who lived on the first may rise on the last day.

Love Poem

Yours is the face that the earth turns to me.
Continuous beyond its human features lie
The mountain forms that rest against the sky.
With your eyes, the reflecting rainbow, the sun's light
Sees me; forest and flowers, bird and beast
Know and hold me forever in the world's thought,
Creation's deep untroubled retrospect.

When your hand touches mine, it is the earth
That takes me—the deep grass,
And rocks and rivers; the green graves,
And children still unborn, and ancestors,
In love passed down from hand to hand from God.
Your love comes from the creation of the world,

From those paternal fingers, streaming through the clouds
That break with light the surface of the sea.

Here, where I trace your body with my hand,
Loves' presence has no end;
For these, your arms that hold me, are the world's.
In us, the continents, clouds and oceans meet
Our arbitrary selves, extensive with the night,
Lost, in the heart's worship, and the body's sleep.

The Pythoness
For John Hayward

I am that serpent-haunted cave
Whose navel breeds the fates of men.
All wisdom issues from a hole in the earth:
The gods form in my darkness, and dissolve again.

From my blind womb all kingdoms come,
And from my grave seven sleepers prophesy.
No babe unborn but wakens to my dream,
No lover but at last entombed in me shall lie.

I am that feared and longed-for burning place
Where man and phoenix are consumed away,
And from my low polluted bed arise
New sons, new suns, new skies.

The Silver Stag

My silver stag is fallen—on the grass
Under the birch-trees he lies, my king of the woods,
That I followed on the mountain, over the swift
    streams,
He is gone under the leaves, under the past.

On the horizon of the dawn he stood,
The target of my eager sight; that shone
Oh from the sun, or from my kindled heart—
Outlined in sky, shaped on the infinite.

What, so desiring, was my will with him,
What wished-for union of blood or thought
In single passion held us, hunter and victim?
Already gone, when into the branched woods I
  pursued him.

Mine he is now, my desired, my awaited, my beloved,
Quiet he lies, as I touch the contours of his proud
  head,
Mine, this horror, this carrion of the wood,
Already melting underground, into the air, out of the
  world.

Oh, the stillness, the peace about me
As the garden lives on, the flowers bloom,
The fine grass shimmers, the flies burn,
And the stream, the silver stream, runs by.

Lying for the last time down on the green ground
In farewell gesture of self-love, softly he curved
To rest the delicate foot that is in my hand,
Empty as a moth's discarded chrysalis.

My bright yet blind desire, your end was this
Death, and my winged heart murderous
Is the world's broken heart, buried in his,
Between whose antlers starts the crucifix.

Worry about Money

Wearing worry about money like a hair shirt
I lie down in my bed and wrestle with my angel.
My bank-manager could not sanction my continuance
  for another day,
But life itself wakes me each morning, and love

Urges me to give although I have no money
In the bank at this moment and ought properly
To cease to exist in a world where poverty
Is a shameful and ridiculous offence.

Having no one to advise me, I open the Bible
And shut my eyes and put my finger on a text
And read that the widow with the young son
Must give first to the prophetic genius
From the little there is in the bin of flour and the
  cruse of oil.

Theodore Roethke (1908–1963)

Two events in Theodore Roethke's life dramatically influenced his later poetry: the death of his father when Roethke was 14 and Roethke's hospitalization in 1934 for a manic-depressive psychosis. His attempt to come to terms with his ambivalent feelings towards his father and his long battle with mental illness define the essence and program of Roethke's writings. Roethke was born May 25, in Saginaw, Michigan. His father, Otto Roethke, and his uncle, Charles, owned the largest greenhouse in the U.S. Some of Theodore Roethke's most powerful poetic images come from his childhood in the greenhouse. In 1923 Charles committed suicide and Otto died of cancer.

Two years later Theodore entered the University of Michigan at Ann Arbor, where he studied the American transcendentalists, being especially influenced by Emerson and Thoreau. He graduated with honors in 1929. Roethke did a year of graduate work at Harvard where he met the poet Robert Hillyer. Hillyer read some of Roethke's poems and encouraged him to start publishing in small magazines. In 1931 Roethke left Harvard to teach, and coach tennis, at Lafayette College in Easton Pennsylvania. Here he honed his twin crafts, teaching and poetry. Roethke decided to accept a post at Michigan State College in 1935 but one month into his teaching duties he was hospitalized for manic depression; his contract was not renewed by Michigan State. He was released from the hospital in 1936 and received his M.A. from the University of Michigan in the same year. Roethke started to teach at Pennsylvania State College in 1936, where he put together his first collection of poems Open House, published in 1941. Open House met with much critical acclaim. One admirer was W. H. Auden who said that the book was "completely successful."

In 1946, after being dismissed from Bennington College for immoral conduct, Roethke suffered another breakdown and was hospitalized for a second time. He began to write a great deal of poems attempting to break out of what he perceived to be the rut of Open House. The result was Lost Son and Other Poems (1948), which contained Roethke's experiments with free forms of verse. He began to play with rhythms and the sounds of words, trying to create an alogical, purely emotional experience. Lost Son is considered Roethke's best book and established him as one of America's premier poets.

In 1947 Roethke was appointed to what turned out to be a permanent teaching position at the University of Washington in Seattle. He married in 1953 and produced The Waking: Poems 1933–1953 for which he won the Pulitzer Prize in 1954. Roethke's Words for the Wind (1957) won the National Book Award and the Bollingen Prize in 1958. On August 1, 1963 Theodore Roethke died suddenly. In 1964 his The Far Field won the National Book Award.

Dolor

I have known the inexorable sadness of pencils,
Neat in their boxes, dolor of pad and paper-weight,
All the misery of manila folders and mucilage,
Desolation in immaculate public places,
Lonely reception room, lavatory, switchboard,
The unalterable pathos of basin and pitcher,
Ritual of multigraph, paper-clip, comma,
Endless duplication of lives and objects.

And I have seen dust from the walls of institutions,
Finer than flour, alive, more dangerous than silica,
Sift, almost invisible, through long afternoons of tedium,
Dropping a fine film on nails and delicate eyebrows,
Glazing the pale hair, the duplicate gray standard faces.

The Lost Son

I. The Flight

At Woodlawn I heard the dead cry:
I was lulled by the slamming of iron,
A slow drip over stones,
Toads brooding in wells.
All the leaves stuck out their tongues;
I shook the softening chalk of my bones,
Saying,
Snail, snail, glister me forward,
Bird, soft-sigh me home,
Worm, be with me.
This is my hard time.

Fished in an old wound,
The soft pond of repose;
Nothing nibbled my line,
Not even the minnows came.

Sat in an empty house
Watching shadows crawl,
Scratching.
There was one fly.

Voice, come out of the silence.
Say something.
Appear in the form of a spider
Or a moth beating the curtain.

Tell me:
Which is the way I take,
Out of what door do I go,
Where and to whom?

      Dark hollows said, lee to the wind,
      The moon said, back of an eel,
      The salt said, look by the sea,
      Your tears are not enough praise,
      You will find no comfort here,
In the kingdom of bank and bang.

Running lightly over spongy ground,
Past the pasture of flat stones,
The three elms,
The sheep strewn on a field,
Over a rickety bridge
Toward the quick-water, wrinkling and rippling.

Hunting along the river,
Down among the rubbish, the bug-riddled foliage,
By the muddy pond-edge, by bog-holes,
By the shrunken lake, hunting, in the heat of summer.

The shape of a rat?

      It's bigger than that.
      It's less than a leg.
      And more than a nose,
      Just under the water
      It usually goes.

It is soft like a mouse?
Can it wrinkle its nose?
Could it come in the house
On the tips of its toes?

      Take the skin of a cat
      And the back of an eel,
      Then roll them in grease,
      That's the way it would feel.

It's sleek as an otter
With wide webby toes,
Just under the water
It usually goes.

II. The Pit

Where do the roots go?
    Look down under the leaves.
Who put the moss there?
    These stones have been here too long.
Who stunned the dirt into noise?
    Ask the mole, he knows.
I feel the slime of a wet nest.
    Beware Mother Mildew.
Nibble again, fish nerves.

III. The Gibber

At the wood's mouth,
By the cave's door,
I listened to something
I had heard before.

Dogs of the groin
Barked and howled,
The sun was against me,
The moon would not have me.

The weeds whined,
The snakes cried,
The cows and briars
Said to me: Die.

What a small song. What slow clouds. What dark water.
Hath the raine a father? All the caves are ice. Only the snow's
  here.
I'm cold. I'm cold all over. Rub me in father and mother.
Fear was my father, Father Fear.
His look drained the stones.

What gliding shape
Beckoning through halls,
Stood poised on the stair,
Fell dreamily down?

From the mouths of jugs
Perched on many shelves,
I saw substance flowing
That cold morning.

Like a slither of eels
That watery cheek
As my own tongue kissed
My lips awake.

Is this the storm's heart? The ground is unstilling itself.
My veins are running nowhere. Do the bones cast out their fire?
Is the seed leaving the old bed? These buds are live as birds.
Where, where are the tears of the world?
Let the kisses resound, flat like a butcher's palm;
Let the gestures freeze; our doom is already decided.
All the windows are burning! What's left of my life?
I want the old rage, the last of primordial milk!
Good-bye, good-bye, old stones, the time-order is going.
I have married my hands to perpetual agitation,
I run, I run to the whistle of money.

    Money money money
    Water water water

How cool the grass is.
Has the bird left?
The stalk still sways.

Has the worm a shadow?
What do the clouds say?
These sweeps of light undo me.
Look, look, the ditch is running white!
I've more veins than a tree!
Kiss me, ashes, I'm falling through a dark swirl.

IV. The Return

The way to the boiler was dark,
Dark all the way,
Over slippery cinders,
Through the long greenhouse.

The roses kept breathing in the dark.
They had many mouths to breathe with.
My knees made little winds underneath
Where the weeds slept.

There was always a single light
Swinging by the fire-pit
Where the fireman pulled out roses,
The big roses, the bloody clinkers.

>Once I stayed all night.
>The light in the morning came slowly over the white
>Snow.
>There were many kinds of cool
>Air.
>Then came
>Steam.
>Pipe-knock.

Scurry of warm over small plants.
Ordnung! ordnung!
Papa is coming!

>A fine haze moved off the leaves;
>Frost melted on far panes;
>The rose, the chrysanthemum turned toward the light.
>Even the hushed forms, the bent yellowy weeds
>Moved in a slow up-sway.

V.

It was beginning winter,
An in-between time,
The landscape still partly brown:
The bones of weeds kept swinging in the wind,
Above the blue snow.

It was beginning winter,
The light moved slowly over the frozen field,
Over the dry seed-crowns,
The beautiful surviving bones
Swinging in the wind.

Light traveled over the wide field;
Stayed.
The weeds stopped swinging.
The mind moved, not alone,
Through the clear air, in silence.

> Was it light?
> Was it light within?
> Was it light within light?
> Stillness becoming alive,
> Yet still?

A lively understandable spirit
Once entertained you.
It will come again.
Be still.
Wait.

Moss-Gathering

To loosen with all ten fingers held wide and limber
And lift up a patch, dark-green, the kind for lining cemetery baskets,
Thick and cushiony, like an old fashioned door-mat,
The crumbling small hollow sticks on the underside mixed with roots,
And wintergreen berries and leaves still stuck to the top—
That was moss-gathering.

But something always went out of me when I dug loose those carpets
Of green, or plunged to my elbows in the spongy yellowish moss of the
    marshes:
And afterwards I always felt mean, jogging back over the logging road,
As if I had broken the natural order of things in that swampland;
Disturbed some rhythm, old and of vast importance,
By pulling off flesh from the living planet;
As if I had committed, against the whole scheme of life, a desecration.

Open House

My secrets cry aloud.
I have no need for tongue.
My heart keeps open house,
My doors are widely swung.
An epic of the eyes
My love, with no disguise.

My truths are all foreknown,
This anguish self-revealed.
I'm naked to the bone,
With nakedness my shield.
Myself is what I wear:
I keep the spirit spare.

The anger will endure,
The deed will speak the truth
In language strict and pure.
I stop the lying mouth:
Rage warps my clearest cry
To witless agony.

Richard Wright (1908–1960)

Richard Wright was born September 4, in a small village two miles east of Natchez, Mississippi. His childhood was a series of hardships and brutal experiences. Before Wright was twelve years old he had been sexually harassed, seen the breakup of his parent's marriage, experienced racial hate, lived in poverty and hunger, and witnessed his mother's long, paralyzing illness. Due to his transient life, Wright was largely self educated, despite a grandmother who regularly burned his books, believing them to be works of the devil. In 1921 though, he was allowed to attend the Jim Hill School, where his brilliant intellect was recognized. Wright went on to the Smith-Robinson school and graduated valedictorian with the ambition to be a writer.

He moved to Memphis in 1925 where he worked at odd jobs while discovering Western literature through a borrowed library card. Deprived of a stimulating cultural environment in the South, Wright traveled to Chicago in 1927 in search of the spiritual and intellectual climate he had read about. Wright won the National Fiction Contest sponsored by *Story Magazine* in 1937 and began to contribute to the leading literary magazines of the day. He also edited the magazine *Challenge*. Wright published his first novel, *Native Son*, in 1940 and an autobiographical novel, *Black Boy*, in 1945. Seeking greater artistic freedom, Wright moved to Paris in 1947 and was enthusiastically accepted into the most sophisticated literary circles. Among his close friends were Gertrude Stein, Simone de Beauvoir, and Sartre. During this French period, Wright published eight more books, including *The Outsider* (1953) and *White Man, Listen* (1957). He died of a heart attack on November 28, 1960.

Between the World and Me

And one morning while in the woods I stumbled suddenly upon the
   thing,
Stumbled upon it in a grassy clearing guarded by scaly oaks and elms.
And the sooty details of the scene rose, thrusting themselves between
   the world and me. . . .

There was a design of white bones slumbering forgottenly upon a
   cushion of ashes.
There was a charred stump of a sapling pointing a blunt finger
   accusingly at the sky.
There were torn tree limbs, tiny veins of burnt leaves, and a scorched
   coil of greasy hemp;
A vacant shoe, an empty tie, a ripped shirt, a lonely hat, and a pair of
   trousers stiff with black blood.
And upon the trampled grass were buttons, dead matches, butt-ends
   of cigars and cigarettes, peanut shells, a drained gin-flask, and
   a whore's lipstick;

Scattered traces of tar, restless arrays of feathers, and the lingering
  smell of gasoline.
And through the morning air the sun poured yellow surprise into the
  eye sockets of a stony skull. . . .
And while I stood my mind was frozen with a cold pity for the life
  that was gone.
The ground gripped my feet and my heart was circled by icy walls of
  fear—
The sun died in the sky; a night wind muttered in the grass and
  fumbled the leaves in the trees; the woods poured forth the
  hungry yelping of hounds; the darkness screamed with thirsty
  voices; and the witnesses rose and lived:
The dry bones stirred, rattled, lifted, melting themselves into my
  bones.
The grey ashes formed flesh firm and black, entering into my flesh.
The gin-flask passed from mouth to mouth; cigars and cigarettes
  glowed, the whore smeared the lipstick red upon her lips,
And a thousand faces swirled around me, clamoring that my life be
  burned. . . .

And then they had me, stripped me, battering my teeth into my
  throat till I swallowed my own blood.
My voice was drowned in the roar of their voices, and my black wet
  body slipped and rolled in their hands as they bound me to
  the sapling.
And my skin clung to the bubbling hot tar, falling from me in limp
  patches.
And the down and quills of the white feathers sank into my raw flesh,
  and I moaned in my agony.
Then my blood was cooled mercifully, cooled by a baptism of
  gasoline.
And in a blaze of red I leaped to the sky as pain rose like water,
  boiling my limbs.

Panting, begging I clutched childlike, clutched to the hot sides of
  death.
Now I am dry bones and my face a stony skull staring in yellow
  surprise at the sun. . . .

I Am a Red Slogan

I AM A RED SLOGAN,
A flaming torch flung to lead the minds of men!
I flaunt my messages from a million banners:
WORKERS OF THE WORLD UNITE!
I AM A RED SLOGAN,
The axe that whacks to the heart of knotty problems:
STOP MUNITION SHIPMENTS!
FIGHT FASCISM!
DEATH TO LYNCHERS!
I bloom in tired brains in sleep:
BREAD!
LAND!
FREEDOM!
I AM A RED SLOGAN,
Brawny knuckles thrust in the face of profiteers:
EXPROPRIATE THE EXPROPRIATORS!
I AM A RED SLOGAN,
Lingering as a duty after my command is shouted:
DEFEND THE U. S. S. R.!
I haunt the doors of your mind until I am taken in:
SELF-DETERMINATION FOR MINORITY PEOPLES!
I am the one red star in the workers' black sky:
TURN IMPERIALIST WAR INTO CIVIL WAR!
I AM A RED SLOGAN,
The crest of the wave that sweeps to victory:
ALL POWER TO THE SOVIETS!

I Have Seen Black Hands

I am black and I have seen black hands, millions and millions of them—
Out of millions of bundles of wool and flannel tiny black fingers have reached restlessly and hungrily for life.
Reached out for the black nipples at the black breasts of black mothers,
And they've held red, green, blue, yellow, orange, white, and purple toys in the childish grips of possession,

And chocolate drops, peppermint sticks, lollypops, wineballs, ice cream cones, and sugared cookies in fingers sticky and gummy,
And they've held balls and bats and gloves and marbles and jack-knives and sling-shots and spinning tops in the thrill of sport and play

And pennies and nickels and dimes and quarters and sometimes on New Year's, Easter, Lincoln's Birthday, May Day, a brand new green dollar bill,
They've held pens and rulers and maps and tablets and books in palms spotted and smeared with ink,
And they've held dice and cards and half-pint flasks and cue sticks and cigars and cigarettes in the pride of new maturity . . .

II

I am black and I have seen black hands, millions and millions of them—
They were tired and awkward and calloused and grimy and covered with hangnails,
And they were caught in the fast-moving belts of machines and snagged and smashed and crushed,
And they jerked up and down at the throbbing machines massing taller and taller the heaps of gold in the banks of bosses,
And they piled higher and higher the steel, iron, the lumber, wheat, rye, the oats, corn, the cotton, the wool, the oil, the coal, the meat, the fruit, the glass, and the stone until there was too much to be used,
And they grabbed guns and slung them on their shoulders and marched and groped in trenches and fought and killed and conquered nations who were customers for the goods black hands had made.
And again black hands stacked goods higher and higher until there was too much to be used,
And then the black hands held trembling at the factory gates the dreaded lay-off slip,
And the black hands hung idle and swung empty and grew soft and got weak and bony from unemployment and starvation,
And they grew nervous and sweaty, and opened and shut in anguish and doubt and hesitation and irresolution . . .

III

I am black and I have seen black hands, millions and millions of them—
Reaching hesitantly out of days of slow death for the goods they had made, but the bosses warned that the goods were private and did not belong to them,
And the black hands struck desperately out in defence of life and there was blood, but the enraged bosses decreed that this too was wrong.
And the black hands felt the cold steel bars of the prison they had made, in despair tested their strength and found that they could neither bend nor break them,
And the black hands fought and scratched and held back but a thousand white hands took them and tied them,
And the black hands lifted palms in mute and futile supplication to the sodden faces of mobs wild in the revelries of sadism,
And the black hands strained and clawed and struggled in vain at the noose that tightened about the black throat,
And the black hands waved and beat fearfully at the tall flames that cooked and charred the black flesh . . .

IV

I am black and I have seen black hands
Raised in fists of revolt, side by side with the white fists of white workers,
And some day—and it is only this which sustains me—
Some day there shall be millions and millions of them,
On some red day in a burst of fists on a new horizon!

Edwin Rolfe (1909–1954)

After Edwin Rolfe's first collection of poems, *To My Contemporaries*, appeared in 1936, he was singled out by *Poetry* magazine to be "the best among these inflammatory young men and women." His next book, *The Lincoln Battalion* (1937) was a history of the unit he served with during the Spanish Civil War. The poetry in his other two collections, *First Love and Other Poems* (1955) and *Permit Me Refuge* (1955), is widely anthologized.

Definition

Knowing this man, who calls himself comrade,
mean, underhanded, lacking all attributes
real men desire, that replenish all worlds
men strive for; knowing that charlatan, fool too,
masquerading always in our colors, must also
be addressed as comrade—knowing these
and others to be false, deficient in knowledge
and love for fellow men that motivates our kind,

nevertheless I answer the salutation proudly,
equally sure that no one can defile it,
feeling deeper than the word the love it bears,
the world it builds. And no man, lying,
talking behind back, betraying trustful friend,
is worth enough to soil this word or mar this world.

Not Men Alone

What, you have never seen a lifeless thing flower,
revive, a new adrenaline in its veins?
Come, I shall show you; not men alone
nor women, but cities also are reborn;
not without labor, not before the hour
when flesh feels lacerated, mangled, torn.

Not only men are resurrected. I have seen
dull cities bloom, grow meaningful
overnight. Wherever class war comes

awareness is its courier, a newer life,
new depths in shallow, parallel streets
which may revert to commonplace, but never
relinquish scenes that have occurred on them.

Toledo's such a city. I remember
its dullness, how I always skirted
its edges on long trips west. Returning east,
I chose roads miles to the north or south
to escape its barrenness; the mind went dead,
the muscles flagged, in passing it.

Then the strike flared: the workers met
and merged at factories. The unions called
Down tools! and the militiamen
sped to the scene of combat. When the smoke
rose with the wind, a hundred men were maimed
but thousands more, the first time in their lives
were conscious of their needs, their role, their destiny.

I passed through Toledo yesterday.
The usual quiet prevailed, but from the eyes
of men and houses a newer spirit flamed.
The deadness I had felt before remained
but it was make-up only, mere disguise
for men aroused, a city awakened,
awaiting the propitious, inevitable day.

Room With Revolutionists
For J.F.

Look at this man in the room before you:
he is young, his skin is dark, his hair
curly and black, his eyes are strangely blue,
he comes from a warmer land under the sun.
He hears a North American speak calmly
of a beautiful and faithless mistress
and is amazed. This man's a revolutionist,

painter of huge areas, editor
of fiery and terrifying words, leader
of the poor who plant, the poor who burrow
under the earth in field and mine.
His life's an always upward-delving battle in
an old torn sweater, the pockets always empty.

And this his companion across the room:
younger than he: the smooth deep forehead
sheathing a subtle and redoubtable brain;
his hair dark, eyes upward-slanting at the corners,
lips clean-etched and full. This man,
nurtured in a northern city,
is a poet, master of strong sensuous words,
artist in his own right. His oratory
before many listeners is like the sudden
startling completeness of summer rain:
warm, clear and clean, soaking into
the very heart of you, the sun just beyond.

This man is my brother, Communist, friend,
counsellor of my youth and manhood. He has crossed
the seething continent a hundred times,
leaving behind him his words
and the sound of them and their meaning.

The heavy drowsy wine of a tropic land
and the sharp bouquet of the northland intermingle
here in this room: these two are held
umbilical to a greater source and destiny,
welded each to each more firmly
than each to his native land.
                       Their vision
parallels their warmth, transcends all frontiers.

Look at them here at ease
relaxed in this pleasant room:
you will not see them again
together for many years.
Tommorrow each will go

his separate way on the maps of the globe
across great distances, talking, painting,
composing poems, organizing,
welding together South- and North-men,
destroying boundaries.

Somebody and Somebody Else and You

Brother, consider as you go your way,
hemmed in by houses or flanked by fields,
conjunctions of roads through midland plains
or grain, watching dried cornstalks sway
dead and cracking in the wind's running:
who spews pennies on the streets of cities?
who jams the faucet, holds rain from crops?
who carves the sagging lines in roofs of barns
   and who reverses this?

They who have reaped your harvest
offer you the stalks. They
have teeth and fangs but their breasts
are dry, sucked empty. They have seen
millions of you stretching skeletal
hands toward them. They have been
deaf to everything you've had to say.

But you go your way, brother. They will go theirs.
By the time you meet you will have gathered
mass enough to challenge their right of way.

Maybe there won't be any doughnuts and coffee,
maybe you'll go a long time before you find
a house to shelter you, a bed to sleep in nights
and somebody to lie with, closely, and feel
here at last you've a moment for breathing
easily, peacefully, without hurry.

But when have you had a house
for nightrest, and a place
to sleep in without rats
gnawing in your head, and
somebody with everything
vital and whole and real?

You can read it in the papers every day
about somebody and somebody else found dead
in a furnished room (and think of all the bother
for the poor landlady, cleaning the mess away)
and nobody knows why they did it or who
they are or where the hell did they come from anyway
and no relations are there to claim the bodies
because their relations are far far away
in Chicago maybe, or Brooklyn, say.

The coroner will chant his Death-by-Suicide dirge
and nobody'll know
that somebody and somebody else have hit the eternal hay.

And maybe in the very same sheet you'll read
how somebody and somebody else are dead,
a couple of Mexicans this time. Headlines:
STARVING MEXICAN PEONS EAT GRASS, DIE.
You probably won't see it (it's in 12-point lightface.
Babe Ruth and Garbo rate 48-point bold)
but read it if you find it among the want ads.
Doughnuts to grass it will leave you cold.

Elsewhere in a city, Milwaukee maybe,
somebody'll say, "Isn't it terrible Mamie?"
staining the newsprint with everready tears
"and just think of it Mamie dear they died
without even an uncle around to bury them."

But you, brother, think as you go your way
reading this in papers under your flophouse mattress,

you know who pours the pennies and the lead, you know
who rots the watered crop, you know
who makes the walls of barns to sag
inward on emptiness
                      who waves a flag
and blows hot air through a star-spangled trumpet

while crops in fields and faces in streets
go slowly empty and yellow.

To My Contemporaries

1.

Jazz notes and Brahms intermittently
fleck the dusk-silence. Through the silhouettes
of sombre trees a lustrous blue
colors the heavens. The note still lingers
of the last thrush; its whistling rings
as if just uttered in the quiet air.
Now there is peace, and sounds are only
heard from afar: the distant train
winding its way along the river shore
bound for the city of tumult; the faint
night-blurred music of a gramophone
from a distant farmhouse; the occasional
noise of the insects
                   and in this lighted room
shadows of moths on the walls, beating against the bulbs.

Now more than ever seems it rich to live,
to pluck the ripened fruit, to plant the seeds
whose growth and blossoming our heirs shall know
in years to come upon a richer earth . . .

But we have lived in furore all our lives.
This quiet stuns us like a fist's impact
against the jaw; and nothing as idyllic
as rural peace can now replace

the accustomed clamor of our daily lives—
the hurried visits, the spasmodic talks,
the too-few interludes that we have known,
the midnight meetings in smoke-filled rooms
and noise of numberless voices arguing.

And so we sit in separate rooms, you
intimidated by the silence, vaguely
feeling all's not well, too tired to read,
too restless to lie still, too stirred
to trace this strangeness to its source.

                              And I
before this page write stray, fugitive thoughts:
things of half-meaning, impressions cut
far less than whole by this silence and its tension.
Here I am not surrendered to my poem
nor master of its words and images;
too great's the doubt in me to synthesize
fragmentary feelings, thought-lines that balk,
grow twisted, fade before they reach their ends.
I sit here only because the typewriter
is my oldest friend in this strange wilderness.
Sitting here thus I feel I've made
some last-straw contact with a friendlier world,
and clutch at it, refuse to let it go
lest I too sink to meaninglessness.

I invoke friends and fellow-Communists,
poets, sharers of my life and thought,
ponder the meaning of our words and deeds,
put questions that are answerless.

2.

You, Funaroff—where's the victory?
We've been composing poems,
each in our separate rooms, for many years.
The scraping of your pen, furious on paper,
quickens the blood of the world, and mine.

A stone in the days of my strength
could crash the window of your tenement
all the distance from Eleventh to Fourteenth.

But where's the victory? I read
in the Daily Worker the other day:
the Chinese peasants seizing arms and bread,
in Mexico they fashion dolls of clay,
chimneys spout red leaflets in Berlin,
Italian flyers bomb the land with calls
of *Avanti popolo!* and in
England a poet quits ancestral halls
to call for the knife, *the major operation.*

The Indians are dying on their reservations,
black men are lynched, the jobless legions creep
from day to hungry day, driven from railway stations.
We have no place to sleep.

But in the subway on a winter morning,
travelling from the Bronx to Union Square,
The *Times* folded at the want-ad page,
we blink from slumber at each station-stop.
The girl across the aisle—her eyes are blue—
reading the *Mirror*. Open your eyes, it's you
she's smiling at. Don't close your eyes again.
Don't surrender to the ache in your limbs,
the heaviness in your head. Look at her!
I look. I see the oval face,
but when the dusty light-bars strike her,
the cheekbones and the hollows; and her eyes
removed from the paper, are blue and wise.
She smiles again.
                    I could arise, I say,
mumbling to myself. I could arise
and go to where she sits and say
nothing that anyone could hear
but take her arm and face the door
and walk away with her,
guiding her to the platform in the rear

and look at her, into her eyes, deep
into her thoughts, and feel that the crowd
had disappeared and that no one was near
except the girl. I could say everything
without a word that any rider'd understand
and she would understand!

Look, Funaroff. Look up from the book!
You're a poet and companion. You can understand
the memories of faces seen on long-ago subway rides,
the persons whom you've known and tried to kill, but can't
They grow the while you comrpomise with newer faces,
less clean-cut, blurred and blunted.
                                        You recall
our fathers' admonition: Covet not, my son,
but take what's yours by right.

It is hard to let go, it is pain to surrender
the fugitive fragments of an earlier self.
But the break must be made, the artery severed
and sewed again, the useless nerve numbed.

3.

The country quite baffles me again.
This silence is deceptive, the flowers a fraud,
the streams polluted. To live here is a lie.
Escape from chaos is impossible;
the world's too muddled, the skies thunder
with guns, projectiles dealing death
but also, remember, the terrible cleansing storm!

To live in villages today a man must also
create a village-suburb in the brain:
partition the skull, decree which part
shall live, observe, feel joy and pain,
and which vast area grow dulled,
the senses, all awareness, killed.

You, Funaroff, and Hayes, and the others:
enter with me the farthest regions
of space and time, the body moving
across huge continents, the brain surveying
the contours of the land, destroying
the cancerous trees and men, restoring
the spark to bodies overwhelmed
by drudgery and dross and dust.
Blueprint the hills and rivers, mark
the meadows and the factories.
Harness the hordes of middlemen,
bankers and bosses, fiddle players
to generals, kings and presidents;
sweep them together and tie their hands
with their servile strings and ticker tape,
and lead the parasite pulp with you
to moldy manors and somnolent suburbs,
into dead lands, beyond the outposts
of workingmen marching. Then lock the doors
and destroy the keys. Leave them to die.

Return with me to cities where the wind
finds chasms between skyscrapers, where men
reveal their thoughts in action, where mills
and factories are continual testament
to the war that only villages can hide.

Rejoin with greater vigor, rejoice
in new days, new companionships.
Revive the rural landscape, the girl
smiling across the subway aisle,
the oppressive silence, the news that flashes
from China to New York
                         and synthesize
these memories within the single self
attendant on the mass of men
who march with us today, who blaze the way
from village to city, from city to the world
our minds foresee, our poems celebrate.

Stephen Spender (Born 1909)

The son of the well-known journalist Edward Harold Spender, Stephen Spender was born in London and educated at the University College School. He attended University College, Oxford where he became friends with W. H. Auden. Subsequently, Spender went to Berlin where he befriended Christopher Isherwood, a friendship which lasts to this day. He spent some time in Spain during the civil war and worked as a London fireman during the Second World War. Spender was also editor of the magazines, *Horizon* and *Encounter*. He has taught at numerous colleges and universities in the U.S. and England. Spender has composed 22 collections of poetry, six plays, and over 25 books of criticism, history and lectures. He was awarded the Queen's Gold Medal for Poetry in 1971.

Though Spender is most often associated with the Auden group, close study of his work reveals that he had little in common with them. Spender was interested in lyricism and emotions; he was a romantic in a cynical time who had a passion for fraternal love and beauty. His later poetry shows the same concern with idealism and romanticism.

An Elementary School Classroom in a Slum

Far far from gusty waves these children's faces.
Like rootless weeds, the hair torn round their pallor.
The tall girl with her weighed-down head. The paper-
seeming boy, with rat's eyes. The stunted, unlucky heir
Of twisted bones, reciting a father's gnarled disease,
His lesson from his desk. At back of the dim class
One unnoted, sweet and young. His eyes live in a dream
Of squirrel's game, in tree room, other than this.

On sour cream walls, donations. Shakespeare's head,
Cloudless at dawn, civilized dome riding all cities.
Belled, flowery, Tyrolese valley. Open-handed map
Awarding the world its world. And yet, for these
Children, these windows, not this world, are world,
Where all their future's painted with a fog,
A narrow street sealed in with a lead sky,
Far far from rivers, capes, and stars of words.

Surely, Shakespeare is wicked, the map a bad example
With ships and sun and love tempting them to steal—
For lives that slyly turn in their cramped holes
From fog to endless night? On their slag heap, these children

Wear skins peeped through by bones and spectacles of steel
With mended glass, like bottle bits on stones.
All of their time and space are foggy slum.
So blot their maps with slums as big as doom.

Unless, governor, teacher, inspecotor, visitor,
This map becomes their window and these windows
That shut upon their lives like catacombs,
Break O break open till they break the town

And show the children to green fields, and make their world
Run azure on gold sands, and let their tongues
Run naked into books, the white and green leaves open
History theirs whose language is the sun.

The Landscape near an Aerodome

More beautiful and soft than any moth
With burring furred antennae feeling its huge path
Through dusk, the air liner with shut-off engines
Glides over suburbs and the sleeves set trailing tall
To point the wind. Gently, broadly, she falls,
Scarcely disturbing charted currents of air.

Lulled by descent, the travellers across sea
And across feminine land indulging its easy limbs
In miles of softness, now let their eyes trained by watching
Penetrate through dusk the outskirts of this town
Here where industry shows a fraying edge.
Here they may see what is being done.

Beyond the winking masthead light
And the landing ground, they observe the outposts
Of work: chimneys like lank black fingers
Or figures, frightening and mad: and squat buildings
With their strange air behind trees, like women's faces
Shattered by grief. Here where few houses
Moan with faint light behind their blinds,
They remark the unhomely sense of complaint, like a dog
Shut out, and shivering at the foreign moon.

In the last sweep of love, they pass over fields
Behind the aerodrome, where boys play all day
Hacking dead grass: whose cries, like wild birds,
Settle upon the nearest roofs
But soon are hid under the loud city.

Then, as they land, they hear the tolling bell
Reaching across the landscape of hysteria,
To where, louder than all those batteries
And charcoaled towers against that dying sky,
Religion stands, the Church blocking the sun.

Marston

Marston, dropping it in the grate, broke his pipe.
Nothing hung on this act, it was no symbol
Ludicrous for calamity, but merely ludicrous.

That heavy-wrought briar with the great pine face
Now split across like a boxer's hanging dream
Of punishing a nigger, he brought from the
   continent;
It was his absurd relic, like bones,
Of stamping on the white-faced mountains,
Early beds in huts, and other journeys.

To hold the bank of the Danube, the slow barges
   down the river,
Those coracles with faces painted on,
Demanded his last money,
A foodless journey home, as pilgrimage.

Polar Exploration

Our single purpose was to walk through snow
With faces swung to their prodigious North
Like compass iron. As clerks in whited banks
With bird-claw pens column virgin paper,
To snow we added foot-prints.
Extensive whiteness drowned
All sense of space. We tramped through
Static, glaring days, Time's suspended blank.
That was in Spring and Autumn. Summer struck
Water over rocks, and half the world
Became a ship with a deep keel, the booming floes
And icebergs with their little birds:
Twittering Snow Bunting, Greenland Wheatear,
Red-throated Divers; imagine butterflies
Sulphurous cloudy yellow; glory of bees
That suck from saxifrage; crowberry,
Bilberry, cranberry, *Pyrola Uniflora*.
There followed Winter in a frozen hut
Warm enough at the kernel, but dare to sleep
With head against the wall—ice gummed my hair!
Hate Culver's loud breathing, despise Freeman's
Fidget for washing; love only the dogs
That whine for scraps, and scratch. Notice
How they run better (on short journeys) with a bitch.
In that, different from us.
Return, return, you warn. We do. There is
A network of railways, money, words, words, words.
Meals, papers, exchanges, debates,
Cinema, wireless: the worst, is Marriage.
We cannot sleep. At night we watch
A speaking clearness through cloud paranoia.
These questions are white rifts:—Was
Ice our anger transformed? The raw, the motionless
Skies, were these the Spirit's hunger?
The continual and hypnotized march through snow,
The dropping nights of precious extinction, were these
Only the wide inventions of the will,
The frozen will's evasion? If this exists

In us as madness here, as coldness
In these summer, civilized sheets: Is the North,
Over there, a tangible, real madness,
A glittering simpleton, one without towns,
Only with bears and fish, a staring eye,
A new and singular sex?

Port Bou

As a child holds a pet
Arms clutching but with hands that do not join
And the coiled animal watches the gap
To outer freedom in animal air,
So the earth-and-rock flesh arms of this harbour
Embrace but do not enclose the sea
Which, through a gap, vibrates to the open sea
Where ships and dolphins swim and above is the sun.
In the bright winter sunlight I sit on the stone parapet
Of a bridge; my circling arms rest on a newspaper
Empty in my mind as the glittering stone
Because I search for an image
And seeing an image I count out the coined words
To remember the childish headlands of this harbour.
A lorry halts beside me with creaking brakes
And I look up at warm waving flag-like faces
Of militiamen staring down at my French newspaper.
'How do they speak of our struggle, over the frontier?'
I hold out the paper, but they refuse,
They did not ask for anything so precious
But only for friendly words and to offer me cigarettes.
In their smiling faces the war finds peace, the famished mouths
Of the rusty carbines brush against their trousers
Almost as fragilely as reeds;
And wrapped in a cloth—old mother in a shawl—
The terrible machine-gun rests.
They shout, salute back as the truck jerks forward
Over the vigorous hill, beyond the headland.
An old man passes, his running mouth,
With three teeth like bullets, spits out 'pom-pom-pom.'

The children run after; and, more slowly, the women
Clutching their clothes, follow over the hill;
Till the village is empty, for the firing practice,
And I am left alone on the bridge at the exact centre
Where the cleaving river trickles like saliva.
At the exact centre, solitary as a target,
Where nothing moves against a background of cardboard houses
Except the disgraceful skirring dogs; and the firing begins,
Across the harbour mouth from headland to headland,
White flecks of foam gashed by lead in the sea;
And the echo trails over its iron lash
Whipping the flanks of the surrounding hills.
My circling arms rest on the newspaper,
My mind seems paper where dust and ink fall,
I tell myself the shooting is only for practice,
And my body seems a cloth which the machine-gun stitches
Like a sewing machine, neatly, with cotton from a reel;
And the solitary, irregular, thin 'paffs' from the carbines
Draw on long needles white threads through my navel.

Seascape
In Memoriam, M. A. S.

There are some days the happy ocean lies
Like an unfingered harp, below the land.
Afternoon gilds all the silent wires
Into a burning music for the eyes.
On mirrors flashing between fine-strung fires
The shore, heaped up with roses, horses, spires,
Wanders on water, walking above ribbed sand.

The motionlessness of the hot sky tires
And a sigh, like a woman's, from inland
Brushes the instrument with shadowing hand
Drawing across its wires some gull's sharp cries
Or bell, or shout, from distant, hedged-in shires;
These, deep as anchors, the hushing wave buries.

Then from the shore, two zig-zag butterflies,
Like errant dog-roses, cross the bright strand
Spiralling over sea in foolish gyres
Until they fall into reflected skies.
They drown. Fishermen understand
Such wings sunk in such ritual sacrifice,

Recalling legends of undersea, drowned cities.
What voyagers, oh what heroes, flamed like pyres
With helmets plumed, have set forth from some island
And them the sea engulfed. Their eyes,
Contorted by the cruel waves' desires
Glitter with coins through the tide scarcely scanned,
While, above them, that harp assumes their sighs.

Song

Stranger, you who hide my love
   In the curved cheek of a smile
And sleep with her upon a tongue
   Of soft lies which beguile,
     Your paradisal ecstasy
     Is justified is justified
By hunger of all beasts beneath
   The overhanging cloud,
     Who, to snatch quick pleasure run,
     Before their momentary sun
Be eclipsed by death.

Lightly, lightly from my sleep
   She stole, our vows of dew to break,
Upon a day of melting rain
   Another love to take;
     Her happy happy perfidy
     Was justified was justified
Since compulsive needs of sense
   Clamour to be satisfied
     And she was never one to miss
     The plausible happiness
Of a new experience.

I, who stand beneath a bitter
   Blasted tree, with the green life
Of summer joy cut from my side
   By that self-justifying knife,
     In my exiled misery
Were justified were justified
If upon two lives I preyed
   Or punished with my suicide,
     Or murdered pity in my heart
     Or two other lives did part
To make the world pay what I paid.

Oh, supposing that I climb
   Alone to a high room of clouds
Up a ladder of the time
And lie upon a bed alone
   And tear a feather from a wing
And listen to the world below
And write round my high paper walls
   Anything and everything
Which I know and do not know!

The Trance

Sometimes, apart in sleep, by chance,
You fall out of my arms, alone,
Into the chaos of your separate trance.
My eyes gaze through your forehead, through the bone,
And see where in your sleep distress has torn
Its violent path, which on your lips is shown
And on your hands and in your dream forlorn.

Restless, you turn to me, and press
Those timid words against my ear
Which thunder at my heart like stones.
"Mercy" you plead, Then "Who can bless?"
You ask. "I am pursued by Time," you moan.
I watch that precipice of fear
You tread, naked in naked distress.

To that deep care we are committed
Beneath the wildness of our flesh
And shuddering horror of our dream,
Where unmasked agony is permitted.
Our bodies, stripped of clothes that seem,
And our souls, stripped of beauty's mesh,
Meet their true selves, their charms outwitted.

This pure trance is the oracle
That speaks no language but the heart,
Our angel with our devil meets
In the atrocious dark nor do they part
But each each forgives and greets,
And their mutual terrors heal
Within our married miracle.

Two Armies

Deep in the winter plain, two armies
Dig their machinery, to destroy each other.
Men freeze and hunger. No one is given leave
On either side, except the dead, and wounded.
These have their leave; while new battalions wait
On time at last to bring them violent peace.

All have become so nervous and so cold
That each man hates the cause and distant words
That brought him here, more terribly than bullets.
Once a boy hummed a popular marching song,
Once a novice hand flapped their salute;
The voice was choked, the lifted hand fell,
Shot through the wrist by those of his own side.

From their numb harvest, all would flee, except
For discipline drilled once in an iron school
Which holds them at the point of the revolver.
Yet when they sleep, the images of home
Ride wishing horses of escape
Which herd the plain in a mass unspoken poem.

Finally, they cease to hate: for although hate
Bursts from the air and whips the earth with hail
Or shoots it up in fountains to marvel at,
And although hundreds fall, who can connect
The inexhaustible anger of the guns
With the dumb patience of those tormented animals?

Clean silence drops at night, when a little walk
Divides the sleeping armies, each
Huddled in linen woven by remote hands.
When the machines are stilled, a common suffering
Whitens the air with breath and makes both one
As though these enemies slept in each other's arms.

Only the lucid friend to aerial raiders
The brilliant pilot moon, stares down
Upon this plain she makes a shining bone
Cut by the shadows of many thousand bones.
Where amber clouds scatter on No-Man's-Land
She regards death and time throw up
The furious words and minerals which destroy.

What I Expected

What I expected, was
Thunder, fighting,
Long struggles with men
And climbing.
After continual straining
I should grow strong;
Then the rocks would shake,
And I rest long.

What I had not foreseen
Was the gradual day
Weakening the will
Leaking the brightness away,
The lack of good to touch,
The fading of body and soul
—Smoke before wind,
Corrupt, unsubstantial.

The wearing of Time,
And the watching of cripples pass
With limbs shaped like questions
In their odd twist,
The pulverous grief
Melting the bones with pity,
The sick falling from earth—
These, I could not foresee.

Expecting always
Some brightness to hold in trust,
Some final innocence
Exempt from dust,
That, hanging solid,
Would dangle through all,
Like the created poem,
Or faceted crystal.

Winter and Summer

Within my head, aches the perpetual winter
Of this violent time, where pleasures freeze.
My inner eye anticipates for ever
Looking through naked trees and running wheels
Onto a blank transparent sky
Leading to nothing; as though, through iron aims,
It was stared back at by the filmy surface
Of a lid covering its own despair.
Thus, when the summer breaks upon my face
With the outward shock of a green wave
Crested with leaves and creamy foam of flowers,
I think the luxurious lazy meadows
Are a deceiving canvas covering
With a balmy paint of leafy billows,
The furious volleys of charioteering power
Behind the sun, racing to destroy.
    When under light lawns, heavy in their soil,
I hear the groaning of the wasted lives
Of those who revolve unreflecting wheels,
    Alas, I prove that I am right,
For if my shadowed mind affirmed the light

It would return to those green, foolish years
When to live seemed to stand knee-deep in flowers:
There, winter was an indoor accident,
Where, with head pressed against the glass, I watched
The garden, falsified by snow,
Waiting to melt, and become real again.

Word

The word bites like a fish
Shall I throw it back free
Arrowing to that sea
Where thoughts lash tail and fin?
Or shall I pull it in
To rhyme upon a dish?

Your Body is Stars

Your body is stars whose million glitter here:
I am lost amongst the branches of this sky
Here near my breast, here in my nostrils, here
Where our vast arms like streams of fire lie.

How can this end? My healing fills the night
And hangs its flags in worlds I cannot hear.
Our movements range through miles, and when we kiss
The moment widens to enclose long years.

* * *

Beholders of the promised dawn of truth
The explorers of immense and simple lines,
Here is our goal, men cried, but it was lost
Amongst the mountain mists and mountain pines.

So with this face of love, whose breathings are
A mystery shadowed on the desert floor:
The promise hangs, this swarm of stars and flowers,
And then there comes the shutting of a door.

Robert Fitzgerald (Born 1910)

Robert Fitzgerald was born in Geneva, New York but grew up in Springfield, Illinois. He attended Choate School in Wallingford, Connecticut and Harvard and Cambridge. After college he worked as a journalist for the *New York Herald-Tribune* and *Time* magazine. He served in the navy in World War II. Fitzgerald resided in Italy from 1953 to 1964 with his family, returning to the U.S. to pursue an academic career. In 1965 he was appointed Boylston Professor of Rhetoric at Harvard. His books of poetry include *Poems* (1935) and *A Wreath for the Sun* (1943). Fitzgerald has translated the *Iliad* and the *Odyssey* and Vergil's *Aneid*, as well as many Greek tragedies. The excellence of these translations, and his devotion to teaching, have overshadowed Fitgerald's poetry, which has not received its due attention.

Colorado

Now the plains come to adore the mountain wall,
Their yellow fields running and bowing like waves
To celebrate in such serene order the fire
And love that bore these stony things. Now fragile
Air, sweet health of a superficial season
Garland a while the majesty of winter.

And I, not long nor with profit hereabouts,
Note merely the blue, the watercolor blue
A descriptive man would like; the rare
And rifted shadowline of trees, the smooth
Peaks too cold for the warm west to redden,
Much, or gild them. They remain sharply vague.

It is so, too, I think, with the remote
Populations of memory: they stand above
Our imperceptible journeys and indulgence,
Easily unseen by a simple turn of the head,
Impossible to grasp in contour, always a little
Shifting, and the same. Death has engraved them
Lovely and lofty, and my metaphysic
Smiles to align them here, the shadowy ones
Tinted so faint, yet luminous as gems.

A property of distance. And distance?
A requisite of the just, which is proportion,
Or holy measure, that the sages loved,
Being so fond of stringed instruments and so
Mild: they liked puppies as well as you;
And saw fit, being profound, not to reflect
Chaos unbounded, but to extract therefrom
Numerous order and magnificence.

So at least I interpret the very thin hostile azure
Wherein these stones are dipt, and I imagine
Of time and the great dead, they too
Correctly make a tune with me; let me
Behold by their grave light my miniscule
Part in the swaying and tranquil grandeur here.

Souls Lake

The evergreen shadow and the pale magnolia
Stripping slowly to the air of May
Stood still in the night of the honey trees.
At rest above a star pool with my friends,
Besides that grove most fit for elegies,
I made my phrase to out-enchant the night.

The epithalamion, the hush were due,
For I had fasted and gone blind to see
What night might be beyond our passages;
Those stars so chevalier in fearful heaven
Could not but lay their steel aside and come
With a grave glitter into my low room.

Vague though the population of the earth
Lay stretched and dry below the cypresses,
It was not round-about but in my night,
Bone of my bone, as an old man would say;
And all its stone weighed my mortality;
The pool would be my body and my eyes,

The air my garment and material
Whereof that wateriness and mirror lived—
The colorable, meek and limpid world.
Though I had sworn my element alien
To the pure mind of night, the cold princes,
Behold them there, and both worlds were the same.

The heart's planet seemed not so lonely then,
Seeing what kin it found in that reclining.
And ah, though sweet the catch of your chorales,
I heard no singing there among my friends;
But still were the great waves, the lions shining,
And infinite still the discourse of the night.

Elizabeth Bishop (1911–1979)

When Elizabeth Bishop was eight months old her father, Thomas Bishop, died and her mother, Gertrude Blumer, suffered a nervous collapse. Bishop was brought up by her maternal grandparents in Nova Scotia. When she was six years old, Bishop was sent to live with her paternal grandparents in Worcester, Massachusetts. There she contracted severe bronchitis and acute asthma, and eventually went to live in Boston with an aunt. Her health slowly began to improve, though she never led a normal childhood. In 1930 she attended Vassar and contributed poetry regularly to the *Vassar Review*.

After graduating from Vassar, Bishop traveled extensively. Between 1935 and 1945 she visited Belgium, France, Brittany, England, North Africa, Spain, Key West, Florida, and Mexico. In 1945 she published her first collection of poetry, *North & South* which chronicled her travels. In 1951 Bishop decided to reside permanently in Brazil where she translated the Brazilian classic *The Diary of 'Helena Morley.'* In 1956 she received the Pulitzer Prize for Poetry. Her third book of poems, *Questions of Travel*, was published in 1965. She died in Cambridge, Massachusetts.

Though her poetical output was sparce, Elizabeth Bishop had a devoted following of readers, poets, and critics. Her poetry lies in the world of appearances, where shapes and colors and textures are intimately bound with the meaning of existence. She differs from impressionistic poets in that her descriptions are precise and exact, indeed some of her poems appear at first to be just a listing of the materials of the thing she is describing (a good example of this is "The Monument" in this anthology). But this is misleading, for just as it is in the colors and brushstrokes a painter uses that we discover his attitude towards his subject, it is in her technique that Bishop reveals the emotion and meaning of her poetry. As the critic Anne Stevenson put it: "But despair, for Elizabeth Bishop, is rarely an occasion for romantic despondency or for virulent sarcasm . . . (it) is rather an opportunity for elegance."

The Monument

Now can you see the monument? It is of wood
built somewhat like a box. No. Built
like several boxes in descending sizes
one above the other.
Each is turned half-way round so that
its corners point toward the sides
of the one below and the angles alternate.
Then on the topmost cube is set
a sort of fleur-de-lys of weathered wood,
long petals of board, pierced with odd holes,
four-sided, stiff, ecclesiastical.
From it four thin, warped poles spring out,
(slanted like fishing-poles or flag-poles)
and from them jig-saw work hangs down,

four lines of vaguely whittled ornament
over the edges of the boxes
to the ground.
The monument is one-third set against
a sea; two-thirds against a sky.
The view is geared
(that is, the view's perspective)
so low there is no 'far away,'
and we are far away within the view.
A sea of narrow, horizontal boards
lies out behind our lonely monument,
its long grains alternating right and left
like floor-boards—spotted, swarming-still,
and motionless. A sky runs parallel,
and it is palings, coarser than the sea's:
splintery sunlight and long-fibred clouds.
'Why does that strange sea make no sound?
Is it because we're far away?
Where are we? Are we in Asia Minor,
or in Mongolia?'
                      An ancient promontory,
an ancient principality whose artist-prince
might have wanted to build a monument
to mark a tomb or boundary, or make
a melancholy or romantic scene of it . . .
'But that queer sea looks made of wood,
half-shining, like a driftwood sea.
And the sky looks wooden, grained with cloud.
It's like a stage-set; it is all so flat!
Those clouds are full of glistening splinters!
What is that ?'
                It is the monument.
'It's piled-up boxes,
outlined with shoddy fret-work, half-fallen off,
cracked and unpainted. It looks old.'
—The strong sunlight, the wind from the sea,
all the conditions of its existence,
may have flaked off the paint, if ever it was painted,
and made it homelier than it was.
'Why did you bring me here to see it?

A temple of crates in cramped and crated scenery,
what can it prove?
I am tired of breathing this eroded air,
this dryness in which the monument is cracking.'

It is an artifact
of wood. Wood holds together better
than sea or cloud or sand could by itself,
much better than real sea or sand or cloud.
It chose that way to grow and not to move.
The monument's an object, yet those decorations,
carelessly nailed, looking like nothing at all,
give it away as having life, and wishing;
wanting to be a monument, to cherish something.
The crudest scroll-work says 'commemorate,'
while once each day the light goes around it
like a prowling animal,
or the rain falls on it, or the wind blows into it.
It may be solid, may be hollow.
The bones of the artist-prince may be inside
or far away on even dryer soil.
But roughly but adequately it can shelter
what is within (which after all
cannot have been intended to be seen).
It is the beginning of a painting,
a piece of sculpture, or poem, or monument,
and all of wood. Watch it closely.

The Weed

I dreamed that dead, and meditating,
I lay upon a grave, or bed,
(at least, some cold and close-built bower).
In the cold heart, its final thought
stood frozen, drawn immense and clear,
stiff and idle as I was there;
and we remained unchanged together
for a year, a minute, an hour.
Suddenly there was a motion,

as startling, there, to every sense
as an explosion. Then it dropped
to insistent, cautious creeping
in the region of the heart,
prodding me from desperate sleep.
I raised my head. A slight young weed
had pushed up through the heart and its
green head was nodding on the breast.
(All this was in the dark.)
It grew an inch like a blade of grass;
next, one leaf shot out of its side
a twisting, waving flag, and then
two leaves moved like a semaphore.
The stem grew thick. The nervous roots
reached to each side; the graceful head
changed its position mysteriously,
since there was neither sun nor moon
to catch its young attention.
The rooted heart began to change
(not beat) and then it split apart
and from it broke a flood of water.
Two rivers glanced off from the sides,
one to the right, one to the left,
two rushing, half-clear streams,
(the ribs made of them two cascades)
which assuredly, smooth as glass,
went off through the fine black grains of earth.
The weed was almost swept away;
it struggled with its leaves,
lifting them fringed with heavy drops.
A few drops fell upon my face
and in my eyes, so I could see
(or, in that black place, thought I saw)
that each drop contained a light,
a small, illuminated scene;
the weed-deflected stream was made
itself, of racing images.
(As if a river should carry all
the scenes that it had once reflected
shut in its waters, and not floating

on momentary surfaces.)
The weed stood in the severed heart.
"What are you doing there?" I asked.
It lifted its head all dripping wet
(with my own thoughts?)
and answered then: 'I grow it,' it said,
'but to divide your heart again.'

Kenneth Patchen (1911–1972)

Kenneth Patchen was born December 13 in Niles, Ohio. His father, Wayne, was a steel worker. The family moved to Warren, Ohio so that the children could attend school. At Harding High School Patchen was an all around student-athlete; while in high school he published two sonnets in the *New York Times*. To earn money for college, Patchen worked in the town's steel mill with his father and brother. This cruel and terrifying work experience profoundly affected his life as a poet and as a man. He spent one year at Alexander Meiklejohn's Experimental College at the University of Wisconsin. The depression ended his studies, and he set off for the road, working odd jobs but always writing.

In 1934 he married Miriam Oikenus, a student at the University of Massachusetts. The young couple moved to Greenwich Village in New York. Patchen's first book of poems, *Before the Brave*, was published in 1936 and in the same year he was awarded a Guggenheim Fellowship. In 1937, after trying to separate the locked bumpers of two cars, Patchen suffered a slipped disc which was not correctly diagnosed until 1950. Thus began a life of tremendous physical and emotional anguish for Patchen. Needless to say, he kept on working, publishing at least one book per year. The Patchens became editors at James Laughlin's fledgling press, New Directions Books, and moved to Connecticut in 1938. Patchen published his first anti-novel in 1941, *The Journal of Albion Moonlight*. After Patchen's back trouble was temporarily relieved in 1950, he and his wife moved to San Francisco where they became identified with the "beat poets"—Lawrence Ferlinghetti, Allen Ginsberg, and Kenneth Rexroth. These poets began their poetry and jazz fusion experiments in 1957. Patchen went on the road to perform with various jazz bands and in 1958 recorded *Kenneth Patchen Reads with the Chamber Jazz Sextet* for Cadence Records. Patchen seemed to be fully recovering from his back ailments. In 1959, while being taken for further surgery, he fell off of the operating cart, causing irreparable harm to his spine. The surgery was canceled and Patchen was sent home to California to live out his days bedridden and in pain. He did not stop creating though, indeed his illness seemed to enhance his art. In 1968 he published his *Collected Poems* and in 1969 the Corcoran Gallery in Washington D.C. had a one man exhibit of his paintings, picture-poems, and concrete poems. Kenneth Patchen died of a heart attack January 8, 1972.

Joe Hill Listens to the Praying

Look at the steady rifles, Joe.
It's all over now—"Murder, first degree,"
The jury said. It's too late now
To go back. Listen Joe, the chaplain is reading:

Lord Jesus Christ who didst
So mercifully promise heaven
To the thief that humbly confessed
His injustice
              throw back your head

Joe: remember that song of yours
We used to sing in jails all over
These United States—tell it to him:
"I'll introduce to you
A man that is a credit to our Red, White
and Blue,
His head is made of lumber and solid as
a rock;
He is a Christian Father and his name is
Mr. Block."
               Remember, Joe—
"You take the cake,
You make me ache,
Tie a rock on your block and jump
in the lake,
Kindly do that for Liberty's sake."

Behold me, I beseech Thee, with
The same eyes of mercy that
                      on the other
Hand we're driftin' into Jungles
From Kansas to the coast, wrapped
   round brake beams on a thousand
   freights; San Joaquin and Omaha
   brush under the wheels—"God made the summer
   for the hobo and the bummer"—we've been
   everywhere, seen everything.
Winning the West for the good citizens;
Driving golden spikes into the U.P.;
Harvest hands, lumbermen drifting—
   now Iowa, now Oregon—
God, how clean the sky; the lovely wine
Of coffee in a can. This land
   is our lover. How greenly beautiful
Her hair; her great pure breasts
   that are
The Rockies on a day of mist and rain.

We love this land of corn and cotton,
   Virginia and Ohio, sleeping on
With our love, with our love—
O burst of Alabama loveliness, sleeping on
In the strength of our love; O Mississippi flowing
Through our nights, a giant mother.

Pardon, and in the end
                        How green is her hair,
  how pure are her breasts; the little farms
  nuzzling into her flanks
  drawing forth life, big rich life
Under the deep chant of her skies
And rivers—but we, we're driftin'
Into trouble from Kansas to the coast, clapped
  into the stink and rot of country jails
  and clubbed by dicks and cops
Becuase we didn't give a damn—
                        remember Joe
How little we cared, how we sang
  the nights away in their filthy jails;
                        and how, when
We got wind of a guy called Marx
  we sang less, just talked
And talked. "Blanket-stiffs" we were
But we could talk, they coudn't jail us
For that—but they did—
                        remember Joe
Of my life be strengthened
                    One Big Union:
  our convention in Chi; the Red Cards,
  leaflets; sleeping in the parks,
  the Boul Mich; "wobblies" now, cheering
  the guys that spoke our lingo, singing
  down the others. "Hear that train blow,
Boys, hear that train blow."

Now confessing my crimes, I may obtain

Millions of stars, Joe—millions of miles.

              Remember Vincent St. John
In the Goldfield strike; the timid little squirt
  with the funny voice, getting onto the platform
  and slinging words at us that rolled
  down our chins and into our hearts,
  like boulders hell-bent down a mountain side.
And Orchard, angel of peace
  —with a stick of dynamite in either hand.
  Pettibone and Moyer: "The strike
Is your weapon, to hell with politics."
                    Big Bill—remember him—
At Boise—great red eye rolling like a lame bull
  through the furniture and men
  of the courtroom—"This bastard,
His Honor."

Hobo Convention:
(Millions of stars, Joe—millions of miles.)
"Hallelujah, I'm a bum,
Hallelujah, I'm a bum." His Honor,
  the sonofabitch!
One Big Strike, Lawrence, Mass—
  23,000 strong, from every neck
  of every woods in America, 23,000,
Joe, remember. "We don't need
  a leader. We'll fix things up
  among ourselves."
"Blackie" Ford and "Double-nose" Suhr in
Wheatland—"I. W. W.'s don't destroy
  property"—and they got life. "I've counted
The stars, boys, counted a million of these prison bars."

  San Diego, soap boxes,
Hundreds of them! And always
  their jail shutting out the sky,
  the clean rhythm of the wheels
  on a fast freight; disinfectant getting
  into the lung-pits, spitting blood

But singing—Christ, how we sang,
                    remember the singing
Joe, One Big Union,
                One Big
                    hope to be
With thee

What do they matter, Joe, these rifles.
They can't reach the towns, the skies, the songs,
   that now are part of more
   than any of us—we were
The homeless, the drifters, but, our songs
   had hair and blood on them.
There are no soap boxes in the sky.
We won't eat pie, now, or ever
   when we die,
            but Joe
We had something they didn't have:
   our love for these States
   was real and deep;
                to be with Thee
In heaven, Amen.
                (How steady are
   the rifles.) We had slept
   naked on this earth on the coldest nights
   listening to the words of a guy named Marx.
Let them burn us, hang us, shoot us,

                        Joe Hill,
For at the last we had what it takes
   to make songs with.

A Letter on the Use of Machine Guns at Weddings

Like the soldier, like the sailor, like the bib and tuck and bailer,
like the corner where we loiter, like the congressman and lawyer,
like the cop on the hill, like the lead in weary Will,
like the kittens in the water, like the names on Hearst's blotter,

like the guys and dames who laugh and chatter,
like the boys and girls who don't matter,
like the preacher and the Pope, like the punks who dish the dope,
like the hungry singing Home on the Range,
like Father Coughlin acting like Red Grange,
like the grumble of the tuba, like the sugar war in Cuba,
like the bill-collectors, like the Law-respecters,
like the pimps and prostitutes, like Mickey Mouse and Puss-in-Boots,
like the churches and the jails, like Astor's hounds and quails,
she's like you like her, now don't you try to spike her,
she's the nuts, she's a mile of Camel butts,
she's honey in the money, she's my pearl,
what am I offered for being alive and willing to marry the girl?
though her insides rumble and her joints are out of whack,
let's give her a whirl, why grumble or try to draw back?
though her hair is false and her teeth are yellow,
let's get chummy, let's all get a break. For what's a fellow
got at stake, for what's a guy to do
who hasn't the guts to deal with sluts, guys like me and you.

A Letter to a Policeman in Kansas City

A lot of men and armies stand to take
no chances with the prisoner Goddamn
them standing there near the bars watch their fingers
flex their eyes proud their legs firm their earth this
time next year last year a hundred years from now
they think it's all ours belongs to us we've got
you where we want for nothing

                                         any painter
can't paint any carpenter can't build any
doctor can't cure any man can't say how deep
it goes inside to watch to stand dumb
in the streets of their cities and know
that your head's crummy your feet drip blood
that your belly rots your life is shot
                                       your days
are spent in two-bit flops because of them

because they get away with murder away
with everything we are or ever were come
to think of it

        Goddamn them standing on
the cover of our world their heavy boots grinding
into our faces their ropes about our necks their guns
shut your mouth you bastard where do you live
what are you doing here look out
look out we don't know anything about that but
I'll tell you where we live and what we're doing here
tomorrow maybe I'll tell you then I'll tell you
when your guard is down when the thing breaks
I'll tell you all you want to know come to
think of it
        I'm not too starved to want food
not too homeless to want a home not too dumb
to answer questions come to think of it
                        it'll take a hell
of a lot more than you've got to stop what's
going on deep inside us when it starts out
when it starts wheels going worlds growing
and any man can live on earth when we're through with it.

Let Us Have Madness Openly

Let us have madness openly, O men
Of my generation. Let us follow
The footsteps of this slaughtered age:
See it trail across Time's dim land
Into the closed house of eternity
With the noise that dying has,
With the face that dead things wear—
                        nor ever say

We wanted more; we looked to find
An open door, an utter deed of love,
Transforming day's evil darkness;
        but

We found extended hell and fog
Upon the earth, and within the head
A rotting bog of lean huge graves.

Street Corner College

Next year the grave grass will cover us.
We stand now, and laugh;
Watching the girls go by;
Betting on slow horses; drinking cheap gin.
We have nothing to do; nowhere to go; nobody.

Last year was a year ago; nothing more.
We weren't younger then; nor older now.

We manage to have the look that young men have;
We feel nothing behind our faces, one way or other.

We shall probably not be quite dead when we die.
We were never anything all the way; not even soldiers.

We are the insulted, brother, the desolate boys.
Sleepwalkers in a dark and terrible land,
Where solitude is a dirty knife at our throats.
Cold stars watch us, chum
Cold stars and the whores

23rd Street Runs into Heaven

You stand near the window as lights wink
On along the street. Somewhere a trolley, taking
Shop-girls and clerks home, clatters through
This before-supper Sabbath. An alley cat cries
To find the garbage cans sealed; newsboys
Begin their murder-into-pennies round.

We are shut in, secure for a little, safe until
Tommorrow. You slip your dress off, roll down
Your stockings, careful against runs. Naked now,
With soft light on soft flesh, you pause
For a moment; turn and face me—
Smile in a way that only women know
Who have lain long with their lover
And are made more virginal.

Our supper is plain but we are very wonderful.

Lawrence Durrell (Born 1912)

Lawrence Durrell was born February 27 in Jullundur, India. Durrell's family moved to England when he was 11 years old. After attending a variety of schools, he opted not to attend a university and worked instead at a series of odd jobs—from playing piano at a nightclub to racing cars. In 1935 Durrell moved to Corfu and he published his first novel, *The Pied Piper of Lovers*. Durrell also came under the influence of Henry Miller after reading the *Tropic of Cancer*. He began a correspondence with Miller, and wrote and published a very Miller-like autobiographical novel, *The Black Book*, in 1938. The book appeared in Paris but was considered too risque for Britain or America.

During World War II, Durrell served in the British Information Office in Egypt, where he gathered material for his later, and most famous work, *The Alexandria Quartet*. After the war Durrell lived in a variety of countries and went through his "gestation period," which ended in 1957 with the publication of the first volume of the *Alexandria Quartet*, a critical and financial success.

Although Durrell's popularity rests upon his novels, he began his career as a poet (his first book was *Ten Poems* (1932)). Some critics consider his most lasting creative achievements to be his poems. Unlike Auden or Eliot, Durrell has limited his themes to five basic categories: short lyrics, meditations, comedy, metaphysical poems, and portraits of artists. Within this framework, Durrell has proved to be a very consistent poet and always a master craftsman.

At Epidaurus

The islands which whisper to the ambitious,
Washed all winter by the surviving stars
Are here hardly recalled: or only as
Stone choirs for the sea-bird,
Stone chairs for the statues of fishermen.
This civilized valley was dedicated to
The cult of the circle, the contemplation
And correction of famous maladies
Which the repeating flesh has bred in us also
By a continuous babyhood, like the worm in meat.

The only disorder is in what we bring here:
Cars drifting like leaves over the glades,
The penetration of clocks striking in London,
The composure of dolls and fanatics,
Financed migrations to the oldest sources:
A theatre where redemption was enacted,
Repentance won, the stones heavy with dew.
The olive signs the hill, signifying revival,
And the swallow's cot in the ruin seems how
Small yet defiant an exaggeration of love!

Here we can carry our own small deaths
With the resignation of place and identity;
A temple set severely like a dice
In the vale's Vergilian shade; once apparently
Ruled from the whitest light of the summer:
A formula for marble when the clouds
Troubled the architect, and the hill spoke
Volumes of thunder, the sibyllic god wept.
Here we are safe from everything but ourselves,
The dying leaves and the reports of love.

The land's lie, held safe from the sea,
Encourages the austerity of the grass chambers,
Provides a context understandably natural
For men who could divulge the forms of gods.
Here the mathematician entered his own problem,
A house built round his identity,
Round the fond yet mysterious seasons
Of green grass, the teaching of summer-astronomy.
Here the lover made his calculations by ferns,
And the hum of the chorus enchanted.

We, like the winter, are only visitors,
To prosper here the breathing grass,
Encouraging petals on a terrace, disturbing
Nothing, enduring the sun like girls
In a town window. The earth's flower
Blows here original with every spring,
Shines in the rising of a man's age
Into cold texts and precedents for time.
Everything is a slave to the ancestor, the order
Of old captains who sleep in the hill.

Then smile, my dear, above the holy wands,
Make the indefinite gesture of the hands,
Unlocking this world which is not our world.
The somnambulists walk again in the north
With the long black rifles, to bring us answers.
Useless a morality for slaves: useless

The shouting at echoes to silence them.
Most useless inhabitants of the kind blue air,
Four ragged travellers in Homer.
All causes end within the great Because.

In Arcadia

By divination came the Dorians,
Under a punishment composed an arch.
They invented this valley they taught
The rock to flow with odourless water.

Fire and a brute art came among them.

Rain fell, tasting of the sky.
Trees grew, composing a grammar.
The river, the river you see was brought down
By force of prayer upon this fertile floor.

Now small skills: the fingers laid upon
The nostrils of flutes, the speech of women
Whose tutors were the birds; who singing
Now civilised their children with the kiss.

Lastly, the tripod sentenced them.

Ash closed on the surviving sons.
The brown bee memorised here, rehearsed
Migration from an inherited habit.
All travellers recorded an empty zone.

Between rocks 'O death', the survivors.
O world of bushes eaten like a moon,
Kissed by the awkward patience of the ant.
Within a concave blue and void of space.

Something died out by this river: but it seems
Less than a nightingale ago.

Nemea

A song in the valley of Nemea:
Sing quiet, quite quiet here.

Song for the brides of Argos
Combing the swarms of golden hair:
Quite quiet, quiet there.

Under the rolling comb of grass,
The sword outrusts the golden helm.

Agamemnon under tumulus serene
Outsmiles the jury of skeletons:
Cool under cumulus the lion queen:

Only the drum can celebrate,
Only the adjective outlive them.

A song in the valley of Nemea:
Sing quiet, quiet, quiet here.

Tone of the frog in the empty well,
Drone of the bald bee on the cold skull,

Quiet, Quiet, Quiet.

On Ithaca Standing

Tread softly, for here you stand
On miracle ground, boy.
A breath would cloud this water of glass,
Honey, bush, berry and swallow.
This rock, then, is more pastoral, than
Arcadia is, Illyria was.

Here the cold spring lilts on sand.
The temperature of the toad
Swallowing under a stone whispers: 'Diamonds,

Boy, diamonds, and juice of minerals!'
Be a saint here, dig for foxes, and water,
Mere water springs in the bones of the hands.

Turn from the hearth of the hero. Think:
Other men have their emblems, I this:
The heart's dark anvil and the crucifix
Are one, have hammered and shall hammer
A nail of flesh, me to an island cross,
Where the kestrel's arrow falls only,
The green sea licks.

A Water-Colour of Venice

Zarian was saying: Florence is youth,
And after it Ravenna, age,
Then Venice, second-childhood.

The pools of burning stone where time
And water, the old siege-masters,
Have run their saps beneath
A thousand saddle-bridges,
Puffed up by marble griffins drinking,

All all set free to float on loops
Of her canals like great intestines
Now snapped off like a berg to float,
Where now, like others, you have come alone,
To trap your sunset in a yellow glass,
And watch the silversmith at work
Chasing the famous salver of the bay . . .

Here sense dissolves, coheres to print only
These bitten choirs of stone on water,
To the rumble of old cloth bells,
The cadging of confetti pigeons,
A boatman singing from his long black coffin . . .

To all that has been said before
You can add nothing, only that here,
Thick as a brushstroke sleep has laid
Its fleecy unconcern on every visage,

At the bottom of every soul a spoonful of sleep.

Roy Fuller (Born 1912)

When Roy Fuller was eight his father died and he and his mother moved from Failsworth to Blackpool, England. He was educated at Blackpool High School and later became a qualified solicitor. He was self-educated in literature and read the new poetry of Pound and Eliot with great interest. In 1928 Fuller began to publish in small English magazines, attracting the attention and encouragement of such editors as Geoffery Grigson and John Lehmann.

1939 marked the beginning of Fuller's dual career: he joined the house-mortgage firm of the Woolwich Building Society, where he worked as a lawyer until 1968, and published his first volume of poetry, *Poems*. During World War II he served in the navy and found plenty of time to write, publishing his second book of verse, *The Middle of War* in 1942.

After the war Fuller returned to his post at Woolwich and wrote two adventure novels for boys, as well as another book of poetry, *Epitaphs and Occasions*, (1949). He did not publish anything for three years, but in 1952 embarked on the second part of his career with a flourish. Between 1952 and 1975 Fuller published eight novels and six poetry books. Upon his retirement from Woolwich in 1968, Fuller was elected professor of poetry at Oxford.

Roy Fuller bridged the gap between the Auden group and English poetry of the fifties. His first collection was greatly influenced by the two great forces of the thirties: Auden and Marxism. Fuller's verse was guided by the socialist belief that poetry should be made accessible to all people and should not be written for a few learned cliques. During World War II Fuller found his distinctive voice. His *Middle of War* and *Lost Season* (1944) are recognized as the most outstanding books of English poetry to come out of the war. The two volumes, though autobiographical, chart the progress of the English people as they prepare for and fight World War II. Fuller also paved the way for "the Movement," the school of English poetry which rejected the experimentation of Pound and Thomas and called for more rigourous and technically proficient verse.

The Hero

When the hero's task was done
And the beast lay underground,
In the time that he had won
From the fates that pushed him round

He had space to contemplate
How the peasants still were bled
And that in the salvaged state
Worms continued at the head.

Little space: already, where
Sweetly he enjoyed his fish,
Seeing through the shouldered hair
Loosening sails and dirty dish,

Gasped a pale new plea for aid.
Cleaning his gun later, he
Felt with awe the old beast's shade
Fall across the wine-dark sea.

Meditation

Now the ambassadors have gone, refusing
Our gifts, treaties, anger, compliance;
And in their place the winter has arrived,
Icing the culture-bearing water.
We brood in our respective empires on
The words we might have said which would have
 breached
The Chinese wall round our superfluous love
And manufactures. We do not brood too deeply.
There are our friends' perpetual, subtle demands
For understanding: visits to those who claim
To show us what is meant by death,
And therefore life, our short and puzzling lives,
And to explain our feelings when we look
Through the dark sky to other lighted worlds—
The well-shaved owners of sanatoria,
And raving, grubby oracles: the books
On diet, posture, prayer and aspirin art:
The claims of frightful weapons to be investigated:
Mad generals to be promoted: and
Our private gulfs to slither down in bed.

Perhaps in spring the ambassadors will return.
Before then we shall find perhaps that bombs,
Books, people, planets, worry, even our wives,
Are not at all important. Perhaps
The preposterous fishing-line tangle of undesired
Human existence will suddenly unravel
Before some staggering equation
Or mystic experience, and God be released
From the moral particle or blue-lit room.
Or, better still, perhaps we shall, before
Anything really happens, be safely dead.

November, 1941

The objects are disposed: the sky is suitable.
Where the coast curves the waves' blown smoke
Blurs with the city's and the pencilled ships
Lumber like toys. The searchers for coal and driftwood
Bend; and the beach is littered with stones and leaves,
Antlers of seaweed, round gulls, to the belt
Of sand, like macadam, watered by the sea.

Well then? It is here one asks the question.
Here, under such a sky, with such that menace of purple,
One confronts the varieties of death and of people
With a certain sense of their inadequacy;
And the grandeur of historical conceptions,
The wheeling empires, appearance of lusty classes,
The alimentary organizations, the clever
Extrications from doom, seize the imagination
As though these forms, like gods, existed cruel,
Aloof, but eventually for our salvation.
And, as the shapes themselves of nature or
The inexorable patterns of nightmare, days
And the sequence of days pull our untidy acts
Into the formidable expression of time and destiny.
The tumbling ocean humps itself to Europe—
There the machines, the armies and the skies,
The stains of movement and the burning regions,
Have all the echoes of a myth and in
My blood reside inhuman power and guilt,
Whose fathers made both myth and progeny.

The Plains

The only blossoms of the plains are black
And rubbery, the spiked spheres of the thorn,
And stuffed with ants. It is before the rains:
The stream is parched to pools, occasional
And green, where tortoise flop; the birds are songless;
Towers of whirling dust glide past like ghosts.

But in the brilliant sun, against the sky,
The river course is vivid and the grass
Flaxen: the strong striped haunches of the zebra,
The white fawn black, like flags, of the gazelles,
Move as emotions or as kindly actions.
The world is nothing but a fairy tale
Where everything is beautiful and good.

At night the stars were faint, the plateau chill;
The great herds gathered, were invisible,
And coughed and made inarticulate noises
Of fear and yearning; sounds of their many hooves
Came thudding quietly. The headlines caught
Eyes and the pallid racing forms. I thought
Of nothing but the word *humanity*:
And I was there outside the square of warmth,
In darkness, in the crowds and padding, crying.
Suddenly the creamy shafts of light
Revealed the lion. Slowly it swung its great
Maned head, then—loose, suede, yellow—loped away.
O purposeful and unapproachable!
Then, later his repugnant hangers-on:
A pair of squint hyenas limping past.
This awful ceremony of the doomed, unknown
And innocent victim has its replicas
Embedded in our memories and in
Our history. The archetypal myths
Stirred in my mind.
      The next day over all
The sun was flooding and the sky rose tall.
Where rock had weathered through the soil I saw
A jackal running, barking, turning his head.
Four vultures sat upon the rock and pecked,
And when I neared them flew away on wings
Like hair. They left a purple scrap of skin.
Have I discovered all the plains can show me?
The animals gallop, spring, are beautiful,
And at the end of every day is night.

F. T. Prince (Born 1912)

Frank Templeton Prince spent his childhood in Kimberly, Cape Province, South Africa. He was educated at the Christian Brother's College in Kimberly and then went on to Balliol College, Oxford where he received his B.A. in 1934. After serving in the Intelligence Corps of the English Army from 1940–1946, Prince began a teaching career which took him to several universities both in the United Kingdom and the U. S., including Oxford, Cambridge, and Amherst College. Prince has published nine verse collections including, in his opinion, his best effort to date, *The Doors of Stone: Poems 1938–1962* (1963). He has also edited numerous poetry collections, most notably those of Milton. Prince's development can be divided into two stages. The first, his early work, deals almost exclusively with the physical beauty of South Africa. The second, his work after he came to Europe, is greatly influenced by European culture, especially the Italian Renaissance. Prince is noted for his exquisite sense of language and carefully polished stanzas.

The Tears of a Muse in America

I

Call out, celebrate the beam
Imprisoning and expressing him.
Fix the mature flash for the end but in advance
Fix in the glow of that sense what shall pass.

II

Give him a pale skin, a long hand
A grey eye with deep eyelids, with deep lids.
Complete with a dark mouth the head
Of Veronese's equerry; though of too confident a grace
His gestures, less fine than his limbs. Allow him also
    to sleep much
As with an effect of wantonness. Then he should
    swim and run
Jump horses and touch music, laugh willingly and
    grow
Among plain manners and legalities, and yet
Say where Monongahela and Alleghany
Have woven preparatives, glistening fall or where
New York assembles brittle towers. And let him,
Pleased to accomplish puposes
Alight in loose dress from a car.

III

He arrives thus with the ray of his intelligence
With what may cluster about it, dispositions
Recollections and curiosity, the state
Of reason and vision, the deceits of passion
Play of reserves, reflections, admirations
I am luminously possessed of. And all of which am
   anxious
To acknowledge makes him another of the many-
   minded, another
Exposed and assaulted, active and passive mind
Engaged in an adventure and interesting and interested
In itself by so being. But here solutions bristle
For the case seems to shine out at me from the moment
I grant him all the mind I can; when I in short
Impute to him an intemperate spirit, a proud wit
And in a springing innocence that still cannot undo
   itself
The pallid fire I cannot if I wish, with-hold. He shall
As he does, overpraise and underprize
And outvalue and condemn all those purities and
   powers
Of sight and speech, the so true so rich fleece
Covertly and attentively and often too
Fastidiously and rashly to neglect.
Here the position, action on his part, his going
In a still preserved uncertainty of light
Waits only for my touch: and there I have him
Amid the impunities of the polluted city
I see him in the stale glare of those follies,
Illiterate illuminations run to seed
Irreconcilables and abominables
Of all kinds swallowed, neither good nor bad
Either remembered or forgotten. In the dusk
There appears the full pallor of his looks
Desiring and desiring to desire
And in fine he proceeds, fanned by this dubious flush
In the way I know. It comes to me afresh
There glimmers out of it upon me that I want

Nothing to come of it at once. It glimmers,
It glimmers from the question of how, how shall it fall
The moment of the simple sight? and where
In what green land the simple sorrow? and
Under what boughs beneath whose hand wherever,
As in a fog upon the perfumed Cape,
A falling together of many gleams
Neither remembered nor forgotten and neither
Undesiring nor desiring the moment of despair?
Only say it should all as it will fall, as it fell
Or will have fallen, hanging back but to take place
All at once in the tacit air and on the ground
Of this period: the process
Of confrontation, reflection, resolution
That follows, it is this that will ascend
To the last point of fitted and related clarity.

IV

Caught in that leisurely and transparent train
Of the soft ostensibility of story
His motions and his thoughts are their own net
And while the beam folds on itself I'll not
Deny it is indefensibly too fine.
For as in smooth seas under dawn, whatever
He does he cannot do amiss
Being in these eyes seen aright
As he questionlessly is
In the white air under dawn
If he lives if he dies
He put plays at all escapes
As a dolphin or salmon leaps
And exquisite heresies
But leave the musing surface with a gleam.
So if all else be but conceivable yet
Of a lucidity that lives, himself
Mirrored may be the same,
Antecedents and foils will palliate. For
How idly miraculous

Or of what tortuous glory
In fact this creature was
How should my mere ingenuity relate?
In the great sweetness of which light
I ask if may be I have made
Though in an ecstasy of loss
At the last too little of it? But at least
Since I have seen him clear,
Whether he fondle a golden mare
Which he has ridden through wet woods
Or in the sunlight by the water
Stand silent as a tree, this verse no longer weeps.

The Token

More beautiful than any gift you gave
You were, a child so beautiful as to seem
To promise ruin what no child can have
Or woman give. And so a Roman gem
I choose to be your token: here a laurel
Springs to its young height, hangs a broken limb.
And here a group of women wanly quarrel
At a sale of Cupids. A hawk looks at them.

Anne Ridler (Born 1912)

Anne Ridler was born July 30 in Rugby, Warwickshire, England. She took a diploma in journalism in 1932 from King's College, London and went to work as an editor at Faber and Faber. She has written seven books of poetry, 17 plays, and edited numerous other literary works, including a revision of Michael Roberts' *The Faber Book of Modern Verse* (1951). Her poetic subjects fall into two broad categories: (1) domestic themes and (2) meditations on love, marriage, children, and places. Though not prolific, her quiet yet strong voice takes its cue from Eliot, thus Ridler has distanced herself in tone from much of the poetry which appears in English women's magazines. In 1954 she won the Oscar Blumenthal Prize.

Christmas and Common Birth

Christmas declares the glory of the flesh:
And therefore a European might wish
To celebrate it not in midwinter but in spring,
When physical life is strong,
When the consent to live is forced even on the young,
Juice is in the soil, the leaf, the vein,
Sugar flows to movement in limbs and brain.
Also, before a birth, in nourishing the child,
We turn again to the earth
With unusual longing—to what is rich, wild,
Substantial: scents that have been stored and
    strengthened
In apple lofts, the underwash of woods, and in barns;
Drawn through the lengthened root; pungent in
    cones
(While the fir wood stands waiting; the beech wood
    aspiring,
Each in a different silence), and breaking out in
    spring
With scent sight sound indivisible in song.

Yet if you think again
It is good that Christmas comes at the dark dream of
    the year
That might wish to sleep for ever.
For birth is awaking, birth is effort and pain;
And now at midwinter are the hints, inklings

(Sodden primrose, honeysuckle greening)
That sleep must be broken.
To bear new life or learn to live is an exacting joy:
The whole self must waken; you cannot predict the
    way
It will happen, or master the responses beforehand.
For any birth makes an inconvenient demand;
Like all holy things
It is frequently a nuisance, and its needs never end;
Strange freedom it brings: we should welcome release
From its long merciless rehearsal of peace.

   So Christ comes
At the iron senseless time, comes
To force the glory into frozen veins:
   His warmth wakes
Green life glazed in the pool, wakes
All calm and crystal trance with living pains.

   And each year
In seasonal growth is good—year
That lacking love is a stale story at best;
   By God's birth
All common birth is holy; birth
Is all at Christmas time and wholly blest.

Deus Absconditus

I selfish and forsaken do still long for you
God for whom I was born and should have died:
Like lovers over miles and miles of sea
I lean my heart toward my comfort uselessly;
Did man or God weep out this sundering tide?

Cut off each sense, withdraw to the inmost secret
    place:
This God absconds from every promised land.
To shrink like a mollusc and to find no grace
This is the lot his lovers face.

And yet the worst is, not to seek you; yet the worst
Is not to know our lack of you. O, Love,
By what cords will you draw us? As at first
The cords of a man? Not splendour but the penal flesh
Taken for love, that moves us most.

Who breaks his tryst in a passionate ritual
May burn in a dry tree, a cold poem,
In the weak limbs of a child, so instant and perpetual
In the stranger's face of a father dying,
Tender still but all the while departing.

Here he is endured, here he is adored.
And anywhere. Yet it is a long pursuit,
Carrying the junk and treasure of an ancient
    creed,
To a love who keeps his faith by seeming mute
And deaf, and dead indeed.

For a Christening

Meditation and Invocation

I

In June the early signs,
And after, the steady labour of subcutaneous growth:
Past the danger of dissolution in the third month,
And in the fifth, quickens.
But hidden while the leaves thicken, through the season when
    smooth corn
Grows bearded, through the peeling of the summer's gold fleece;
Hidden but with heart throbbing, while stars sharpen and throb in
    the skies,
While sunsets grow cold and orange, while winter airs are whirled
    and torn;
And at Candlemas with pain is born.
Lying with a right occipital position, what prompts it we may
    never know,

But at the appointed time dives down, down into the light—
Blinding snow-light, piercing the darkest corner with white,
Brightness of prick-eared cyclamen pink against the snow—
So long hidden, so sudden into sight.

II

You are our darling and our foreign guest;
We know all your origins, and this is to know nothing.
Distinguished stranger to whom we offer food and rest;
Yet made of our own natures; yet looked for with such longing.
Helpless wandering hands, the miniature of mine,
Fine skin and furious look and little raging voice—
Your looks are full human, your qualities all hidden:
It is your mere existence we have by heart, and rejoice.
The wide waters of wonder and comprehension pour
Through this narrow weir, and irresistible their power.
The rainbow multiple glory of our humanity cannot pierce
As does the single white beam of your being.
This makes your presence so shattering a grace,
Unsheathed sudddenly from the womb: it was none of our intending
To set in train a miracle; and yet it is merely
Made palpable in you, missed elsewhere by diffusion.
Therefore we adore God-in-our-flesh as a baby:
Whose Being is His Essence, and outside It, illusion.
Later, the fulfilment, the example, death, misprison—
Here the extraordinary fact of Being, which we see
Stripped and simple as the speechless stranger on my knee.

III

Blessing, sleep and grow taller in sleeping.
Lie ever in kind keeping.
Infants curl in a cowrie of peace
And should lie lazy. After this ease,
When the soul out of its safe shell goes,
Stretched as you stretch those knees and toes,
What should I wish you? Intelligence first,

In a credulous age by instruction cursed.
Take from us both what immunity
We have from the germ of the printed lie.
Your father's calm temper I wish you, and
The shaping power of his confident hand.
Much, too, that is different and your own;
And may we learn to leave you alone.
For your part, forgive us the pain of living.
Grow in that harsh sun great-hearted and loving.

Sleep, little honey, then; sleep while the powers
Of the Nine Bright Shiners and the Seven Stars
Harmless, encircle: the natural world
Lifegiving, neutral, unless despoiled
By our greed or scorn. And wherever you sleep—
My arms outgrown—or waking weep,
Life is your lot: you lie in God's hand,
In His terrible mercy, world without end.

A Mile from Eden

With buds embalmed alive in ice,
Flies in amber, the wood lies:
On snow even the shadows are white,
And we walk tipsy with too much light.
In slanting rays, like the damned
Our footsteps flame but make no sound.
While in this waste we wander
I tell him again of the godlike Flounder,
The garish desires of the fisherman's wife
(Desires we saw from the first unsafe,
For the same sin, though tropical,
Is in the Garden and the Fall).
But as I describe the granted glories,
The crowns, candles, golden floors,
I see his longing in his eyes:
Eyes of the humble hoping for Heaven,
Eyes of Adam a mile from Eden.
I see him a child with his joys round him,

One foot still on the coral strand,
The sun like a locket hung from his hand,
Now a man with his griefs about him.

If his hunger is holy, where hers was greed,
Can he always avoid the wish to be God?
Heaven revolves, distant, perfect,
Placid and impregnable as in a Collect;
And we walk in a waste of snows,
Yet see that power before our eyes
Which if we learn its usage can
Break up the amber, reverse the sun,
The bird's-eye glory to full sight
Bring, and outcasts into delight.

Now Philippa Is Gone

Now Philippa is gone, that so divinely
Could strum and sing, and is rufus and gay,
Have we the heart to sing, or at midday
Dive under Trotton Bridge? We shall only
Doze in the yellow spikenard by the wood
And take our tea and melons in the shade.

Piero Della Francesca

The body is not fallen like the soul:
For these are godlike, being
Creatures of flesh, and in that being whole.
Founded on earth, they seem to be built not painted—
These huge girls, the mountain marble and
The valley clays were mixed for them,
The cleanness of lavender and the coolness of sand,
Also the tints of the deep sea;
And from the sea were made
The shell-like apse, and the pillars that echo each other
As waves do, in the Virgin's grey colonnade.

This gentle Jerome, with his Christ nailed
To the brown hill behind his head,
In speech with a stolid Donor, could not be—
Surely—by Manichaean doubts assailed;
In bodily peace this Solomon is wise:
Nothing is tortured, nothing ethereal here,
Nor would transcend the limits of material
Being, for in the flesh is nothing to fear
And nothing to despise.
The singing choir is winged, but who would wish
To fly, whose feet may rest on earth?
Christ with his banner, Christ in Jordan's water,
Not humbled by his human birth.

George Barker (Born 1913)

George Barker was born to an English father, and an Irish mother, on February 26th. When he was six months old his family moved to Chelsea in London where his father worked as a constable. At the age of 14 Barker left secondary school and began to educate himself in the arts and literature; he intended to become a poet. For the next six years he worked at various jobs around London, including stints as a wall paper designer and a garage mechanic.

In 1933 Barker published his first novel, *Alanna Autumnal* and his first book of poetry, *Thirty Preliminary Poems*. He was then introduced to T. S. Eliot who became his life long mentor. With the publication of his second novel, *Janus*, and his second book of poetry, *Poems*, Barker's reputation was set. He married Jessica Woodward and went to live in a Dorset cottage supported by grants from Faber and Faber, the Royal Society of Literature, and the King's Bounty. Barker's magnum opus, *Calamiterror*, a long poem on the anxiety of modern life and the integration of the self, was published in 1937.

1939 marked the beginning of a self-imposed exile for Barker. He traveled to Japan to teach English literature at the Imperial Tohoku University in Sendai. Between 1940 and 1943 Barker resided in the United States, dividing his time between New York and California. During his stay in America he informally ended his marriage. In 1941 his first American publication, *Selected Poems*, appeared. He also wrote a series of book reviews for the *Nation*, and prose and poetry for the *New Republic*. Barker returned to England in 1944, but left for Italy in 1950. Between 1951 and 1959 he spent much of his time in Spain.

Barker's nomadic life-style reveals his attitude toward poetry. Though he was a contemporary of Auden, Spender, and Day Lewis, Barker wrote in the Romantic tradition and believed that a poet creates through suffering: "I am in the grip of a struggle which is far more terrible and far less noisy . . ." Barker differed from many modern English poets in that he was in search of the Ideal; he was a modern romantic caught between the vulgarity of the world and his vision of how the world ought to be. Though largely ignored by contemporary poets and critics, condemned for its romanticism when reviewed, Barker's poetry has enjoyed a revaluation in recent years.

First Cycle of Love Poems

I

This morning take a holiday from unhappiness because
It is the greatest day there ever was
When he stepped down out of the nuptial arch
With the cross in his face and he shall search
For ever for the wreath and not even at his death
Really regret this day that gave him birth.

O history be kind and Time be short to him
Where he is anonymous and let him come to no harm
From the hammer of the diurnal, or the drum,

The sweatbox and the wheel where the dog's dream
Turns and is interminable. O be near always
You whom from far I shall not the less praise!

Let the gentle solstice, like the Fierral Bay
Where the Eleven Thousand Virgins keep
The fishes quiet in their arms, keep him asleep
All his life long in a long summer's day:
With the empty hourglass, the four-leafed clover,
The rock for the resurrection, and much love.

II

Here at my hand here at my heart lie still.
Will then the prince of index finger, your caduceus,
Alight on my lip like a dove on a window sill
Delivering in its claw the symbolic oleander?

Here at my heart here at my hand lie still
Till the dog-rose springs off its beds of bush
To run in circles leaping at your heel,
And nature, happy, curls up at your kiss.

Lie still, lie still, here at my heart lie still
Sleeping like thunderheads. Be over me dominant
So I shall sleep as the river sleeps under the hill
Kissing the foot and giving back the element.

Here at my hand lie still; lie still at my heart.
Sesame is on his tongue and the unicorn rages
Round the abdominal amphitheatre. I hear
His double engines drumming up the passages

O till his cumulus, over the angry bed
Arching, is rainbows. Volplane my bomber
Shuttling silver through the night I bride;
He spins his disc of kisses in my slumber.

And I lie still in heart and hand lie still,
All the streamers of welcome flaunting in my marrow
And flares I lift my arms are, because he will
Come down alighting on my bed like a meadow.

Then here in my heart he lies as dark as pillage
Where in my arms I hold
The murderer who, Samsoning up my five pillars,
Lies quiet now, for here at my heart I fold him.

III

The kiss is maypole where my seven
Happiest sins truss me to the rod:
The lightning cracks my face of heaven
When he leans down, when he leans down like a diver
Out of his breast's cloud.

The flammenwerfer and the fish
And also I acknowledge him creator.
Between his horizon of arms meaures my wish,
My mirage of marriage that, one moment later,
Comes true in a flash.

O at your work you patient hundred thousand
With the hammer, the hour and the pen,
His harder labour is love. He has emblazoned
Everything, overnight everything has blossomed
With Love again.

IV

Then like the ship at rest in the bay
   I drop my sails and come home
To harbour in his arms and stay
    For ever harboured from harm.

On his foot's beach my combers ride
    The vaulted coral where he stands,
And spray against his rock of side
    Showers that fill his hands.

O whirlwinds catching up the sea
    And folding islands in your shawls,
Give him to me, give him to me,
    And I will wrap him in my shallows.

O the Red Sea parted long ago
    When the angel went whistling through,
My seas rise up in pride also
    To let his chariots through.

The masculine cliff-face gazes out
    At the smile of the horizon,
And disregards the sea that flaunts
    Her beauties by the dozen.

So he looks out over my subjugation
    Where the combers coil at his feet,
And sees, the far side of adulation,
My Hesperides rise singing, one moment, from the ocean,
    And the next, sinking, weep.

But from the altitude of his domination
    O sometimes, like waterfalls,
His hand comes down through a gravity of anticipation
    And a constellation of nuptials.

Nightly to his archipelagoes where
    Apples adorn the pillar,
My kiss of fishes moves in schools and bears
    The body to him on a silver platter.

The syzygies, over our Balkan bed,
    Shed silver on the peninsula,
Against whose shores my waters beat their head
    Like rain on a red star.

The narwhal with a spike on its brow
   Spins thrashing through the wave:
His love is mine, who lashes now
   In the sweat of seas I gave.

Then morning, like a monument
   Glittering in a tree,
Reminds me of a former moment
When the first star was immanent
And the mountain, dominant,
   Leaned down and kissed me.

V

My joy, my jockey, my Gabriel
Who bares his horns above my sleep
Is sleeping now. And I shall keep him
In valley and on pinnacle
And marvellous in my tabernacle.

My peace is where his shoulder holds
My clouds among his skies of face;
His plenty is my peace, my peace.
And like a serpent by a boulder
His shade I rest in glory coiled.

Time will divide us, and the sea
Wring its sad hands all day between;
The autumn bring a change of scene.
But always and for ever he
At night will sleep and keep by me.

Galway Bay

With the gulls' hysteria above me
I walked near these breakneck seas
This morning of mists, and saw them,
Tall the mysterious queens
Waltzing in on the broad
Ballroom of the Atlantic.

All veils and waterfalls and
Wailings of the distraught,
These effigies of grief moved
Like refugees over the water;
The icy empresses of the Atlantic
Rising to bring me omen.

These women woven of ocean
And sorrows, these far sea figures,
With the fish and skull in their
Vapour of faces, the icicles
Salting down from their eyelashes,
As I walked by the foreshore

Moved towards me, ululating:
O dragnet of the sweet heart
Bind us no longer! The cage
Bursts with passions and bones,
And every highspirited fish
Lives off our scuttled love!

I stood on a stone, the gulls
Crossed my vision with wings
And my hearing with caterwauling;
The hurdling wave, backbroken,
Died at my feet. Taller
Than the towering hour above me

The homing empresses of the sea
Came among me. And, shivering,
I felt death nuzzling in the nest
Of the diurnally shipwrecked
Drowned nocturnally breast.

Holy Poems
C.B. In Memoriam, June, MCMXXXIX

I

I am Saint John on Patmos of my heart
Towered and tabernacled with illusion;
Black Michaels and gold Satans stand at hand
Gulling me with their gestures of temptation
To bring me down from the marvelous mountains
Where in Babylonian gardens I find
Spinoza's face hanging from every tree
Murmuring love of all our kith and kind:
Or I feel, cold as a draught on my arm,
The spiralling universe like a worm
Coiling for comfort; and in my mind
The three-winged dove among my dreams
Moaning for its apocalyptic home.

II

I bleed Sebastian's brother on the ground,
No good it does me: or I hang my hand
My harp-hand on the Haman tree, but no—
My blood smiles from the ground in pride,
My hand makes music when winds blow.
There is no martyrdom worse than a life,
Nor can it be bought off with a sacrifice.
I cannot cut my body to St. Peter's key,
Or, nipping off the hip-rose with a knife
Make me archangel, nor with a kiss
Claim thirty shillings, for no one will buy
The plaster Jesus that my master is,
Crossed on my pain and crucified in my eye.

III

The monarch who wears a shrieking crown
Is us. All whipping tongues and words
Flash at our head and doom us down:
The sex of our cherubim is swords.
When we step down out of our beds or doors
The burning bush springs up between our feet;
Our smile is bright with tiger, and the days
Turn us like dogs in their drums. Then comes
Spinning and shining among us like wheels,
Throwing off visions to lead us home,
God—snatches me up in finger and thumb,
Douses me like a glimmer, And I see
Cruel to be kind to all his kind is he.

News of the World II

In the first year of the last disgrace
    Peace, turning her face away,
Coughing in laurelled fires, weeping,
    Drags out from her hatcheted heart
    The sunset axe of the day.

And leaning up against the red sky
    She mourns over evening cities:
The milky morning springs from her mothering
        breast
    Half choked with happy memories
    And fulfilment of miseries.

'I am the wife of the workman world
    With an apron full of children—
And happy, happy any hovel was
    With my helping hand under his gifted head
    And for my sleep his shoulder.

'I wish that the crestfallen stars would fall
   Out of his drunken eye and strike
My children cold. I wish the big sea
   Would pity them, and pity me,
   And smother us all alike.

'Bitter sun, bitter sun, put out your lions
   As I have put out my hope.
For he will take them in his clever hand
And teach them how to dismember love
   Just as though it was Europe.

'O washing-board Time, my hands are sore
   And the backs of the angels ache.
For the redhanded husband has abandoned me
To drag his coat in front of his pride,
   And I know my heart will break.

In the first year of the last disgrace
   Peace, turning her face away,
Coughing in fire and laurels, weeping,
   Bared again her butchered heart
   To the sunrise axe of the day.

News of the World III

Let her lie naked here, my hand resting
Light on her broken breast, the sleeping world
Given into our far from careful keeping,
Terrestrial daughter of a disaster of waters
No master honours. Let her lie to-night
Attended by those visions of bright swords
That never defended but ended life.
My emerald trembler, my sky skipping scullion,
See, now, your sister, dipping into the horizon,
Leaves us in darkness; you, nude, and I
Seeking to loose what the day retrieves,
An immoderation of love. Bend your arm
Under my generation of heads. The seas enfold

My sleepless eye and save it weeping
For the dishonoured star. I hear your grave
Nocturnal lamentation, where, abandoned, far,
You, like Arabia in her tent, mourn through an
    evening
Of wildernesses. O what are you grieving for?
From the tiara'd palaces of the Andes
And the last Asiatic terraces, I see
The wringing of the hands of all of the world,
I hear your long lingering disillusion.
Favour the viper, heaven, with one vision
That it may see what is lost. The crime is blended
With the time and the cause. But at your
Guilty and golden bosom, O daughter of laws,
I happy lie to-night, the fingering zephyr
Light and unlikely as a kiss. The shades creep
Out of their holes and graves for a last
Long look at your bare empire as it rolls
Its derelict glory away into darkness. Turn, liar,
Back. Our fate is in your face. Whom do you love
But those whom you doom to the happy disgrace
Of adoring you with degradations? I garb my wife,
The wide world of a bride, in devastations.
She has curled up in my hand, and, like a moth,
Died a legend of splendour along the line of my life.
But the congregation of clouds paces in dolour
Over my head and her never barren belly
Where we lie, summered, together, a world and I.
Her birdflecked hair, sunsetting the weather,
Feathers my eye, she shakes an ear-ring sky,
And her hand of a country trembles against me.
The glittering nightriders gambol through
A zodiac of symbols above our love
Promising, O my star-crossed, death and disasters.
But I want breath for nothing but your possession
Now, now, this summer midnight, before the dawn
Shakes its bright gun in the sky, before
The serried battalions of lies and organizations of
    hate

Entirely encompass us, buried; before the wolf and
    friend
Renders us enemies. Before all this,
Lie one night in my arms and give me peace.

Resolution of Dependence

We poets in our youth begin in gladness
But thereof come in the end despondency and madness.
    (Wordsworth: *Resolution and Independence*)

I encountered the crowd returning from amusements,
The Bournemouth Pavilion, or the marvellous
    gardens,
The Palace of Solace, the Empyrean Cinema: and
    saw
William Wordsworth was once, tawdrily conspicuous,
Obviously emulating the old man of the mountain-
    moor,
Traipsing along on the outskirts of the noisy crowd.
Remarkable I reflected that after all it is him.
The layers of time falling continually on Grasmere
    Churchyard,
The accumulation of year and year like calendar,
The acute superstition that Wordsworth is after all
    dead,
Should have succeeded in keeping him quiet and
    cold.
I resent the resurrection when I feel the updraft of
    fear.

But approaching me with a watch in his hand, he
    said:
'I fear you are early; I expected a man; I see
That already your private rebellion has been quelled.
Where are the violent gestures of the individualist?
I observe the absence of the erratic, the strange;
Where is the tulip, the rose, or the bird in hand?'

I had the heart to relate the loss of my charms,
The paradise pets I kept in my pocket, the bird,
The tulip trumpet, the penis water pistol;
I had the heart to have mourned them, but no word.
'I have done little reading,' I murmured, 'I have
Most of the time been trying to find an eqation.'

He glanced over my shoulder at the evening
    promenade.
The passing people, like Saint Vitus, averted their
    eyes:
I saw his eyes like a bent pin searching for eyes
To grip and catch. 'It is a species', he said,
'I feel I can hardly cope with—it is ghosts,
Trailing, like snails, an excrement of blood.
'I passed my hand like a postman's into them;
The information I dropped in at once dropped out.'
'No,' I answered, 'they received your bouquet of
    daffodils,
They speak of your feeling for Nature even now.'
He glanced at his watch. I admired a face.
The town clock chimed like a cat in a well.

'Since the private rebellion, the personal turn,
Leads down to the river with the dead cat and dead
    dog,
Since the single act of protest like a foggy film
Looks like women bathing, the Irish Lakes, or Saint
    Vitus,
Susceptible of innumerable interpretations,
I can only advise a suicide or a resolution.'

'I can resolve,' I answered, 'if you can absolve.
Relieve me of my absurd and abysmal past.'
'I cannot relieve or absolve—the only absolution
Is final resolution to fix on the facts.
I mean more and less than Birth and Death; I also
    mean
The mechanical paraphernalia in between.

'Not you and not him, not me, but all of them.
It is the conspiracy of five hundred million
To keep alive and kick. This is the resolution,
To keep us alive and kicking with strength or joy.
The past's absolution is the present's resolution.
The equation is the interdependence of parts.'

Sacred Elegy V

I

These errors loved no less than the saint loves arrows
Repeat, Love has left the world. He is not here.
O God, like Love revealing yourself in absence
So that, though farther than stars, like Love that sorrows
In separation, the desire in the heart of hearts
To come home to you makes you most manifest.
The booming zero spins as his halo where
Ashes of pride on all the tongues of sense
Crown us with negatives. O deal us in our deserts
The crumb of falling vanity. It is eucharist.

II

Everyone walking everywhere goes in a glow
Of geometrical progression, all meteors, in praise:
Hosannas on the tongues of the dumb shall raise
Roads for the gangs in chains to return to
God. They go hugging the traumas like halleluias
To the bodies that earn this beatitude. The Seven
Seas they crowd like the great sailing clippers,
Those homing migrants that, with their swallow-like sails set,
Swayed forward along the loneliness that opposed,
For nothing more than a meeting in heaven.

III

Therefore all things, in all three tenses,
Alone like the statue in an alcove of love,
Moving in obedient machinery, sleeping
Happy in impossible achievements, keeping
Close to each other because the night is dark;
The great man dreaming on the stones of circumstances,
The small wringing hands because rocks will not move:
The beast in its red kingdom, the star in its arc:
O all things, therefore, in shapes or in senses,
Know that they exist in the kiss of his Love.

IV

Incubus. Anaesthetist with glory in a bag,
Foreman with a sweatbox and a whip. Asphyxiator
Of the ecstatic. Sergeant with a grudge
Against the lost lovers in the park of creation,
Fiend behind the fiend behind the fiend behind the
Friend. Mastodon with mastery, monster with an ache
At the tooth of the ego, the dead drunk judge:
Wheresover Thou art our agony will find Thee
Enthroned on the darkest altar of our heartbreak
Perfect. Beast, brute, bastard. O dog my God!

Sonnet of Fishes

Bright drips the morning from its trophied nets
Looped along a sky flickering fish and wings,
Cobbles like salmon crowd up waterfalling
Streets where life dies thrashing as the sea forgets,
True widow, what she has lost; and, ravished, lets
The knuckledustered sun shake bullying
A fist of glory over her. Everything,
Even the sly night, gives up its lunar secrets.

And I with pilchards cold in my pocket make
Red-eyed a way to bed, But in my blood
Crying I hear, still, the leap of the silver diver
Caught in four cords after his fatal strake:
And then, the immense imminence not understood,
Death, in a dark, in a deep, in a dream, for ever.

Summer Idyll

Sometimes in summer months, the matrix earth
Loaded to gold, the boughs arching downward
Burdened, the shallow and glucose streams
Teeming, flowers out, all gold camouflage
Of the collusive summer; but under the streams
Winter lies coldly, and coldly embedded in
The corn hunger lies germinally, want under
The abundance, poverty pulling down
The tautened boughs, and need is the seed.

Robe them in superb summer, at angles
Their bones penetrate, or with a principality
Of Spring possess them, under the breast
Space of a vacancy spreads like a foul
Ghost flower, want; and the pressure upon
The eyeball of their spirits, upon the organs
Of their spare bodies, the pressure upon
Their movement and their merriment, loving and
Living, the pressure upon their lives like deep
Seas, becomes insufferable.

Sometimes the summer lessens a moment the pressure.
Large as the summer rose some rise
Bathing in rivers or at evening harrying rabbits,
Indulging in games in meadows—and some are idle, strewn
Over the parks like soiled paper like summer
Insects, bathed in sweat or at evening harried
By watchmen, park-keepers, policemen—indulge in games
Dreaming as I dream of rest and cleanliness and cash.

And the gardens exhibit the regalia of the season
Like debutante queans, between which they wander
Blown with vague odours, seduced by the pure
Beauty, like drowned men floating in bright coral.
Summer, denuding young women, also denudes
Them, removes jackets, exposing backs—
Summer moves many up the river in boats

Trailing their fingers in the shadowed water; they
Too move by the river, and in the water shadows
Trail a hand, which need not find a bank,
Face downward, like bad fruit. Cathedrals and Building
Societies, as they appear, disappear; and Beethoven
Is played more loudly to deafen the Welsh echoes,
And Summer, blowing over the Mediterranean
Like swans, like perfect swans.

Summer Song

I looked into my heart to write
    And found a desert there.
But when I looked again I heard
Howling and proud in every word
    The hyena despair.

Great summer sun, great summer sun,
    All loss burns in trophies;
And in the cold sheet of the sky
Lifelong the fishlipped lovers lie
    Kissing catastrophes.

O loving garden where I lay
    When under the breasted tree
My son stood up behind my eyes
And groaned: Remember that the price
    Is vinegar for me.

Great summer sun, great summer sun,
    Turn back to the designer:
I would not be the one to start
The breaking day and the breaking heart
    For all the grief in China.

My one, my one, my only love,
    Hide, hide your face in a leaf,
And let the hot tear falling burn
The stupid heart that will not learn
    The everywhere of grief.

Great summer sun, great summer sun,
    Turn back to the never-never
Cloud-cuckoo, happy, far-off land
Where all the love is true love, and
    True love goes on for ever.

To My Mother

Most near, most dear, most loved and most far,
Under the window where I often found her
Sitting as huge as Asia, seismic with laughter,
Gin and chicken helpless in her Irish hand,
Irresistible as Rabelais, but most tender for
The lame dogs and hurt birds that surround her,—
She is a procession no one can follow after
But be like a little dog following a brass band.

She will not glance up at the bomber, or condescend
To drop her gin and scuttle to the cellar,
But lean on the mahogany table like a mountain
Whom only faith can move, and so I send
O all my faith and all my love to tell her
That she will move from mourning into morning.

Muriel Rukeyser (1913–1980)

Muriel Rukeyser was born December 25, in New York City. Her father, Lawrence Rukeyser, a construction engineer, introduced his daughter to the technology which would dominate her early poems. She was educated at the Ethical Culture School, the Fieldston School, and attended Vassar College from 1930 to 1932. In 1935 Rukeyser worked as an editor and wrote verse commentaries for photographs appearing in *Coronet* and *Life* magazines. Her first collection of poetry, *Theory of Flight* won the Yale Younger Poets Prize in 1935. She has also won the Oscar Blumenthal Prize (1940), the Harriet Monroe Poetry Award (1941), and was elected to the National Institute for Arts and Letters in 1967. Always politically active, Rukeyser was arrested in Alabama in 1933 while she reported on the Scottsboro trials; she visited Hanoi in 1972 and was jailed that same year in Washington D.C. in protest of the Vietnam war. Rukeyser has written 25 collections of verse, and numerous filmscripts, translations, and plays.

Boy with His Hair Cut Short

Sunday shuts down on this twentieth-century evening.
The El passes. Twilight and bulb define
the brown room, the overstuffed plum sofa,
the boy, and the girl's thin hands above his head.
A neighbor radio sings stocks, news, serenade.

He sits at the table, head down, the young clear neck
      exposed,
watching the drugstore sign from the tail of his eye;
tattoo, neon, until the eye blears, while his
solicitous tall sister, simple in blue, bending
behind him, cuts his hair with her cheap shears.

The arrow's electric red always reaches its mark,
successful neon! He coughs, impressed by that precision.
His child's forehead, forever protected by his cap,
is bleached against the lamplight as he turns head
and steadies to let the snippets drop.

Erasing the failure of weeks with level fingers,
she sleeks the fine hair, combing: "You'll look fine tomorrow!
You'll surely find something, they can't keep turning you down;
the finest gentleman's not so trim as you!" Smiling, he raises
the adolescent forehead wrinkling ironic now.

He sees his decent suit laid out, new-pressed,
his carfare on the shelf. He lets his head fall, meeting
her earnest hopeless look, seeing the sharp blades splitting,
the darkened room, the impersonal sign, her motion,
the blue vein, bright on her temple, pitifully beating.

Mediterranean

On the evening of July 25, 1936, five days after the outbreak of the Spanish civil war, the Americans with the anti-fascist Olympic games were evacuated from Barcelona at the order of the Catalonian government. In a small Spanish boat, the *Ciudad di Ibiza*, which the Belgians had chartered, they and a group of five hundred, including the Hungarian and Belgian teams as well as the American, sailed overnight to Sète, the first port in France. The only men who remained were those who had volunteered in the loyalist forces: the core of the future International Brigades.

I

At the end of July, exile. We watched the gangplank go
cutting the boat away, indicating: sea.

Barcelona, the sun, the fire-bright harbor, war.
Five days.

    Here at the rail, foreign and refugee,
we saw the city, remembered that zero of attack,
chase in the groves, snares through the olive hills,
rebel defeat: leaders, two regiments,
broadcasts of victory, tango, surrender.
The truckride to the city, barricades,
bricks pried at corners, rifle-shot in street,
car-burning, bombs, blank warnings, fists up, guns
busy sniping, the torn walls, towers of smoke.
And order making, committees taking charge, foreigners
commanded out by boat.

I saw the city, sunwhite flew on glass,
trucewhite from window, the personal lighting found
eyes on the dock, sunset-lit faces of singers,
eyes, goodbye into exile. Saw where Columbus rides
black-pillared: discovery, turn back, explore
a new-found Spain, coast-province, city-harbor.
Saw our parades ended, the last marchers on board
listed by nation.

I saw first of those faces going home into war
the brave man, Otto Boch, the German exile, knowing
he quieted tourists during machine-gun battle,
he kept his life straight as a single issue—
left at that dock we left, his gazing Brueghel face,
square forehead and eyes, strong square breast fading,
the narrow runner's hips diminishing dark.
I see this man, dock, war, a latent image.

The boat *Ciudad di Ibiza,* built for two hundred,
loaded with five hundred, manned by loyal sailors,
chartered by Belgians when consulates were helpless,
through a garden of gunboats, margin of the port,
entered: Mediterranean.

II

Frontier of Europe, the tideless sea, a field of power
touching desirable coasts, rocking in time conquests,
fertile, the moving water maintains its boundaries,
layer on layer, Troy-seven civilized worlds,
Egypt, Greece, Rome, jewel Jerusalem,
giant feudal Spain, giant England, this last war.

The boat pulled into evening, underglaze blue
flared instant fire, blackened towards Africa.
Over the city alternate light occurred;
   and pale
in the pale sky emerging stars.
No city now, a besieged line of light
masking the darkness where the country lay,

but we knew guns
bright through mimosa
singe of powder
and reconnoitering plane
flying anonymous
scanning the Pyrenees
tall black above the Catalonian sea.

Boat of escape, dark on the water, hastening, safe,
holding non-combatants, the athlete, the child,
the printer, the boy from Antwerp, the black boxer,
lawyer and Communist.
    The games had not been held.

A week of games, theater and festival;
world anti-fascist week. Pistol starts race.
Machine-gun marks the war. Answered unarmed,
charged the Embarcadero, met those guns.
And charging through the province, joined that army.
Boys from the hills, the unmatched guns,
the clumsy armored cars.
Drilled in the bullring. Radio cries:
To Saragossa! And this boat.

Escape, dark on the water, an overloaded ship.
Crowded the deck. Spoke little. Down to dinner.
Quiet on sea: no guns.
The printer said, In Paris there is time,
but where's its place now; where is poetry?

This is the sea of war; the first frontier
blank on the maps, blank sea; Minoan boats
maybe achieved this shore;
mountains whose slope divides
one race, old insurrections, Narbo, now
moves at the colored beach
destroyer, wardog. "Do not burn the church,
compañeros, it is beautiful. Besides,
it brings tourists." They smashed only the image
madness and persecution.

Exterminating wish; they forced the door,
lifted the rifle, broke the garden window,
removed only the drawings: cross and wrath.
Whenever we think of these, the poem is,
that week, the beginning, exile
remembered in continual poetry.

Voyage and exile, a midnight cold return,
dark to our left mountains begin the sky.
There, pointed the Belgian, I heard a pulse of war,
sharp guns while I ate grapes in the Pyrenees.
Alone, walking to Spain, the five o'clock of war.
In those cliffs run the sashed and sandaled men,
capture the car, arrest the priest, kill captain,
fight our war.
The poem is the fact, memory falls
under and seething lifts and will not pass.

Here is home-country, who fights our war.
Street-meeting speaker to us:
". . . came for games,
  you stay for victory; foreign? your job is:
  go tell your countries what you saw in Spain."
The dark unguarded army left all night.
M. de Paîche said, "We can learn from Spain."
The face on the dock that turned to find the war.

III

Seething, and falling black, a sea of stars,
black marked with virile silver. Peace all night,
over that land, planes
death-lists——a frantic bandage
the rubber tires burning——monuments,
sandbag, overturned wagon, barricade
girl's hand with gun——food failing, water failing
the epidemic threat
the date in a diary——a blank page opposite
no entry—

however, met
the visible enemy heroes: madness, infatuation
the cache in the crypt, the breadline shelled,
the yachtclub arsenal, the foreign check.
History racing from an assumed name, peace,
a time used to perfect weapons.

If we had not seen fighting
if we had not looked there
   the plane flew low
   the plaster ripped by shot
   the peasant's house
if we had stayed in our world
between the table and the desk
between the town and the suburb
slow disintegration
male and female
If we had lived in our cities
sixty years might not prove
   the power this week
   the overthrown past
   tourist and refugee
Emeric in the bow speaking his life
and the night on this ship
and the night over Spain
quick recognition
male and female

And the war in peace, the war in war, the peace,
the face on the dock
the faces in those hills.

IV

Near the end now, morning. Sleepers cover the decks,
cabins full, corridors full of sleep. But the light
vitreous, crosses water; analyzed darkness
crosshatched in silver, passes up the shore,
touching limestone massif, deserted tableland,
bends with the down-warp of the coastal plain.

The colored sun stands on the route to Spain,
builds on the waves a series of mirrors
and on the scorched land rises hot.
Coasts change their names as the boat goes to
France, Costa Brava softens to Côte Vermeil,
Spain's horizon ghost behind the shapeless sea.

Blue praising black, a wind above the waves
moves pursuing a jewel, this hieroglyph
boat passing under the sun to lose it on the
attractive sea, habitable and old.
A barber sun, razing three races; met
from the north with a neurotic eagerness.

They rush to the solar attraction; local daybreak finds
them on the red earth of the colored cliffs; the little islands
tempt worshipers, gulf-purple, pointed bay;
we crowd the deck,
welcome the islands with a sense of loss.

V

The wheel in the water, green, behind my head.
Turns with its light-spokes. Deep. And the drowning eyes
find under the water figures near
in their true picture, moving true,
the picture of that war enlarging clarified
as the boat perseveres away, always enlarging,
to become clear.

Boat of escape, your water-photograph.
I see this man, dock, war, a latent image.
And at my back speaking the black boxer,
telling his education: porter, fighter, no school,
no travel but this, the trade union sent a team.
I saw Europe break apart
and artifice or martyr's will
cannot anneal this war, nor make
the loud triumphant future start
shouting from its tragic heart.

Deep in the water the Spanish shadows turn,
assume their brightness past a cruel lens,
quick vision of loss. The pastoral lighting takes
the boat, deck, passengers, the pumice cliffs,
the winedark sweatshirt at my shoulder.
Cover away the fighting cities
but still your death-afflicted eyes
must hold the print of flowering guns,
bombs whose insanity craves size,
the lethal breath, the iron prize.

The clouds upon the water-barrier pass,
the boat may turn to land; these shapes endure,
rise up into our eyes, to bind
us back; an accident of time
set it upon us, exile burns it in.
Once the fanatic image shown,
enemy to enemy,
past and historic peace wear thin;
hypocrite sovereignties go down
before this war the age must win.

VI

The sea produced that town: Sète, which the boat turns to,
at peace. Its breakwater, casino, vermouth factory, beach.
They searched us for weapons. No currency went out.
The sign of war was the search for cameras,
pesetas and photographs go back to Spain,
the money for the army. Otto is fighting now, the lawyer said.
No highlight hero. Love's not a trick of light.

But.—The town lay outside, peace, France.
And in the harbor the Russian boat *Schachter*;
sharp paint-smell, the bruise-colored shadow swung
under its side. Signaling to our decks
sailors with fists up, greeting us, asking news,
making the harbor real.
          Barcelona.

Slow-motion splash. Anchor. Small from the beach
the boy paddles to meet us, legs hidden in canoe,
curve of his blade that drips.
Now gangplank falls to dock.
          Barcelona
everywhere, Spain everywhere, the cry of planes for Spain.
The picture at our eyes, past memory, poems,
to carry and spread and daily justify.
The single issue, the live man standing tall,
on the hill, the dock, the city, all the war.
Exile and refugee, we land, we take
nothing negotiable out of the new world;
we believe, we remember, we saw.
Mediterranean gave
image and peace, tideless for memory.

For that beginning
make of us each
a continent and inner sea
Atlantis buried outside
to be won.

More of a Corpse Than a Woman

Give them my regards when you go to the school reunion;
and at the marriage-supper, say that I'm thinking about them.
They'll remember my name; I went to the movies with that one,
feeling the weight of their death where she sat at my elbow;
      she never said a word,
      but all of them were heard.

All of them alike, expensive, girls, the leaden friends:
one used to play the piano, one of them once wrote a sonnet,
one even seemed awakened enough to photograph wheatfields—
the dull girls with the educated minds and technical passions—
      pure love was their employment,
      they tried it for enjoyment.

Meet them at the boat: they've brought the souvenirs of boredom,
a seashell from the faltering monarchy;
the nose of a marble saint; and from the battlefield,
an empty shell divulged from a flower-bed.
        The lady's wealthy breath
        perfumes the air with death.

The leaden lady faces the fine, voluptuous woman,
faces a rising world bearing its gifts in its hands.
Kisses her casual dreams upon the lips she kisses,
risen, she moves away; takes others; moves away.
        Inadequate to love,
        supposes she's enough.

Give my regards to the well-protected woman,
I knew the ice-cream girl, we went to school together.
There's something to bury, people, when you begin to bury.
When your women are ready and rich in their wish for the world,
        destroy the leaden heart,
        we've a new race to start.

Reading Time: 1 Minute 26 Seconds

The fear of poetry is the
fear: mystery and fury of a midnight street
of windows whose low voluptuous voice
issues, and after that there is no peace.

That round waiting moment in the
theatre: curtain rises, dies into the ceiling
and here is played the scene with the mother
bandaging a revealed son's head. The bandage is torn off.
Curtain goes down. And here is the moment of proof.

That climax when the brain acknowledges the world,
all values extended into the blood awake.
Moment of proof. And as they say Brancusi did,
building his bird to extend through soaring air,
as Kafka planned stories that draw to eternity
through time extended. And the climax strikes.

Love touches so, that months after the look of
blue stare of love, the footbeat on the heart
is translated into the pure cry of birds
following air-cries, or poems, the new scene.
Moment of proof. That strikes long after act.

They fear it. They turn away, hand up palm out
fending off moment of proof, the straight look, poem.
The prolonged wound-consciousness after the bullet's shot.
The prolonged love after the look is dead,
the yellow joy after the song of the sun,
aftermath proof, extended radiance.

Delmore Schwartz (1913–1966)

Delmore Schwartz was born December 8, in New York City, the eldest of two sons. His parents had a very unhappy marriage, finally separating when Schwartz was still young. Despite a traumatic homelife, he was an enthusiastic, albeit erratic, student at George Washington High School. He graduated with a B.A. in philosophy from New York University in 1935 and went on to Harvard with the intention of becoming a professional philosopher. Though Schwartz was encouraged by the likes of Alfred North Whitehead, he left Harvard in 1937 without taking a degree. He claimed that he left school because he was "bursting with the book he had to get out so that he could then marry the girl." The real reason, however, may have been his failure to procure a fellowship. In any case, "the book" was Schwartz' 1938 masterpiece, *In Dreams Begin Responsibilities*. The greatest writers of the thirties—Wallace Stevens, Mark Van Doren, John Crowe Ransom, Philip Rahv, and even W. H. Auden—lined up to praise his first work. It was the first collection to capture the disillusionment of America in the thirties, especially the malaise of first generation Americans.

With the critical success of *In Dreams Begin Responsibilities*, Schwartz returned to Harvard as the Briggs-Copeland Instructor of English Composition. He remained at Harvard until 1947. In the meantime he became one of the editors at the *Partisan Review* and came out with his second book, *Genesis* (1943). Schwartz was greatly disappointed at the reaction to his second effort, for while a few critics were complimentary, most were merciless in their attacks. This was due to at least two factors: (1) the instant recognition of his first book had made many people in literary circles jealous; (2) *In Dreams Begin Responsibilities* was the best work Schwartz ever did, and though *Genesis* is a fine book by most standards, it pales in comparison to its predecessor. Nevertheless, Schwartz, always fearful that he would lose his talent, began to exhibit the manic-depressive traits which would later consume his personality and cause him to end his career.

His 1948 collection of short stories, *The World is a Wedding*, met with better critical appraisal, but was not a financial success. From 1949 to 1957, Schwartz taught at various universities including Princeton and Kenyon College. He was a consultant with New Directions Publishers and the poetry editor and film critic of the *New Republic*. His one published book during this period, *Vaudeville for a Princess*, was not received warmly and Schwartz sunk deeper and deeper into alcoholism, paranoia, and manic-depression.

The end of the fifties brought Schwartz a brief reprieve. His *Summer Knowledge* (1959) was praised for breaking with his former analytical style and exploring free verse and intuitive knowledge, (hence the title). He was awarded the Bollingen Prize in 1960, the youngest poet ever to receive that prestigious honor. Schwartz taught at Syracuse University from 1962 to 1965 but was not tenured due to his aberrant behavior. He began to frequent the seedy hotels off New York's Times Square and on July 11, 1966 died of a heart attack in the Hotel Dixie.

For One Who Would Not Take His Life in His Hands

Athlete, virtuoso,
Training for happiness,
Bend arm and knee, and seek
The body's sharp distress;
For pain is pleasure's cost,
Denial is the route
To speech before the millions
Or personal with the flute.

The ape and great Achilles,
Heavy with their fate,
Batter doors down, strike
Small children at the gate;
Driven by love to this,
As knock-kneed Hegel said,
To seek with a sword for peace
That the child may be lifted from
The recent dead.

"Ladies and Gentlemen," said
The curious Socrates,
"I have asked: What is this life
But a childermass,
As Abraham recognized,
A working with the knife
At animal, maid, and stone
Until we have cut down
All but the soul alone:
Through hate we come to love,
No other means is known."

The Heavy Bear Who Goes with Me

"the withness of the body"
Whitehead

The heavy bear who goes with me,
A manifold honey to smear his face,
Clumsy and lumbering here and there,
The central ton of every place,
The hungry beating brutish one
In love with candy, anger, and sleep,
Crazy factotum, dishevelling all,
Climbs the building, kicks the football,
Boxes his brother in the hate-ridden city.

Breathing at my side, that heavy animal,
That heavy bear who sleeps with me,
Howls in his sleep for a world of sugar,
A sweetness intimate as the water's clasp,
Howls in his sleep because the tight-rope
Trembles and shows the darkness beneath.
—The strutting show-off is terrified,
Dressed in his dress-suit, bulging his pants,
Trembles to think that his quivering meat
Must finally wince to nothing at all.

That inescapable animal walks with me,
Has followed me since the black womb held,
Moves where I move, distorting my gesture,
A caricature, a swollen shadow,
A stupid clown of the spirit's motive,
Perplexes and affronts with his own darkness,
The secret life of belly and bone,
Opaque, too near, my private, yet unknown,
Stretches to embrace the very dear
With whom I would walk without him near,
Touches her grossly, although a word
Would bare my heart and make me clear,
Stumbles, flounders, and strives to be fed
Dragging me with him in his mouthing care,
Amid the hundred million of his kind,
The scrimmage of appetite everywhere.

The Starlight's Intuitions Pierced the Twelve

The starlight's intuitions pierced the twelve,
The brittle night sky sparkled like a tune
Tinkled and tapped out on the xylophone.
Empty and vain, a glittering dune, the moon
Arose too big, and, in the mood which ruled,
Seemed like a useless beauty in a pit;
And then one said, after he carefully spat:
"No matter what we do, he looks at it!

"I cannot see a child or find a girl
Beyond his smile which glows like that spring moon."
"—Nothing no more the same," the second said,
"Though all may be forgiven, never quite healed
The wound I bear as witness, standing by;
No ceremony surely appropriate,
Nor secret love, escape or sleep because
No matter what I do, he looks at it—"

"Now," said the third, "no thing will be the same:
I am as one who never shuts his eyes,
The sea and sky no more are marvellous,
I know no more true freshness or surprise!"
"Now," said the fourth, "nothing will be enough,
—I heard his voice accomplishing all wit:
No word can be unsaid, no deed withdrawn,
—No matter what is said, he measures it!"

"Vision, imagination, hope or dream
Believed, denied, the scene we wished to see?
It does not matter in the least: for what
Is altered if it is not true? That we
Saw goodness, as it is—*this* is the awe
And the abyss which we will not forget,
His story now the skull which holds all thought:
No matter what I think, I think of it!"

"And I will never be what once I was,"
Said one for long as single as a knife,
"And we will never be as once we were;
We have died once, this is a second life."
"My mind is spilled in moral chaos," one
Righteous as Job exclaimed, "now infinite
Suspicion of my heart stems what I will,
—No matter what I choose, he stares at it!"

"I am as one native in summer places,
—Ten weeks' excitement paid for by the rich;
Debauched by that, and then all winter bored,"
The sixth declared, "his peak left us a ditch."
"He came to make this life more difficult,"
The seventh said, "No one will ever fit
His measures' heights, all is inadequate:
No matter what we have, what good is it?"

"He gave forgiveness to us: what a gift!"
The eighth chimed in. "But now we know *how much*
Must be forgiven. But if forgiven, what?
The crime which was will be; and the least touch
Revives the memory: what is forgiveness worth?"
The ninth spoke thus: "Who now will ever sit
At ease in Zion at the Easter feast?
No matter what the place, he touches it!"

"And I will always stammer, since he spoke,"
One, who had been most eloquent, said, stammering,
"I looked too long at the sun; like too much light,
Too much of goodness is a boomerang,"
Laughed the eleventh of the troop, "I must
Try what he tried: I saw the infinite
Who walked the lake and raised the hopeless dead:
No matter what the feat, he first accomplished it!"

So spoke the twelfth; and then the twelve in chorus:
"Unspeakable unnatural goodness is
Risen and shines, and never will ignore us;
He glows forever in all consciousness;
Forgiveness, love, and hope possess the pit,
And bring our endless guilt, like shadow's bars:
No matter what we do, he stares at it!
What pity can each deny? what debt defer?
We know he looks at us like all the stars,
And we shall never be as once we were,
This life will never be what once it was!"

Karl Shapiro (Born 1913)

Karl Shapiro was born November 10 in Baltimore. Shapiro was a poor student and only lasted one semester at the University of Virginia. In 1932 he decided to educate himself in the arts. He privately printed a collection of poetry, *Poems*, in 1935 which won him a scholarship to Johns Hopkins University in 1937. Shapiro lost the scholarship in 1939 due to a poor grade in history. An ardent anti-intellectual, he dropped out to devote himself to poetry. In the same year, 1941, that he was drafted into the United States Army, many of his poems which were published in various magazines, most notably *Poetry*, were collected in the New Directions anthology *Five Young American Poets*. While serving in the military Shapiro's career as a poet flourished. He won the Jeanette Sewell Davis Prize (1942), the Levinson Prize (1943), the Contemporary American Poetry Prize (1944), and the Pulitzer Prize (1945). In 1944 Shapiro published what is perhaps his most famous collection, *V-Letter and Other Poems*. After being discharged from the army in 1946, Shapiro taught at Johns Hopkins University. He became editor of *Poetry* magazine in 1950 and editor of *Prairie Schooner* in 1956. He won the Bollingen Prize with John Berryman in 1969. Shapiro has taught at various universities across the country and is the author of one novel, *Edsel*, and one film, *Karl Shapiro's America*.

The Dome of Sunday

With focus sharp as Flemish-painted face
In film of varnish brightly fixed
And through a polished hand-lens deeply seen,
Sunday at noon through hyaline thin air
Sees down the street,
And in the camera of my eye depicts
Row-houses and row-lives:
Glass after glass, door after door the same,
Face after face the same, the same,
The brutal visibility the same;

As if one life emerging from one house
Would pause, a single image caught between
Two facing mirrors where vision multiplies
Beyond perspective,
A silent clatter in the high-speed eye
Spinning out photo-circulars of sight.

I see slip to the curb the long machines
Out of whose warm and windowed rooms pirouette
Shellacked with silk and light
The hard legs of our women.
Our women are one woman, dressed in black.
The carmine printed mouth
And cheeks as soft as muslin-glass belong

Outright to one dark dressy man,
Merely a swagger at her curvy side.
This is their visit to themselves:
All day from porch to porch they weave
A nonsense pattern through the even glare,
Stealing in surfaces
Cold vulgar glances at themselves.

And high up in the heated room all day
I wait behind the plate glass pane for one,
Hot as a voyeur for a glimpse of one,
The vision to blot out this woman's sheen;
All day my sight records expensively
Row-houses and row-lives.

But nothing happens; no diagonal
With melting shadow falls across the curb:
Neither the blinded negress lurching through fatigue,
Nor exiles bleeding from their pores,
Nor that bright bomb slipped lightly from its rack
To splinter every silvered glass and crystal prism,
Witch-bowl and perfume bottle
And billion candle-power dressing-bulb,
No direct hit to smash the shatter-proof
And lodge at last the quivering needle
Clean in the eye of one who stands transfixed
In fascination of her brightness.

Elegy for a Dead Soldier

I

A white sheet on the tail-gate of a truck
Becomes an altar; two small candlesticks
Sputter at each side of the crucifix
Laid round with flowers brighter than the blood,
Red as the red of our apocalypse,
Hibiscus that a marching man will pluck
To stick into his rifle or his hat,
And great blue morning-glories pale as lips
That shall no longer taste or kiss or swear.
The wind begins a low magnificat,
The chaplain chats, the palmtrees swirl their hair,
The columns come together through the mud.

II

We too are ashes as we watch and hear
The psalm, the sorrow, and the simple praise
Of one whose promised thoughts of other days
Were such as ours, but now wholly destroyed,
The service record of his youth wiped out,
His dream dispersed by shot, must disappear.
What can we feel but wonder at a loss
That seems to point at nothing but the doubt
Which flirts our sense of luck into the ditch?
Reader of Paul who prays beside this fosse,
Shall we believe our eyes or legends rich
With glory and rebirth beyond the void?

III

For this comrade is dead, dead in the war,
A young man out of millions yet to live,
One cut away from all that war can give,
Freedom of self and peace to wander free.

Who mourns in all this sober multitude
Who did not feel the bite of it before
The bullet found its aim? This worthy flesh,
This boy laid in a coffin and reviewed—
Who has not wrapped himself in this same flag,
Heard the light fall of dirt, his wound still fresh,
Felt his eyes closed, and heard the distant brag
Of the last volley of humanity?

IV

By chance I saw him die, stretched on the ground,
A tattooed arm lifted to take the blood
Of someone else sealed in a tin. I stood
During the last delirium that stays
The intelligence a tiny moment more,
And then the strangulation, the last sound.
The end was sudden, like a foolish play,
A stupid fool slamming a foolish door,
The absurd catastrophe, half-prearranged,
And all the decisive things still left to say.
So we disbanded, angrier and unchanged,
Sick with the utter silence of dispraise.

V

We ask for no statistics of the killed,
For nothing political impinges on
This single casualty, or all those gone,
Missing or healing, sinking or dispersed,
Hundreds of thousands counted, millions lost.
More than an accident and less than willed
Is every fall, and this one like the rest.
However others calculate the cost,
To us the final aggregate is *one*,
One with a name, one transferred to the blest;
And though another stoops and takes the gun,
We cannot add the second to the first.

VI

I would not speak for him who could not speak
Unless my fear were true: he was not wronged,
He knew to which decision he belonged
But let it choose itself. Ripe in instinct,
Neither the victim nor the volunteer,
He followed, and the leaders could not seek
Beyond the followers. Much of this he knew;
The journey was a detour that would steer
Into the Lincoln Highway of a land
Remorselessly improved, excited, new,
And that was what he wanted. He had planned
To earn and drive. He and the world had winked.

VII

No history deceived him, for he knew
Little of times and armies not his own;
He never felt that peace was but a loan,
Had never questioned the idea of gain.
Beyond the headlines once or twice he saw
The gathering of a power by the few
But could not tell their names; he cast his vote,
Distrusting all the elected but not law.
He laughed at socialism; *on mourrait
Pour les industriels?* He shed his coat
And not for brotherhood, but for his pay.
To him the red flag marked the sewer main.

VIII

Above all else he loathed the homily,
The slogan and the ad. He paid his bill
But not for Congressmen at Bunker Hill.
Ideals were few and those there were not made
For conversation. He belonged to church
But never spoke of God. The Christmas tree,

The Easter egg, baptism, he observed,
Never denied the preacher on his perch,
And would not sign Resolved That or Whereas.
Softness he had and hours and nights reserved
For thinking, dressing, dancing to the jazz.
His laugh was real, his manners were home made.

IX

Of all men poverty pursued him least;
He was ashamed of all the down and out,
Spurned the panhandler like an uneasy doubt,
And saw the umemployed as a vague mass
Incapable of hunger or revolt.
He hated other races, south or east,
And shoved them to the margin of his mind.
He could recall the justice of the Colt,
Take interest in a gang-war like a game.
His ancestry was somehwere far behind
And left him only his peculiar name.
Doors opened, and he recognized no class.

X

His children would have known a heritage,
Just or unjust, the richest in the world,
The quantum of all art and science curled
In the horn of plenty, bursting from the horn,
A people bathed in honey, Paris come,
Vienna transferred with the highest wage,
A World's Fair spread to Phoenix, Jacksonville,
Earth's capitol, the new Byzantium,
Kingdom of man—who knows? Hollow or firm,
No man can ever prophesy until
Out of our death some undiscovered germ,
Whole toleration or pure peace is born.

XI

The time to mourn is short that best becomes
The military dead. We lift and fold the flag,
Lay bare the coffin with its written tag,
And march away. Behind, four others wait
To lift the box, the heaviest of loads.
The anesthetic afternoon benumbs,
Sickens our senses, forces back our talk.
We know that others on tommorrow's roads
Will fall, ourselves perhaps, the man beside,
Over the world the threatened, all who walk:
And could we mark the grave of him who died
We would write this beneath his name and date:

Epitaph

Underneath this wooden cross there lies
A Christian killed in battle. You who read,
Remember that this stranger died in pain;
And passing here, if you can lift your eyes
Upon a peace kept by a human creed,
Know that one soldier has not died in vain.

Elegy Written on a Frontporch

The sun burns on its sultry wick;
Stratus and cumulus unite.
I who am neither well nor sick
Sit in a wicker chair and write.

A hot wind presses at my lips.
I peel. Am totally undressed.
Pinkish, as though a part-eclipse,
Heat licks upon my naked breast.

Angles in quick succession rise.
Eyesight is stereopticon
As roof and roof geometrize
Perspective deviously drawn.

I face a heaven half-destroyed,
A skyscape alabaster, dead.
One living shadow on the void,
A Flying Fortress drones ahead.

Motion and fixity take shape;
The fallow rays intensify
Distinctness. Nothing can escape
The clean hard focus of the eye.

Noise into humming noise constricts;
The traffic mumbles deeper down.
Only a trolley contradicts,
Ticks by neurotically to town.

Stretched taut upon the light I scorch,
Writhe in my sweat and smoke and sun.
The evening paper hits the porch;
My honeymoon of peace is done.

Unmasticated pulp of life . . .
Decision finds me blind and deaf.
I do not finger for the strife
Of Delano and Mutt and Jeff,

Or bend upon my nudity's
Umbilicus, the fact of facts,
As one who drowns in light and sees
The newsreel of his private acts.

I do not hug my feet with glee
And smile into my cul-de-sac
Enamoured of the dignity
Of facing forward moving back.

But set my wired sight, reclaim
The rotted friendship and the fresh;
Tune in on him who changed his name
And her who stultified the flesh.

I see who came to marriage raw
With poverty and self-abuse;
Defendants to the general law,
Their ignorance was no excuse.

Instructors, graduates I see,
Scholars who sneered into their books,
The female doctors pouring tea,
Hundreds of victims of their looks.

The money-poise of some, the pride
Of those who whored on easy checks,
Sons of The Business, dressy, snide,
Disfigured in expensive wrecks.

Believers in the songhit, thin
With pounding to the hebroid jazz;
The studious drinkers feeding in
The cloaca of the middle-class.

I see too many who romanced
Defeat, unmasculine, debased;
The striptease puritans who danced
The long lewd ritual of waste.

All these I bury out of sight
Sans benefit of epitaph.
I turn my legs into the light,
Punch out a cigaret and laugh.

For one, the best against that rout,
Deserted, obdurate to see
Their weakly literate wear out
The old Horatian fallacy;

Spoke of the beauty-to-obey,
The life-expectancy of bone,
She turned her back upon the day
But will not lie at night alone.

Haircut

O wonderful nonsense of lotions of Lucky Tiger,
Of savory soaps and oils of bottle-bright green,
The gold of liqueurs, the unguents of Newark and Niger,
Powders and balms and waters washing me clean,

In mirrors of marble and silver I see us forever
Increasing, decreasing the puzzles of luminous spaces
As I turn, am revolved and pumped in the air on a lever,
With the backs of my heads in chorus with all of my faces.

Scissors and comb are mowing my hair into neatness,
Now pruning my ears, now smoothing my neck like a pain;
In the harvest of hair and the chaff of powdery sweetness
My snow-covered slopes grow dark with the wooly rain.

And the little boy cries, for it hurts to sever the curl,
And we too are quietly bleating to part with our coat.
Does the barber want blood in a dish? I am weak as a girl,
I desire my pendants, the fatherly chin of a goat.

I desire the pants of a bear, the nap of a monkey
Which trousers of friction have blighted down to my skin.
I am bare as a tusk, as jacketed up a flunkey,
With the chest of moth-eaten camel growing within.

But in death we shall flourish, you summer-dark leaves of my head.
While the flesh of the jaw ebbs away from the shores of my teeth;
You shall cover my sockets and soften the boards of my bed
And lie on the flat of my temples as proud as a wreath.

Nostalgia

My soul stands at the window of my room,
    And I ten thousand miles away;
My days are filled with Ocean's sound of doom,
    Salt and cloud and the bitter spray.
Let the wind blow, for many a man shall die.

My selfish youth, my books with gilded edge,
    Knowledge and all gaze down the street;
The potted plants upon the window ledge
    Gaze down with selfish lives and sweet.
Let the wind blow, for many a man shall die.

My night is now her day, my day her night,
    So I lie down, and so I rise;
The sun burns close, the star is losing height,
    The clock is hunted down the skies.
Let the wind blow, for many a man shall die.

Truly a pin can make the memory bleed,
    A word explode the inward mind
And turn the skulls and flowers never freed
    Into the air, no longer blind.
Let the wind blow, for many a man shall die.

Laughter and grief join hands. Always the heart
    Clumps in the breast with heavy stride;
The face grows lined and wrinkled like a chart,
    The eyes bloodshot with tears and tide.
Let the wind blow, for many a man shall die.

The Potomac

    The thin Potomac scarcely moves
But to divide Virginia from today;
    Rider, whichever is your way
You go due south and neither South improves;
Not this, of fractured columns and queer rents

And rags that charm the nationalist,
Not that, the axle of the continents,
Nor the thin sky that flows unprejudiced
This side and that, cleansing the poisoned breath.

For Thomas died a Georgian death
And now the legion bones of Arlington
   Laid out in marble alphabets
Stare on the great tombs of the capitol
   Where heroes calcified and cool
   Ponder the soldier named Unknown
Whose lips are guarded with live bayonets.

Yet he shall speak though sentries walk
And columns with their cold Corinthian stalk
   Shed gold-dust pollen on Brazil
   To turn the world to Roman chalk;
Yet he shall speak, yet he shall speak
   Whose sulphur lit the flood-lit Dome,
   Whose hands were never in the kill,
Whose will was furrows of Virginia loam.

But not like London blown apart by boys
Who learned the books of love in English schools,
His name shall strike the fluted columns down;
These shall lie buried deep as fifty Troys,
The money fade like leaves from green to brown,
And embassies dissolve to molecules.

V-Letter

I love you first because your face is fair,
        Because your eyes Jewish and blue,
Set sweetly with the touch of foreignness
Above the cheekbones, stare rather than dream.
Often your countenance recalls a boy
        Blue-eyed and small, whose silent mischief
Tortured his parents and compelled my hate
        To wish his ugly death.

Because of this reminder, my soul's trouble,
And for your face, so often beautiful,
         I love you, wish you life.

I love you first because you wait, because
         For your own sake, I cannot write
Beyond these words. I love you for these words
That sting and creep like insects and leave filth.
I love you for the poverty you cry
         And I bend down with tears of steel
That melt your hand like wax, not for this war
         The droplets shattering
Those candle-glowing fingers of my joy,
But for your name of agony, my love,
         That cakes my mouth with salt.

And all your imperfections and perfections
         And all your magnitude of grace
And all this love explained and unexplained
Is just a breath. I see you woman-size
And this looms larger and more goddess-like
         Than silver goddesses on screens.
I see you in the ugliness of light,
         Yet you are beautiful,
And in the dark of absence your full length
Is such as meets my body to the full
         Though I am starved and huge.

You turn me from these days as from a scene
         Out of an open window far
Where lies the foreign city and the war.
You are my home and in your spacious love
I dream to march as under flaring flags
         Until the door is gently shut.
Give me the tearless lesson of your pride,
         Teach me to live and die
As one deserving anonymity,
The mere devotion of a house to keep
         A woman and a man.

Give me the free and poor inheritance
　　　　　Of our own kind, not furniture
Of education, nor the prophet's pose,
The general cause of words, the hero's stance,
The ambitions incommensurable with flesh,
　　　　　But the drab makings of a room
Where sometimes in the afternoon of thought
　　　　　The brief and blinding flash
May light the enormous chambers of your will
And show the gracious Parthenon that time
　　　　　Is ever measured by.

As groceries in a pantry gleam and smile
　　　　　Because they are important weights
Bought with the metal minutes of your pay,
So do these hours stand in solid rows,
The dowry for a use in common life.
　　　　　I love you first because your years
Lead to my matter-of-fact and simple death
　　　　　Or to our open marriage,
And I pray nothing for my safety back,
Not even luck, because our love is whole
　　　　　Whether I live or fail.

John Berryman (1914–1972)

The oldest of two brothers, John Berryman was born in McAlester, Oklahoma on October 25th to John Smith, a banker, and Martha (Little) Smith, a school teacher. When he was ten years old the family moved to Tampa, Florida where his parents began to suffer severe marital problems. When Berryman was 12 years old he witnessed his father's suicide—an event which would haunt him the rest of his life.

After his father's death, Berryman's family moved to Gloucester, Massachusetts and finally settled in New York City. His mother married a wall street broker, John Angus McAlpin Berryman, who adopted her two sons. Berryman was sent to South Kent School in Kent, Connecticut where his literary ambitions took seed despite an anti-intellectual atmosphere of the school at the time. In 1932 he attended Columbia University studying literature and philosophy and coming under the influence of Mark Van Doren. After reading Van Doren's *A Winter Day* Berryman decided to become a poet.

After graduating from Columbia, Phi Beta Kapa, Berryman was awarded a traveling scholarship to Clare College, Cambridge. While overseas he met W. B. Yeats, Dylan Thomas, and W. H. Auden. After two years he returned to the United States and began his academic career, first teaching at Harvard and Princeton, then settling down at the University of Minnesota in 1955. In 1940 Berryman's first group of poems, "Twenty Poems," was published in *Five Young American Poets* and in 1942 his first book, *Poems,* appeared. Also in 1942 he married his first wife, Eileen Mulligan, but the marriage ended in 1953 due to Berryman's heavy drinking, personality problems, and compulsive work habits. In 1956, while at the University of Minnesota, Berryman married Ann Levine, but they were divorced just three years later, once again due to his drinking habits and disorderly behavior. Berryman married Kate Donahue in 1961.

In 1952 he was awarded a Guggenheim Fellowship and in 1953 he published his most ambitious poem, "Homage to Mistress Bradstreet," in the *Partisan Review*. "Homage" is a long narrative dealing with the seventeenth century poet Anne Bradstreet, but it is also Berryman's attempt to break out of the modern tradition of narrative poetry initiated by Eliot's *The Wasteland*.

In 1965 he received his greatest honor, being awarded the Pulitzer Prize for *77 Dreams*. He followed this in 1968 with what is considered his best work, *His Toy, His Dream, His Rest,* which won the National Book Award and a share of the Bollingen Prize.

On January 7, 1972 Berryman jumped off a bridge into the frozen Mississippi and died instantly. Though no one is sure of the exact reason for his suicide, certainly his failing health, the death of his father, and the fear of losing his talent contributed to his depression.

John Berryman's literary reputation varied throughout his career. In the 1940's he was considered a rising young poet of restrained and well crafted academic verse. With the publication of the experimental "Homage to Mistress Bradstreet" his reputation declined, but in the 1960's he attained a permanent position as one of America's finest poets—his 1969 *The Dream Songs* is one of the few volumes of poetry to become a book-club selection.

Canto Amor

Dream in a dream the heavy soul somewhere
struck suddenly & dark down to its knees.
A griffin sighs off in the orphic air.

If (Unknown Majesty) I not confess
praise for the rack the rock the live sailor
under the blue sea,—yet I may You bless

always for hér, in fear & joy for hér
whose gesture summons ever when I grieve
me back and is my mage and minister.

—Muses, whose whorship I may never leave
but for this pensive woman, now I dare,
teach me her praise! with her my praise receive.—

Three years already of the round world's war
had rolled by stoned & disappointed eyes
when she and I came where we were made for.

Pale as a star lost in returning skies,
more beautiful than midnight stars more frail
she moved towards me like chords, a sacrifice;

entombed in body trembling through the veil
arm upon arm, learning our ancient wound,
we see our one soul heal, recovering pale.

Then priestly sanction, then the drop of sound.
Quickly part to the cavern ever warm
deep from the march, body to body bound,

descend (my soul) out of dismantling storm
into the darkness where the world is made.
Come back to the bright air. Love is multiform.

Heartmating hesitating unafraid
although incredulous, she seemed to fill
the lilac shadow with light wherein she played,

whom sorry childhood had made sit quite still,
an orphan silence, unregarded sheen,
listening for any small soft note, not hopeful:

caricature: as once a maiden Queen,
flowering power comeliness kindness grace,
shattered her mirror, wept, would not be seen.

These pities moved. Also above her face
serious or flushed, swayed her fire-gold
not earthly hair, now moonless to unlace,

resistless flame, now in a sun more cold
great shells to whorl about each secret ear,
mysterious histories, strange shores, unfold.

New musics! One the music that we hear
this is the music which the masters make
out of their minds, profound solemn & clear.

And then the other music, in whose sake
all men perceive a gladness but we are drawn
less for that joy than utterly to take

our trial, naked in the music's vision,
the flowing ceremony of trouble and light,
all Loves becoming, none to rest upon.

Such Mozart made,—an ear so delicate
he fainted at a trumpet-call, a child
so delicate. So merciful that sight,

so stern, we follow rapt who ran awild.
Marriage is the second music, and thereof
we hear what we can bear, faithful & mind.

Therefore the streaming torches in the grove
through dark or bright, swiftly & now more near
cherish a festival of anxious love.

Dance for this music, Mistress to music dear,
more, that full storm through the disordered wood
ravens at midnight of my thirtieth year

and only the trial of our music should
still this irresolute air, only your voice
spelling the tempest may compel our good:

Sing then beyond my song: whirl & rejoice!

The Song of the Demented Priest

I put those things there.—See them burn.
The emerald the azure and the gold
Hiss and crack, the blues and greens of the world
As if I were tired. Someone interferes
Everywhere with me. The clouds the clouds are torn
In ways I do not understand or love.

Licking my long lips, I looked upon God
And he flamed and was friendlier
Than you were, and he was small. Showing me—
Serpents and thin flowers; these were cold.
Dominion waved and glittered like the flare
From ice under a small sun. I wonder.

Afterward the violent and formal dancers
Came out, shaking their pithless heads.
I would instruct them but I cannot now,—
Because of the elements. They rise and move,
I nod a dance and they dance in the rain
In my red coat. I am the king of the dead.

Randall Jarrell (1914–1965)

Born May 6 in Nashville, Tennessee, Randall Jarrell divided his childhood years between Hollywood, California and Nashville. He finally settled in Nashville, where he attended high school and Vanderbilt University. While at Vanderbilt he came under the influence of John Crowe Ransom who, impressed by Jarrell's creativity and intelligence, persuaded him to study English. Under the tutelage of Ransom, Jarrell began to compose poetry and published his first poem, "Above the waters in their toil" in *American Review* in 1934. In 1937, while still working on his M.A. thesis, Jarrell taught at Kenyon College where he became life long friends with Robert Lowell. After completing his M. A. in 1938, Jarrell went to teach at the University of Texas at Austin. In 1940 he contributed 20 poems to John Ciardi's *Five Young American Poets*; in 1942 Jarrell published his first book of poems, *Blood for a Stranger*.

He served as an Air Force instructor during World War II. From this experience, Jarrell produced some of the most memorable war poetry to come out that era: *Little Friend, Little Friend* (1945), *Losses* (1948), and *The Seven-League Crutches* (1951). After the war Jarrell taught at Sarah Lawrence College, and became the New York literary editor of *The Nation*. In 1947 he joined the faculty of the Women's College of the University of North Carolina at Greensboro. His literary fame, as a critic, teacher, and poet, began to spread. His 1953 book of criticism, *Poetry and the Age*, was heralded as a revolutionary step away from the domination of the New Critics. Jarrell's first and only novel appeared in 1954, *Pictures from an Institution*, a satire on American academic circles that met with mixed reviews. At the same time he was a guest lecturer at several universities and held a Consultantship in Poetry at the Library of Congress. In 1960 Jarrell reached the height of critical acclaim with *The Woman at the Washington Zoo*, a collection of poems which won the National Book Award. Jarrell is also well known for the children's stories he wrote in collaboration with the illustrator Maurice Sendak, *The Animal Family* (1965), *The Bat Poet* (1964), and *Fly by Night* (1976). In 1965 Jarrell was hospitalized with a nervous breakdown, but was soon released and began working on what some consider his best poetry, published in 1968 and entitled *The Lost World*. But before he could complete *The Lost World*, Jarrell was fatally hit by a car on October 17, 1965.

Robert Lowell described Randall Jarrell as "the most heartbreaking English poet of his generation." His poems concentrate on the loss of innocence and the pain and loneliness of the adult world. Though Jarrell never solves these problems, his verse has the sound of authentic, everyday human emotions and he offers the reader the consolation of compassion.

The Death of the Ball Turret Gunner

From my mother's sleep I fell into the State,
And I hunched in its belly till my wet fur froze.
Six miles from earth, loosed from its dream of life,
I woke to black flak and the nightmare fighters.
When I died they washed me out of the turret with a hose.

Losses

It was not dying: everybody died.
It was not dying: we had died before
In the routine crashes—and our fields
Called up the papers, wrote home to our folks,
And the rates rose, all because of us.
We died on the wrong page of the almanac,
Scattered on mountains fifty miles away;
Diving on haystacks, fighting with a friend,
We blazed up on the lines we never saw.
We died like aunts or pets or foreigners.
(When we left high school nothing else had died
For us to figure we had died like.)

In our new planes, with our new crews, we bombed
The ranges by the desert or the shore,
Fired at towed targets, waited for our scores—
And turned into replacements and woke up
One morning, over England, operational.
It wasn't different: but if we died
It was not an accident but a mistake
(But an easy one for anyone to make).
We read our mail and counted up our missions—
In bombers named for girls, we burned
The cities we had learned about in school—
Till our lives wore out; our bodies lay among
The people we had killed and never seen.
When we lasted long enough they gave us medals;
When we died they said, "Our casualties were low."

They said, "Here are the maps"; we burned the cities.

It was not dying—no, not ever dying;
But the night I died I dreamed that I was dead,
And the cities said to me: "Why are you dying?
We are satisfied, if you are; but why did I die?"

A Pilot from the Carrier

Strapped at the center of the blazing wheel,
His flesh ice-white against the shattered mask,
He tears at the easy clasp, his sobbing breaths
Misting the fresh blood lightening to flame,
Darkening to smoke; trapped there in pain
And fire and breathlessness, he struggles free
Into the sunlight of the upper sky—
And falls, a quiet bundle in the sky,
The miles to warmth, to air, to waking:
To the great flowering of his life, the hemisphere
That holds his dangling years. In its long slow sway
The world steadies and is almost still. . . .
He is alone; and hangs in knowledge
Slight, separate, estranged: a lonely eye
Reading a child's first scrawl, the carrier's wake—
The travelling milk-like circle of a miss
Beside the plant-like genius of the smoke
That shades, on the little deck, the little blaze
Toy-like as the glitter of the wing-guns,
Shining as the fragile sun-marked plane
That grows to him, rubbed silver tipped with flame.

Second Air Force

Far off, above the plain the summer dries,
The great loops of the hangars sway like hills.
Buses and weariness and loss, the nodding soldiers
Are wire, the bare frame building, and a pass
To what was hers; her head hides his square patch
And she thinks heavily: My son is grown.
She sees a world: sand roads, tar-paper barracks,
The bubbling asphalt of the runways, sage,
The dunes rising to the interminable ranges,
The dim flights moving over clouds like clouds.
The armorers in their patched faded green,
Sweat-stiffened, banded with brass cartridges,
Walk to the line; their Fortresses, all tail,

Stand wrong and flimsy on their skinny legs,
And the crews climb to them clumsily as bears.
The head withdraws into its hatch (a boy's),
The engines rise to their blind laboring roar,
And the green, made beasts run home to air.
Now in each aspect death is pure.
(At twilight they wink over men like stars
And hour by hour, through the night, some see
The great lights floating in—from Mars, from Mars.)
How emptily the watchers see them gone.

They go, there is silence; the woman and her son
Stand in the forest of the shadows, and the light
Washes them like water. In the long-sunken city
Of evening, the sunlight stills like sleep
The faint wonder of the drowned; in the evening,
In the last dreaming light, so fresh, so old,
The soldiers pass like beasts, unquestioning,
And the watcher for an instant understands
What there is then no need to understand;
But she wakes from her knowledge, and her stare,
A shadow now, moves emptily among
The shadows learning in their shadowy fields
The empty missions.
                    Remembering,
She hears the bomber calling, *Little Friend!*
To the fighter hanging in the hostile sky,
And sees the ragged flame eat, rib by rib,
Along the metal of the wing into her heart:
The lives stream out, blossom, and float steadily
To the flames of the earth, the flames
That burn like stars above the lands of men.

She saves from the twilight that takes everything
A squadron shipping, in its last parade—
Its dogs run by it, barking at the band—
A gunner walking to his barracks, half-asleep,
Starting at something, stumbling (above, invisible,
The crews in the steady winter of the sky
Tremble in their wired fur); and feels for them

The love of life for life. The hopeful cells
Heavy with someone else's death, cold carriers
Of someone else's victory, grope past their lives
Into her own bewilderment: The years meant *this?*

But for them the bombers answer everything.

Laurie Lee (Born 1914)

Laurie Lee, born June 26, grew up in Stroud, Gloucestershire, England, where he was educated at the Slad village school and the Stroud Central School. When he was 19, Lee walked from his small village to Spain, where he was trapped by the Civil War; he recorded these experiences in *As I Walked Out One Morning*. During World War II he made documentary movies for the General Post Office film unit. Lee was Caption Writer-in-Chief and Curator of Eccentricities for the Festival of Britain in 1950. In 1952 he was made a Member, Order of the British Empire.

Laurie Lee has written over 15 plays, memoirs, and travel books. His verse works include *The Sun My Monument* (1944), *The Bloom of Candles* (1947), *The Many-Coated Man* (1955), and *Pocket Poems* (1960). Lee's poetry is always charming, and poetic in the traditional sense—his favorite images are the sea, the moon, flowers, stars, girls, animals, etc. Lee virtually ignores the world of politics and society; rather he concentrates on nature and his personal reminiscences.

Day of These Days

Such a morning it is when love
leans through geranium windows
and calls with a cockerel's tongue.

When red-haired girls scamper like roses
over the rain-green grass,
and the sun drips honey.

When hedgerows grow venerable,
berries dry black as blood,
and holes suck in their bees.

Such a morning it is when mice
run whispering from the church,
dragging dropped ears of harvest.

When the partridge draws back his spring
and shoots like a buzzing arrow
over grained and mahogany fields.

When no table is bare,
and no breast dry,
and the tramp feeds off ribs of rabbit.

Such a day it is when time
piles up the hills like pumpkins,
and the streams run golden.

When all men smell good,
and the cheeks of girls
are as baked bread to the mouth.

As bread and beanflowers
the touch of their lips,
and their white teeth sweeter than cucumbers.

Milkmaid

The girl's far treble, muted to the heat,
calls like a fainting bird across the fields
to where her flock lies panting for her voice,
their black horns buried deep in marigolds.

They climb awake, like drowsy butterflies,
and press their red flanks through the tall branched
 grass,
and as they go their wandering tongues embrace
the vacant summer mirrored in their eyes.

Led to the limestone shadows of a barn
they snuff their past embalmed in the hay,
while her cool hand, cupped to the udder's fount,
distils the brimming harvest of their day.

Look what a cloudy cream the earth gives out,
fat juice of buttercups and meadow-rye;
the girl dreams milk within her body's field
and hears, far off, her muted children cry.

The Three Winds

The hard blue winds of March
shake the young sheep
and flake the long stone walls;
now from the gusty grass
comes the horned music of rams,
and plovers fall out of the sky
filling their wings with snow.

Tired of this northern tune
the winds turn soft
blowing white butterflies
out of the dog-rose hedges,
and schoolroom songs are full
of boy's green cuckoos
piping the summer round

Till August sends at last
its brick-red breath
over the baking wheat and blistered poppy,
brushing with feathered hands
the skies of brass,
with dreams of river moss
my thirst's delirium.

Norman Nicholson (Born 1914)

An only child, Norman Nicholson was born January 8, the son of a tailor, Joseph Nicholson. Norman Nicholson grew up and has spent the entire of his life in the small mining town of Millom, Cumberland, England. This region, with its combination of beautiful landscape and decayed industrialism, is the major subject and backdrop for most of Nicholson's poetry. In 1925 he won a scholarship to Millom Secondary Grammar School. He was a brilliant student and seemed destined to an academic career. Nicholson was also devoutly religious and was confirmed by the Church of England in 1929. His whole life changed the next year, though, as he contracted tuberculosis. Nicholson had to cancel his university plans and spend 15 months in a sanatorium in Hampshire. Subsequently his health was too unstable for him to hold a full time job, so he turned to writing. Nicholson's poetry was encouraged by several friends and acquaintances, most notably T. S. Eliot. Nicholson's first published poem, "Song for 7 p.m." appeared in the magazine *Poetry* in 1938. In the same year he gave a series of lectures on modern literature to the Millom branch of the Worker's Educational Association; these lectures formed the basis of his 1943 book of criticism, *Man and Literature*. Despite these early successes the late thirties were a dry period for Nicholson, he could not get any work published. His conviction in Christianity grew more pronounced during these hard times.

In 1944, Nicholson's fortune changed when T. S. Eliot accepted his collection of poems, *The Five Rivers*, for publication. He also published in the same year a novel, *The Fire of the Lord*. *The Five Rivers* met with immediate acceptance and praise. Nicholson was awarded the Heinemann Prize and appointed a Fellow of the Royal Society of Literature in 1945. With his literary reputation set, Nicholson has written over 16 plays, novels, books of criticism, and verse collections. In 1967 he was given the Cholmondeley Prize for Poetry.

Norman Nicholson's poetry turns on two influences, his faith, and his devotion to the region of Cumberland. For Nicholson, the commonplace serves to reveal his insights into human psychology and the deeper significance of life. Recently his provincialism has been attacked, but his is not a provincialism which is narrow minded, rather its limited scope is a tool by which Nicholson addresses the timeless concerns of humanity.

Caedmon

Above me the abbey, grey arches on the cliff,
The lights lit in the nave, pale prayers against the
    night,
For still the Blessed Hilda burns like a brand
Among the black thorns, the thickets of darkness,
The ways and walls of a wild land,
Where the spade grates on stone, on the grappling
    gorse,
And the Norse gods clamber on the Christian
    crosses.
Below me the sea, the angry, the hungered,

Gnashing the grey chalk, grinding the cobbles.
The snow falls like feathers, the hail like quills,
The sun sets, and the night rises like a sea-mist,
And the fog is in the bones of the drowned. Here fare
    far out
Mariners and marauders, foragers and fishermen.
Tearing their treasure from the teeth of the waves,
    from the gullet of the gaping shores—
Over the heaped and heaving hills they return to the
    wistful harbours,
The freeman's blood and the sea's salt frozen on the
    gold.
Honour to warriors and wanderers, honour to the
    wise,
Honour to kings and kinsmen of kings, honour to
    councillors,
Honour to priests, honour to pilgrims,
Honour even to minstrels, the many-songed migrants.
But never have I ventured forth, neither on the
    northern tides,
Nor more than a shin's depth down the steep and
    staggering shore;
I have not roamed with the fighting men nor fired the
    Scotsmen's byres.
Yet I, even I, have heard the angels speak,
I, who never learned the liturgical tongue,
Who cannot read the written revelation,
Walking at night on the shingle, waking at dawn in
    the straw,
I have seen long spears of lighting lance at my eyes,
And felt the words, pricked out with fire,
Notched in my bones and burning in my body.
The angels crawled like gold lice through my
    dreams.
By the grey sea, under the grimacing clouds,
I hack and hammer at the handiwork of verse,
Feeling the sting of words, fearing the angels'
    threats,
Hoping that when the tide is full I may seek my
    unhaunted bed.

Cleator Moor

From one shaft at Cleator Moor
They mined for coal and iron ore.
This harvest below ground could show
Black and red currants on one tree.

In furnaces they burnt the coal,
The ore was smelted into steel,
And railway lines from end to end
Corseted the bulging land.

Pylons sprouted on the fells,
Stakes were driven in like nails,
And the ploughed fields of Devonshire
Were sliced with the steel of Cleator Moor.

The land waxed fat and greedy too,
It would not share the fruits it grew,
And coal and ore, as sloe and plum,
Lay black and red for jamming time.

The pylons rusted on the fells,
The gutters leaked beside the walls,
And women searched the ebb-tide tracks
For knobs of coal or broken sticks.

But now the pits are wick with men,
Digging like dogs dig for a bone:
For food and life *we* dig the earth—
In Cleator Moor they dig for death.

Every waggon of cold coal
Is fire to drive a turbine wheel;
Every knuckle of soft ore
A bullet in a soldier's ear.

The miner at the rockface stands,
With his segged and bleeding hands
Heaps on his head the fiery coal,
And feels the iron in his soul.

Michaelmas

Like a hound with nose to the trail
The 'bus follows the road;
The road leaps up the hill.
In the valley the railway line is carved like a groove
    in wood;
The little towns smoke in the hollows;
The slagbanks are grey beneath the brown,
    bludgeoning fell.

This is the day the air has eyes,
And the Devil falls like hail
From the bright and thundering skies,
And soaks into soil and rock,
And the bad blood rises in nettle and dock,
And toadstools burst like boils between the toes of
    the trees.

The war that began in heaven still goes on.
Thorn trees twist like spears,
The owl haunts the grain,
The coursed rabbit weeps icicles of tears;
But the feathers of the clouds foretell
St. Michael's victory in the purged and praising rain.

Song at Night

'Music for a while'
Make audible the smile
   That eyes no longer see;
With crying crayon write
Across the unhearing night
   The shape of sighs for me.

Music for a time
Resolve the brawls of rhyme
   That chord within my head;
Sweet as starlight, shine,
Illuminate the line,
   Setting the word unsaid.

When Dryden's page is bare,
And silent Purcell's air,
   And mute the singing sky,
Then let me pluck one name
And echo clear proclaim
   Not I, my dear, not I.

The Tame Hare

She came to him in dreams—her ears
Diddering like antennae, and her eyes
Wide as dark flowers where the dew
Holds and dissolves a purple hoard of shadow.
The thunder clouds crouched back, and the world
   opened
Tiny and bright as a celandine after rain.
A gentle light was on her, so that he
Who saw the talons in the vetch
Remembered now how buttercup and daisy
Would bounce like springs when a child's foot stepped
   off them.
Oh, but never dared he touch—
Her fur was still electric to the fingers.

Yet of all the beasts blazoned in gilt and blood
In the black-bound missal of his mind,
Pentecostal dove and paschal lamb,
Eagle, lion, serpent, she alone
Lived also in the noon of ducks and sparrows;
And the cleft-mouthed kiss which plugged the night
   with fever
Was sweetened by a lunch of docks and lettuce.

The Undiscovered Planet

Out on the furthest tether let it run
Its hundred-year-long orbit, cold
As solid mercury, old and dead
Before *this* world's fermenting bread
Had got a crust to cover it; landscape of lead
Whose purple voes and valleys are
Lit faintly by a sun
No nearer than a measurable star.

No man has seen it; nor the lensed eye
That pin-points week by week the same patch of sky
Records even a blur across its pupil; only
The errantry of Saturn, the wry
Retarding of Uranus, speak
Of the pull beyond the pattern:—
The unknown is shown
Only by a bend in the known.

Henry Reed (Born 1914)

Born in Birmingham, Warwickshire, England, Henry Reed was educated at the King Edward School in Birmingham and took his M.A. from the University of Birmingham. While in college he was good friends with W. H. Auden and Louis MacNeice. After graduation, Reed worked as a teacher and a journalist, but in 1945 became a radio playwright. He has devoted his career to radio work. Reed has written two books of verse: *A Map of Verona* (1946) and *Lessons of the War* (1970). His *Map of Verona* contains a brilliant parody of T. S. Eliot, entitled "Chard Whitlow," as well as poems about the Second World War, dramatic monologues (precursors of his radio plays), and the famous "Tintagel" sequence.

Lessons of the War
To Alan Michell

Judging Distances

Not only how far away, but the way that you say it
Is very important. Perhaps you may never get
The knack of judging a distance, but at least you know
How to report on a landscape: the central sector,
The right of arc and that, which we had last Tuesday,
    And at least you know

That maps are of time, not place, so far as the Army
Happens to be concerned—the reason being,
Is one which need not delay us. Again you know
There are three kinds of tree, three only, the fir and
    the poplar,
And those which have bushy tops to; and lastly
    That things only seem to be things.

A barn is not called a barn, to put it more plainly,
Or a field in the distance, where sheep may be safely
    grazing.
You must never be over-sure. You must say, when
    reporting:
At five o'clock in the central sector is a dozen
Of what appear to be animals; whatever you do,
    Don't call the bleeders *sheep*.

I am sure that's quite clear; and suppose, for the sake
    of example,
The one at the end, asleep, endeavours to tell us
What he sees over there to the west, and how far away, HENRY
After first having come to attention. There to the west, REED
On the fields of summer the sun and the shadows bestow
    Vestments of purple and gold.

The still white dwellings are like a mirage in the heat,
And under the swaying elms a man and a woman
Lie gently together. Which is, perhaps, only to say
That there is a row of houses to the left of arc,
And that under some poplars a pair of what appear to
    be humans
    Appear to be loving.

Well that, for an answer, is what we might rightly call
Moderately satisfactory only, the reason being,
Is that two things have been omitted, and those are
    important.
The human beings, now: in what direction are they,
And how far away, would you say? And do not forget
    There may be dead ground in between.

There may be dead ground in between; and I may not
    have got
The knack of judging a distance; I will only venture
A guess that perhaps between me and the apparent
    lovers,
(Who, incidentally, appear by now to have finished,)
At seven o'clock from the houses, is roughly a distance
    Of about one year and a half.

Dylan Thomas (1914–1953)

Dylan Thomas was born October 27 in Swansea, South Wales, the son of a grammar school teacher and frustrated poet, D. J. Thomas. As a child, Dylan Thomas suffered from lung hemorrhages, which prevented him from attending school on a regular basis. His holidays were spent at Fern Hill where Thomas' Uncle James and Aunt Ann Jones had a farm. These vacations were an idyllic time for Thomas and he incorporated many of these experiences in his beautiful country poems, and, of course, in the famous "Fern Hill" and "After the Funeral." At grammar school, though he detested academics, Thomas began to write poems; he appeared in the school literary magazine during his first term. These early poems were basically pastiches of Housman and Rupert Brooke, but showed a fascination with the sound of words divorced from their content or meaning—a concern which would dominate his early work and contribute to charges that his poetry was too inaccessible and obscure. Though Thomas ignored his school work, he had a solid knowledge of contemporary literature—Joyce, Eliot, the Sitwells, etc.—and published an extraordinary article, given that he was only 14 at the time, entitled "Modern Poetry," in which he argued that the most important aspect of poetry was " . . . freedom—essential and unlimited—freedom of form, of structure, of imagery, and of idea."

Thomas quit grammar school and, opting to not go to a college, stayed at his parents' home to compose poetry. This period, 1931–1934, is regarded as the most important in Thomas' creative life. It was here that Thomas developed the technique and voice which were to become his trademarks. During this time, he wrote almost all of the poems that appeared in his first book, *18 Poems* (1934), and indeed composed about half of all the poems that he ever wrote.

After years of struggling to get anything published, Thomas' first collection, *18 Poems,* won the *Sunday Referee* Book Prize for Poetry and received very fine critical reviews. He moved to London in 1934 and began to establish his reputation as both an innovative poet and unique personality. After spending time alone in Ireland, Thomas finished his second collection, *25 Poems,* in 1936. This publication culminated his early experimental period, and poems such as the enigmatic masterpiece "Altarwise by Owllight" foreshadowed his more mature poetry. The book received enthusiastic praise from Edith Sitwell: "I could not name one poet of this, the youngest generation, who shows so great a promise, and even so great an achievement." For "serious" poetry, *25 Poems* was a great commercial success as it went through four printings almost immediately after it was published.

In 1937 Thomas married Caitlin Macnamara. His marriage and *25 Poems* marked the end of his "difficult" surreal early period. Thomas became more humanistic—he wrote about Caitlin, love and his home. Thus the poetry had a wider world view and became more objective and less self-centered. This shift in style is best summed up in the 1938 "Poem to Caitlin." Though Thomas was gaining recognition, he and Caitlin lived in abject poverty in a fisherman's cottage, relying on the generosity of friends and publishers to survive.

Thomas published his third volume of verse, *Map of Love,* in 1939 and followed with a collection of autobiographical short stories in 1940, *Portrait of the Artist as a Young Dog.* When Britain entered World War II Thomas did not relish the idea of becoming a soldier. To excuse himself from the draft he got a job as a scriptwriter for the BBC and Strand Films. The forties were a gestation period. Thomas worked on documentaries and did broadcasts for the BBC, but wrote very little for the first half of the decade. In fact, in 1941, Thomas sold all of his old notebooks, notebooks he had been keeping since he was a teenager, to a rare manuscript dealer. This represented a significant rejection of his past achievements and a resolve to progress. In 1946 Thomas came out with *Deaths and Entrances.* Poems such as "Poem in October," "Fern Hill," and "In my craft or sullen art" marked the beginning of Thomas' mature and most accomplished stage. Due to *Portrait of the Artist as*

Young Dog and his BBC broadcasts, Thomas was a popular figure and *Deaths and Entrances* was widely read and accepted as a masterpiece.

The Thomas family moved to Laugharne in 1948 and settled in the isolated, but now famous, Boat House—the subject of "Sir John's Hill." By now Thomas was making, for the first time in his life, a substantial sum of money. But both Thomas and Caitlin were poor managers and they and their children continued to live on the brink of starvation, always in tremendous debt. To alleviate the situation, Thomas agreed to do a series of readings in America. His first of four visits to the U.S. lasted from February to June, 1950. Here Thomas charmed audiences with his original and powerful readings, and shocked the literary establishment with his indecorous behavior and unabashed alcoholism. He did another tour of America in 1952, solidifying his legend. His 1952 *Collected Poems* was a bestseller and critical success and gave Thomas his first semblance of financial stability. But he still could not handle his money and had to go on another U.S. tour in 1953. While in New York he suffered a nervous collapse brought about by the severe stress of his schedule and his addiction to alcohol. He died November 9 in St. Vincent's Hospital in Greenwich Village. Dylan Thomas is buried in St. Martin's churchyard, Laugharne, Wales.

After the Funeral
In Memory of Ann Jones

After the funeral, mule praises, brays,
Windshake of sailshaped ears, muffle-toed tap
Tap happily of one peg in the thick
Grave's foot, blinds down the lids, the teeth in black,
The spittled eyes, the salt ponds in the sleeves,
Morning smack of the spade that wakes up sleep,
Shakes a desolate boy who slits his throat
In the dark of the coffin and sheds dry leaves,
That breaks one bone to light with a judgment clout,
After the feast of tear-stuffed time and thistles
In a room with a stuffed fox and a stale fern,
I stand, for this memorial's sake, alone
In the snivelling hours with dead, humped Ann
Whose hooded, fountain heart once fell in puddles
Round the parched worlds of Wales and drowned each sun
(Though this for her is a monstrous image blindly
Magnified out of praise; her death was a still drop;
She would not have me sinking in the holy
Flood of her heart's flame; she would lie dumb and deep
And need no druid of her broken body).
But I, Ann's bard on a raised hearth, call all
The seas to service that her wood-tongued virtue

Babble like a bellbuoy over the hymning heads,
Bow down the walls of the ferned and foxy woods
That her love sing and swing through a brown chapel,
Bless her bent spirit with four, crossing birds.
Her flesh was meek as milk, but this skyward statue
With the wild breast and blessed and giant skull
Is carved from her in a room with a wet window
In a fiercely mourning house in a crooked year.
I know her scrubbed and sour humble hands
Lie with religion in their cramp, her threadbare
Whisper in a damp word, her wits drilled hollow,
Her fist of a face died clenched on a round pain;
And sculptured Ann is seventy years of stone.
These cloud-sopped, marble hands, this monumental
Argument of the hewn voice, gesture and psalm
Storm me forever over her grave until
The stuffed lung of the fox twitch and cry Love
And the strutting fern lay seeds on the black sill.

Altarwise by Owl-Light

I

Altarwise by owl-light in the halfway-house
The gentleman lay graveward with his furies;
Abaddon in the hang-nail cracked from Adam,
And, from his fork, a dog among the fairies,
The atlas-eater with a jaw for news,
Bit out the mandrake with to-morrow's scream.
Then, penny-eyed, that gentleman of wounds,
Old cock from nowheres and the heaven's egg,
With bones unbuttoned to the halfway winds,
Hatched from the windy salvage on one leg,
Scraped at my cradle in a walking word
That night of time under the Christward shelter:
I am the long world's gentleman, he said,
And share my bed with Capricorn and Cancer.

II

Death is all metaphors, shape in one history;
The child that sucketh long is shooting up,
The planet-ducted pelican of circles
Weans on an artery the gender's strip;
Child of the short spark in a shapeless country
Soon sets alight a long stick from the cradle;
The horizontal cross-bones of Abaddon,
You by the cavern over the black stairs,
Rung bone and blade, the verticals of Adam,
And, manned by midnight, Jacob to the stars.
Hairs of your head, then said the hollow agent,
Are but the roots of nettles and of feathers
Over these groundworks thrusting through a pavement
And hemlock-headed in the wood of weathers.

III

First there was the lamb on knocking knees
And three dead seasons on a climbing grave
That Adam's wether in the flock of horns,
Butt of the tree-tailed worm that mounted Eve,
Horned down with skullfoot and the skull of toes
Of thunderous pavements in the garden time;
Rip of the vaults, I took my marrow-ladle
Out of the wrinkled undertaker's van,
And, Rip Van Winkle from a timeless cradle,
Dipped me breast-deep in the descended bone;
The black ram, shuffling of the year, old winter,
Alone alive among his mutton fold,
We rung our weathering changes on the ladder,
Said the antipodes, and twice spring chimed.

IV

What is the metre of the dictionary?
The size of genesis? the short spark's gender?

Shade without shape? the shape of Pharaoh's echo?
(My shape of age nagging the wounded whisper).
Which sixth of wind blew out the burning gentry?
(Questions are hunchbacks to the poker marrow).
What of bamboo man among your acres?
Corset the boneyards for a crooked boy?
Button your bodice on a hump of splinters,
My camel's eyes will needle through the shrowd.
Love's reflection of the mushroom features,
Stills snapped by night in the bread-sided field,
Once close-up smiling in the wall of pictures,
Arc-lamped thrown back upon the cutting flood.

V

And from the windy West came two-gunned Gabriel,
From Jesu's sleeve trumped up the king of spots,
The sheath-decked jacks, queen with a shuffled heart;
Said the fake gentleman in suit of spades,
Black-tongued and tipsy from salvation's bottle.
Rose my Byzantine Adam in the night.
For loss of blood I fell on Ishmael's plain,
Under the milky mushrooms slew my hunger,
A climbing sea from Asia had me down
And Jonah's Moby snatched me by the hair,
Cross-stroked salt Adam to the frozen angel
Pin-legged on pole-hills with a black medusa
By waste seas where the white bear quoted Virgil
And sirens singing from our lady's sea-straw.

VI

Cartoon of slashes on the tide-traced crater,
He in a book of water tallow-eyed
By lava's light split through the oyster vowels
And burned sea silence on a wick of words.
Pluck, cock, my sea eye, said medusa's scripture,
Lop, love, my fork tongue, said the pin-hilled nettle;

And love plucked out the stinging siren's eye,
Old cock from nowheres lopped the minstrel tongue
Till tallow I blew from the wax's tower
The fats of midnight when the salt was singing;
Adam, time's joker, on a witch of cardboard
Spelt out the seven seas, an evil index,
The bagpipe-breasted ladies in the deadweed
Blew out the blood guaze through the wound of manwax.

VII

Now stamp the Lord's Prayer on a grain of rice,
A Bible-leaved of all the written woods
Strip to this tree: a rocking alphabet,
Genesis in the root, the scarecrow word,
And one light's language in the book of trees.
Doom on deniers at the wind-turned statement.
Time's tune my ladies with the teats of music,
The scaled sea-sawers, fix in a naked sponge
Who sucks the bell-voiced Adam out of magic,
Time, milk, and magic, from the world beginning.
Time is the tune my ladies lend their heartbreak,
From bald pavilions and the house of bread
Time tracks the sound of shape on man and cloud,
On rose and icicle the ringing handprint.

VIII

This was the crucifixion on the mountain,
Time's nerve in vinegar, the gallow grave
As tarred with blood as the bright thorns I wept;
The world's my wound, God's Mary in her grief,
Bent like three trees and bird-papped through her shift,
With pins for teardrops is the long wound's woman.
This was the sky, Jack Christ, each minstrel angle
Drove in the heaven-driven of the nails
Till the three-coloured rainbow from my nipples
From pole to pole leapt round the snail-waked world.

I by the tree of thieves, all glory's sawbones,
Unsex the skeleton this mountain minute,
And by this blowclock witness of the sun
Suffer the heaven's children through my heartbeat.

IX

From the oracular archives and the parchment,
Prophets and fibre kings in oil and letter,
The lamped calligrapher, the queen in splints,
Buckle to lint and cloth their natron footsteps,
Draw on the glove of prints, dead Cairo's henna
Pour like a halo on the caps and serpents.
This was the resurrection in the desert,
Death from a bandage, rants the mask of scholars
Gold on such features, and the linen spirit
Weds my long gentleman to dusts and furies;
With priest and pharaoh bed my gentle wound,
World in the sand, on the triangle landscape,
With stones of odyssey for ash and garland
And rivers of the dead around my neck.

X

Let the tale's sailor from a Christian voyage
Atlaswise hold half-way off the dummy bay
Time's ship-racked gospel on the globe I balance:
So shall winged harbours through the rockbirds' eyes
Spot the blown word, and on the seas I image
December's thorn screwed in a brow of holly.
Let the first Peter from a rainbow's quayrail
Ask the tall fish swept from the bible east,
What rhubarb man peeled in her foam-blue channel
Has sown a flying garden round that sea-ghost?
Green as beginning, let the garden diving
Soar, with its two bark towers, to that Day
When the worm builds with the gold straws of venom
My nest of mercies of the rude, red tree.

Ballad of the Long-Legged Bait

The bows glided down, and the coast
Blackened with birds took a last look
At his thrashing hair and whale-blue eye;
The trodden town rang its cobbles for luck.

Then good-bye to the fishermanned
Boat with its anchor free and fast
As a bird hooking over the sea,
High and dry by the top of the mast,

Whispered the affectionate sand
And the bulwarks of the dazzled quay.
For my sake sail, and never look back,
Said the looking land.

Sails drank the wind, and white as milk
He sped into the drinking dark;
The sun shipwrecked west on a pearl
And the moon swam out of its hulk.

Funnels and masts went by in a whirl.
Good-bye to the man on the sea-legged deck
To the gold gut that sings on his reel
To the bait that stalked out of the sack,

For we saw him throw to the swift flood
A girl alive with his hooks through her lips;
All the fishes were rayed in blood,
Said the dwindling ships.

Good-bye to chimneys and funnels,
Old wives that spin in the smoke,
He was blind to the eyes of candles
In the praying windows of waves

But heard his bait buck in the wake
And tussle in a shoal of loves.
Now cast down your rod, for the whole
Of the sea is hilly with whales,

She longs among horses and angels,
The rainbow-fish bend in her joys,
Floated the lost cathedral
Chimes of the rocked buoys.

Where the anchor rode like a gull
Miles over the moonstruck boat
A squall of birds bellowed and fell,
A cloud blew the rain from its throat;

He saw the storm smoke out to kill
With fuming bows and ram of ice,
Fire on starlight, rake Jesu's stream;
And nothing shone on the water's face

But the oil and bubble of the moon,
Plunging and piercing in his course
The lured fish under the foam
Witnessed with a kiss.

Whales in the wake like capes and Alps
Quaked the sick sea and snouted deep,
Deep the great bushed bait with raining lips
Slipped the fins of those humpbacked tons

And fled their love in a weaving dip.
Oh, Jericho was falling in their lungs!
She nipped and dived in the nick of love,
Spun on a spout like a long-legged ball

Till every beast blared down in a swerve
Till every turtle crushed from his shell
Till every bone in the rushing grave
Rose and crowed and fell!

Good luck to the hand on the rod,
There is thunder under its thumbs;
Gold gut is a lightning thread,
His fiery reel sings off its flames,

The whirled boat in the burn of his blood
Is crying from nets to knives,
Oh the shearwater birds and their boatsized brood
Oh the bulls of Biscay and their calves

Are making under the green, laid veil
The long-legged beautiful bait their wives.
Break the black news and paint on a sail
Huge weddings in the waves,

Over the wakeward-flashing spray
Over the gardens of the floor
Clash out the mounting dolphin's day,
My mast is a bell-spire,

Strike and smoothe, for my decks are drums,
Sing through the water-spoken prow
The octopus walking into her limbs
The polar eagle with his tread of snow.

From salt-lipped beak to the kick of the stern
Sing how the seal has kissed her dead!
The long, laid minute's bride drifts on
Old in her cruel bed.

Over the graveyard in the water
Mountains and galleries beneath
Nightingale and hyena
Rejoicing for that drifting death

Sing and howl through sand and anemone
Valley and sahara in a shell,
Oh all the wanting flesh his enemy
Thrown to the sea in the shell of a girl

Is old as water and plain as an eel;
Always good-bye to the long-legged bread
Scattered in the paths of his heels
For the salty birds fluttered and fed

And the tall grains foamed in their bills;
Always good-bye to the fires of the face,
For the crab-backed dead on the sea-bed rose
And scuttled over her eyes,

The blind, clawed stare is cold as sleet.
The tempter under the eyelid
Who shows to the selves asleep
Mast-high moon-white women naked

Walking in wishes and lovely for shame
Is dumb and gone with his flame of brides.
Sussanah's drowned in the bearded stream
And no-one stirs at Sheba's side

But the hungry kings of the tides;
Sin who had a woman's shape
Sleeps till Silence blows on a cloud
And all the lifted waters walk and leap.

Lucifer that bird's dropping
Out of the sides of the north
Has melted away and is lost
Is always lost in her vaulted breath,

Venus lies star-struck in her wound
And the sensual ruins make
Seasons over the liquid world,
White springs in the dark.

Always good-bye, cried the voices through the shell,
Good-bye always for the flesh is cast
And the fisherman winds his reel
With no more desire than a ghost

Always good luck, praised the finned in the feather
Bird after dark and the laughing fish
As the sails drank up the hail of thunder
And the long-tailed lightning lit his catch.

The boat swims into the six-year weather,
A wind throws a shadow and it freezes fast.
See what the gold gut drags from under
Mountains and galleries to the crest!

See what clings to hair and skull
As the boat skims on with drinking wings!
The statues of great rain stand still,
And the flakes fall like hills.

Sing and strike his heavy haul
Toppling up the boatside in a snow of light!
His decks are drenched with miracles.
Oh miracle of fishes! The long dead bite!

Out of the urn the size of a man
Out of the room the weight of his trouble
Out of the house that holds a town
In the continent of a fossil

One by one in dust and shawl,
Dry as echoes and insect-faced,
His fathers cling to the hand of the girl
And the dead hand leads the past,

Leads them as children and as air
On to the blindly tossing tops;
The centuries throw back their hair
And the old men sing from newborn lips:

Time is bearing another son.
Kill Time! She turns in her pain!
The oak is felled in the acorn
And the hawk in the egg kills the wren.

He who blew the great fire in
And died on a hiss of flames
Or walked on the earth in the evening
Counting the denials of the grains

Clings to her drifting hair, and climbs;
And he who taught their lips to sing
Weeps like the risen sun among
The liquid choirs of his tribes.

The rod bends low, divining land,
And through the sundered water crawls
A garden holding to her hand
With birds and animals

With men and women and waterfalls
Trees cool and dry in the whirlpool of ships
And stunned and still on the green, laid veil
Sand with legends in its virgin laps

And prophets loud on the burned dunes;
Insects and valleys hold her thighs hard,
Time and places grip her breast bone,
She is breaking with seasons and clouds;

Round her trailed wrist fresh water weaves,
With moving fish and rounded stones
Up and down the greater waves
A separate river breathes and runs;

Strike and sing his catch of fields
For the surge is sown with barley,
The cattle graze on the covered foam,
The hills have footed the waves away,

With wild sea fillies and soaking bridles
With salty colts and gales in their limbs
All the horses of the haul of miracles
Gallop through the arched, green farms.

Trot and gallop with gulls upon them
And thunderbolts in their manes.
O Rome and Sodom To-morrow and London
The country tide is cobbled with towns,

And steeples pierce the cloud on her shoulder
And the streets that the fisherman combed
When his long-legged flesh was a wind on fire
And his loin was a hunting flame

Coil from the thoroughfares of her hair
And terribly lead him home alive
Lead her prodigal home to his terror,
And furious ox-killing house of love.

Down, down, down, under the ground,
Under the floating villages,
Turns the moon-chained and water-wound
Metropolis of fishes,

There is nothing left of the sea but its sound,
Under the earth the loud sea walks,
In deathbeds of orchards the boat dies down
And the bait is drowned among hayricks,

Land, land, land, nothing remains
Of the pacing, famous sea but its speech,
And into its talkative seven tombs
The anchor dives through the floors of a church.

Good-bye, good luck, struck the sun and the moon,
To the fisherman lost on the land.
He stands alone at the door of his home,
With his long-legged heart in his hand.

Ceremony after a Fire Raid

I

Myselves
The grievers
Grieve
Among the street burned to tireless death
A child of a few hours

With its kneading mouth
Charred on the black breast of the grave
The mother dug, and its arms full of fires.

Begin
With singing
Sing
Darkness kindled back into beginning
When the caught tongue nodded blind,
A star was broken
Into the centuries of the child
Myselves grieve now, and miracles cannot atone.

Forgive
Us forgive
Us your death that myselves the believers
May hold it in a great flood
Till the blood shall spurt,
And the dust shall sing like a bird
As the grains blow, as your death grows, through our heart.

Crying
Your dying
Cry,
Child beyond cockcrow, by the fire-dwarfed
Street we chant the flying sea
In the body bereft.
Love is the last light spoken. Oh
Seed of sons in the loin of the black husk left.

II

I know not whether
Adam or Eve, the adorned holy bullock
Or the white ewe lamb
Or the chosen virgin
Laid in her snow
On the altar of London,
Was the first to die

In the cinder of the little skull,
O bride and bride groom
O Adam and Eve together
Lying in the lull
Under the sad breast of the head stone
White as the skeleton
Of the garden of Eden.

I know the legend
Of Adam and Eve is never for a second
Silent in my service
Over the dead infants
Over the one
Child who was priest and servants,
Word, singers, and tongue
In the cinder of the little skull,
Who was the serpent's
Night fall and the fruit like a sun,
Man and woman undone,
Beginning crumbled back to darkness
Bare as the nurseries
Of the garden of wilderness.

III

Into the organpipes and steeples
Of the luminous cathedrals,
Into the weathercocks' molten mouths
Rippling in twelve-winded circles,
Into the dead clock burning the hour
Over the urn of sabbaths
Over the whirling ditch of daybreak
Over the sun's hovel and the slum of fire
And the golden pavements laid in requiems,
Into the bread in a wheatfield of flames,
Into the wine burning like brandy,
The masses of the sea
The masses of the sea under
The masses of the infant-bearing sea

Erupt, fountain, and enter to utter for ever
Glory glory glory
The sundering ultimate kingdom of genesis' thunder.

Ears in the Turrets Hear

Ears in the turrets hear
Hands grumble on the door,
Eyes in the gables see
The fingers at the locks.

Shall I unbolt or stay
Alone till the day I die
Unseen by stranger-eyes
In this white house?
Hands, hold you poison or grapes?

Beyond this island bound
By a thin sea of flesh
And a bone coast,
The land lies out of sound
And the hills out of mind.
No bird or flying fish
Disturbs this island's rest.

Ears in this island hear
The wind pass like a fire,
Eyes in this island see
Ships anchor off the bay.
Shall I run to the ships
With the wind in my hair,
Or stay till the day I die
And welcome no sailor?
Ships, hold you poison or grapes?

Hands grumble on the door,
Ships anchor off the bay,
Rain beats the sand and slates.
Shall I let in the stranger,
Shall I welcome the sailor,
Or stay till the day I die?

Hands of the stranger and holds of the ships,
Hold you poison or grapes?

Fern Hill

Now as I was young and easy under the apple boughs
About the lilting house and happy as the grass was green,
   The night above the dingle starry,
     Time let me hail and climb
   Golden in the heydays of his eyes,
And honoured among wagons I was prince of the apple towns
And once below a time I lordly had the trees and leaves
     Trail with daisies and barley
   Down the rivers of the windfall light.

And as I was green and carefree, famous among the barns
About the happy yard and singing as the farm was home,
   In the sun that is young once only,
     Time let me play and be
   Golden in the mercy of his means,
And green and golden I was huntsman and herdsman, the calves
Sang to my horn, the foxes on the hills barked clear and cold,
     And the sabbath rang slowly
   In the pebbles of the holy streams.

All the sun long it was running, it was lovely, the hay
Fields high as the house, the tunes from the chimneys, it was air
   And playing, lovely and watery
     And fire green as grass.
   And nightly under the simple stars
As I rode to sleep the owls were bearing the farm away,
All the moon long I heard, blessed among stables, the nightjars
   Flying with the ricks, and horses
     Flashing into the dark.

And then to awake, and the farm, like a wanderer white
With the dew, come back, the cock on his shoulder: it was all
   Shining, it was Adam and maiden,
     The sky gathered again
   And the sun grew round that very day.
So it must have been after the birth of the simple light
In the first, spinning place, the spellbound horses walking warm
   Out of the whinnying green stable
     On to the fields of praise.

And honoured among foxes and pheasants by the gay house
Under the new made clouds and happy as the heart was long
   In the sun born over and over,
     I ran my heedless ways,
   My wishes raced through the house high hay
And nothing I cared, at my sky blue trades, that time allows
In all his tuneful turning so few and such morning songs
   Before the children green and golden
     Follow him out of grace.

Nothing I cared, in the lamb white days, that time would take me
Up to the swallow thronged loft by the shadow of my hand,
   In the moon that is always rising,
     Nor that riding to sleep
   I should hear him fly with the high fields
And wake to the farm forever fled from the childless land.
Oh as I was young and easy in the mercy of his means,
   Time held me green and dying
     Though I sang in my chains like the sea.

The Hunchback in the Park

The hunchback in the park
A solitary mister
Propped between trees and water
From the opening of the garden lock
That lets the trees and water enter
Until the Sunday sombre bell at dark

Eating bread from a newspaper
Drinking water from the chained cup
That the children filled with gravel
In the fountain basin where I sailed my ship
Slept at night in a dog kennel
But nobody chained him up.

Like the park birds he came early
Like the water he sat down
And Mister they called Hey mister
The truant boys from the town
Running when he had heard them clearly
On out of sound

Past lake and rockery
Laughing when he shook his paper
Hunchbacked in mockery
Through the loud zoo of the willow groves
Dodging the park keeper
With his stick that picked up leaves.

And the old dog sleeper
Alone between nurses and swans
While the boys among willows
Made the tigers jump out of their eyes
To roar on the rockery stones
And the groves were blue with sailors

Made all day until bell time
A woman figure without fault
Straight as a young elm
Straight and tall from his crooked bones
That she might stand in the night
After the locks and chains

All night in the unmade park
After the railings and shrubberies
The birds the grass the trees the lake
And the wild boys innocent as strawberries
Had followed the hunchback
To his kennel in the dark.

Poem in October

      It was my thirtieth year to heaven
Woke to my hearing from harbour and neighbor wood
         And the mussel pooled and the heron
             Priested shore
            The morning beckon
With water praying and call of seagull and rook
And the knock of sailing boats on the net webbed wall
         Myself to set foot
            That second
     In the still sleeping town and set forth.

      My birthday began with the water-
Birds and the birds of the winged trees flying my name
         Above the farms and the white horses
           And I rose
            In rainy autumn
And walked abroad in a shower of all my days.
High tide and the heron dived when I took the road
         Over the border
            And the gates
     Of the town closed as the town awoke.

      A springful of larks in a rolling
Cloud and the roadside bushes brimming with whistling
         Blackbirds and the sun of October
            Summery
            On the hill's shoulder,
Here were fond climates and sweet singers suddenly
Come in the morning where I wandered and listened
         To the rain wringing
            Wind blow cold
     In the wood faraway under me.

      Pale rain over the dwindling harbour
And over the sea wet church the size of a snail
         With its horns through mist and the castle
            Brown as owls
            But all the gardens

Of spring and summer were blooming in the tall tales
Beyond the border and under the lark full cloud.
    There could I marvel
        My birthday
    Away but the weather turned around.

It turned away from the blithe country
And down the other air and the blue altered sky
    Streamed again a wonder of summer
        With apples
        Pears and red currants
And I saw in the turning so clearly a child's
Forgotten mornings when he walked with his mother
    Through the parables
        Of sun light
    And the legends of the green chapels

    And the twice told fields of infancy
That his tears burned my cheeks and his heart moved in mine.
    These were the woods the river and sea
        Where a boy
        In the listening
Summertime of the dead whispered the truth of his joy
To the trees and the stones and the fish in the tide.
    And the mystery
        Sang alive
    Still in the water and singingbirds.

    And there could I marvel my birthday
Away but the weather turned around. And the true
    Joy of the long dead child sang burning
        In the sun.
        It was my thirtieth
Year to heaven stood there then in the summer noon
Though the town below lay leaved with October blood.
    O may my heart's truth
        Still be sung
    On this high hill in a year's turning.

A Refusal to Mourn the Death, by Fire of a Child in London

Never until the mankind making
Bird beast and flower
Fathering and all humbling darkness
Tells with silence the last light breaking
And the still hour
Is come of the sea tumbling in harness

And I must enter again the round
Zion of the water bead
And the synagogue of the ear of corn
Shall I let pray the shadow of a sound
Or sow my salt seed
In the least valley of sackcloth to mourn

The majesty and burning of the child's death.
I shall not murder
The mankind of her going with a grave truth
Nor blaspheme down the stations of the breath
With any further
Elegy of innocence and youth.

Deep with the first dead lies London's daughter,
Robed in the long friends,
The grains beyond age, the dark veins of her mother,
Secret by the unmourning water
Of the riding Thames.
After the first death, there is no other.

A Winter's Tale

      It is a winter's tale
That the snow blind twilight ferries over the lakes
And floating fields from the farm in the cup of the
    vales,
Gliding windless through the hand folded flakes,
The pale breath of cattle at the stealthy sail,

      And the stars falling cold,
And the smell of hay in the snow, and the far owl
Warning among the folds, and the frozen hold
Flocked with the sheep white smoke of the farm house
    cowl
In the river wended vales where the tale was told.

      Once when the world turned old
On a star of faith pure as the drifting bread,
As the food and flames of the snow, a man unrolled
The scrolls of fire that burned in his heart and head,
Torn and alone in a farm house in a fold.

      Of fields. And burning then
In his firelit island ringed by the winged snow
And the dung hills white as wool and the hen
Roosts sleeping chill till the flame of the cock crow
Combs through the mantled yards and the morning men

      Stumble out with their spades,
The cattle stirring, the mousing cat stepping shy,
The puffed birds hopping and hunting, the milk maids
Gentle in their clogs over the fallen sky,
And all the woken farm at its white trades,

      He knelt, he wept, he prayed,
By the spit and the black pot in the log bright light
And the cup and the cut bread in the dancing shade,
In the muffled house, in the quick of night,
At the point of love, forsaken and afraid.

      He knelt on the cold stones,
He wept from the crest of grief, he prayed to the
    veiled sky
May his hunger go howling on bare white bones
Past the statues of the stables and the sky roofed sties
And the duck pond glass and the blinding byres alone

>   Into the home of prayers
> And fires where he should prowl down the cloud
> Of his snow blind love and rush in the white lairs.
> His naked need struck him howling and bowed
> Though no sound flowed down the hand folded air
>
>   But only the wind strung
> Hunger of birds in the fields of the bread of water,
>   tossed
> In high corn and the harvest melting on their tongues
> And his nameless need bound him burning and lost
> When cold as snow he should run the wended vales
>   among
>
>   The rivers mouthed in night,
> And drown in the drifts of his need, and lie curled
>   caught
> In the always desiring centre of the white
> Inhuman cradle and the bride bed forever sought
> By the believer lost and the hurled outcast of light.
>
>   Deliver him, he cried,
> By losing him all in love, and cast his need
> Alone and naked in the engulfing bride,
> Never to flourish in the fields of the white seed
> Or flower under the time dying flesh astride.
>
>   Listen. The minstrels sing
> In the departed villages. The nightingale,
> Dust in the buried wood, flies on the grains of her
>   wings
> And spells on the winds of the dead his winter's tale.
> The voice of the dust of water from the withered spring
>
>   Is telling. The wizened
> Stream with bells and baying water hounds. The dew
>   rings
> On the gristed leaves and the long gone glistening
> Parish of snow. The carved mouths in the rock are
>   wind swept strings.
> Time sings through the intricately dead snow drop.
>   Listen.

It was a hand or sound
In the long ago land that glided the dark door wide
And there outside on the bread of the ground
A she bird rose and rayed like a burning bride.
A she bird dawned, and her breast with snow and
     scarlet downed.

     Look. And the dancers move
On the departed, snow bushed green, wanton in
     moon light
As a dust of pigeons. Exulting, the grave hooved
Horses, centaur dead, turn and tread the drenched
     white
Paddocks in the farms of birds. The dead oak walks
     for love.

     The carved limbs in the rock
Leap, as to trumpets. Calligraphy of the old
Leaves is dancing. Lines of age on the stones weave
     in a flock.
And the harp shaped voice of the water's dust
     plucks in a fold
Of fields. For love, the long ago she bird rises. Look.

     And the wild wings were raised
Above her folded head, and the soft feathered voice
Was flying through the house as though the she bird
     praised
And all the elements of the slow fall rejoiced
That a man knelt alone in the cup of the vales,

     In the mantle and calm,
By the spit and the black pot in the log bright light.
And the sky of birds in the plumed voice charmed
Him up and he ran like a wind after the kindling flight
Past the blind barns and byres of the windless farm.

       In the poles of the year
When black birds died like priests in the cloaked
       hedge row
And over the cloth of counties the far hills rode near,
Under the one leaved trees ran a scarecrow of snow
And fast through the drifts of the thickets antlered
       like deer,

       Rags and prayers down the knee-
Deep hillocks and loud on the numbled lakes,
All night lost and long wading in the wake of the she-
Bird through the times and lands and tribes of the
       snow flakes.
Listen and look where she sails the goose plucked sea,

       The sky, the bird, the bride,
The cloud, the need, the planted stars, the joy beyond
The fields of seed and the time dying flesh astride,
The heavens, the heaven, the grave, the burning font.
In the far ago land the door of his death glided wide,

       And the bird descended.
On a bread white hill over the cupped farm
And the lakes and floating fields and the river wended
Vales where he prayed to come to the last harm
And the home of prayers and fires, the tale ended.

       The dancing perishes
On the white, no longer growing green, and,
       minstrel dead,
The singing breaks in the snow shoed villages of
       wishes
That once cut the figures of birds on the deep bread
And over the glazed lakes skated the shapes of fishes

        Flying. The rite is shorn
Of nightingale and centaur dead horse. The springs
        wither
Back. Lines of age sleep on the stones till trumpeting
        dawn.
Exultation lies down. Time buries the spring weather
That belled and bounded with the fossil and the dew
        reborn.

        For the bird lay bedded
In a choir of wings, as though, she slept or died,
And the wings glided wide and he was hymned and
        wedded,
And through the thighs of the engulfing bride,
The woman breasted and the heaven headed

        Bird, he was brought low,
Burning in the bride bed of love, in the whirl-
Pool at the wanting centre, in the folds
Of paradise, in the spun bud of the world.
And she rose with him flowering in her melting snow.

Alun Lewis (1915–1944)

Alun Lewis, born July 1 in Aberdare, South Wales, was a grammar school teacher before he enlisted in the British army in 1940. He was transferred to India in 1942 where he insisted on seeing active duty, despite being offered a desk job. He was killed in a shooting accident while on patrol. His best work is his 1942 *Raider's Dawn*, a book of verse which details the lonely and alienating experience of the soldier at war. His poetry about India, *Ha! Ha! Among the Trumpets*, appeared in 1945.

Dawn on the East Coast

From Orford Ness to Shingle Street
The grey disturbance spreads
Washing the icy seas on Deben Head.

Cock pheasants scratch the frozen fields,
Gulls lift thin horny legs and step
Fastidiously among the rusted mines.

The soldier leaning on the sandbagged wall
Hears in the combers' curling rush and crash
His single self-centered monotonous wish;

And time is a froth of such transparency
His drowning eyes what they wish to see;
A girl laying his table with a white cloth.
      .   .   .   .
The light assails him from a flank,
Two carbons touching in his brain
Crumple the cellophane lanterns of his dream.

And then the day, grown feminine and kind,
Stoops with the gulfing motion of the tide
And pours his ashes in a tiny urn.

From Orford Ness to Shingle Street
The grey disturbance lifts its head
And one by one, reluctantly,
The living come back slowly from the dead.

The Jungle

I

In mole-blue indolence the sun
Plays idly on the stagnant pool
In whose grey bed black swollen leaf
Holds Autumn rotting like an unfrocked priest.
The crocodile slides from the ochre sand
And drives the great translucent fish
Under the boughs across the running gravel.
Windfalls of brittle mast crunch as we come
To quench more than our thirst—our selves—
Beneath this bamboo bridge, the mantled pool
Where sleep exudes a sinister content
As though all strength of mind and limb must pass
And all fidelities and doubts dissolve,
The weighted world a bubble in each head,
The warm pacts of the flesh betrayed
By the nonchalance of a laugh,
The green indifference of this sleep.

II

Wandering and fortuitous the paths
We followed to this rendezvous today
Out of mines and offices and dives,
The sidestreets of anxiety and want,
Huge cities known and distant as the stars,
Wheeling beyond our destiny and hope.
We did not notice how the accent changed
As shadows ride from precipice to plain
Closing the parks and cordoning the roads,
Clouding the humming cultures of the West—
The weekly bribe we paid the man in black,
The day shift sinking from the sun,
The blinding arc of rivets blown through steel,
The patient queues, headlines and slogans flung
Across a frightened continent, the town
Sullen and out of work, the little home

Semi-detached, suburban, transient
As fever or the anger of the old,
The best ones on some specious pretext gone.

But we who dream beside this jungle pool
Prefer the instinctive rightness of the poised
Pied kingfisher deep darting for a fish
To all the banal rectitude of states,
The dew-bright diamonds on a viper's back
To the slow poison of a meaning lost
And the vituperations of the just.

III

The banyan's branching clerestories close
The noon's harsh splendour to a head of light.
The black spot in the focus grows and grows:
The vagueness of the child, the lover's deep
And inarticulate bewilderment,
The willingness to please that made a wound,
The kneeling darkness and the hungry prayer;
Cargoes of anguish in the holds of joy,
The smooth deceitful stranger in the heart,
The tangled wrack of motives drifting down
An oceanic tide of Wrong.
And though the state has enemies we know
The greater enmity within ourselves.

Some things we cleaned like knives in earth,
Kept from the dew and rust of Time
Instinctive truths and elemental love,
Knowing the force that brings the teal and quail
From Turkestan across Himalayan snows
To Kashmir and the South alone can guide
That winging wildness home again.

Oh you who want us for ourselves,
Whose love can start the snow-rush in the woods
And melt the glacier in the dark coulisse,
Forgive this strange inconstancy of soul,
The face distorted in the jungle pool
That drowns its image in a mort of leaves.

IV

Gray monkeys gibber, ignorant and wise.
We are the ghosts, and they the denizens;
We are like them anonymous, unknown,
Avoiding what is human, near,
Skirting the villages, the paddy fields
Where boys sit timelessly to scare the crows
On bamboo platforms raised above their lives.

A trackless wilderness divides
Joy from its cause, the motive from the act:
The killing arm uncurls, strokes the soft moss;
The distant world is an obituary,
We do not hear the tappings of its dread.
The act sustains; there is no consequence.
Only aloneness, swinging slowly
Down the cold orbit of an older world
Than any they predicted in the schools,
Stirs the cold forest with a starry wind,
And sudden as the flashing of a sword
The dream exalts the bowed and golden head
And time is swept with a great turbulence,
The old temptation to remold the world.

The bamboos creak like an uneasy house;
The night is shrill with crickets, cold with space.
And if the mute pads on the sand should lift
Annihilating paws and strike us down
Then would some unimportant death resound
With the imprisoned music of the soul?
And we become the world we could not change?
Or does the will's long struggle end
With the last kindness of a foe or friend?

The Peasants

The dwarf barefooted, chanting
Behind the oxen by the lake,
Stepping lightly and lazily among the thorntrees
Dusky and dazed with sunlight, half awake;

The women breaking stones upon the highway,
Walking erect with burdens on their heads,
One body growing in another body,
Creation touching verminous straw beds.

Across scorched hills and trampled crops
The soldiers straggle by.
History staggers in their wake.
The peasants watch them die.

To a Comrade in Arms

Red fool, my laughing comrade,
Hiding your woman's love
And your man's madness,
Patrolling farther than nowhere
To gain what is nearer than here,
Your face will grow grey as Christ's garments
With the dust of ditches and trenches,
So endlessly faring.

Red fool, my laughing comrade,
Hiding your mystic symbols
Of bread broken for eating
And palm-leaves strewn for welcome,
What foe will you make your peace with
This summer that is more cruel
Than the ancient God of the Hebrews?

When bees swarm in your nostrils
And honey drips from the sockets
Of eyes that today are frantic
With love that is frustrate,
What vow shall we vow who love you
For the self that you did not value?

David Gascoyne (Born 1916)

Born on October 10 in Harrow, Middlesex, England, David Gascoyne was educated at Salisbury Cathedral Choir School and Regent Street Polytechnic in London. He began his literary career while still in his teens, writing surrealist poetry and introducing continental European surrealism to England. Gascoyne's early experience with surrealism gave him a firm grounding in image creation, especially the juxtaposition of paradoxical ideas to produce disturbing effects. His major poems appeared in *Poems 1937–1942*, where he expressed himself on existential philosophy, the Second World War, and Christian symbolism. He has published 11 books of verse overall, and many essays on the history of the surrealist movement.

An Autumn Park

Dark suffocates the world; but such
Ubiquity of shadow is unequal. Here
At the spiked gates which crown the hill begins
A reign as of suspense within suspense;
Outside our area of sand-bagged mansions and of tense
But inarticulate expectancy of roars,
The unhistoric park
Extends indifference through all its air.

During these present days
None but the lonely and reflective care to walk
Through the unworldly and concealed preserves
Of vegetable integrity (where trees
Though murmurous at least are without words . . .)
For such unsocial ones the park negates
With its consistently non-human peace
All the loud mind-polluted world outside its gates.

When sudden sunrays break the brooding haze
Which makes monotonous these grounds,
Livid the little wind-flaked lakes appear,
Vivid the fever-mottled leaves still bound
By mouldering stalks to idly shaken boughs;
Brief light and breath intensify the scene
With glitter drifting across wet grass wastes
And odour of crushed bracken and raw sand . . .

These acres bordering on plains of brick
And brain and coin and newspaper and noise,
Still store for townsmen such as seek
Remembrance of the simpler earth that was
Our dwelling and contentment once, a chance
Of re-beholding that lost innocence; may show
To those that walk to-day there to forget, the true
And imminent glory breaking through Man's circumstance.

Ecce Homo

Whose is this horrifying face,
This putrid flesh, discoloured, flayed,
Fed on by flies, scorched by the sun?
Whose are these hollow red-filmed eyes
And thorn-spiked head and spear-stuck side?
Behold the Man: He is Man's Son.

Forget the legend, tear the decent veil
That cowardice or interest devised
To make their mortal enemy a friend,
To hide the bitter truth all His wounds tell,
Lest the great scandal be no more disguised:
He is in agony till the world's end.
And we must never sleep during that time!
He is suspended on the cross-tree now
And we are onlookers at the crime,
Callous contemporaries of the slow
Torture of God. Here is the hill
Made ghastly by His spattered blood

Whereon He hangs and suffers still:
See, the centurions wear riding-boots,
Black shirts and badges and peaked caps,
Greet one another with raised-arm salutes;
They have cold eyes, unsmiling lips;
Yet these His brothers know not what they do.

And on His either side hang dead
A labourer and a factory hand,

Or one is maybe a lynched Jew
And one a Negro or a Red,
Coolie or Ethiopian, Irishman,
Spaniard or German democrat.

Behind His lolling head the sky
Glares like a fiery cataract
Red with the murders of two thousand years
Committed in His name and by
Crusaders, Christian warriors
Defending faith and property.

Amid the plain beneath His transfixed hands,
Exuding darkness as indelible
As guilty stains, fanned by funereal
And lurid airs, beseiged by drifting sands
And clefted landslides, our about-to-be
Bombed and abandoned cities stand.

He who wept for Jerusalem
Now sees His prophecy extend
Across the greatest cities of the world,
A guilty panic reason cannot stem
Rising to raze them all as He foretold;
And He must watch this drama to the end.

Though often named, He is unknown
To the dark kingdoms at His feet
Where everything disparages His words,
And each man bears the common guilt alone
And goes blindfolded to his fate,
And fear and greed are sovereign lords.

The turning point of history
Must come. Yet the complacent and the proud
And who exploit and kill, may be denied—
Christ of Revolution and of Poetry—
The resurrection and the life
Wrought by your spirit's blood.

Involved in their own sophistry
The black priest and the upright man
Faced by subversive truth shall be struck dumb,
Christ of Revolution and of Poetry,
While the rejected and condemned become
Agents of the divine.

Not from a monstrance silver-wrought
But from the tree of human pain
Redeem our sterile misery,
Christ of Revolution and of Poetry,
That man's long journey through the night
May not have been in vain.

An Elegy
R.R. 1916–41

Friend, whose unnatural early death
In this year's cold, chaotic Spring
Is like a clumsy wound that will not heal:
What can I say to you, now that your ears
Are stoppered-up with distant soil?
Perhaps to speak at all is false; more true
Simply to sit at times alone and dumb
And with most pure intensity of thought
And concentrated inmost feeling, reach
Towards your shadow on the years' crumbling wall.

I'll say not any word in praise or blame
Of what you ended with the mere turn of a tap;
Nor to explain, deplore nor yet exploit
The latent pathos of your living years—
Hurried, confused and unfulfilled—
That were the shiftless years of both our youths
Spent in the monstrous mountain-shadow of
Catastrophe that chilled you to the bone:
The certain imminence of which always pursued
You from your heritage of fields and sun . . .

I see your face in hostile sunlight, eyes
Wrinkled against its glare, behind the glass
Of a car's windscreen, while you seek to lose
Yourself in swift devouring of white roads
Unwinding across Europe or America;
Taciturn at the wheel, wrapped in a blaze
Of restlessness that no fresh scent can quench;
In cities of brief sojourn that you pass
Through in your quest for respite, heavy drink
Alone enabling you to bear each hotel night.

Sex, Art and Politics: those poor
Expedients! You tried them each in turn,
With the wry inward smile of one resigned
To join in every complicated game
Adults affect to play. Yet girls you found
So prone to sentiment's corruptions; and the joy
Of sensual satisfaction seemed so brief, and left
Only new need. It proved hard to remain
Convinced of the Word's efficacy; or even quite
Certain of World-Salvation through 'the Party
    Line' . . .

Cased in the careful armour that you wore
Of wit and nonchalance, through which
Few quizzed the concealed countenance of fear,
You waited daily for the sky to fall;
At moments wholly panic-stricken by
A sense of stifling in your brittle shell;
Seeing the world's damnation week by week
Grow more and more inevitable; till
The conflagration broke out with a roar,
And from those flames you fled through whirling
    smoke,

To end at last in bankrupt exile in
That sordid city, scene of *Ulysses*; and there,
While War sowed all the lands with violent graves,
You finally succumbed to a black, wild
Incomprehensibility of fate that none could share . . .

Yet even in your obscure death I see
The secret candour of that lonely child
Who, lost in the storm-shaken castle-park,
Astride his crippled mastiff's back was borne
Slowly away into the utmost dark.

Jardin Du Palais Royal
To B. Von M.

The sky's a faded blue and taut-stretched flag
Tenting the quadrangle. On three
Sides the arcade (tenebrous lanes
Down which at times patchouli'd ghosts flit by,—
Furtive reflections on the filmy panes
Of shops which seem to store only the dusts
And atmospheres of antiquated years,—
Intent on fusty vice), restricts the garden-
Statues' timeless gaze. Here inside this
Shut-off and bygone place, brown urchin birds
Play tag and twitter, jittering around
The central fountain's dance; while children chase
Their ragged shadows round about
The palinged trees, with screams; and iron chairs
With pattern-perforated seats drop their design
Like black lace on the gravel. There we sat
And watched that liquid trembling spire the wind
Made sway and break and spatter a thin spray
Like tears upon our hair and tight-clenched hands . . .
How long? I have forgotten. But you rocked
Backwards and forwards, scraping up small stones,
And never spoke. The day was in July,
Full of a whitish and exhausting glare. And I
Could only stare in silence, trying to see
Into the constantly disintegrating core
Round which the fountain ever climbed again;
Hearing the clack of feet that died away
Down the dim passage, and the unnerving din
Child-voices made behind us. O but then

You turned, and asked me with inconsolable eyes
The meaning of the pain that kept us dumb;
And then we both knew that our pact had been betrayed;
And that cold moment made the garden seem
Too like our lives, abandoned in a wilderness of Time,
Boxed-in by the frustrating and decayed
Walls of the haunted Memory's arcade.

Orpheus in the Underworld

Curtains of rock
And tears of stone,
Wet leaves in a high crevice of the sky:
From side to side the draperies
Drawn back by rigid hands.

And he came carrying the shattered lyre,
And wearing the blue robes of a king.
And looking through eyes like holes torn in a screen;
And the distant sea was faintly heard,
From time to time, in the suddenly rising wind,
Like a broken song.

Out of his sleep, from time to time,
From between half open lips,
Escaped the bewildered words which try to tell
The tale of his bright night
And his wing-shadowed day
The soaring flights of thought beneath the sun
Above the islands of the seas
And all the deserts, all the pastures, all the plains
Of the distracting foreign land.

He sleeps with the broken lyre between his hands,
And round his slumber are drawn back
The rigid draperies, the tears and wet leaves,
Cold curtains of rock concealing the bottomless sky.

Robert Lowell (1917–1977)

Robert Lowell, the great grandson of James Russell Lowell and a distant cousin of Amy Lowell, was born March 1 in Boston, Massachusetts. He attended Harvard briefly, and received his A.B. from Kenyon College in 1940. He spent part of World War II in prison as a conscientious objector. Lowell won the Pulitzer Prize in 1947 for *Lord Weary's Castle*. Considered by some critics to be the best American poet of his generation, Lowell's career was marked by constant experimentation and growth. His early poems adhered to rigorous formal constraints. He later turned to narrative lyrics, and his 1959 *Life Studies* was written entirely in free verse. The late fifties were a time of tremendous personal trauma for Lowell: he was divorced, left the Catholic church, and began to have the first fits of madness which would plague him for the rest of his life. Lowell's later work, reflecting a calmer period in his life, returned to his early formal style.

After the Surprising Conversions

September twenty-second, Sir: today
I answer. In the latter part of May,
Hard on our Lord's Ascension, it began
To be more sensible. A gentleman
Of more than common understanding, strict
In morals, pious in behavior, kicked
Against our goad. A man of some renown,
An useful, honored person in the town,
He came of melancholy parents; prone
To secret spells, for years they kept alone—
His uncle, I believe, was killed of it:
Good people, but of too much or little wit.
I preached one Sabbath on a text from Kings;
He showed concernment for his soul. Some things
In his experience were hopeful. He
Would sit and watch the wind knocking a tree
And praise this countryside our Lord has made.
Once when a poor man's heifer died, he laid
A shilling on the doorsill; though a thirst
For loving shook him like a snake, he durst
Not entertain much hope of his estate
In heaven. Once we saw him sitting late
Behind his attic window by a light
That guttered on his Bible; through that night
He meditated terror, and he seemed

Beyond advice or reason, for he dreamed
That he was called to trumpet Judgment Day
To Concord. In the latter part of May
He cut his throat. And though the coroner
Judged him delirious, soon a noisome stir
Palsied our village. At Jehovah's nod
Satan seemed more let loose amongst us: God
Abandoned us to Satan, and he pressed
Us hard, until we thought we could not rest
Till we had done with life. Content was gone.
All the good work was quashed. We were undone.
The breath of God had carried out a planned
And sensible withdrawal from this land;
The multitude, once unconcerned with doubt,
Once neither callous, curious nor devout,
Jumped at broad noon, as though some peddler groaned
At it in its familiar twang: "My friend,
Cut your own throat. Cut your own throat. Now! Now!"
September twenty-second, Sir, the bough
Cracks with the unpicked apples, and at dawn
The small-mouth bass breaks water, gorged with spawn.

As a Plane Tree by the Water

Darkness has called to darkness, and disgrace
Elbows about our windows in this planned
Babel of Boston where our money talks
And multiplies the darkness of a land
Of preparation where the Virgin walks
And roses spiral her enamelled face
Or fall to splinters on unwatered streets.
Our Lady of Babylon, go by, go by,
I was once the apple of your eye;
Flies, flies are on the plane tree, on the streets.

The flies, the flies, the flies of Babylon
Buzz in my ear-drums while the devil's long
Dirge of the people detonates the hour
For floating cities where his golden tongue
Enchants the masons of the Babel Tower

To raise tomorrow's city to the sun
That never sets upon these hell-fire streets
Of Boston, where the sunlight is a sword
Striking at the withholder of the Lord:
Flies, flies are on the plane tree, on the streets.

Flies strike the miraculous waters of the iced
Atlantic and the eyes of Bernadette
Who saw Our Lady standing in the cave
At Massabielle, saw her so squarely that
Her vision put out reason's eyes. The grave
Is open-mouthed and swallowed up in Christ.
O walls of Jericho! And all the streets
To our Atlantic wall are singing: "Sing,
Sing for the resurrection of the King."
Flies, flies are on the plane tree, on the streets.

Colloquy in Black Rock

Here the jack-hammer jabs into the ocean;
My heart, you race and stagger and demand
More blood-gangs for your nigger-brass percussions,
Till I, the stunned machine of your devotion,
Clanging upon this cymbal of a hand,
Am rattled screw and footloose. All discussions

End in the mud-flat detritus of death.
My heart, beat faster, faster. In Black Mud
Hungarian workmen give their blood
For the martyre Stephen, who was stoned to death.

Black Mud, a name to conjure with: O mud
For watermelons gutted to the crust,
Mud for the mole-tide harbor, mud for mouse,
Mud for the armored Diesel fishing tubs that thud
A year and a day to wind and tide; the dust
Is on this skipping heart that shakes my house,

House of our Savior who was hanged till death.
My heart, beat faster, faster. In Black Mud
Stephen the martyre was broken down to blood:
Our ransom is the rubble of his death.

Christ walks on the black water. In Black Mud
Darts the kingfisher. On Corpus Christi, heart,
Over the drum-beat of St. Stephen's choir
I hear him, *Stupor Mundi*, and the mud
Flies from his hunching wings and beak—my heart,
The blue kingfisher dives on you in fire.

The Drunken Fisherman

Wallowing in this bloody sty,
I cast for fish that pleased my eye
(Truly Jehovah's bow suspends
No pots of gold to weight its ends);
Only the blood-mouthed rainbow trout
Rose to my bait. They flopped about
My canvas creel until the moth
Corrupted its unstable cloth.

A calendar to tell the day;
A handkerchief to wave away
The gnats; a couch unstuffed with storm
Pouching a bottle in one arm;
A whiskey bottle full of worms;
And bedroom slacks: are these fit terms
To mete the worm whose moltem rage
Boils in the belly of old age?

Once fishing was a rabbit's foot—
O wind blow cold, O wind blow hot,
Let suns stay in or suns step out:
Life danced a jig on the sperm-whale's spout—
The fisher's fluent and obscene
Catches kept his conscience clean.
Children, the raging memory drools
Over the glory of past pools.

Now the hot river, ebbing, hauls
Its bloody waters into holes;
A grain of sand inside my shoe
Mimics the moon that might undo
Man and Creation too; remorse,
Stinking, has puddled up its source;
Here tantrums thrash to a whale's rage.
This is the pot-hole of old age.

Is there no way to cast my hook
Out of this dynamited brook?
The Fisher's sons must cast about
When shallow waters peter out.
I will catch Christ with a greased worm,
And when the Prince of Darkness stalks
My bloodstream to its Stygian term . . .
On water the Man-Fisher walks.

Falling Asleep over the Aeneid

An old man in Concord forgets to go to morning service.
He falls asleep, while reading Vergil, and dreams that he is
    Aeneas at the funeral of Pallas, an Italian prince.

>   The sun is blue and scarlet on my page,
>   And *yuck-a, yuck-a, yuck-a, yuck-a,* rage
>   The yellowhammers mating. Yellow fire
>   Blankets the captives dancing on their pyre,
>   And the scorched lictor screams and drops his rod.
>   Trojans are singing to their drunken God,
>   Ares. Their helmets catch on fire. Their files
>   Clank by the body of my comrade—miles
>   Of filings! Now the scythe-wheeled chariot rolls
>   Before their lances long as vaulting poles,
>   And I stand up and heil the thousand men,
>   Who carry Pallas to the bird-priest. Then
>   The bird-priest groans, and as his birds foretold,
>   I greet the body, lip to lip. I hold

The sword that Dido used. It tries to speak,
A bird with Dido's sworded breast. Its beak
Clangs and ejaculates the Punic word
I hear the bird-priest chirping like a bird.
I groan a little. "Who am I, and why?"
It asks, a boy's face, though its arrow-eye
Is working from its socket. "Brother, try,
O Child of Aphrodite, try to die:
To die is life." His harlots hang his bed
With feathers of his long-tailed birds. His head
Is yawning like a person. The plumes blow;
The beard and eyebrows ruffle. Face of snow,
You are the flower that country girls have caught,
A wild bee-pillaged honey-suckle brought
To the returning bridegroom—the design
Has not yet left it, and the petals shine;
The earth, its mother, has, at last, no help:
It is itself. The broken-winded yelp
Of my Phoenician hounds, that fills the brush
With snapping twigs and flying, cannot flush
The ghost of Pallas. But I take his pall,
Stiff with its gold and purple, and recall
How Dido hugged it to her, while she toiled,
Laughing—her golden threads, a serpent coiled
In cypress. Now I lay it like a sheet;
It clinks and settles down upon his feet,
The careless yellow hair that seemed to burn
Beforehand. Left foot, right foot—as they turn,
More pyres are rising: armored horses, bronze,
And gagged Italians, who must file by ones
Across the bitter river, when my thumb
Tightens into their wind-pipes. The beaks drum;
Their headman's cow-horned death's-head bites its tongue,
And stiffens, as it eyes the hero slung
Inside his feathered hammock on the crossed
Staves of the eagles that we winged. Our cost
Is nothing to the lovers, whoring Mars
And Venus, father's lover. Now his car's
Plumage is ready, and my marshals fetch
His squire, Acoetes, white with age, to hitch

Aethon, the hero's charger, and its ears
Prick, and it steps and steps, and stately tears
Lather its teeth; and then the harlots bring
The hero's charms and baton—but the King,
Vain-glorious Turnus, carried off the rest.
"I was myself, but Ares thought it best
The way it happened." At the end of time,
He sets his spear, as my descendants climb
The knees of Father Time, his beard of scalps,
His scythe, the arc of steel that crowns the Alps.
The elephants of Carthage hold those snows,
Turms of Numidian horse unsling their bows,
The flaming turkey-feathered arrows swarm
Beyond the Alps. "Pallas," I raise my arm
And shout, "Brother, eternal health. Farewell
Forever." Church is over, and its bell
Frightens the yellowhammers, as I wake
And watch the whitecaps wrinkle up the lake.
Mother's great-aunt, who died when I was eight,
Stands by our parlor sabre. "Boy, it's late.
Vergil must keep the Sabbath." Eighty years!
It all comes back. My Uncle Charles appears.
Blue-capped and bird-like. Phillips Brooks and Grant
Are frowning at his coffin, and my aunt,
Hearing his colored veterans parade
Through Concord, laughs, and tells her English maid
To clip his yellow nostril hairs, and fold
His colors on him . . . It is I, I hold
His sword to keep from falling, for the dust
On the stuffed birds is breathless, for the bust
Of young Augustus weighs on Vergil's shelf:
It scowls into my glasses at itself.

Mr. Edwards and the Spider

I saw the spiders marching through the air,
Swimming from tree to tree that mildewed day
   In latter August when the hay
     Came creaking to the barn. But where
        The wind is westerly,
Where gnarled November makes the spiders fly
Into the apparitions of the sky,
They purpose nothing but their ease and die
Urgently beating east to sunrise and the sea;

What are we in the hands of the great God?
It was in vain you set up thorn and briar
   In battle array against the fire
     And treason crackling in your blood;
        For the wild thorns grow tame
And will do nothing to oppose the flame;
Your lacerations tell the losing game
You play against a sickness past your cure.
How will the hands be strong? How will the heart endure?

A very little thing, a little worm,
Or hourglass-blazoned spider, it is said,
   Can kill a tiger. Will the dead
     Hold up his mirror and affirm
        To the four winds the smell
And flash of his authority? It's well
If God who holds you to the pit of hell,
Much as one holds a spider, will destroy,
Baffle and dissipate your soul. As a small boy

On Windsor Marsh, I saw the spider die
When thrown into the bowels of fierce fire:
   There's no long struggle, no desire
     To get up on its feet and fly—
        It stretches out its feet
And dies. This is the sinner's last retreat;
Yes, and no strength exerted on the heat
Then sinews the abolished will, when sick
And full of burning, it will whistle on a brick.

But who can plumb the sinking of that soul?
Josiah Hawley, picture yourself cast
  Into a brick-kiln where the blast
  Fans your quick vitals to a coal—
    If measured by a glass,
How long would it seem burning! Let there pass
A minute, ten, ten trillion; but the blaze
Is infinite, eternal: this is death,
To die and know it. This is the Black Widow, death.

The Quaker Graveyard in Nantucket
For Warren Winslow, Dead at Sea

Let man have dominion over the fishes of the sea and the fowls of the air and the beasts and the whole earth, and every creeping creature that moveth upon the earth.

I

A brackish reach of shoal off Madaket,—
The sea was still breaking violently and night
Had steamed into our North Atlantic Fleet,
When the drowned sailor clutched the drag-net. Light
Flashed from his matted head and marble feet,
He grappled at the net
With the coiled, hurdling muscles of his thighs:
The corpse was bloodless, a botch of reds and whites,
Its open, staring eyes
Were lustreless dead-lights
Or cabin-windows on a stranded hulk
Heavy with sand. We weight the body, close
Its eyes and heave it seaward whence it came,
Where the heel-headed dogfish barks its nose
On Ahab's void and forehead; and the name
Is blocked in yellow chalk.
Sailors, who pitch this portent at the sea
Where dreadnaughts shall confess

Its hell-bent deity,
When you are powerless
To sand-bag this Atlantic bulwark, faced
By the earth-shaker, green, unwearied, chaste
In his steel scales: ask for no Orphean lute
To pluck life back. The guns of the steeled fleet
Recoil and then repeat
The hoarse salute.

II

Whenever winds are moving and their breath
Heaves at the roped-in bulwarks of this pier,
The terns and sea-gulls tremble at your death
In these home waters. Sailor, can you hear
The Pequod's sea wings, beating landward, fall
Headlong and break on our Atlantic wall
Off 'Sconset, where the yawing S-boats splash
The bellbuoy, with ballooning spinnakers,
As the entangled, screeching mainsheet clears
The blocks: off Madaket, where lubbers lash
The heavy surf and throw their long lead squids
For blue-fish? Sea-gulls blink their heavy lids
Seaward. The winds' wings beat upon the stones,
Cousin, and scream for you and the claws rush
At the sea's throat and wring it in the slush
Of this old Quaker graveyard where the bones
Cry out in the long night for the hurt beast
Bobbing by Ahab's whaleboats in the East.

III

All you recovered from Poseidon died
With you, my cousin, and the harrowed brine
Is fruitless on the blue beard of the god,
Stretching beyond us to the castles in Spain,
Nantucket's westward haven. To Cape Cod
Guns, cradled on the tide,

Blast the eelgrass about a waterclock
Of bilge and backwash, roil the salt and sand
Lashing earth's scaffold, rock
Our warships in the hand
Of the great God, where time's contrition blues
Whatever it was these Quaker sailors lost
In the mad scramble of their lives. They died
When time was open-eyed,
Wooden and childish; only bones abide
There, in the nowhere, where their boats were tossed
Sky-high, where mariners had fabled news
Of IS, the whited monster. What it cost
them is their secret. In the sperm-whale's slick
I see the Quakers drown and hear their cry:
"If God himself had not been on our side,
If God himself had not been on our side,
When the Atlantic rose against us, why,
Then it had swallowed us up quick."

IV

This is the end of the whaleroad and the whale
Who spewed Nantucket bones on the thrashed swell
And stirred the troubled waters to whirlpools
To send the Pequod packing off to hell:
This is the end of them, three-quarters fools,
Snatching at straws to sail
Seaward and seaward on the turntail whale,
Spouting out blood and water as it rolls,
Sick as a dog to these Atlantic shoals:
Clamavimus, O depths. Let the sea-gulls wail

For water, for the deep where the high tide
Mutters to its hurt self, mutters and ebbs.
Waves wallow in their wash, go out and out,
Leave only the death-rattle of the crabs,
The beach increasing, its enormous snout
Sucking the ocean's side.
This is the end of running on the waves;

We are poured out like water. Who will dance
The mast-lashed master of Leviathans
Up from this field of Quakers in their unstoned graves?

V

When the whale's viscera go and the roll
Of its corruption overruns this world
Beyond tree-swept Nantucket and Wood's Hole
And Martha's Vineyard, Sailor, will your sword
Whistle and fall and sink into the fat?
In the great ash-pit of Jehoshaphat
The bones cry for the blood of the white whale,
The fat flukes arch and whack about its ears,
The death-lance churns into the sanctuary, tears
The gun-blue swingle, heaving like a flail,
And hacks the coiling life out: it works and drags
And rips the sperm-whale's midriff into rags,
Gobbets of blubber spill to wind and weather,
Sailor, and gulls go round the stoven timbers
Where the morning stars sing out together
And thunder shakes the white surf and dismembers
The red flag hammered in the mast-head. Hide
Our steel, Jonas Messias, in Thy side.

VI

Our Lady of Walsingham

There once the penitents took off their shoes
And then walked barefoot the remaining mile;
And the small trees, a stream and hedgerows file
Slowly along the munching English lane,
Like cows to the old shrine, until you lose
Track of your dragging pain.
The stream flows down under the druid tree,
Shiloah's whirlpools gurgle and make glad
The castle of God. Sailor, you were glad
And whistled Sion by that stream. But see:

Our Lady, too small for her canopy,
Sits near the altar. There's no comeliness
At all or charm in that expressionless
Face with its heavy eyelids. As before,
This face, for centuries a memory,
Non est species, neque decor,
Expressionless, expresses God: it goes
Past castled Sion. She knows what God knows,
Not Calvary's Cross nor crib at Bethlehem
Now, and the world shall come to Walsingham.

VII

The empty winds are creaking and the oak
Splatters and splatters on the cenotaph,
The boughs are trembling and a gaff
Bobs on the untimely stroke
Of the greased wash exploding on a shoal-bell
In the old mouth of the Atlantic. It's well;
Atlantic, you are fouled with the blue sailors,
Sea-monsters, upward angel, downward fish:

Unmarried and corroding, spare of flesh,
Mart once of supercilious, wing'd clippers,
Atlantic, where your bell-trap guts its spoil
You could cut the brackish winds with a knife
Here in Nantucket, and cast up the time
When the Lord God formed man from the sea's slime
And breathed into his face the breath of life,
And blue-lung'd combers lumbered to the kill.
The Lord survives the rainbow of His will.

Where the Rainbow Ends

I saw the sky descending, black and white,
Not blue, on Boston where the winters wore
The skulls to jack-o'-lanterns on the slates,
And Hunger's skin-and-bone retrievers tore

The chickadee and shrike. The thorn tree waits
Its victim and tonight
The worms will eat the deadwood to the foot
Of Ararat: the scythers, Time and Death,
Helmed locusts, move upon the tree of breath;
The wild ingrafted olive and the root

Are withered, and a winter drifts to where
The Pepperpot, ironic rainbow, spans
Charles River and its scales of scorched-earth miles.
I saw my city in the Scales, the pans
Of judgment rising and descending. Piles
Of dead leaves char the air—
And I am a red arrow on this graph
Of Revelations. Every dove is sold
The Chapel's sharp-shinned eagle shifts its hold
On serpent-Time, the rainbow's epitaph.

In Boston serpents whistle at the cold.
The victim climbs the altar steps and sings:
"Hosannah to the lion, lamb, and beast
Who fans the furnace-face of IS with wings:
I breathe the ether of my marriage feast."
At the high altar, gold
And a fair cloth. I kneel and the wings beat
My cheek. What can the dove of Jesus give
You now but wisdom, exile? Stand and live,
The dove has brought an olive branch to eat.

William Sydney Graham (Born 1918)

Born in Greenock, Scotland, W.S. Graham was educated at Greenock High School and the Workers Educational Association College, Newbattle Abbey, in Edinburgh. He lectured at New York University in 1947 and 1948, but returned to Scotland to devote himself to poetry. He has published ten volumes of verse. After a 15 year hiatus, Graham came out with *Malcolm Mooney's Land* in 1970 to critical and popular acclaim. Graham has stated that he works with four recurrent themes: the difficulty of human communication, the crisis of identity, the nature of aesthetic experience, and the celebration of life in the English language. His poems are structured as vehicles for self-discovery, and show a joy in the sounds and rhythms of words in themselves.

At Whose Sheltering Shall the Day Sea

At whose sheltering shall the day sea
Captain his ships of foam to save
Them weary of air, their hair gently
Afloat above them on prongs of water?
Now, prince in the seacircling tower,
Emigrant to grief, furious seafarer swept over

The seven wounds and multiple five
Senses of drowning; he fills his voice
With land-dry prayers and the sea above.
His 'help' or 'save me' like a bird
Bore back only the stretched whitefingered
Hand of the swelling sea and found him sheltered,

Sheltered in soon all of us to be
That memory against the scuppering rocks,
The spilling aprons of the sea.
Grief fills the voice with water, building
Ruin on the ruining land. Sheltering
In sea he breathes dry land, dry grave and dwelling.

Gigha

That firewood pale with salt and burning green
Outfloats its men who waved with a sound of
  drowning
Their saltcut hands over mazes of this rough bay.

Quietly this morning beside the subsided herds
Of water I walk. The children wade the shallows.
The sun with long legs wades into the sea.

Listen. Put on Morning

Listen. Put on morning.
Waken into falling light.
A man's imagining
Suddenly may inherit
The handclapping centuries
Of his one minute on earth.
And hear the virgin juries
Talk with his own breath
To the corner boys of his street.
And hear the Black Maria
Searching the town at night.
And hear the playropes caa
The sister Mary in.
And hear Willie and Davie
Among the bracken of Narnain
Sing in a mist heavy
With myrtle and listeners.
And hear the higher town
Weep a petition of fears
At the poorhouse close upon
The public heartbeat.
And hear the children tig
And run with my own feet
Into the netting drag
Of a suiciding principle.
Listen. Put on lightbreak.

Waken into miracle.
The audience lies awake
Under the tenements
Under the sugar docks
Under the printed moments.
The centuries turn their locks
And open under the hill
Their inherited books and doors
All gathered to distil
Like happy berry pickers
One voice to talk to us.
Yes listen. It carries away
The second and the years
Till the heart's in a jacket of snow
And the head's in a helmet white
And the song sleeps to be wakened
By the morning ear bright.
Listen. Put on morning.
Waken into falling light.

Night's Fall Unlocks the Dirge of the Sea

Night's fall unlocks the dirge of the sea
To pour up from the shore and befriending
Gestures of water waving, to find me
Dressed warm in a coat of land in a house
Held off the drowned by my blood's race
Over the crops of my step to meet some praise.

The surge by day by night turns lament
And by this night falls round the surrounding
Seaside and countryside and I can't
Sleep one word away on my own for that
Grief sea with a purse of pearls and debt
Wading the land away with salt in his throat.

By this loud night traded into evidence
Of a dark church of voices at hand
I lie, work of the gruff sea's innocence
And lie, work of the deaths I find
On the robbed land breathing air and
The friendly thief sea wealthy with the drowned.

To My Father

Yes as alike as entirely
You my father I see
That high Greenock tenement
And whole shipyarded front.

As alike as a memory early
Of 'The Bonny Earl o'Moray'
Fiddled in our high kitchen
Over the sleeping town

These words this one night
Feed us and will not
Leave us without our natures
Inheriting new fires.

The March whinfires let fall
From the high Greenock hill
A word fetched so bright
Out of the forehead that

A fraction's wink and I
And my death change round softly.
My birth and I so softly
Change round the outward journey.

Entirely within the fires
And winter-harried natures
Of your each year, the still
Foundered man is the oracle

Tented within his early
Friendships. And he'll reply
To us locked in our song.
This night this word falling

Across the kindling skies
Takes over over our bodies.

Keith Douglas (1920–1944)

Keith Douglas was born January 24, an only child. He was a brilliant student, athlete, and actor while in school. Douglas' first poem was published in *New Verse* when he was only 16. He studied at Merton College, Oxford with Edmund Blunden and edited *The Cherwell*. Douglas joined the English army in 1940 and was sent to the Middle East, where he took part in the Battle of El Alamein. He recorded his experiences in the desert campaign in *Alamein to Zem Zem* (1947). Douglas transferred to the European theatre and was killed on a Normandy beach shortly after the D Day invasion. His *Collected Poems*, culled from Douglas' many magazine publications, appeared in 1951.

The Deceased

He was a reprobate I grant
and always liquored till his money went.

His hair depended on a noose from
a Corona Veneris. His eyes, dumb

like prisoners in their cavernous slots, were
settled in attitudes of despair.

You who God bless you never sunk so low
censure and pray for him that he was so;

and with his failings you regret the verses
the fellow made, probably between curses,

probably in the extremes of moral decay,
but he wrote them in a sincere way:

and appears to have felt a refined pain
to which your virtue cannot attain.

Respect him. For this
He had an excellence which you miss.

Desert Flowers

Living in a wide landscape are the flowers—
Rosenberg I only repeat what you were saying—
the shell and the hawk, every hour
Are slaying men and jerboas, slaying

the mind: but the body can fill
the hungry flowers and dogs who cry words
at nights, the most hostile things of all.
But that is not new. Each time the night discards

draperies on the eyes and leaves the mind awake
I look each side of the door of sleep
for the little coin it will take
to buy the secret I shall not keep.

I see men as trees suffering
or confound the detail and the horizon.
Lay the coin on my tongue and I will sing
of what the others never set eyes on.

Mersa

This blue half circle of sea
moving transparently
on the sand as pale as salt
was Cleopatra's hotel:

here is a guesthouse built
and broken utterly since
an amorous modern prince
lived in this scoured shell.

Now from the ruined hive of a town
the cherry-skinned soldiers stroll down
to undress to idle on the white beach.
Up there, the immensely long road goes by

to Tripoli: the wind and dust reach
the secrets of the whole
poor town whose masks would still
deceive a passer by,

faces with sightless doors
for eyes, with cracks like tears
oozing at corners. A dead tank alone
leans where the gossips stood.

I see my feet like stones
underwater. The logical little fish
converge and nip the flesh
imagining I am one of the dead.

Time Eating

Ravenous Time has flowers for his food
in Autumn, yet can cleverly make good
each petal: devours animals and men,
but for ten dead he can create ten.

If you enquire how secretly you've come
to mansize from the smallness of a stone
it will appear his effort made you rise
so gradually to your proper size.

But as he makes he eats; the very part
where he began, even the elusive heart
Time's ruminative tongue will wash
and slow juice masticate all flesh.

That volatile huge intestine holds
material and abstract in its folds:
thought and ambition melt and even the world
will alter, in that catholic belly curled.

But Time, who ate my love, you cannot make
such another; you who can remake
the lizard's tail and the bright snakeskin
cannot, cannot. That you gobbled in
too quick, and though you brought me from a boy
you can make no more of me, only destroy.

Richard Wilbur (Born 1921)

Richard Wilbur was born March 1 in New York City, the son of portrait artist Lawrence Wilbur. Richard graduated from Amherst College in 1942 and took an A.M. from Harvard in 1947. He taught at Wesleyan University from 1957 to 1977 and is presently writer-in-residence at Smith College. He won the Pulitzer Prize and the National Book Award for his 1957 *Things of This World*. The ostensible subjects of Wilbur's numerous poetry collections are familiar objects in the world. But one should not be misled by the seemingly simple and traditional structure of many of Wilbur's poems—his is a poetry of ideas which find their expression in the common experiences of humanity.

O

The idle dayseye, the laborious wheel,
The osprey's tours, the pointblank matin sun
Sanctified first the circle; thence for fun
Doctors deduced a shape, which some called real
(So all games spoil), a shape of spare appeal.
Cryptic and clean, and endlessly spinning unspun.
Now I go backward, filling by one and one
Circles with hickory spokes and rich soft shields
Of petalled dayseyes, with herehastening steel
Volleys of daylight, writhing white looks of sun;
And I toss circles skyward to be undone
By actual wings, for wanting this repeal
I should go whirling a thin Euclidean reel,
No hawk or hickory to true my run.

Still, Citizen Sparrow

Still, citizen sparrow, this vulture which you call
Unnatural, let him but lumber again to air
Over the rotten office, let him bear
The carrion ballast up, and at the tall

Tip of the sky lie cruising. Then you'll see
That no more beautiful bird is in heaven's height,
No wider more placid wings, no watchfuller flight;
He shoulders nature there, the frightfully free,

The naked-headed one. Pardon him, you
Who dart in the orchard aisles, for it is he
Devours death, mocks mutability,
Has heart to make an end, keeps nature new.

Thinking of Noah, childheart, try to forget
How for so many bedlam hours his saw
Soured the song of birds with its wheezy gnaw,
And the slam of his hammer all the day beset

The people's ears. Forget that he could bear
To see the towns like coral under the keel,
And the fields so dismal deep. Try rather to feel
How high and weary it was, on the waters where

He rocked his only world, and everyone's.
Forgive the hero, you who would have died
Gladly with all you knew; he rode that tide
To Ararat; all men are Noah's sons.

Sidney Keyes (1922–1943)

Sidney Keyes, the son of Captain Reginald Keyes, was born May 27. His mother died soon after and young Sidney was brought up and educated, until the age of nine, by his paternal grandfather. Keyes was then sent off to Dartford Grammar School and the Tonbridge School where he was a scholarly and distant student. At the age of 16, with encouragement from the poet Tom Staveley, Keyes produced his first poem, an elegy to his grandfather. In 1940 he won a history scholarship to Queen's College, Oxford where he edited *The Cherwell*. In April, 1942 Keyes entered the army and in July of the same year came out with his first book of verse, *The Iron Laurel*. Keyes was killed while on a reconnaissance mission in Tunisia. His second volume of poetry, *The Cruel Solstice*, published posthumously in 1944, won the Hawthornden Prize.

Early Spring

Now that the young buds are tipped with a falling sun—
Each twig a candle, a martyr, St. Julian's branched
   stag—
And the shadows are walking the cobbled square like
   soldiers
With their long legs creaking and their pointed hands
Reaching the railings and fingering the stones
Of what expended, unprojected graves:
The soil's a flirt, the lion Time is tamed,
And pain like a cat will come home to share your
   room.

Elegy
In Memoriam S.K.K.

April again and it is a year again
Since you walked out and slammed the door
Leaving us tangled in your words, Your brain
Lives in the bank-book, and your eyes look up
Laughing from the carpet on the floor:
And we still drink from your silver cup.

It is a year again since they poured
The dumb ground into your mouth:
And yet we know, by some recurring word
Or look caught unawares, that you still drive
Our thoughts like the smart cobs of your youth—
When you and the world were alive.

A year again, and we have fallen on bad times
Since they gave you to the worms.
I am ashamed to take delight in these rhymes
Without grief; but you need no tears.
We shall never forget nor escape you, nor make terms
With your enemies, the swift-devouring years.

Glaucus

The various voices are his poem now.

Under the currents, under the shifting lights
Of midway water, rolls his fleshy wreck:
Its gurnard eye reflects those airy heights
Where once it noted white Arcturus set.

Gull-swift and swerving, the wet spirit freed
Skims the huge breakers. Watching at the prow
Of any southbound vessel, sailor, heed
Never that petrel spirit, cruel as pride.

Let no cliff-haunting woman, no girl claim
Kinship with Glaucus, neither sow
The tide with daffodils, nor call his name
Into the wind, for he is glorified—
And cold Aegean voices speak his fame.

The Grail

The great cup tumbled, ringing like a bell
Thrown down upon the lion-guarded stair
When the cloud took Him; and its iron voice
Challenged the King's dead majesty to fear.

Rise up, Arthur. Galahad grail-seeker
Wails with the pale identical queens on the river.
The sculptured lion raises a clumsy paw:
Bors has lain down beneath the stones of law.

Lie uneasy, Guenever. Lancelot sword-lover
Burnt like a blade will share your bed no more.
Bared his red head, he weeps with shame and
   sickness—
His pride the sword-bridge to your heart of Gorre.

But the dead girl, the flower-crowned, alone
Walks without fear the bannered streets of heaven;
Lies nightly in the hollow of His hand—
The cradle of your fear her fort and haven.

She alone
Knew from her birth the mystic Avalon.

Holstenwall

We're going to the fair at Holstenwall;
It is my eyes you've taken out—
My bright eyes and my hollow heart
Stare and ring at Holstenwall.

I stand up straight, strong master, stand
Straight as a man, and am no man:
My pulses beat, O master, yet
I can help nothing. This is a wicked land.

Standing and stiff, send me forth, send
My fear forth, master. Cold boards hamper
My fingers, masters, that would grope and clamber
Precise as spiders, grope and rend.

Swift and desiring, master, as a hound,
Let me get life, strong master, tear and wound
These dead crowds into life. O set
My course at this loud land, speed my swift feet.

Set me against the lover and the pope—
I need the living heart, the holy knowledge.
Give me the frightened girl and I will rape
Her life alive and cross the guarded bridge.

We're going to the fair at Holstenwall.
Remember your puppet; life lies in my hand:
Yet no dead doll or clockwork nightingale.
Have pity, master. This is a wicked land.

The Kestrels

When I would think of you, my mind holds only
The small defiant kestrels—how they cut
The raincloud with sharp wings, continually circling
About a storm-rocked elm, with passionate cries.
It was an early month. The plow cut hard.
The may was knobbed with chilly buds. My folly
Was great enough to lull away my pride.

There is no virtue now in blind reliance
On place or person or the forms of love.
The storm bears down the pivotal tree, the cloud
Turns to the net of an inhuman fowler
And drags us from the air. Our wings are clipped.
Yet still our love and luck lies in our parting:
Those cries and wings surprise our surest act.

INDEX

Author, title, first line, and subject index to Supplements I and II of *The World's Best Poetry*.

Poet names are in roman; poem titles are in italics; poem first lines are in quotations; subject heads are in boldface.

"Abelard was: God is," II, 34.
Abercrombie, Lascelles. I, 1–5.
"About suffering they were never wrong," II, 164.
"Above me the abbey, grey arches on the cliff," II, 338.
"Above the hemispheres there floats," II, 78.
"Ace—Pride of Parents," II, 148.
Adam and Eve
Ave Eva. John Wheelwright. II, 52.
Eve. Ralph Hodgson. I, 163.
A Mile from Eden. Anne Ridler. II, 275.
Adams, Leonie. II, 70–71.
Adventure
Terror. Robert Penn Warren. II, 133.
A.E. (See George William Russell.) I, 274.
Aeneid, The (Vergil)
Falling Asleep over the Aeneid. Robert Lowell. II, 390.
Africa
Heritage. Countee Cullen. I, 96.
The Plains. Roy Fuller. II, 265.
"After hot loveless nights, when cold winds stream," II, 95.
"After rain, through afterglow, the unfolding fan," II, 56.
After Ronsard. Charles Williams. I, 315.
After the Funeral. Dylan Thomas. II, 347.
After the Surprising Conversions. Robert Lowell. II, 386.
After Winter. Sterling A. Brown. II, 82.
The After Woman. Francis Joseph Thompson. I, 300.
Aging
The First of May. Alfred Edward Housman. I, 169.
It Is Time That I Wrote My Will. William Butler Yeats. I, 330.
Leavetaking. William Watson. I, 313.
Listen. Put on Morning. William Sydney Graham. II, 401.
Loveliest of Trees. Alfred Edward Housman. I, 166.
Missing Dates. William Empson. II, 144.

What I Expected. Stephen Spender. II, 236.
When First My Way. Alfred Edward Housman. I, 170.
The Youth with Red-gold Hair Edith Sitwell. II, 22.
Aiken, Conrad. I, 12–14.
Air Travel
The Black Vulture. George Sterling. I, 288.
Air Warfare
The Death of the Ball Turret Gunner. Randall Jarrell. II, 330.
Losses. Randall Jarrell. II, 331.
A Pilot from the Carrier. Randall Jarrell. II, 332.
Second Air Force. Randall Jarrell. II. 332.
The Airman's Alphabet. W. H. Auden. II, 148.
Alienation
The Little Boy Lost. Stevie Smith. II, 103.
All Goats. Elizabeth Jane Coatsworth. I, 85.
All Gone. Cecil Day Lewis. II, 109.
"All Greece hates," II, 4.
"All I could see from where I stood," I, 214.
"All in green went my love riding," I, 101.
"All night the cocks crew, under a moon like day," I, 61.
The Alligator. Beatrice Ravenel. I, 261.
"Aloof within the day's enormous dome," I, 288.
Altarwise by Owl-Light. Dylan Thomas. II, 348.
"Although she feeds me bread of bitterness." I, 203.
Amazons (mythology)
The White Women. Mary Elizabeth Coleridge. I, 87.
America. Claude McKay. I, 203.
"Amid the thunders of the falling dark," II, 10.
"Among the smoke and fog of a December afternoon," I, 116.
An Ancient to Ancients. Thomas Hardy. I, 161.
"And here face down beneath the sun," I, 204.
"And now she cleans her teeth into the lake," II, 140.

"And one morning while in the woods I stumbled," II, 212.
Animals
Dark Song. Edith Sitwell. II, 12.
"Ant and shrew," I, 312.
Apple Trees
Moonlit Apples. John Drinkwater. I, 109.
"April again and it is a year again," II, 411.
"The Archer is wake!" I, 319.
"Are the living so much use," II, 29.
"Are you awake, Gemelli," I, 149.
Arizona Poems. John Gould Fletcher. I, 126.
Army, English
Lessons of the War. Henry Reed. II, 344.
"Arrested like marble horses," II, 24.
Art
Boats In a Fog. Robinson Jeffers. I, 173.
The Monument. Elizabeth Bishop. II, 243.
Arthurian Legend
The Grail. Sidney Keyes. II, 413.
"As a child holds a pet," II, 231.
"As a naked man I go," I, 286.
As a Plane Tree by the Water. Robert Lowell. II, 387.
"As Jesus and his followers," I, 152.
As One Who Wanders Into Old Workings. Cecil Day Lewis. II, 110.
Astrology
Peace On Earth. William Carlos Williams. I, 319.
Astronomy
The Undiscovered Planet. Norman Nicholson. II, 343.
At Epidaurus. Lawrence Durrell. II, 257.
"At noon, Tithonus, withered by his singing," I, 14.
"At Rochecoart," I, 251.
"At sunrise, swimming out to sea," I, 141.
At the Cenotaph. Hugh MacDiarmid. II, 29.
"At the end of July," II, 296.
At the Grave of Henry James. W. H. Auden. II, 150.
"At the top of the house the apples are laid," I, 109.
At Whose Sheltering Shall the Day Sea. William Sydney Graham. II, 400.
"At Woodlawn," II, 205.
"Athlete, virtuoso," II, 307.
Atlantis
Leviathan. Peter Quennel. I, 254.
Auden, W.H. II, 148–169.
Auslander, Joseph. I, 16.
Autobiography. Louis MacNeice. II, 171.

Autumn
Maple and Sumach. Cecil Day Lewis. II, 117
Autumn Morning at Cambridge. Frances Cornford. I, 91.
An Autumn Park. David Gascoyne. II, 379.
Ave Eva. John Wheelwright. II, 52.
Aviation
The Landscape Near An Aerodome. Stephen Spender. II, 228.
Aviation and Aviators
The Airman's Alphabet. W. H. Auden. II, 148.
"Avoid the reeking herd," Elinor Wylie. I, 326

Babel Falls. Anna Hempstead Branch. I, 68.
Babies
The First Year, (sels.) E.J. Scovell. II, 188
For a Christening. Anne Ridler. II, 273.
Bacon, Leonard. I, 21.
Ballad of the Goodly Fere. Ezra Pound. I, 249
Ballad of the Long-Legged Bait. Dylan Thomas II, 353.
Barbers
Haircut. Karl Shapiro. II, 321.
"Barefoot I went and made no sound," II, 51
Barker, George. II, 278–294.
Battle of Britain
Still Falls the Rain. Edith Sitwell. II, 21.
Bax, Clifford. I. 27–29.
Beauty
The Enamel Girl. Genevieve Taggard. I, 292
Leisure. William Henry Davies. I, 105.
Romantic Fool. Harold Monro. I, 224.
"Because he had spoken harshly to his mother," II, 131.
"Before she first had smiled or looked with calm," II, 188.
"Before the Roman came to Rye or out of Severn," I, 83.
"Before the spring had flowered away full summer," I, 29.
"Before this generous time," I, 150.
"Begotten by the meeting of rock with rock," I 12.
Belloc, Hilaire. I, 31–33.
Bells
Bredon Hill. Alfred Edward Housman. I 166.
"Beneath the poplars o'er the sacred pool," I 145.
Benet, Stephen Vincent. I, 46–47.
The Bereaved Swan. Stevie Smith. II, 102.

Berkshire Holiday. Clifford Bax. I, 29.
Berryman, John. II, 327–329.
Betjeman, John. II, 136–138.
Betrayals
Song. Stephen Spender. II, 233.
Between the World and Me. Richard Wright. II, 212.
Beyond Good and Evil. George Edward Woodberry. I, 322.
Bible–Old Testament
Babel Falls. Anna Hempstead Branch. I, 68.
Nimrod Wars With the Angels. Anna Hempstead Branch. I, 67.
Binyon, Laurence. I, 50–53.
Birch Trees
Birches. Robert Frost. I, 131.
The Turning Of the Leaves. Vernon Watkins. II, 191.
Birds
The Darkling Thrush. Thomas Hardy. I, 156.
The Different Day. Grace Hazard Conkling. I, 88.
The Falconer of God. William Rose Benet. I, 46.
The Kingfisher. William Henry Davies. I, 105.
The Riddlers. Walter John De La Mare. I, 108.
Birth
Christmas and Common Birth. Anne Ridler. II, 271.
The Death of the Ball Turret Gunner. Randall Jarrell. II, 330.
For a Christening. Anne Ridler. II, 273.
Birthday Poem for Thomas Hardy. Cecil Day Lewis. II, 111.
Birthdays
Poem in October. Dylan Thomas. II, 366.
Bishop, Elizabeth. II, 243–245.
Bishop, John Peale. II, 24–27.
Bitterness. Victoria Mary Sackville-West. I, 277.
The Black Rock of Kiltearn. Andrew Young. II, 2.
The Black Vulture. George Sterling. I, 288.
Blackmur, Richard P. II, 107.
Blues
The Weary Blues. Langston Hughes. I, 171.
Blunden, Edmund. II, 44–46.
Boats in a Fog. Robinson Jeffers. I, 173.
Bodenheim, Maxwell. I, 56.
Body (human)

The Heavy Bear Who Goes With Me. Delmore Schwartz. II, 308.
Piero Della Francesca. Anne Ridler. II, 276.
Bogan, Louise. I, 61.
Bombing Casualties in Spain. Herbert Read. II, 32.
"Borrowed wings on his ankles," II, 182.
Boston, Massachusetts
As a Plane Tree By the Water. Robert Lowell. II, 387.
Where the Rainbow Ends. Robert Lowell. II, 398.
Bottomley, Gordon. I, 62–63.
Bourgeoisie
Dirge. Kenneth Fearing. II, 99.
The Dome of Sunday. Karl Shapiro. II, 319.
Bourne, Randolph (about)
Salvos For Randolph Bourne. Horace Gregory. II, 65.
"Bowed by the weight of centuries he leans," I, 205.
"The bows glided down," II, 353.
The Boy out of Church. Robert Graves. I, 152.
Boy with His Hair Cut Short. Muriel Rukeyser. II, 295.
"A brackish reach of shoal off Madaket," II, 394.
Branch, Anna Hempstead. I, 67–71.
Bread-Word Giver. John Wheelwright. II, 53.
"The breath of dew, and twilight's grace," I, 154.
Bredon Hill. Alfred Edward Housman. I, 166.
A Bride in the '30's. W. H. Auden. II, 154.
Bridges, Robert. I, 73–75.
"Bright drips the morning from its trophied nets," II, 291.
The British Museum
Homage to the British Museum. William Empson. II, 141.
Brooke, Rupert. I, 76–80.
Brother Fire. Louis MacNeice. II, 172.
"Brother, consider as you go your way," II, 220.
Brotherhood
Definition. Edwin Rolfe. II, 217.
Brown, Sterling A. II, 82–88.
Bullfights
Death of the Bull. Roy Campbell. II, 91.
But for Lust. Ruth Pitter. II, 48.
"But God sent forth a pale and spectral host," I, 67.
"But it could never be true," II, 98.
"But to reach the archimedean point," II, 128.

"By divination came the Dorians, " II, 259.
"By night they haunted a thicket of April mist," I, 258.
"By the old Moulmein Pagoda," I, 180.

C Stands for Civilization. Kenneth Fearing. II, 97.
Caedmon. Norman Nicholson. II, 338.
"Call out, celebrate the beam," II, 267.
"The Cambridge ladies who live in furnished souls." I, 104.
"Camoes, alone, of all the lyric race," II, 94.
Campbell, Roy. II, 91–95.
Camping
 Camping Out. William Empson. II, 140.
Canto Amor. John Berryman. II, 327.
Cargoes. John Masefield. I, 210.
Carry Her over the Water. W. H. Auden. II, 157.
Casino. W. H. Auden. II, 158.
Castles
 Gold. John Drinkwater. I, 110.
Cemeteries
 The Hill above the Mine. Malcolm Cowley. II, 60.
 The Worms at Heaven's Gate. Wallace Stevens. I, 291.
Ceremony after a Fire Raid. Dylan Thomas. II, 359.
"Cherish you then the hope I shall forget," I, 224.
Cherry Trees
 Loveliest of Trees. Alfred Edward Housman. I, 166.
Chesterton, Gilbert Keith. I, 83–84.
Chicago. Carl Sandburg. I, 283.
The Chief Centurions. John Masefield. I, 208.
"The child not yet is lulled to rest," I, 212.
China
 The Chinese Nightingale. Vachel Lindsay. I, 189.
"Chloe is false, but the fire in her eyes," I, 144.
Choosing a Mast. Roy Campbell. II, 92.
Christianity
 The After Woman. Francis Joseph Thompson. I, 300.
 Altarwise by Owl-Light. Dylan Thomas. II, 348.
 As a Plane Tree by the Water. Robert Lowell. II, 387.
 Colloquy in Black Rock. Robert Lowell. II, 388.

 Stylite. Louis MacNeice. II, 183.
 To a Comrade in Arms. Alun Lewis. II, 378.
Christmas
 The Oxen. Thomas Hardy. I, 159.
 Christmas and Common Birth. Anne Ridler. II, 271.
 "Christmas Eve, and twelve of the clock," I, 159.
Circles
 O. Richard Wilbur. II, 409.
Circus
 The End of the World. Archibald MacLeish. I, 203.
 The Menagerie. William Vaughn Moody. I, 228.
Cities
 To My Contemporaries. Edwin Rolfe. II, 222.
Civil War, American
 Ode to the Confederate Dead. Allen Tate. II, 73.
Civil War, Spanish
 Bombing Casualties in Spain. Herbert Read. II, 32.
 Mediterranean. Muriel Rukeyser. II, 296.
Cleator Moor. Norman Nicholson. II, 340.
Clouds
 Clouds across the Canyon. John Gould Fletcher. I, 129.
 Most Lovely Shade. Edith Sitwell. II, 15.
 Windmills. John Gould Fletcher. I, 126.
Clouds across the Canyon. John Gould Fletcher. I, 129.
The Coat of Fire. Edith Sitwell. II, 10.
Coatsworth, Elizabeth Jane. I, 85.
Coleridge, Mary Elizabeth. I, 87.
The Collier. Vernon Watkins. II, 189.
Colloquy in Black Rock. Robert Lowell. II, 388.
Colloquy with a King-Crab. John Peale Bishop. II, 24.
Colorado. Robert Fitzgerald. II, 240.
"Colorado Morton's riding far," I, 21.
Columbus, Christopher
 The Discovery. John Collings ("Solomon Eagle"). I, 285.
"'Come in out of the night,' said the landlord," I, 259.
Come, Live with Me, and Be My Love. Cecil Day Lewis. II, 112.
Communism
 I Am a Red Slogan. Richard Wright. II, 214.
 Joe Hill Listens to the Praying. Kenneth Patchen. II, 248.
The Conflict. Cecil Day Lewis. II, 112.

Conkling, Grace Hazard. I, 88.
Conscience
The Contrary Experience. Herbert Read. II, 32.
Contentment
The Sunlight on the Garden. Louis MacNeice. II, 185.
The Contrary Experience. Herbert Read. II, 32.
Conversation. Louis MacNeice. II, 173.
"The core of him is hate," I, 311.
Cornford, Frances. I, 90–91.
Corpses
The Worms at Heaven's Gate. Wallace Stevens. I, 291.
"Count up those books whose pages you have read," II, 190
Country Summer. Leonie Adams. II, 70–71.
Cowley, Malcolm. II, 59–60.
Crabs
The Dead Crab. Andrew Young. II, 2.
"Cracked by that accurate beak," I, 85.
Cradle-Song at Twilight. Alice Meynell. I, 212.
Crane, Hart. I, 92.
Creation. Alfred Noyes. I, 245.
Creation
He Made This Screen. Marianne Moore. I, 233.
Crucifixion
Ecce Homo. David Gascoyne. II, 380.
Cullen, Countee. I, 96–100.
Cummings Edward Estlin. I, 101–104.
"Curtains of rock," II, 385.
Cynicism
C Stands for Civilization. Kenneth Fearing. II, 97.
The King of Spain. Maxwell Bodenheim. I, 56.

"Daisies are broken," I, 320.
Dark Song, (from *Facade*). Edith Sitwell. II, 12.
"Dark suffocates the world," II, 379.
The Darkling Thrush. Thomas Hardy. I, 156.
"Darkness has called to darkness, and disgrace," II, 387.
"Daughter of the ancient Eve," I, 300.
David
That Harp You Play So Well. Marianne Moore. I, 234.
King David. Stephen Vincent Benet. I, 34.
Davies, William Henry. I, 105.
Dawn on the East Coast. Alun Lewis. II, 374.

Day Lewis, Cecil. II, 109–125.
Day of These Days. Laurie Lee. II, 335.
De La Mare, Walter John. I, 107–108.
The Dead Crab. Andrew Young. II, 2.
The Dead Ride Fast. Richard P. Blackmur. II, 107.
"Dear Boys, they've killed our woods: the ground," I, 5.
Death
The Chief Centurions. John Masefield. I, 208.
The Dead Ride Fast. Richard P. Blackmur. II, 107.
Desire. Kathleen Raine. II, 197.
Epitaph. Lascelles Abercrombie. I, 5.
For a Dead Lady. Edwin Arlington Robinson. I, 271.
Friends Beyond. Thomas Hardy. I, 157.
Go Down Death. James Weldon Johnson. I, 176.
The Groundhog. Richard Eberhart. II, 127.
Hagen. Horace Gregory. II, 63.
It Is Time That I Wrote My Will. William Butler Yeats. I, 330.
The Midnight Skaters. Edmund Blunden. II, 45.
Missing Dates. William Empson. II, 144.
"Out, Out–." Robert Frost. I, 133.
Salutation. Thomas Stearns Eliot. I, 114.
Sister Lou. Sterling A. Brown. II, 88.
Song of the Three Seeds in the Macaw's Beak. Elizabeth Jane Coatsworth. I, 85.
Sonnet XVIII. Hilaire Belloc. I, 33.
Sonnet: "Go, spend your penny." John Masefield. I, 209.
Swimmers. Louis Untermeyer. I, 309.
The Vanishing Boat. Edmund William Gosse. I, 146.
Watch Any Day. W. H. Auden. II, 169.
The Death of the Ball Turret Gunner. Randall Jarrell. II, 330.
Death of the Bull. Roy Campbell. II, 91.
The Death of the Hired Man. Robert Frost. I, 135.
The Deceased. Keith Douglas. II, 405.
"Deep in the winter plain, two armies," II, 235.
Deer
Song. Edward Estlin Cummings. I, 101.
Definition. Edwin Rolfe. II, 217.
Dejection. Robert Bridges. I, 73.
"Delphic and Theban and Corinthian," II, 143.
Dempsey, Dempsey. Horace Gregory. II, 62.
Departure in the Dark. Cecil Day Lewis. II, 113.

Depressions (economic)
Devil's Dream. Kenneth Fearing. II, 98.
Hellbabies. Horace Gregory. II, 64.
Desert Flowers. Keith Douglas. II, 406.
Deserts
Rain in the Desert. John Gould Fletcher. I, 128.
Desire. Kathleen Raine. II, 197.
Despair
The Weary Blues. Langston Hughes. I, 171.
Winter and Summer. Stephen Spender. II, 237.
With Rue My Heart is Laden. Alfred Edward Housman. I, 169.
Deus Absconditus. Anne Ridler. II, 272.
Devil's Dream. Kenneth Fearing. II, 98.
Dialectics
For One Who Would Not Take His Life in His Hands. Delmore Schwartz. II, 307.
Diana and Endymion
The May-Tree. Alfred Noyes. I, 242.
The Different Day. Grace Hazard Conkling. I, 88.
The Dinner-Party, (sels.). Amy Lowell. I, 201.
Dirge. Kenneth Fearing. II, 99.
The Discovery. John Collings ("Solomon Eagle") Squire. I, 285.
Dividends. Kenneth Fearing. II, 100.
"Dolls' faces are rosier but these were children," II, 32.
Dolor. Theodore Roethke. II, 204.
The Dome of Sunday. Karl Shapiro. II, 312.
The Donkey. Gilbert Keith Chesterton. I, 84.
Doolittle, Hilda. II, 4–6.
Douglas, Keith. II, 405–407.
"Down the railroad in a green valley," I, 303.
Down by the Salley Gardens. William Butler Yeats. I, 328.
"Down the road someone is practicing scales," II, 184.
"Down, you mongrel, Death" I, 219.
"Dream in a dream the heavy soul somewhere," II, 327.
The Dreamer. Clifford Bax. I, 27.
Dreams
Autobiography. Louis MacNeice. II, 171.
The Lesson. W. H. Auden. II, 162.
Tears in Sleep. Louise Bogan. I, 61.
Drinkwater, John. I, 109–110.
"Droning a drowsy syncopated tune," I, 171.
Drowning
At Whose Sheltering Shall the Day Sea. William Sydney Graham. II, 400.

Gigha. William Sydney Graham. II, 401.
Night's Fall Unlocks the Dirge of the Sea. William Sydney Graham. II, 402.
The Drum. Edith Sitwell. II, 12.
The Drunken Fisherman. Robert Lowell. II, 389.
Ducks
Flighting for Duck. William Empson. II, 142.
Durrell, Lawrence. II, 257–261.
"The dwarf barefooted, chanting," II, 377.
"Dwarf pines; the wild plum on the wind-grassed," II, 24.
The Eagle and the Mole. Elinor Wylie. I, 326.
Eagles
The Eagle and the Mole. Elinor Wylie. I, 326.
Early Spring. Sidney Keyes. II, 411.
"Early sun on Beaulieu water," II, 138.
Ears in the Turrets Hear. Dylan Thomas. II, 362.
"Easily, my dear, you move, easily your head," II, 154.
Eberhart, Richard. II, 126–128.
Ecce Homo. David Gascoyne. II, 380.
An Eclogue for Christmas. Louis MacNeice. II, 174.
Education
An Elementary School Classroom in a Slum. Stephen Spender. II, 227.
Edwards, Jonathan
Mr. Edwards and the Spider. Robert Lowell. II, 393.
"Egyptian banks, an avenue of clay," II, 142.
Elegy. Sidney Keyes. II, 411.
Elegy for a Dead Soldier. Karl Shapiro. II, 314.
Elegy Written on a Frontporch. Karl Shapiro. II, 318.
An Elegy. David Gascoyne. II, 382.
An Elementary School Classroom in a Slum. Stephen Spender. II, 227.
The Elements. Oscar Williams. II, 78.
Eliot, Thomas Stearns. I, 114–120.
Empson, William. II, 140–145.
Empty Vessel. Hugh MacDiarmid II, 29.
The Enamel Girl. Genevieve Taggard. I, 292.
The End of the World. Archibald MacLeish. I, 203.
England
Sonnet: Realities I. Edward Estlin Cummings. I, 104.
England and the English
Autumn Morning at Cambridge. Frances Cornford. I, 91.
Cargoes. John Masefield. I, 210.

In the Train. Clifford Bax. I, 27.
The Old Vicarage, Grantchester. Rupert Brooke. I, 76.
Parliament Hill Fields. John Betjeman. II, 136.
Perhaps. W. H. Auden. II, 165.
The Rolling English Road. Gilbert Keith Chesterton. I, 83.
The South Country. Hilaire Belloc. I, 31.
Upper Lambourne. John Betjeman. II, 138.
The Welsh Marches. Alfred Edward Housman. I, 167.
Epilogue from Emblems of Love. Lascelles Abercrombie. I, 1.
Epitaph. Lascelles Abercrombie. I, 5.
Epitaphs
After the Funeral. Dylan Thomas. II, 347.
Elegy. Sidney Keyes. II, 411.
Tombstone with Cherubim. Horace Gregory. II, 66.
Erotic Love
O Wha's Been Here Afore Me, Lass. Hugh MacDiarmid. II, 30.
23rd Street Runs into Heaven. Kenneth Patchen. II, 255.
Eternity
Desire. Kathleen Raine. II, 197.
Iliad. Humbert Wolfe. I, 321.
Eve. Ralph Hodgson. I, 163.
Evening Scene. E. J. Scovell. II, 187.
"The evergreen shadow and the pale magnolia," II, 241.
"Everybody give the big boy a hand," II, 62.
"Everybody loved Chick Lorimer in our town," I, 281.
Evolution
The Menagerie. William Vaughn Moody. I, 228.
Exodus From Egypt
Departure in the Dark. Cecil Day Lewis. II, 113.
Experience
The Lost Son. Theodore Roethke. II, 205.
Explorations. Louis MacNeice. II, 178.
Eye-Witness. Ridgely Torrence. I, 303.

Failure
To a Friend Whose Work Has Come to Nothing. William Butler Yeats. I, 329.
Fairs
Hostenwall. Sidney Keyes. II, 413.
Faith

Deus Absconditus. Anne Ridler. II, 272.
It Is Time That I Wrote My Will. William Butler Yeats. I, 330.
Mysticism Has Not the Patience To Wait For God's Revelation. Richard Eberhart. II, 128.
The Oxen. Thomas Hardy. I, 159.
A Winter's Tale. Dylan Thomas. II, 368.
The Falconer of God. William Rose Benet. I, 46.
The Fall. Kathleen Riane. II, 198.
Falling Asleep over the Aeneid. Robert Lowell. I, 390.
"False dreams, all false," I, 321.
"Far far from gusty waves these children's faces," II, 227.
"Far off, above the plain the summer dries," II, 332.
Farming and Farmers
After Winter. Sterling A. Brown. II, 82.
Country Summer. Leonie Adams. II, 70.
Foreclosure. Sterling A. Brown. II, 83.
Fatalism
The Hero. Roy Fuller. II, 263.
Fate
The Fall. Kathleen Raine. II, 198.
The Fates (mythology)
Ode. John Peale Bishop. II, 25.
Foreclosure. Sterling A. Brown. II, 83.
Fathers
To My Father. William Sydney Graham. II, 403.
Fear
In Waste Places. James Stephens. I, 286.
Reading Time: 1 Minute 26 Seconds. Muriel Rukeyser. II, 304.
"Fearful of beauty, I always went," I, 292.
Fearing, Kenneth. II, 97–101.
Feelings
Open House. Theodore Roethke. II, 211.
Fern Hill. Dylan Thomas. II, 363.
Festoons of Fishes. Alfred Kreynborg. I, 121.
Ficke, Arthur Davison. I, 121.
The Finding of Love. Robert Graves. I, 150.
Fire
Brother Fire. Louis MacNeice. II, 172.
The Prairie Fire. John G. Neihardt. I, 240.
A Refusal to Mourn the Death, by Fire, of a Child in London. Dylan Thomas. II, 368.
"The fire was furry as a bear," II, 12.
"The firewood pale with salt and burning green," II, 401.
"The firm, familiar world," I, 240.

First Cycle of Love Poems. George Barker. II, 278.
The First of May. Alfred Edward Housman. I, 169.
"The first time that I dreamed, we were in flight," II, 162.
The First Year (sel.) E. J. Scovell. II, 188.
Fishing and Fisherman
  Ballad of the Long-Legged Bait. Dylan Thomas. II, 353.
  The Drunken Fisherman. Robert Lowell. II, 389.
  Sonnet of Fishes. George Barker. II, 291.
  The Trout Map. Allen Tate. II, 76.
Fitzgerald, Robert. II, 240–241.
Flecker, James Elroy. I, 122.
Fletcher, John Gould. I, 126–129.
Flighting for Duck. William Empson. II, 142.
A Flower is Looking through the Ground. Harold Monro. I, 225.
"A Flying word from here and there," I, 272.
For a Christening. Anne Ridler. II, 273.
For a Dead Lady. Edwin Arlington Robinson. I, 271.
"For infants time is like a humming shell," II, 118.
For One Who Would Not Take His Life in His Hands. Delmore Schwartz. II, 307.
For St. Bartholomew's Eve. Malcolm Cowley. II, 59.
"For those who had the power," II, 124.
Foreclosure. Sterling A. Brown. II, 83.
"Foremost of false philosophies," I, 264.
Forests
  The Little Boy Lost. Stevie Smith. II, 103.
Forgetfulness
  Let It Be Forgotten. Sara Teasdale. I, 293.
Four Legs, Three Legs, Two Legs. William Empson. II, 143.
"Four pelicans went over the house," I, 173.
France
  Provincia Deserta. Ezra Pound. I, 251.
Free Will
  Explorations. Louis MacNeice. II, 178.
Freud, Sigmund
  In Memory of Sigmund Freud. W. H. Auden. II, 158.
A Friend's Song for Simoisius. Louise Imogen Guiney. I, 154.
"Friend, whose unnatural early death," II, 382.
Friends Beyond. Thomas Hardy. I, 157.
Friendship

Portrait of a Lady. Thomas Stearns Eliot. I, 116.
Tableau. Countee Cullen. I, 100.
A Frieze. John Peale Bishop. II, 24.
"From my mother's sleep I fell into the State," II, 330.
"From one shaft at Cleator Moor," II, 340.
"From Orford Ness to Shingle Street," II, 374.
"From what proud star I know not, but I found," II, 44.
Frost, Robert. I, 130–134.
Fuller, Roy. II, 263–265.
Funerals
  After the Funeral. Dylan Thomas. II, 347.
  Ceremony after a Fire Raid. Dylan Thomas. II, 359.

Galway Bay. George Barker. II, 283.
Gambling
  Casino. W. H. Auden. II, 158.
Gascoyne, David. II, 379–385.
Ghosts
  The Listeners. Walter John De La Mare. I, 107.
The Giant Puffball. Edmund Blunden. II, 44.
Gibson, Wilfrid Wilson. I, 141.
The Gift. George William Russell. I, 274.
Gifts and Giving
  The Gift. George William Russell. I, 274.
  The Token. F. T. Prince. II, 267–270.
Gigha. W. S. Graham. II, 401.
"The girl's far treble, muted to the heat," II, 336.
"Give them my regards when you go to the school," II, 303.
Glaucus. Sidney Keyes. II, 412.
Gloucester Moors. William Vaughn Moody. I, 225.
Go Down Death. James Weldon Johnson. I, 176.
"Go, spend your penny, Beauty, when you will," I, 209.
The Goal of Intellectual Man. Richard Eberhart. II, 126.
Goats
  All Goats. Elizabeth Jane Coatsworth. I, 85.
God
  Deus Absconditus. Anne Ridler. II, 272.
  The Dreamer. Clifford Bax. I, 27.
  First Cycle of Love Poems. George Barker. II, 278.
  The Hound of Heaven. Francis Joseph Thompson. I, 295.

Nimrod Wars with the Angels. Anna Hempstead Branch. I, 67.
Noon. Robinson Jeffers. I, 175.
Recessional. Rudyard Kipling. I, 179.
Renascence. Edna St. Vincent Millay. I, 214.
Report on Experience. Edmund Blunden. II, 46.
Sacred Elegy V. George Barker. II, 290.
"God of our fathers, known of old," I, 179.
Gold. John Drinkwater. I, 110.
"The gold-armoured ghost from the Roman road," II, 22.
The Golden Corpse. Stephen Vincent Benet. I, 42.
The Golden Journey to Samarkand. James Elroy Flecker. I, 122.
Gone. Carl Sandburg. I, 281.
Gorman, Herbert. I, 141–143.
The Gorse. Wilfrid Wilson Gibson. I, 141.
Gosse, Edmund William. I, 145–146.
Graham, William Sydney. II, 400–403.
The Grail. Sidney Keyes. II, 413.
Graves, Robert. I, 149–152.
"The great cup tumbled, ringing like a bell," II, 413.
The Great Lover. Rupert Brooke. I, 80.
Greece
   At Epidaurus. Lawrence Durrell. II, 257.
   A Frieze. John Peale Bishop. II, 24.
   Glaucus. Sidney Keyes. II, 412.
   In Arcadia. Lawrence Durrell. II, 259.
   Nemea. Lawrence Durrell. II, 260.
   On Ithaca Standing. Lawrence Durrell. II, 260.
"The green corn waving in the dale," I, 74.
Gregory, Horace. II, 62–67.
Grieve, Christopher Murray. (See MacDiarmid, Hugh.)
The Groundhog. Richard Eberhart. II, 127.
Growing Up
   Autobiography. Louis MacNeice. II, 171.
   The Enamel Girl. Genevieve Taggard. I, 292.
   The Lost Son. Theodore Roethke. II, 205.
   The Runner With the Lots. Leonie Adams. II, 71.
Gruach. Gordon Bottomley. I, 63.
Guilt
   Number Five. John Crowe Ransom. I, 259.
Guiney, Louise Imogen. I, 153–154.
Gulls
   A Talisman. Marianne Moore. I, 233.
Guns
   Port Bou. Stephen Spender. II, 231.

Gypsy Man. Langston Hughes. I, 171.

"Ha' we lost the goodliest fere o' all," I, 249.
Hagen. Horace Gregory. II, 63.
Haircut. Karl Shapiro. II, 321.
"The hard blue winds of March," II, 337.
Hardy, Thomas. I, 156–161.
Hardy, Thomas (about)
   Birthday Poem for Thomas Hardy. Cecil Day Lewis. II, 111.
"He is dying," I, 146.
He Made This Screen. Marianne Moore. I, 233.
"He roars in the swamp," I, 261.
"He snuggles his fingers," II, 82.
"He strides across the grassy corn," II, 3.
"He was a reprobate I grant," II, 405.
Heart and Mind. Edith Sitwell. II, 14.
Heaven
   The Heavenly City. Stevie Smith. II, 103.
   The Heavy Bear Who Goes With Me. Delmore Schwartz. II, 308.
Helen. Hilda Doolittle. II, 4.
Hell
   The Pythoness. Kathleen Raine. II, 201.
   The Tunnel. Hart Crane. I, 92.
Hellbabies. Horace Gregory. II, 64.
Heloise and Abelard
   Sic et Non. Herbert Read. II, 34.
"Her mist of primroses within her breast," I, 274.
"Here the jack-hammer jabs into the ocean," II, 388.
"Here we go a-walking, so softly, so softly," I, 315.
Heritage. Countee Cullen. I, 96.
The Hero. Roy Fuller. II, 263.
"High the vanes of Shrewsbury gleam," I, 167.
The Hill above the Mine. Malcolm Cowley. II, 60.
"His naked skin clothed in the torried mist," II, 94.
History
   November, 1941. Roy Fuller. II, 265.
Hodgson, Ralph. I, 163–165.
"Hog Butcher for the World," I, 283.
Holstenwall. Sidney Keyes. II, 413.
Holy Poems. George Barker. II, 284.
The Holy War. Rudyard Kipling. I, 182.
Homage to the British Museum. William Empson. II, 141.
"Homer and Hesoid and Virgil knew," I, 276.
"Honey," II, 88.

"Hoofs of thunder, fetlocks splashed with sunrise," I, 143.
"The hop-poles stand in cones," II, 45.
Hope
After Winter. Sterling A. Brown. II, 82.
The Darkling Thrush. Thomas Hardy. I, 156.
A Time to Dance. Cecil Day Lewis. II, 124.
Horses
Loreine: A Horse. Arthur Davison Ficke. I, 121.
Horseshoe Crabs
Colloquy with a King-Crab. John Peale Bishop. II, 24.
The Hound of Heaven. Francis Joseph Thompson. I, 295.
Housman, Alfred Edward. I, 166–170.
"'How, how,' he said. Friend Chang,' I said," I, 189.
"The huge red-buttressed mesa over yonder," I, 128.
Hughes, Langston. I, 171.
Humanism (philosophy)
I Walked Out to the Graveyard to see the Dead. Richard Eberhart. II, 128.
Humanity
The Coat of Fire. Edith Sitwell. II, 10.
The Hunchback in the Park. Dylan Thomas. II, 364.
"The hunchback on the corner, with gum," II, 132.
Hunchbacks
The Hunchback in the Park. Dylan Thomas. II, 364.
Hunting and Hunters
Flighting for Duck. William Empson. II, 142.
Song. Edward Estlin Cummings. I, 101.
"The hurdy-gurdy, public piano of the past," II, 80.
Hussar's Song. Thomas Hardy. I, 159.
"Hymn the Finders!" I, 53.

"—I am a gentleman in a dustcoat trying," I, 260.
I Am a Red Slogan. Richard Wright. II, 214.
"I am a witch, and a kind old witch," I, 90.
"I am black and I have seen black hands," II, 214.
"I am Saint John on Patmos of my heart," II, 284.
"I am that serpent-haunted cave," II, 201.
"I come from nothing; but from where," I, 213.
"I did not make the conditions of my life whereby," II, 197.

"I don't know how he came," I, 282.
"I dreamed that dead, and meditating," II, 245.
"I encountered the crowd returning from amusements," II, 288.
"I fled him, down the nights and down the days," I, 295.
"I flung my soul to the air like a falcon flying," I, 46.
"I had come to the house, in a cave of trees," I, 61.
"I have been so great a lover: filled my days," I, 80.
"I have been wandering in the lonely valleys," I, 243.
"I have been young, and now am not too old," II, 46.
"I have known the inexorable sadness of pencils," II, 204.
I Have Seen Black Hands. Richard Wright. II, 214.
I Hear an Army Charging upon the Land. James Joyce. II, 1.
"I leant upon a coppice gate," I, 156.
"I looked into my heart to write," II, 293.
"I love my little son, and yet when he was ill," II, 31.
"I love you first because your face is fair," II, 323.
"I may be smelly and I may be old," II, 104.
"I meet you in an evil time," II, 174.
"I met ayont the cairney," II, 29.
"I put those things there. —See them burn," II, 329.
"I ran out in the morning, when the air was clean," I, 91.
I Remembered. Sara Teasdale, I, 294.
"I rode in the dark of the spirit," I, 322.
"I sang as one," II, 112.
I Saw a Stable, Low and Very Bare. Mary Elizabeth Coleridge. I, 87.
"I saw the sky descending, black and white," II, 398.
"I saw the spiders marching through the air," II, 393.
"I selfish and forsaken do still long for you," II, 272.
"I sigh for the heavenly country," II, 103.
"I talked to old Lem," II, 85.
"I thought, beloved, to have brought you," I, 274.
"I took the crazy short-cut to the bay," I, 309.
"I walk, I only," I, 302.
I Walked Out to the Graveyard to See the Dead. Richard Eberhart. II, 128.

INDEX 425

I Will Not Let Thee Go. Robert Bridges. I, 72.
"I wonder if the hawk knew," I, 88.
"I wonder where it could of went to," I, 314.
"I'm going to be a pirate with a bright brass pivot," I, 207.
"I, an old woman in the light of the sun," II, 16.
"The idle dayseye, the laborious wheel," II, 409.
"If I should die, think only this of me," I, 76.
"If you would know why men dread nonchalance," I, 56.

Ignorance
Festoons of Fishes. Alfred Kreymborg. I, 184.
No Credit. Kenneth Fearing. II, 101.
Iliad. Humbert Wolfe. I, 321.

Imagination
Walking Song. Charles Williams. I, 315.

Immortality
A Frieze. John Peale Bishop. II, 24.
In Heaven I Suppose, Lie Down Together. Cecil Day Lewis. II, 115.
A Song of Derivations. Alice Meynell. I, 213.
"In a garden shady this holy lady," II, 167.
In Arcadia. Lawrence Durrell. II, 259.
"In dream, again within the clean, cold hell," I, 141.
In Heaven I Suppose, Lie Down Together. Cecil Day Lewis. II, 115.
"In his tall senatorial," II, 12.
In January. Gordon Bottomley. I, 62.
"In June, the early signs," II, 273.
"In June, amid the golden fields," II, 127.
In Memory of Sigmund Freud. W. H. Auden. II, 158.
"In mole-blue indolence the sun," II, 375.
"In my childhood trees were green," II, 171.
In Poets' Defence. John Wheelwright. II, 54.
"In summertime on Bredon," I, 166.
"In the beginning there was nought," I, 245.
"In the bowl of buildings *alias* the back yard," II, 79.
"In the first year of the last disgrace," II, 285.
In the Heart of Contemplation. Cecil Day Lewis. II, 115.
In the Train. Clifford Bax. I, 27.
"In the wild soft summer darkness," I, 294.
In Waste Places. James Stephens. I, 286.

Incense
The Red Lacquer Music-Stand. Amy Lowell. I, 198.
"Incognitos of masquerading moons," I, 184.

Indians of America
March-Patrol of the Naked Heroes. Herbert Gorman. I, 143.
Ossawatomie. Carl Sandburg. I, 282.

Individuality
Time Eating. Keith Douglas. II, 407.
Indolence. Vernon Watkins. II, 190.

Innocence
A Summer Night. George Will Russell. I, 274.

Intellect
Solutions. Edmund Blunden. II, 46.
"Into the silver night," I, 145.
Invitation to Juno. William Empson. II, 141.

Ireland
It Is Time That I Wrote My Will. William Butler Yeats. I, 330.
Neutrality. Louis MacNeice. II, 181.
September, 1913. William Butler Yeats. I, 328.
"Is it a wish—that tiny tin whistle," I, 185.
"Is it birthday weather for you, dear soul?" II, 111.
"'Is there anybody there?' said the Traveller." I, 107.
Isis Wanderer. Kathleen Raine. II, 199.
"The islands which whisper to the ambitious," II, 257.
"It is a winter's tale," II, 368.
"It is the fall, the eternal fall of water," II, 198.
It Is Time That I Wrote My Will. William Butler Yeats. I, 330.
"It was my thirtieth year to heaven," II, 366.
"It was not dying: everybody died," II, 331.
"It was the Rainbow gave thee birth," I, 105.

James, Henry (about)
At the Grave of Henry James. W. H. Auden. II, 150.
Jardin du Palais Royal. David Gascoyne. II, 384.
Jarrell, Randall. II, 330–332.
"Jazz notes and Brahms intermittently," II, 222.
Jeffers, Robinson. I, 173–175.

Jesus Christ
Ballad of the Goodly Fere. Ezra Pound. I, 249.
The Drunken Fisherman. Robert Lowell. II, 389.
Eye-Witness. Ridgely Torrence. I, 303.
I Saw a Stable, Low and Very Bare. Mary Elizabeth Coleridge. I, 87.
The Starlight's Intuitions Pierced the Twelve. Delmore Schwartz. II, 309.

Still Falls the Rain. Edith Sitwell. II, 21.
To a Contemporary Bunkshooter. Carl Sandburg. I, 279.
Joe Hill Listens to the Praying. Kenneth Patchen. II, 248.
"John begins like Genesis," II, 57.
John Bunyan
The Holy War. Rudyard Kipling. I, 182.
John Winter. Laurence Binyon. I, 50.
"John, founder of towns,–dweller in none," II, 53.
Johnson, James Weldon. I, 176.
Joyce, James. II, 1.
Judgement Day
Where the Rainbow Ends. Robert Lowell. II, 398.
June Thunder. Louis MacNeice. II, 179.
The Jungle. Alun Lewis. II, 375.
"Just as my fingers on these keys," I, 289.
"Just now the lilac is in bloom," I, 76.

The Kestrels. Sidney Keyes. II, 414.
Keyes, Sidney. II, 411–414.
King David. Stephen Vincent Benet. I, 34.
The King of Spain. Maxwell Bodenheim. I, 56.
The Kingfisher. William Henry Davies. I, 105.
Kings and Rulers
The Queen Forgets. George Sterling. I, 287.
The Kings. Louise Imogen Guiney. I, 153.
Kipling, Rudyard, I, 179–182.
"Knowing this man, who calls himself comrade," II, 217.
Knowledge
The Falconer of God. William Rose Benet. I, 46.
In Heaven I Suppose, Lie Down Together. Cecil Day Lewis. II, 115.
The Undiscovered Planet. Norman Nicholson. II, 343.
Kreymborg, Alfred. I, 184–185.

La Figlia Che Piange. Thomas Stearns Eliot. I, 120.
Labor and Laborers
The Death of the Hired Man. Robert Frost. I, 135.
The Man with the Hoe. Edwin Markham. I, 205.
Reflections in an Iron Works. Hugh MacDiarmid. II, 30.
The Scullion of the Queen. Maxwell Bodenheim. I, 56.

Steel. Joseph Auslander. I, 16.
Tom Mooney. William Ellery Leonard. I, 186.
The Word is Deed. John Wheelwright. II, 57.
The Lady Poverty. Alice Meynell. I, 212.
"Lady, three white leopards sat under a juniper," I, 114.
Lakes
Nocturne in a Deserted Brickyard. Carl Sandburg. I, 278.
The Land. Victoria Mary Sackville-West. I, 276.
The Landscape near an Aerodrome. Stephen Spender. II, 228.
Laurel
Mountain Laurel. Alfred Noyes. I, 243.
Law and Lawyers
Legal Fiction. William Empson. II, 144.
Leavetaking. William Watson. I, 313.
Lee Laurie. II, 335–337.
Legal Fiction. William Empson. II, 144.
Legend. John V. A. Weaver. I, 314.
Leisure. William Henry Davies. I, 105.
Leonard, William Ellery. I, 186.
Leonardo da Vinci
There Lived a Lady in Milan. William Rose Benet. I, 47.
Les Sylphides. Louis MacNeice. II, 185.
The Lesson. W. H. Auden. II, 162.
Lessons Of the War: Judging Distances. Henry Reed. II, 344.
"Let her lie naked here, my hand resting," II, 286.
"Let It Be Forgotten." Sara Teasdale. I, 293.
Let Us Have Madness Openly. Kenneth Patchen II, 254.
"Let us walk in the white snow," I, 326.
A Letter on the Use of Machine Guns at Weddings. Kenneth Patchen. II, 252.
A Letter to a Policeman in Kansas City. Kenneth Patchen. II, 253.
Leviathan. Peter Quennell. I, 254.
Lewis, Alun. II, 374–378.
Life
Dejection. Robert Bridges. I, 73.
Ears in the Turrets Hear. Dylan Thomas. II 362.
Elegy Written on a Frontporch. Karl Shapiro II, 318.
Meditation. Roy Fuller. II, 264.
An Old Woman. Edith Sitwell. II, 16.
The Rolling English Road. Gilbert Keith Chesterton. I, 81.
Train Ride. John Wheelwright. II, 56.

The Valley of the Shadow. Edwin Arlington Robinson. I, 267.
"Life in a day: he took his girl to the ballet," II, 185.
Conduct of Life
  A World Within a War. Herbert Read. II, 36.
  "Like a hound with nose to the trail," II, 341.
  "Like the soldier, like the sailor, like the bib," II, 252.
  Lilacs. Amy Lowell. I, 195.
Lincoln, Abraham
  The Master. Edwin Arlington Robinson. I, 272.
  Lindsay, Vachel. I, 189.
  Listen. Put on Morning. W. S. Graham. II, 401.
  The Listeners. Walter John De La Mare. I, 107.
  The Little Boy Lost. Stevie Smith. II, 103.
  "Living in a wide landscape are the flowers," II, 406.
  "Locked arm in arm they cross the way," I, 100.
London
  Walking Song. Charles Williams. I, 315.
Loneliness
  Miranda's Song. W. H. Auden. II, 164.
  The Mixer. Louis MacNeice. II, 180.
Longing
  John Winter, Laurence Binyon. I, 50.
  "Look at the steady rifles, Joe," II, 248.
  "Look at this man in the room before you," II, 218.
  Loreine: A Horse. Arthur Davison Ficke. I, 121.
Loss
  The Golden Journey to Samarkand. James Elroy Flecker. I, 122.
  The Runner with the Lots. Leonie Adams. II, 71.
  The Sea Holly. Conrad Aiken. I, 12.
  When You Are Old. William Butler Yeats. I, 332.
  Losses. Randall Jarrell. II, 331.
  The Lost Son. Theodore Roethke. II, 205.
  "A lot of men and armies stand to take," II, 253.
Love, Nature of
  A Bride in the '30's. W. H. Auden. II, 154.
  Chloe Is False. Edmund William Gosse. I, 145.
  The Goal of Intellectual Man. Richard Eberhart. II, 126.
  Gypsy Man. Langston Hughes. I, 171.
  Heart and Mind. Edith Sitwell. II, 14.
  The Kestrels. Sidney Keyes. II, 414.

The Old Witch in the Copse. Frances Cornford. I, 90.
Revelation. Robert Penn Warren. II, 131.
Sacred Elegy V. George Barker. II, 290.
So Sweet Love Seemed that April Morn. Robert Bridges. I, 75.
Somebody's Song. Dorothy Parker. I, 248.
To the Tune of the Coventry Carol. Stevie Smith. II, 105.
V-Letter. Karl Shapiro. II, 323.
Watch Any Day. W. H. Auden. II, 169.
The Wedding. Conrad Aiken. I, 14.
Your Body Is Stars. Stephen Spender. II, 238.
Love—Plaints and Protests
  Bitterness. Victoria Mary Sackville-West. I, 277.
  Epilogue from Emblems of Love. Lascelles Abercrombie. I, 1.
  I Will Not Let Thee Go. Robert Bridges. I, 72.
  The Lesson. W. H. Auden. II, 162.
  Love Song. William Carlos Williams. I, 320.
  Summer Song. George Barker. II, 293.
  The Suppliant. Edmund William Gosse. I, 145.
  To the Unimplored Beloved. Edward Shanks. I, 284.
Love
  The Finding of Love. Robert Graves. I, 150.
  For One Who Would Not Take His Life in His Hands. Delmore Schwartz. II, 307.
  The Gift. George William Russell. I, 274.
  Gold. John Drinkwater. I, 110.
  The Great Lover. Rupert Brooke. I, 80.
  I Remembered. Sara Teasdale. I, 294.
  Love Poem. Kathleen Raine. II, 200.
  Nocturn. Francis Joseph Thompson. I, 302.
  O Vocables of Love. Laura (Jackson) Riding. I, 265.
  Piazza Piece. John Crowe Ransom. I, 260.
  Revelation. Edmund William Gosse. I, 145.
  Scunner. Hugh MacDiarmid. II, 31.
  Sonnet from Second April. Edna St. Vincent Millay. I, 224.
  Spectral Lovers. John Crowe Ransom. I, 258.
  Summer Night, Riverside. Sara Teasdale. I, 294.
  To Earthward. Robert Frost. I, 134.
  To the Beloved. Alice Meynell. I, 211.
  The Token. F. T. Prince. II, 270.
  A Virginal. Ezra Pound. I, 251.
  "Love at the lips was touch," I, 134.
  Love Poem. Kathleen Raine. II, 200.
  Love Song. William Carlos Williams. I, 320.

Loveliest of Trees. Alfred Edward Housman. I, 166.
Lowell, Amy. I, 195–198.
Lowell, Robert. II, 386–398.
"Lucretius could not credit centaurs," II, 141.
Luis De Camoes. Roy Campbell. II, 94.
Lust
  But for Lust. Ruth Pitter. II, 48.
  Peter Quince at the Clavier. Wallace Stevens. I, 289.
  Sic et Non. Herbert Read. II, 34.

MacDiarmid, Hugh. II, 29–31.
MacLeish, Archibald. I, 203–204.
MacNeice, Louis. II, 171–185.
"Man is a sacred city, built of marvellous earth," I, 208.
"A Man said unto his Angel," I, 153.
The Man With the Hoe. Edwin Markham. I, 205.
"The Management Area of Cherokee," II, 76.
Mandalay. Rudyard Kipling. I, 180.
Mankind
  Petition. W. H. Auden. II, 167.
  Titanic Litany. John Wheelwright. II, 55.
"Many know you now by virtue of that music," I, 28.
"Maple and sumach down this autumn ride," II, 117.
March-Patrol of the Naked Heroes. Herbert Gorman. I, 143.
Markham, Edwin. I, 205.
Marriage
  Canto Amor. John Berryman. II, 327.
  Carry Her over the Water. W. H. Auden. II, 157.
  Invitation to Juno. William Empson. II, 141.
  Les Sylphides. Louis MacNeice. II, 185.
Marston. Stephen Spender. II, 229.
"Mary sat musing on the lamp-flame at the table," I, 135.
Masefield, John. I, 207–210.
The Master. Edwin Arlington Robinson. I, 272.
The May-Tree. Alfred Noyes. I, 242.
McKay, Claude. I, 203.
Meditation. Roy Fuller. II, 264.
Mediterranean. Muriel Rukeyser. II, 296.
Medusa. Louise Bogan. I, 61.
Melancholy
  Now Philippa Is Gone. Anne Ridler. II, 276.
Memories
  Colorado. Robert Fitzgerald. II, 240.

Jardin Du Palais Royal. David Gascoyne. II, 384.
Musician. Clifford Bax. I, 28.
Nostalgia. Karl Shapiro, II, 322.
With Rue My Heart Is Laden. Alfred Edward Housman. I, 169.
The Menagerie. William Vaughn Moody. I, 228.
Mending Wall. Robert Frost. I, 130.
Mersa. Keith Douglas. II, 406.
Mexico and Mexicans
  Windmills. John Gould Fletcher. I, 126.
Meynell, Alice. I, 210–213.
Michaelmas. Norman Nicholson. II, 341.
The Midnight Skaters. Edmund Blunden. II, 45.
"A mile behind is Gloucester town," I, 225.
A Mile from Eden. Anne Ridler. II, 275.
The Military Harpist. Ruth Pitter. II, 48.
Milk and Milking.
  Milkmaid. Laurie Lee. II, 336.
  Milk At the Bottom Of the Sea. Oscar Williams. II, 79.
Milkmaid. Laurie Lee. II, 336.
Millay, Edna St. Vincent. I, 214–224.
Mills and Millers
  Steel Mill. Louis Untermeyer. I, 311.
  The Windmill. Robert Bridges. I, 74.
  Windmills. John Gould Fletcher. I, 126.
Mining and Miners
  Cleator Moor. Norman Nicholson. II, 340.
  The Collier. Vernon Watkins. II, 189.
Miranda's Song. W. H. Auden. II, 164.
Missing Dates. William Empson. II, 144.
Missouri River
  Foreclosure. Sterling A. Brown. II, 83.
The Mixer. Louis MacNeice. II, 180.
Moles
  The Eagle and the Mole. Elinor Wylie. I, 326.
Money
  Dividends. Kenneth Fearing. II, 100.
  "The monk sat in his den," II, 106.
Monro, Harold. I, 224–225.
The Monument. Elizabeth Bishop. II, 243.
Moody, William Vaughn. I, 225–228.
Moon
  Moonlit Apples. John Drinkwater. I, 109.
Moore, Marianne. I, 233–234.
Moore, Thomas Sturge. I, 235.
Morality
  Beyond Good and Evil. George Edward Woodberry. I, 322.
  "More beautiful than any gift you gave," II, 270.

"More beautiful and soft than any moth," II, 228.
More of a Corpse Than a Woman. Muriel Rukeyser. II, 303.
Morning
Day of These Days. Laurie Lee. II, 335.
Prelude. John Drinkwater. I, 110.
A Wood Song. Ralph Hodgson. I, 165.
Mortality
The Heavy Bear Who Goes With Me. Delmore Schwartz. II, 308.
O Dreams, O Destinations. Cecil Day Lewis. II, 118.
Moss
Moss-Gathering. Theodore Roethke. II, 210.
"Most holy Night, that still dost keep," I, 33.
Most Lovely Shade. Edith Sitwell. II, 15.
"Most near, most dear, most loved and most far," II, 294.
Mothers and Motherhood
Milkmaid. Laurie Lee. II, 336.
Second Air Force. Randall Jarrell. II, 332.
The Tigress. Ruth Pitter. II, 50.
To My Mother. George Barker. II, 294.
Mountain Laurel. Alfred Noyes. I, 243.
Mowing and Mowers
The Translation. Mark Van Doren. I, 312.
Mr. Edwards and the Spider. Robert Lowell. II, 393.
Musée des Beaux Arts. W. H. Auden. II, 164.
Museums. Louis MacNeice. II, 180.
Music and Musicians
The Military Harpist. Ruth Pitter. II, 48.
Peter Quince at the Clavier. Wallace Stevens. I, 289.
Song at Night. Norman Nicholson. II, 341.
Song for St. Cecilia's Day. W. H. Auden. II, 167.
The Weary Blues. Langston Hughes. I, 171.
"A Music-Stand of crimson lacquer, long since," I, 198.
"Music for a while," II, 341.
Musician. Clifford Bax. I, 28.
"My Dear One is mine as mirrors are lonely," II, 164.
"My man's a gypsy," I, 171.
"My secrets cry aloud," II, 211.
"My soul stands at the window of my room," II, 322.
"Myselves," II, 359.
Mystery. John Drinkwater. I, 113.

Mysticism Has Not the Patience to Wait for God's Revelation. Richard Eberhart. II, 128.

Nature
Boats in a Fog. Robinson Jeffers. I, 173.
Indolence. Vernon Watkins. II, 190.
Pelicans. Robinson Jeffers. I, 173.
Tamar. Robinson Jeffers. I, 174.
Nearing Again the Legendary Isle. Cecil Day Lewis. II, 117.
"The nearly right/And yet not quite," II, 105.
Negroes
I Have Seen Black Hands. Richard Wright. II, 214.
Neighbors
Mending Wall. Robert Frost. I, 130.
Neihardt, John G. I, 240.
Nemea. Lawrence Durrell. II, 260.
"The neutral island facing the Atlantic," II, 181.
"Never until the mankind making," II, 368.
New England
Lilacs. Amy Lowell. I, 195.
New Jersey
Legend. John V. A. Weaver. I, 314.
New York City
Shame On Thee, O Manhattan. Anna Hempstead Branch. I, 71.
The Tunnel. Hart Crane. I, 92.
News of the World II. George Barker. II, 285.
News of the World III. George Barker. II, 286.
"Next year the grave grass will cover us," II, 255.
Nicholson, Norman. II, 338–343.
Nietzsche, Friederic (about)
Beyond Good and Evil. George Edward Woodberry. I, 322.
Night
Cradle-Song at Twilight. Alice Meynell. I, 212.
Souls Lake. Robert Fitzgerald. II, 241.
You, Andrew Marvell. Archibald MacNeice. I, 204.
"Night and we heard heavy and cadenced hoofbeats," II, 27.
Night's Fall Unlocks the Dirge Of the Sea. W. S. Graham. II, 402.
The Night. Hilaire Belloc. I, 33.
Nimrod Wars with the Angels. Anna Hempstead Branch. I, 67.
No Credit. Kenneth Fearing. II, 101.

"No more with overflowing light," I, 271.
"No notice in the papers," II, 66.
"No, no! Go from me I have left her lately," I, 251.
Noah
Still, Citizen Sparrow. Richard Wilbur. II, 409.
"Nobody comes to the graveyard on the hill," II, 60.
"Nobody ever galloped on this road," II, 107.
Nocturn. Francis Joseph Thompson. I, 302.
Nocturne in a Deserted Brickyard. Carl Sandburg. I, 278.
Noon. Robinson Jeffers. I, 175.
North Pole
Polar Exploration. Stephen Spender. II, 230.
Nostalgia. Karl Shapiro. II, 322.
Nostalgia
Berkshire Holiday. Clifford Bax. I, 29.
Not Honey. Hilda Doolittle. II, 5.
Not Men Alone. Edwin Rolfe. II, 217.
"Not of silver nor of coral," I, 233.
"Not only how far away, but the way that you say it," II, 344.
"Not picnics or pageants or the improbable," II, 133.
"Not yet! Do not yet touch," II, 191.
Note on Local Flora. William Empson. II, 145.
"Nothing so sharply reminds a man he is mortal," II, 113.
November, 1941. Roy Fuller. II, 265.
"Now all the truth is out," I, 329.
"Now as I was young and easy under the apple boughs," II, 363.
"Now can you see the monument! It is of wood," II, 243.
"Now one and all, you rose," I, 165.
Now Philippa Is Gone. Anne Ridler. II, 276.
"Now that the young buds are tipped with," II, 411.
"Now the ambassadors have gone, refusing," II, 264.
"Now the plains come to adore the mountain wall," II, 240.
"Now the rich cherry, whose sleek wood," II, 70.
"Now, when my life is more than half consumed," I, 63.
Noyes, Alfred. I, 242–245.
Number Five. John Crowe Ransom. I, 259.

O. Richard Wilbur. II, 409.

"O bitterness never spoken, the death mask etched," II, 65.
"O David, if I had," I, 234.
O Dreams, O Destinations. Cecil Day Lewis. II, 118.
"O Love, the interest itself in thoughtless Heaven," II, 165.
"O Shepherd, up upon the snow," I, 62.
"O Swiftness of the swallow and strength," I, 174.
O Vocables of Love. Laura (Jackson) Riding. I, 265.
O Wha's Been Here Afore Me, Lass. Hugh MacDiarmid. II, 30.
"O wonderful nonsense of lotions of Lucky Tiger," II, 321.
"The objects are disposed: the sky is suitable," II, 265.
Obscurity
Portrait—II. Edward Estlin Cummings. I, 102.
Portrait—X. Edward Estlin Cummings. I, 103.
The Weak Monk. Stevie Smith. II, 106.
Ode. John Peale Bishop. II, 25.
Ode to the Confederate Dead. Allen Tate. II, 73.
"Of evident invisibles," I, 102.
"Oh, not more subtly silence strays," I, 211.
"Oh, thou great Babel–out of nothing reared," I, 68.
Old Age
After Ronsard. Charles Williams. I, 315.
An Ancient to Ancients. Thomas Hardy. I, 161.
An Old Woman. Edith Sitwell. II, 16.
Piazza Piece. John Crowe Ransom. I, 260.
When You Are Old. William Butler Yeats. I, 332.
Old Lem. Sterling A. Brown. II, 85.
"An old man in Concord forgets," II, 390.
The Old Vicarage, Grantchester. Rupert Brooke. I, 76.
The Old Witch in the Copse. Frances Cornford. I, 90.
An Old Woman. Edith Sitwell. II, 16.
On Ithaca Standing. Lawrence Durrell. II, 260.
"1-2-3 was the number he played but today," II, 99.
"The only blossoms of the plains are black," Roy Fuller. II, 265.
"Only the hands are living; to the wheel attracted," II, 158.

Open House. Theodore Roethke. II, 211.
"The Orchards half the way," I, 169.
"Ordinary people are peculiar too," II, 173.
Orient
  The Golden Journey to Samarkand. James Elroy Flecker. I, 122.
  Mandalay. Rudyard Kipling. I, 180.
Orpheus—(mythology)
  Orpheus In The Underworld. David Gascoyne. II, 385.
Ossawatomie. Carl Sandburg. I, 282.
"Our single purpose was to walk through snow," II, 230.
"Out of the tomb we bring Badroulbadour," I, 291.
"Out on the furthest tether let it run," II, 343.
"Out, Out—." I, 133.
The Oxen. Thomas Hardy. I, 159.

Paganism
  Stylite. Louis MacNeice. II, 183.
Painting and Painters
  Musée de Beaux Arts. W. H. Auden. II, 164.
  The Sitting. Cecil Day Lewis. II, 122.
Paranoia
  The Woman Who Disapproved of Music At the Bar. Horace Gregory. II, 67.
Parenthood
  The Two Parents. Hugh MacDiarmid. II, 31.
  The Voice. Wilfrid Wilson Gibson. I, 141.
Parker, Dorothy. I, 248.
Parks
  An Autumn Park. David Gascoyne. II, 379.
Parliament Hill Fields. John Betjeman. II, 136.
Parties
  The Dinner-Party, (sels.). Amy Lowell. I, 201.
"Pass, thou wild light," I, 313.
Patchen, Kenneth. II, 248–255.
Patriotism
  The Soldier. Rupert Brooke. I, 76.
Peace
  News of the World II. George Barker. II, 285.
  Peace on Earth. William Carlos Williams. I, 319.
Peasants
  The Peasants. Alun Lewis. II, 377.
PeeWee. Alfred Kreymborg. I, 185.
Pelicans. Robinson Jeffers. I, 173.
"Performances, assortments, resumes," I, 92.
Perhaps. W. H. Auden. II, 165.
Perseus. Louis MacNeice. II, 182.

Perseverance
  The Conflict. Cecil Day Lewis. II, 112.
  The Dead Ride Fast. Richard P. Blackmur. II, 107.
  Homage to the British Museum. William Empson. II, 141.
  Rest from Loving and Be Living. Cecil Day Lewis. II, 122.
  This Last Pain. William Empson. II, 145.
Peter Quince at the Clavier. Wallace Stevens. I, 289.
Petition. W. H. Auden. II, 167.
Piazza Piece. John Crowe Ransom. I, 260.
Piero Della Francesca. Anne Ridler. II, 276.
A Pilot From the Carrier. Randall Jarrell. II, 332.
Pine Trees
  Choosing a Mast. Roy Campbell. II, 92.
Pirates
  The Tarry Buccaneer. John Masefield. I, 207.
Pitter, Ruth. II, 48–51.
The Plains. Roy Fuller. II, 265.
Plants and Planting
  Note on Local Flora. William Empson. II, 145.
Plowing and Plowmen
  The Land. Victoria Mary Sackville-West. I, 276.
Poem in October. Dylan Thomas. II, 366.
The Poet and His Book. Edna St. Vincent Millay. I, 219.
Poetry and Poets
  At the Grave of Henry James. W. H. Auden. II, 150.
  The Deceased. Keith Douglas. II, 405.
  Gruach. Gordon Bottomley. I, 63.
  Iliad. Humbert Wolfe. I, 321.
  In Poets' Defence. John Wheelwright. II, 54.
  The Poet and His Book. Edna St. Vincent Millay. I, 219.
  Reading Time: 1 Minute 26 Seconds. Muriel Rukeyser. II, 304.
  Room with Revolutionists. Edwin Rolfe. II, 218.
  Word. Stephen Spender. II, 238.
Polar Exploration. Stephen Spender. II, 230.
Policemen
  A Letter to a Policeman in Kansas City. Kenneth Patchen. II, 253.
Politics and Politicians
  The Road from Election to Christmas. Oscar Williams. II, 80.
Port Bou. Stephen Spender. II, 231.

Portrait—II. Edward Estlin Cummings. I, 102.
Portrait—X. Edward Estlin Cummings. I, 103.
Portrait of a Lady. Thomas Stearns Eliot. I, 116.
The Potomac. Karl Shapiro. II, 322.
Pound, Ezra. I, 249–251.
Poverty
  Come, Live with Me, and Be My Love. Cecil Day Lewis. II, 112.
  An Elementary School Classroom in a Slum. Stephen Spender. II, 227.
  Hagen. Horace Gregory. II, 63.
  The Lady Poverty. Alice Meynell. I, 212.
  Worry about Money. Kathleen Raine. II, 202.
  The Prairie Fire. John G. Neihardt. I, 240.
  Prelude. John Drinkwater. I, 110.
Priests
  The Song of the Demented Priest. John Berryman. II, 329.
  Prince. F. T.. II, 267–270.
Prisons and Prisoners
  The Gorse. Wilfrid Wilson Gibson. I, 141.
Progress
  As One Who Wanders into Old Workings. Cecil Day Lewis. II, 110.
  An Autumn Park. David Gascoyne. II, 379.
  C Stands for Civilization. Kenneth Fearing. II, 97.
  Cleator Moor. Norman Nicholson. II, 340.
  The Elements. Oscar Williams. II, 78.
Prometheus
  Titanic Litany. John Wheelwright. II, 55.
Promiscuity
  Watch Any Day. W. H. Auden. II, 169.
Provincia Deserta. Ezra Pound. I, 251.
Puffballs
  The Giant Puffball. Edmund Blunden. II, 44.
"The pure air trembles, O pitiless God," I, 175.
Pursuit. Robert Penn Warren. II, 132.
The Pythoness. Kathleen Raine. II, 201.

The Quaker Graveyard in Nantucket. Robert Lowell. II, 394.
The Queen Forgets. George Sterling. I, 287.
Quennell, Peter. I, 254.
"Quinquireme of Nineveh from distant Ophir," I, 210.
"Quite unexpectedly as Vasserot," I, 203.

Rabbits
  The Tame Hare. Norman Nicholson. II, 342.

Racial Prejudice
  I Have Seen Black Hands. Richard Wright. II, 214.
  Old Lem. Sterling A. Brown. II, 85.
"The raging and the ravenous," II, 50.
Rain
  June Thunder. Louis MacNeice. II, 179.
  Rain in the Desert. John Gould Fletcher. I, 128.
Raine, Kathleen. II, 196–202.
Ransom, John Crowe. I, 258–260.
Ravenel, Beatrice. I, 261.
"Ravenous time has flowers for his food," II, 407.
Read, Herbert. II, 32–36.
Reading Time: 1 Minute 26 Seconds. Muriel Rukeyser. II, 304.
"Rebel poets, who've given vicar aid," II, 54.
Recessional. Rudyard Kipling. I, 179.
"Red fool, my laughing comrade," II, 378.
The Red Lacquer Music-Stand. Amy Lowell. I, 198.
Reed, Henry. II, 344.
Reflections in an Iron Works. Hugh MacDiarmid. II, 30.
A Refusal to Mourn the Death, by Fire, of a Child in London. Dylan Thomas. II, 368.
Regret
  La Figlia Che Piange. Thomas Stearns Eliot. I, 120.
Religion
  After the Surprising Conversions. Robert Lowell. II, 386.
  Caedmon. Norman Nicholson. II, 338.
  Heritage. Countee Cullen. I, 96.
  Holy Poems. George Barker. II, 284.
  The Landscape near an Aerodrome. Stephen Spender. II, 228.
  "Remain, for me, chaste, unapproached, unstirred," I, 284.
  Remembering Nat Turner. Sterling A. Brown. II, 87.
  Renascence. Edna St. Vincent Millay. I, 214.
Report on Experience. Edmund Blunden. II, 46.
Repression
  The Weed. Elizabeth Bishop. II, 245.
Resolution of Dependence. George Barker. II, 288.
Responsiblities
  In the Heart of Contemplation. Cecil Day Lewis. II, 115.
  Rest from Loving and Be Living. Cecil Day Lewis. II, 122.
Resurrection

Isis Wanderer. Kathleen Raine. II, 199.
The Return. John Peale Bishop. II, 27.
Revelation. Edmund William Gosse. I, 145.
Revelation. Robert Penn Warren. II, 131.
Revolution
  Bread-Word Giver. John Wheelwright. II, 53.
  In Poets' Defence. John Wheelwright. II, 54.
  The Serf. Roy Campbell. II, 94.
  Tom Mooney. William Ellery Leonard. I, 186.
  You That Love England. Cecil Day Lewis. II, 125.
Revolutionaries
  Room With Revolutionists. Edwin Rolfe. II, 218.
  Richard Cory. Edwin Arlington Robinson. I, 266.
The Riddlers. Walter John De La Mare. I, 108.
Riding, Laura (Jackson). I, 264–265.
Ridler, Anne. II, 271–276.
The River God. Stevie Smith. II, 104.
The Road from Election to Christmas. Oscar Williams. II, 80.
Robinson, Edwin Arlington. I, 266–272.
Roethke, Theodore. II, 204–211.
Rolfe, Edwin. II, 217–222.
The Rolling English Road. Gilbert Keith Chesterton. I, 83.
"Romantic fool who cannot speak!" I, 224.
Room with Revolutionists. Edwin Rolfe. II, 218.
Roses
  Sonnet: Roses are Beauty. John Masefield. I, 209.
"A rosy shield upon its back," II, 2.
"Row after row with strict impunity," II, 73.
Rukeyser, Muriel. II, 295–304.
"Rumbling under blackened girders, Midland, bound," II, 136.
The Runner with the Lots. Leonie Adams. II, 71.
Russell, George William. I, 274.
Ryton Firs. Lascelles Abercrombie. I, 5.

Sabbath
  The Boy Out of Church. Robert Graves. I, 152.
Sackville-West, Victoria Mary. I, 276–277.
Sacred Elegy V. George Barker. II, 290.
Sacrifice
  Colorado Morton's Ride. Leonard Bacon. I, 21.
Sahara Desert
  Mersa. Keith Douglas. II, 406.

"Said the Lion to the Lioness–'When you are amber.'" II, 14.
Sailors and Sailing
  John Winter. Laurence Binyon. I, 50.
  The Quaker Graveyard in Nantucket. Robert Lowell. II, 394.
Saint Bartholomew
  For St. Bartholomew's Eve. Malcolm Cowley. II, 59.
"The saint on the pillar stands," II, 183.
Salutation. Thomas Stearns Eliot. I, 114.
Salvos for Randolph Bourne. Horace Gregory. II, 65.
Sandburg, Carl. I, 278–283.
The Scarecrow. Andrew Young. II, 3.
Schwartz, Delmore. II, 307–309.
Scovell, E. J.. II, 187–188.
"The scullion of the Queen was grieved because," I, 56.
Scunner. Hugh MacDiarmid. II, 31.
Sea
  At Whose Sheltering Shall The Day Sea. W. S. Graham. II, 400.
  Gigha. W. S. Graham. II, 401.
  Night's Fall Unlocks the Dirge of the Sea. W. S. Graham. II, 402.
  Sea, False Philosophy. Laura (Jackson) Riding. I, 264.
"The sea drained off, my poverty's uncovered–," II, 109.
Sea, False Philosophy. Laura (Jackson) Riding. I, 264.
The Sea Holly. Conrad Aiken. I, 12.
Seascape. Stephen Spender. II, 232.
Seashore
  Evening Scene. E. J. Scovell. II, 187.
The Seasons
  The Three Winds. Laurie Lee. II, 337.
Second Air Force. Randall Jarrell. II, 332.
Seed
  Song of the Three Seeds in Macaw's Mouth. Elizabeth Jane Coatsworth. I, 85.
Seekers
  Pursuit. Robert Penn Warren. II, 132.
Segragation
  Tableau. Countee Cullen. I, 100.
Self
  Not Honey. Hilda Doolittle. II, 5.
  There is a Spell, for Instance. Hilda Doolittle. II, 6.
"September twenty-second, Sir: today," II, 386.
September, 1913. William Butler Yeats. I, 328.

The Serf. Roy Campbell. II, 94.
Sex
  The Sisters. Roy Campbell. II, 95.
"Shadows of clouds," I, 129.
"Shame on thee, O Manhattan, whom I love!" I, 71.
Shanks, Edward. I, 284.
Shapiro, Karl. II, 312–323.
"She came to him in dreams–her ears," II, 342.
"She lifted up her head," I, 121.
"She walks–the lady of my delight–," I, 210.
Shepherds and Shepherdesses
  In January. Gordon Bottomley. I, 62.
  The Shepherdess. Alice Meynell. I, 210.
Sic et Non. Herbert Read. II, 34.
Sidgwick, Henry (about)
  The Vanishing Boat. Edmund William Gosse. I, 146.
"Silence before/Sound./Sycamore," II, 192.
Sin
  Ballad of the Long-Legged Bait. Dylan Thomas. II, 353.
  King David. Stephen Vincent Benet. I, 34.
  "Sir, no man's enemy, forgiving all," W. H. Auden. II, 167.
Sirens (mythology)
  "Hymn the Finders!" Laurence Binyon. I, 53.
  Nearing Again the Legendary Isle. Cecil Day Lewis. II, 117.
Sister Lou. Sterling A. Brown. II, 88.
The Sisters. Roy Campbell. II, 95.
The Sitting. Cecil Day Lewis. II, 122.
Sitwell, Edith. II, 10–22.
"Sixteen years ago I built this house," II, 36.
Skating and Skaters
  The Midnight Skaters. Edmund Blunden. II, 45.
"The sky's a faded blue and taut-stretched flag," II, 384.
Sleep
  The Night. Hilaire Belloc. I, 33.
  Tears in Sleep. Louise Bogan. I, 61.
Slow Movement. Louis MacNeice. II, 182.
"Slowly the poison the whole blood stream fills," II, 144.
Smith, Stevie. II, 102–106.
Snakes
  The Viper. Ruth Pitter. II, 51.
Snow
  Milk at the Bottom of the Sea. Oscar Williams. II, 79.
  Velvet Shoes. Elinor Wylie. I, 326.

"'So . . .'they said," I, 201.
"So like a god I sit here," II, 122.
So Sweet Love Seemed That April Morn. Robert Bridges. I, 75.
Social Problems — United States
  I Have Seen Black Hands. Richard Wright. II, 214.
  Joe Hill Listens to the Praying. Kenneth Patchen. II, 248.
  A Letter on the Use of Machine Guns at Weddings. Kenneth Patchen. II, 252.
  A Letter to a Policeman in Kansas City. Kenneth Patchen. II, 253.
  Salvos for Randolph Bourne. Horace Gregory. II, 65.
  Somebody and Somebody Else and You. Edwin Rolfe. II, 220.
  Street Corner College. Kenneth Patchen. II, 255.
The Soldier. Rupert Brooke. I, 76.
Soldiers
  Elegy for a Dead Soldier. Karl Shapiro. II, 314.
  Hussar's Song. Thomas Hardy. I, 159.
  Two Armies. Stephen Spender. II, 235.
Solitude
  Souls Lake. Robert Fitzgerald. II, 241.
Solomon Eagle. (See Squire, John Collings.)
Solutions. Edmund Blunden. II, 46.
Somebody and Somebody Else and You. Edwin Rolfe. II, 220.
"Somebody knew Lincoln somebody Xerxes," I, 103.
Somebody's Song. Dorothy Parker. I, 248.
"Something there is that doesn't love a wall," I, 130.
"Sometimes in summer months, the matrix earth," II, 292.
"Sometimes, apart in sleep, by chance," II, 234.
Song. Edward Estlin Cummings. I, 101.
Song. Stephen Spender. II, 233.
Song at Night. Norman Nicholson. II, 341.
Song for St. Cecilia's Day. W. H. Auden. II, 167.
"A song in the valley of Nemea," II, 260.
A Song of Derivations. Alice Meynell. I, 213.
The Song of the Demented Priest. John Berryman. II, 329.
Song of the Three Seeds in the Macaw's Beak. Elizabeth Jane Coatsworth. I, 85.
Songs and Singing
  Empty Vessel. Hugh MacDiarmid. II, 29.

Sonnet—Realities I. Edward Estlin Cummings. I, 104.
Sonnet from Second April. Edna St. Vincent Millay. I, 224.
Sonnet of Fishes. George Barker. II, 291.
Sonnet XVIII. Hilaire Belloc. I, 33.
Sonnet: Go, Spend Your Penny. John Masefield. I, 209.
Sorrow
Dolor. Theodore Roethke. II, 204.
The Riddlers. Walter John De La Mare. I, 108.
Soul
The Eagle and the Mole. Elinor Wylie. I, 326.
Souls Lake. Robert Fitzgerald. II, 241.
The South Country. Hilaire Belloc. I, 31.
Spain
Epilogue from Emblems of Love. Lascelles Abercrombie. I, 1.
Spectral Lovers. John Crowe Ransom. I, 258.
Spender, Stephen. II, 227–238.
The Sphinx
Four Legs, Three Legs, Two Legs. William Empson. II, 143.
Spiders
Mr. Edwards and the Spider. Robert Lowell. II, 393.
"Sports and gallantries, the stage, the arts," I, 173.
Spring
Early Spring. Sidney Keyes. II, 411.
Stay, Spring. Andrew Young. II, 3.
Squire, John Collings ("Solomon Eagle"). I, 285.
St. Michael
Michaelmas. Norman Nicholson. II, 341.
"Stand on the highest pavement of the stair—," I, 120.
Star Talk. Robert Graves. I, 149.
The Starlight's Intuitions Pierced the Twelve, Delmore Schwartz. II, 309.
Stars
Peace on Earth. William Carlos Williams. I, 319.
Star Talk. Robert Graves. I, 149.
Stay, Spring. Andrew Young. II, 3.
Steel. Joseph Auslander. I, 16.
Steel Mill. Louis Untermeyer. I, 311.
Stephens, James. I, 286.
Sterling, George. I, 287–288.
Stevens, Wallace. I, 289–291.
Still Falls the Rain. Edith Sitwell. II, 21.
Still, Citizen Sparrow. Richard Wilbur. II, 409.

"Strangely assorted, the shape of song," II, 48.
"Stranger, you who hide my love." II, 233.
"Strapped at the center of the blazing wheel," II, 332.
Street Corner College. Kenneth Patchen. II, 255.
Strikes and Strikers
Not Men Alone. Edwin Rolfe. II, 217.
"Stripped country, shrunken as a beggar's heart," I, 42.
"Stuff of the moon," I, 278.
Stylite. Louis MacNeice. II, 183.
Subways
The Tunnel. Hart Crane. I, 92.
"Such a morning it is when love," II, 335.
"Suddenly from a wayside station," I, 27.
Suicide
Dirge. Kenneth Fearing. II, 99.
An Elegy. David Gascoyne. II, 382.
Richard Cory. Edwin Arlington Robinson. I, 266.
Steel. Joseph Auslander. I, 16.
Summer
Country Summer. Leonie Adams. II, 70.
Summer Idyll. George Barker. II, 292.
Summer Night, Riverside. Sara Teasdale. I, 294.
A Summer Night. George William Russell. I, 274.
Summer Song. George Barker. II, 293.
Sun
The Youth with Red-gold Hair. Edith Sitwell. II, 22.
"Sun burns on its sultry wick," II, 318.
Sunday
Sunday Morning. Louis MacNeice. II, 184.
"Sunday shuts down on this twentieth-century evening," II, 295.
The Sunlight on the Garden. Louis MacNeice. II, 185.
The Suppliant. Edmund William Gosse. I, 145.
"The swallow flew like lightning over the green," II, 46.
The Swan's Feet. E. J. Scovell. II, 188.
Swans
The Bereaved Swan. Stevie Smith. II, 102.
The Swan's Feet. E. J. Scovell. II, 188.
"Sweet Stay-At-Home, sweet Well-Content," I, 106.
Swimmers. Louis Untermeyer. I, 309.

Tableau. Countee Cullen. I, 100.

Taggard, Genevieve. I, 292.
A Talisman. Marianne Moore. I, 233.
Tamar. Robinson Jeffers. I, 174.
The Tame Hare. Norman Nicholson. II, 342.
Tarred and Feathered
  Between the World and Me. Richard Wright. II, 212.
The Tarry Buccaneer. John Masefield. I, 207.
Tate, Allen. II, 73–76.
Tears in Sleep. Louise Bogan. I, 61.
The Tears of a Muse In America. F. T. Prince. II, 267.
Teasdale, Sara. I, 294.
The Tempest (Shakespeare)
  Miranda's Song. W. H. Auden. II, 164.
Terror. Robert Penn Warren. II, 133.
"Thank God my brain is not inclined to cut," I, 228.
That Harp You Play So Well. Marianne Moore. I, 234.
"The buzz-saw snarled and rattled in the yard," I, 133.
"The fear of poetry is the/fear," II, 304.
"The snow, less intransigeant than their marble," II, 150.
Theatre
  At Epidaurus. Lawrence Durrell. II, 257.
"The die!" II, 59.
"There are some days the happy ocean lies," II, 232.
"There is a castle on a hill," I, 110.
"There is a supreme god in the ethnological section," II, 141.
There Is a Spell, for Instance. Hilda Doolittle. II, 6.
"There is a tree native in Turkestan," II, 145.
There Lived a Lady in Milan. William Rose Benet. I, 47.
"There never was a mood of mine," I, 294.
"There was an Indian, who had known no change," I, 285.
"There were faces to remember in the Valley," I, 267.
"These errors loved no less than the saint loves," II, 290.
"These, who desired to live, went out to death," I, 5.
Theseus. T. Sturge Moore. I, 235.
"They are able, with science, to measure," II, 97.
"They named it Aultgraat—Ugly Burn," II, 2.
"The thin Potomac scarcely moves," II, 322.
"Think not that mystery has place," I, 113.

"This advantage to be seized; and here an escape," II, 100.
"This blue half circle sea," II, 406.
"This is what I vow," I, 248.
"This last pain for the damned the Fathers found," II, 145.
"This man is dead," I, 16.
"This mast, new-shaved," II, 92.
"This morning take a holiday from unhappiness," II, 278.
"This too is an experience of the soul," II, 199.
Thomas, Dylan. II, 347–368.
Thompson, Francis Joseph. I, 295–302.
"Those Horns, the envy of the moon," II, 91.
" 'Thou Solitary!' the Blackbird cried," I, 108.
"Though black the night, I know upon the sky," I, 110.
The Three Winds. Laurie Lee. II, 337.
Tigers
  The Tigress. Ruth Pitter. II, 50.
Time
  For a Dead Lady. Edwin Arlington Robinson. I, 271.
  Slow Movement. Louis MacNeice. II, 182.
  Time Eating. Keith Douglas. II, 407.
A Time To Dance. Cecil Day Lewis. II, 124.
"A Tinker out of Bedford," I, 182.
Titanic Litany. John Wheelwright. II, 55.
To a Comrade in Arms. Alun Lewis. II, 378.
To a Contemporary Bunkshooter. Carl Sandburg. I, 279.
To a Friend Whose Work Has Come To Nothing. William Butler Yeats. I, 329.
To Earthward. Robert Frost. I, 134.
"To loosen with all ten fingers held wide," II, 210.
To My Contemporaries. Edwin Rolfe. II, 222.
To My Father. W. S. Graham. II, 403.
To My Mother. George Barker. II, 294.
To the Beloved. Alice Meynell. I, 211.
To the Tune of the Coventry Carol. Stevie Smith. II, 105.
To the Unimplored Beloved. Edward Shanks. I, 284.
The Token. F. T. Prince. II, 270.
Toledo, July 1936. Roy Campbell. II, 95.
Toledo, Ohio
  Not Men Alone. Edwin Rolfe. II, 217.
Toledo, Spain
  Toledo, July 1936. Roy Campbell. II, 95.
"Toledo, when I saw you die," II, 95.
Tom Mooney. William Ellery Leonard. I, 186.

Tombstone with Cherubim. Horace Gregory. II, 66.
Tools
The Word is Deed. John Wheelwright. II, 57.
Torrence, Ridgely. I, 303.
Train Ride. John Wheelwright. II, 56.
The Trance. Stephen Spender. II. 234.
The Translation. Mark Van Doren. I, 312.
Travel
Marston. Stephen Spender. II, 229.
Sweet Stay-At-Home. William Henry Davies. I, 106.
"When I Set Out For Lyonnesse." Thomas Hardy. I, 160.
"Tread softly, for here you stand," II, 260.
Trees
Ryton Firs. Lascelles Abercrombie. I, 5.
The Trout Map. Allen Tate. II, 76.
Truth
All Gone. Cecil Day Lewis. II, 109.
Open House. Theodore Roethke. II, 211.
The Tunnel. Hart Crane. I, 92.
Turner, Nat
Remembering Nat Turner. Sterling A. Brown. II, 87.
The Turning of the Leaves. Vernon Watkins, II, 191.
23rd Street Runs into Heaven. Kenneth Patcher. II, 255.
Twentieth Century Life
A Bride in the '30's. W. H. Auden. II, 154.
Dolor. Theodore Roethke. II, 204.
An Eclogue For Christmas. Louis MacNeice. II, 174.
Let Us Have Madness Openly. Kenneth Patchen. II, 254.
To My Contemporaries. Edwin Rolfe. II, 222.
Twilight
Leavetaking. William Watson. I, 315.
Two Armies. Stephen Spender. II, 235.
The Two Parents. Hugh MacDiarmid. II, 31.

The Unconscious
The Trance. Stephen Spender. II, 234.
"Under the bridge of stone the river shuddered by," I, 27.
"Under a splintered mast," I, 233.
The Undiscovered Planet. Norman Nicholson. II, 343.
Unemployment
Boy with His Hair Cut Short. Muriel Rukeyser. II, 295.

United States
America. Claude McKay. I, 203.
The Tears of a Muse in America. F. T. Prince. II, 267.
Untermeyer, Louis. I, 309–311.
"Up the ash tree climbs the ivy," II, 138.

V-Letter. Karl Shapiro. II, 323.
Vagabonds
The Hunchback in the Park. Dylan Thomas. II, 364.
Street Corner College. Kenneth Patchen. II, 255.
The Valley of the Shadow. Edwin Arlington Robinson. I, 267.
Van Doren, Mark. I, 312.
The Vanishing Boat. Edmund William Gosse. I, 146.
"The various voices are his poem now," II, 412.
Velvet Shoes. Elinor Wylie. I, 326.
Venice, Italy
A Water-Colour of Venice. Lawrence Durrell. II, 261.
The Viper. Ruth Pitter. II, 51.
A Virginal. Ezra Pound. I, 251.
The Voice. Wilfrid Wilson Gibson. I, 141.
Volcanoes
The Different Day. Grace Hazard Conkling. I, 88.
Vultures
The Black Vulture. George Sterling. I, 288.
Still, Citizen Sparrow. Richard Wilbur. II, 409.

"Waking, he found himself in a train, andante," II, 182.
Walking Song. Charles Williams. I, 315.
"Wallowing in this bloody sty," II, 389.
Walls
Mending Wall. Robert Frost. I, 130.
"Wan/Swan/On the Lake," II, 102.
War
At the Cenotaph. Hugh MacDiarmid. II, 29.
The Contrary Experience. Herbert Read. II, 32.
Dawn on the East Coast. Alun Lewis. II, 374.
Desert Flowers. Keith Douglas. II, 406.
Elegy for a Dead Soldier. Karl Shapiro. II, 314.
A Friend's Song for Simoisius. Louise Imogen Guiney. I, 154.

I Hear an Army Charging Upon the Land. James Joyce. II, 1.
The Kings. Louise Imogen Guiney. I, 153.
March-Patrol of the Naked Heroes. Herbert Gorman. I, 143.
News of the World III. George Barker. II, 286.
The Peasants. Alun Lewis. II, 377.
Reflections in an Iron Works. Hugh MacDiarmid. II, 30.
The Return. John Peale Bishop. II, 27.
The Welsh Marches. Alfred Edward Housman. I, 167.
Warren, Robert Penn. II, 131–133.
Washington, D.C.
The Potomac. Karl Shapiro. II, 322.
Watch Any Day. W. H. Auden. II, 169.
A Water-Colour of Venice. Lawrence Durrell. II, 261.
Waterfalls
The Black Rock of Kiltearn. Andrew Young. II, 2.
Watkins, Vernon. II, 189–192.
Watson, William. I, 313.
"The waves lay down their trail," II, 187.
"We heard her speaking of Chinese musicians," II, 67.
"We, listen, wind from where," II, 71.
"We saw a bloody sunset over Courtland," II, 87.
"We who with songs beguile your pilgrimage," I, 122.
"We're going to the fair at Holstenwall," II, 413.
The Weak Monk. Stevie Smith. II, 106.
"Wearing worry about money like a hair shirt," II, 202.
The Weary Blues. Langston Hughes. I, 171.
Weaver, John V. A.. I, 314.
The Wedding. Conrad Aiken. I, 14.
The Weed. Elizabeth Bishop. II, 245.
Weeds. Edna St. Vincent Millay. I, 223.
"Weep not, weep not," I, 176.
The Welsh Marches. Alfred Edward Housman. I, 167.
"The whale butting through scarps of moving marble," II, 178.
"What ails John Winter," I, 50.
"What am I? O thou sea, with all thy noise," I, 235.
"What came before and afterward," I, 287.
What I Expected. Stephen Spender. II, 236.
"What is Africa to me," I, 96.

"What is this life if, full of care," I, 105.
"What need you, being come to sense," I, 328.
"What shall we do for Love these days?" I, 1.
"What, you have never seen a lifeless thing flower," II, 217.
Wheelwright, John. II, 52–57.
When First My Way. Alfred Edward Housman. I, 170.
"When I am living in the Midlands," I, 31.
"When I see birches bend to left and right," I, 131.
"When I set out for Lyonnesse," I, 160.
"When I was born on Amman hill," II, 189.
"When I would think of you, my mind holds only," II, 414.
"When our brother Fire was having his dog's day," II, 172.
"When the fishes flew and forest walked," I, 84.
"When the hero's task was done," II, 263.
"When there are so many we shall have to mourn," II, 158.
"When we lay where Budmouth Beach is," I, 159.
"When you are old, and I—if that should be," I, 315.
"When you are old and gray and full of sleep," I, 332.
"When you to Acheron's ugly water come," I, 33.
"Whenever Richard Cory went down town," I, 266.
"Where dwell the lovely, wild white women fold," I, 87.
"Where once we danced, where once we sang," I, 161.
Where the Rainbow Ends. Robert Lowell. II, 398.
"Wherefore to-night so full of care," I, 73.
"Whether dinner was pleasant, with the windows lit," II, 101.
Whistles and Whistling
PeeWee. Alfred Kreymborg. I, 185.
"White sheet on the tail-gate of a truck," I, 314.
"White with daisies and red with sorrel," I, 223.
The White Women. Mary Elizabeth Coleridge. I, 87.
"Who is this whose feet," II, 188.
"Whose is this horrifying face," II, 380.
"Why will they never sleep," II, 25.
Wilbur, Richard. II, 409.

"Wild strawberries, gooseberries, trampled," II, 52.
"William Dewy, Tranter Reuben, Farmer Ledlow late," I, 157.
Williams, Charles. I, 315.
Williams, Oscar. II, 78–80.
Williams, William Carlos. I, 319–320.
Wind
  The Three Winds. Laurie Lee. II, 337.
  The Windmill. Robert Bridges. I, 74.
  Windmills. John Gould Fletcher. I, 126.
  Winter and Summer. Stephen Spender. II, 237.
  A Winter's Tale. Dylan Thomas. II, 368.
Witchcraft
  The Drum. Edith Sitwell. II, 12.
  The Old Witch in the Copse. Frances Cornford. I, 90.
"With a pert moustache and a ready candid smile," II, 180.
"With buds embalmed alive in ice," II, 275.
"With focus sharp as Flemish-painted face," II, 312.
With Rue My Heart Is Laden. Alfred Edward Housman. I, 169.
"With the gulls' hysteria above me," II, 283.
"Within my head, aches the perpetual winter," II, 237.
Wolfe, Humbert. I, 321.
The Woman Who Disapproved of Music at the Bar. Horace Gregory. II, 67.
Women—Bourgeoisie
  More of a Corpse Than a Woman. Muriel Rukeyser. II, 303.
Women
  Gone. Carl Sandburg. I, 281.
  There Lived a Lady in Milan. William Rose Benet. I, 47.
Wonders
  Mystery. John Drinkwater. I, 113.
  A Wood Song. Ralph Hodgson. I, 165.
"The wood was rather old and dark," II, 103.
Woodberry, George Edward. I, 322.
Word. Stephen Spender. II, 238.
The Word Is Deed. John Wheelwright. II, 57.
Words
  Word. Stephen Spender. II, 238.
Wordsworth, William (about)
  Resolution of Dependence. George Barker. II, 288.
World War II
  November, 1941. Roy Fuller. II, 265.
  A World Within a War. Herbert Read. II, 36.
  The Worms At Heaven's Gate. Wallace Stevens. I, 291.

Worry About Money. Kathleen Raine. II, 202.
"Would you resembled the metal you work with," II, 30.
Wright, Richard. II, 212–214.
Wylie, Elinor. I, 326.

Yeats, William Butler. I, 328–330.
"Yes as alike as entirely," II, 403.
"Yes, they were kind exceedingly; most mild," I, 277.
"You come along . . . tearing your shirt . . . yelling," I, 279.
"You cry as the gull cries," II, 32.
"You stand near the window as lights wink," II, 255.
You That Love England. Cecil Day Lewis. II, 125.
You, Andrew Marvell. Archibald MacLeish. I, 204.
Young, Andrew. II, 2–3.
"Your body derns, II, 31.
Your Body Is Stars. Stephen Spender. II, 238.
"Yours is the face that the earth turns to me," II, 200.
Youth
  Down by the Salley Gardens. William Butler Yeats. I, 328.
  An Elegy. David Gascoyne. II, 382.
  Epitaph. Lascelles Abercrombie. I, 5.
  Fern Hill. Dylan Thomas. II, 363.
  A Flower Is Looking through the Ground. Harold Monro. I, 225.
  The Golden Corpse. Stephen Vincent Bent. I, 42.
  Musician. Clifford Bax. I, 28.
  "*Out, Out*–." Robert Frost. I, 133.
  Poem in October. Dylan Thomas. II, 366.
  Portrait—II. Edward Estlin Cummings. I, 102.
  A Summer Night. George William Russell. I, 274.
  Youth and Age on Beaulieu River, Hants. John Betjeman. II, 138.
  The Youth with Red-gold Hair. Edith Sitwell. II, 22.

Zacchaeus (mythology)
  Zacchaeus in the Leaves. Vernon Watkins. II, 192.
"Zarian was saying: Florence is youth," II, 261.

ACKNOWLEDGEMENTS

(Continued from p. iv)

OXFORD UNIVERSITY PRESS, for "The Goal of Intellectual Man;" "I Walked Out to the Graveyard;" "Mysticism Has Not the . . ." from *Collected Poems 1930–1976* by Richard Eberhart. Copyright 1960, 1976 by Richard Eberhart.

RANDOM HOUSE, INC., for "The Airman's Alphabet," from *The Orators: An English Study* by W.H. Auden, Copyright 1937 by The Modern Library, Inc. and renewed 1962 by W.H. Auden. "Perhaps" and "Petition" from *The English Auden*, edited by Edward Mendelson, copyright 1937 and renewed 1965 by W.H. Auden, copyright 1934 and renewed 1962 by W.H. Auden. "At the Grave of Henry James," copyright 1941 and renewed 1969 by W.H. Auden; "A Bride in the 30's" copyright 1937 and renewed 1965 by W.H. Auden; "Carry Her over Water;" Copyright 1941 by Hawkes & Son (London) Ltd.; "Casino," Copyright 1937 by Random House, Inc.; "In Memory of Sigmund Freud," Copyright 1940 and renewed 1968 by W.H. Auden; "The Lesson," Copyright 1945 by W.H. Auden; "Miranda's Song," Copyright 1944 by W.H. Auden; "Musée des Beaux Arts;" copyright 1940 and renewed 1968 by W. H. Auden. "Song for St. Cecilia's Day," Copyright 1945 by W.H. Auden; "Watch Any Day His Nonchalant Pauses," Copyright 1934 and renewed 1962 by W.H. Auden, from *W.H. Auden: Collected Poems*, edited by Edward Mendelson. "An Elementary School Classroom," Copyright 1942 and renewed 1970 by Stephen Spender: "The Landscape near an Aerodrome," Copyright 1934 and renewed 1962 by Stephen Spender; "Marston, dropping it," Copyright 1934 and renewed 1961 by Stephen Spender; "Polar Exploration," Copyright 1942 by Stephen Spender; "Port Bou," Copyright 1942 by Stephen Spender, "Seascape," Copyright 1946 by Stephen Spender; "Song," Copyright 1942 by Stephen Spender; "The Trance," Copyright 1947 by Stephen Spender; "Two Armies," Copyright 1942 by Stephen Spender, "What I expected, was," Copyright 1934 and renewed 1962 by Stephen Spender; "Word," Copyright 1948 by Stephen Spender; "Your Body Is Stars;" Copyright 1934 and renewed 1962 by Stephen Spender, from *Collected Poems, 1928–1953* by Stephen Spender. "Winter and Summer," Copyright 1942 by Stephen Spender, from *Ruins and Visions: Poems 1934–1942* by Stephen Spender. "Pursuit;" "Revelation;" "Terror;" Copyright 1942 by Robert Penn Warren, from *Selected Poems 1923–1975* by Robert Penn Warren. "The Dome of Sunday;" Copyright 1942 by Karl Shapiro; "Elegy for a Dead Soldier," Copyright 1944 by Karl Shapiro; "Elegy Written on a Front Porch," Copyright 1942 by Karl Shapiro; "Haircut," Copyright 1942 by Karl Shapiro; "The Potomac," Copyright 1941 by Karl Shapiro; "V-Letter," Copyright 1943 by Karl Shapiro, from *Collected Poems, 1940–1978* by Karl Shapiro.

RUSSELL & VOLKENING, INC., for "C Stands for Civilization;" "Devil's Dream;" "Dirge;" "Dividends;" "No Credit;" from *New and Selected Poems* by Kenneth Fearing, Copyright 1956.

CHARLES SCRIBNER'S SONS, for "Ode" and "The Return" from *Now With His Love,* by John Peale Bishop, Copyright 1933 by Charles Scribner's Sons, copyright renewed. "Frieze," from *The Collected Poems of John Peale Bishop*, Copyright 1948 by Charles Scribner's Sons, Copyright renewed. "Colloquy with a King Crab" from *Selected Poems* by John Peale Bishop, Copyright 1941 by Charles Scribner's Sons, Copyright renewed.